AMERICAN LAW AND LEGAL SYSTEMS

JAMES V. CALVI, *1949—*
West Texas State University

SUSAN COLEMAN
West Texas State University

Prentice Hall, Englewood Cliffs, New Jersey 07632

Library of Congress Cataloging-in-Publication Data

Calvi, James V.
   American law and legal systems.

   Bibliography
   Includes index.
   1. Law--United States. I. Coleman, Susan
II. Title.
KF387.C28 1989   349.73   87-29269
ISBN 0-13-027566-2   347.3

Editorial/production supervision and interior design: *Marjorie Shustak*
Cover design: *Zak Design*
Manufacturing buyer: *Peter Havens*

With love and gratitude

To my wife Leesa and my daughter Jennifer
and

To my parents, John and Sue Coleman

 © 1989 by Prentice-Hall, Inc.
A Division of Simon & Schuster
Englewood Cliffs, New Jersey 07632

Printed in the United States of America

10 9 8 7 6 5 4 3 2 1

ISBN 0-13-027566-2

Prentice-Hall International (UK) Limited, *London*
Prentice-Hall of Australia Pty. Limited, *Sydney*
Prentice-Hall Canada Inc., *Toronto*
Prentice-Hall Hispanoamericana, S.A., *Mexico*
Prentice-Hall of India Private Limited, *New Delhi*
Prentice-Hall of Japan, Inc., *Tokyo*
Simon & Schuster Asia Pte. Ltd., *Singapore*
Editora Prentice-Hall do Brasil, Ltda., *Rio de Janeiro*

Contents

Preface

We decided to write an introductory law book for a simple reason: We were dissatisfied with the existing choices. We felt that some introductory law books—often the ones written by lawyers—were too legalistic in their approach. These books often contained excerpts from Supreme Court cases and basically taught law the same way as their lawyer-authors had been taught law. Other introductory law books leaned too much toward social science in their orientation. We decided a more balanced approach was needed. We also wanted to write a book that could be easily understood by a layperson, but which had enough technical information to introduce the beginner to the intricacies of the law. To that end, we have included chapters that deal with what is commonly known as "everyday law": contracts, wills, family law, and torts. We have included a glossary to call special attention to important legal terms and doctrines. We divided the chapters so that each of us could write in his or her own area of expertise. Consequently, the chapters dealing with the more technical aspects of the law were written by Susan Coleman, a licensed attorney; the chapters dealing with the social and political aspects of the law were written by Jim Calvi, an unlicensed political scientist. We reviewed each other's chapters as they were written in order to achieve the necessary balance. We are happy to report that the incidents of bruised egos were minimal.

It is with heartfelt gratitude that we thank those people who helped us in this endeavor. Naturally, we want to thank our families, who put up with us through endless rewrites and self-imposed deadlines—especially Sue Coleman, who helped compile the Index and Table of Cases. We would also like to thank our colleagues at West Texas State University for the personal and institutional support provided. We would especially like to thank Dr. Jim Woodyard of the Killgore Research Center, who displayed untiring effort and unending patience as we learned (and relearned) the deep, dark secrets of word processing and computer usage. It is no exaggeration to say that we could not have done it without him. We wish to thank the following professors who graciously reviewed the manuscript: Karl Andresen, University of Wisconsin–Eau Claire; Robert L. Bock, Western New England College; James Magee, University of Delaware; and Lee S. Weinberg, University of Pittsburgh.

We want to thank the people of Prentice Hall for their patience and understanding in leading two relative novices through the intricacies of book publishing. First, Karen Horton, Political Science editor, who gave us the opportunity to bring this idea to fruition. Second, Marjorie Shustak, who served as production editor and answered our numerous inquiries about the process. Third and finally, Nancy Morgan Andreola, copy editor, who showed us that we don't write nearly as well as we thought.

1

Introduction

In order to understand the American legal system, one must first come to terms with the question, What is law? Americans have always had ambivalent feelings about law. Our rhetoric is full of noble ideals such as "equal justice under law" and the "rule of law." We pride ourselves on having a "government of laws, not men," and on the assertion that "no one is above the law." At the same time, disregard for the rule of law has been part of our political tradition. We are a nation born of violent revolution, and during our frontier period, vigilante groups often took the law into their own hands. Even in our own time we debate the role of civil disobedience in the civil rights, antiwar, and antinuclear movements.

In many ways the questions we ask ourselves about the nature of law are the same ones we ask about our political system and about society at large. How do we account for the conflicting attitudes Americans have toward law? How can persons who are law abiding one minute turn into a lynch mob the next? How can a nation founded on the basis of its citizens' "inalienable rights" systematically deny those rights to black Americans and other minorities? How can we explain these contradictions? The answers to these questions are not easy, but we can begin to understand the paradox by understanding the nature of law both in general terms and in American society specifically.

In this chapter we will focus on several aspects of law in America. First, we will examine the functions of law in society. Second, we will discuss the source of law in society in order to help us understand why people do or do not obey the law. Next, we will define the different kinds of law in our legal system, with examples of the various forms the law takes. Finally, we will conclude with a case study of *Bob Jones University v. United States*, which illustrates a number of the chapter's major points.

FUNCTIONS OF LAW IN SOCIETY

Society tends to place far too much emphasis on the negative aspects of law. Many view the law as a list of things they are forbidden to do. Perhaps this attitude is only natural, given our socialization. As children we were continually told, "Don't do this" and "Don't touch that," so it is understandable that our first contact with authority has negative connotations. Law, like the restrictions placed on us by our parents, defines the boundaries of acceptable and unacceptable behavior. But law is more than just a list of forbidden activities; it touches every aspect of our lives and should be viewed as a positive force. Following is a list of some of the functions of law in our society.

Law Bestows Benefits on People.   One of the positive aspects of law that perhaps we seldom consider is that it bestows benefits upon people. Government, no matter what its form, uses its law-making power to determine who receives certain benefits and who does not. Laws deciding eligibility for programs like Social Security, food stamps, unemployment compensation, and veterans' benefits are just a few examples; laws determining who may operate an automobile, practice law, sell real estate, or receive tax deductions are some others. Law is thus closely connected to the political system, since it is government that determines "who gets what, when, and how."[1] The law becomes a major concern of interest groups who try to secure the passage of laws beneficial to them while blocking the passage of those which harm their interests. Finally, it is the government's ability to meet the demands of interest groups and its fairness in allocating benefits that provide an important measure of governmental effectiveness.

Law Creates New Programs.   The next function of law is closely related to the aforementioned one. Government, by passing laws that bestow benefits, must create both new programs and the bureaucracies to administer them. Programs such as flood control, crop insurance, welfare benefits, and highway construction by their very nature benefit people in varying degrees. Some programs, like highway construction and flood control, are seemingly for the general welfare but also bestow benefits (like big profits) on highway contractors and insurance companies. Battles between the President and Congress over the nation's budget are actually struggles over the funding levels of new and existing programs that have been created by the government.

Law Proscribes Certain Activities.   As we have noted, most of our thinking about law centers around what we may not do. Law forbids behavior that causes harm to other people or to their property. Some behavior is termed *malum in se,* or "wrong in itself." Consequently, the law forbids murder, rape, arson, theft, and other forms of antisocial behavior. There are also laws banning activities that, while not harmful in themselves, are forbidden simply because society disapproves of them. Neither parking in a "no parking" zone nor letting the meter expire is really wrong in itself, but both are against the law. These are examples of *malum prohibitum*—acts that are wrong merely because they have been prohibited by government. Finally, some forms of behavior—such as gambling, prostitution, or homosexual activities—are debatable as to whether they are wrong in themselves or simply wrong because a majority in society thinks they should be prohibited. In any case, it is only by banning and punishing certain activities that people can live together in society in relative harmony.

Law Provides Predictability.   One final function of law is to provide a measure of predictability so that we can conduct our affairs with some certainty. Contract law is a good example of law fulfilling the need for predictability; without contracts enforceable in courts, businesspersons could not conduct their affairs. We also seek predictability because we want some assurance that those in power will not act arbitrarily. One element of due process is the requirement that a law forbidding an activity cannot be "void for vagueness."[2] Some Supreme Court justices, for example, have expressed concern over upholding pornography laws when the Court itself has such difficulty defining pornography.[3] Lawyers want some assurance that the law governing the outcome of yesterday's cases will serve as guideposts for today's decisions and tomorrow's cases. That assurance is why lawyers so eagerly look for *precedents* when presenting cases. Lawyers hope that such precedents will help guide the judge's decision and make the outcome more predictable.

These functions of law give us some clues as to the nature of law by making us aware of its purpose for a society. Law can be seen as a battle for scarce resources, as a way of organizing society, or as a source of predictability and stability. But understanding the functions of law in society is not enough. Another important aspect of law is the *source* of law in a society. We now turn our attention toward understanding why people obey the law.

SOURCES OF LAW IN SOCIETY

It is because law performs such important functions that it becomes necessary to examine the source of law in society. The source of law concerns not only the legitimacy of the law in the eyes of the people, but also the legitimacy of the lawmaker. In an absolute monarchy, the will of a single individual and the law are one and the same. In the film *The Ten Commandments,* Pharaoh had only to say, "So let it be written, so let it be done," and his word became law. How can the will of a single person be so readily accepted by others as binding? In other words, from where did Pharaoh derive his power, and why did his people obey him?

The answer to why humans obey can be as varied as humans themselves, but generally the reasons can be reduced to two: People obey either because they believe that they should or because they are afraid not to. Compliance with the law is much easier to effect if the lawmaker can convince the people that he or she has the right to make the law. In some societies—ancient Egypt and pre–World War II Japan, for example—the lawmaker was seen as a god. Thus, people obeyed Pharaoh and the Japanese Emperor out of both religious respect and fear. During the Age of Absolutism in Europe, the theory of the ***divine right of kings*** governed people's thinking about the source of the king's power. In Roman Catholic theology, the Pope was chosen by God to be the "Vicar of Christ" on earth and was considered to be infallible in matters of Church doctrine. Similarly, people believed that the king was chosen by God to rule over them in secular matters. Just as the Pope was infallible in Church matters, the belief that "the king can do no wrong" was based upon the belief that God had chosen the king and guided him. But what if the king should suffer the misfortune of being dethroned? Did this disprove the theory that the king was king "by the grace of God"? No, because in the Bible, as everyone knew, God had replaced Saul as king of Israel with David when Saul displeased Him. As a result, all law, spiritual and temporal, was inspired by God, and to disobey God's earthly representative was to disobey God Himself; the punishment was eternal damnation, a powerful penalty in the minds of medieval people.

Law, as understood by medieval thinkers, came from God and was considered to be eternal and immutable. During the Age of the Enlightenment, however, both religious and political thinkers began to challenge the absolutism of popes and kings. The idea developed that the lawmaker received his authority, not from God by virtue of his fortunate birth, but from the consent of the governed. Thomas Jefferson incorporated the concept of natural law into the Declaration of Independence when he invoked the notion that persons are endowed by their Creator with certain "inalienable rights." But he also emphatically stated that governments are instituted among men to protect those natural rights and that when a government no longer does so, it is the right of the people to alter or abolish it. Jefferson then chronicled a long list of abuses of power by George III to justify the drastic step the Colonies were about to take.

The Declaration of Independence and the philosophy behind it added a new wrinkle to the relationship between the people and their government. Government derived its power from the consent of the governed, not by some accident of royal birth. Implicit in the concept of government by consent is the idea of majority rule. American democracy, of course, links majority rule with representative government, wherein elected representatives of the people make the laws that bind all members of society. The legitimacy of both the law and the lawmaker rests on what we refer to simply as the democratic process. As long as laws are passed in accordance with the democratic "rules of the game," people are likely to obey them willingly.

Why have we discussed the question of legitimacy at such length? At the beginning of this chapter, we stated a paradox of law in America: We are a nation born of revolution, and yet we strongly believe in the rule of law. How do we reconcile these two apparently contradictory ideas? In order to do so, we must look at three approaches to the nature of law.[4]

The Natural-Law Approach. **Natural-law** theorists believe that the laws that govern relationships among people, like the laws that govern the physical universe, are sown in nature. These laws are eternal and immutable, just as God, the source of all law, is eternal. Natural law is often referred to as a form of "higher law," in order to distinguish it from lesser—that is, man-made—law. Natural law has moral overtones, and those who invoke it often call it "God's law." Ascertaining just what is and is not God's law can be risky business, but its advocates echo the belief of Justice Potter Stewart that they "know it when they see it."

Appeal to natural, or higher, law provides a justification for *civil disobedience.* For example, if one's conscience tells one that war is morally wrong, then one has a moral obligation not only to resist induction into the military, but also to commit overt acts of civil disobedience in order to raise the consciousness of the community about the evils of war. It was by appealing to the conscience of society that Mahatma Gandhi and Martin Luther King, Jr., were able to make both those in authority and the general public see the immorality of colonialism and segregation.[5] Opponents of nuclear war have tried to make the question of nuclear disarmament into a moral issue which justifies admittedly illegal behavior such as sit-ins and trespassing on nuclear facilities. Invoking this higher law is one way in which a minority can hope to convince the majority to change its mind by appealing to the majority's sense of morality.

Positive-Law Approach.   A second approach, **positive law,** is the belief that law should simply reflect the will of the majority. Law is stripped of any moral overtones and boils down to the old adage "Might makes right." Despite the immorality of segregation or colonialism, if a majority wishes to have a segregated society or a colonial policy, then they may have it. Those who disagree with the law can certainly work within the democratic process to change it (albeit an unlikely occurrence), but they must accept it as the legitimate reflection of the will of the majority. Under no circumstances may the minority resort to unlawful methods to effect change. The law, then, becomes whatever a majority wants at a particular point in time.

Sociological Approach.   The **sociological theory of law** holds that law represents a reflection of the values, mores, and culture of the society that produces it, and that as the society changes, the law will also change. For example, we have seen tremendous change in our own society as a result of the women's movement. As traditional views of the role of women have changed, laws dealing with the rights of women in employment, pension plans, credit, and child support have changed to keep pace. Although the law may lag behind a bit, it eventually catches up and reflects society's prevalent views.

The sociological approach is even more evident in our view of criminal behavior. Criminal law, you will recall, defines what type of behavior is antisocial and therefore proscribed. Some behavior is wrong in itself and is almost universally condemned. Other acts are wrong merely because they have been prohibited. At one time the manufacture and sale of alcoholic beverages were against the law, but after some experience with Prohibition, the measure was finally repealed. Today the use of marijuana is against the law in most states, but as society's views change, we may expect some change in marijuana laws as well. Many states have already reduced the crime of possession of marijuana from a felony offense to a misdemeanor.

How would each of the three approaches just described deal with an issue such as homosexual marriages? The natural-law theorist might argue that such marriages are a sin against God, violate natural law, and should not be legalized. The positive-law theorist would argue that the morality of homosexual marriages is irrelevant; a majority of people are still opposed to them (assuming this to be true), and they should therefore remain illegal. The advocate of the sociological appr⟨ argue that while our society is not yet ready to accept such n a more tolerant atmosphere may prevail at some future time.

In a sense, American law encompasses all three of these appr⟨ ⟩ries. The resulting paradox is the same one that is inherent in our political system and in society in general. On one hand, we believe that law should reflect the will of the majority; on the other hand, we accept the notion that minorities also have rights under the law. It is a source of frustration to many who wonder why we have busing if a majority of Americans oppose it, and why we do not have prayer in the schools when a majority favor it. Is the law a manifestation of the majority's will or isn't it? Reconciling this paradox is never easy and seldom satisfying.

KINDS OF LAW

It should be clear by now that one's feelings about the origins of law and the functions it performs in society are crucial to understanding the legal system itself. One final obstacle remains: understanding the kinds of law that exist in the legal environment. This section will introduce the various kinds of law, and the final section will use a case study of *Bob Jones University v. United States* to illustrate them. We will begin by distinguishing substantive law from procedural law.

Substantive v. Procedural Law. It is important at the outset to differentiate between the substance of the law and the process or procedures of the law. The former—that is, **substantive law**—is concerned with the content, or substance, of the law. In criminal law, for example, the substantive law will define what kind of behavior is considered to be antisocial and prescribe the kind of punishment that will be imposed for engaging in it. The substantive law will clearly define the elements of the crime (for example, the necessary evil intent) and the range of punishment (5 to 10 years' imprisonment) that may be handed out upon conviction. As previously discussed, the determination of what behavior is forbidden and what punishment is appropriate is made by elected representative bodies such as the Congress and the state legislatures. Likewise, in civil law, the legislature of each state is free to specify the legal grounds for a civil action, such as a divorce proceeding. Mental cruelty, adultery, irreconcilable differences, and incompatibility are common substantive grounds for a divorce.

Procedural law governs the *process* of the law. In a political system such as ours, we are as much concerned about *how* the law is applied as about the substance of the law itself. Terms like *kangaroo court* and *railroading a defendant* indicate that our system of law is also concerned about fundamental fairness. Consequently, we guarantee everyone, especially those charged with criminal offenses, **due process of law.** We make this guarantee because our system of constitutional government is based upon the idea that there are limits to governmental power and that even those in authority must adhere to the rule of law. We wish to prevent government from acting toward us in an arbitrary fashion, and so we believe that even a person charged with the most heinous crime is entitled to "have his day in court" governed by a set of preordained rules of fairness. Thus, we guarantee the accused the right to remain silent before his accusers, the right to a trial by jury, and the right to counsel. Even after a conviction, the Constitution protects the condemned person from cruel and unusual punishment.

Of the two types, substantive and procedural, the latter tends to generate more controversy. Although debate rages over questions like whether marijuana should be a crime or whether the punishment for using it is too severe, people generally defer to their elected representatives on these issues. However, procedural due process comes under attack because it provides the "loopholes" through which criminals are sometimes allowed to slip. All of us are aware of cases in which a criminal has been set free because the police failed to comply with certain "technicalities" in the law. Astounded citizens want to know the justice in letting a factually guilty person go free because "the constable blunders."[6]

There is no satisfactory answer to the question, What about the rights of the victim? But we should understand that the Framers of our Constitution had first-hand experience with a tyrannical government and believed that in the long run it was better to risk letting the guilty go free than to risk creating an arbitrary and tyrannical government. Even though most citizens will never need the protection of the Bill of Rights, it is also true that it is better to have them and not need them than to need them and not have them. Understanding this fact does not necessarily make it acceptable to many people, however, and so the debate over how much "process" is due to those accused of crime will undoubtedly continue.

Criminal and Civil Law.   Several references have already been made to criminal and civil law, but now we want to define them more clearly. **Criminal law,** as we have indicated, deals with activities that have been formally forbidden by a society's government. The range of crimes extends from parking violations to murder. As we have seen, some crimes are "wrong in themselves," and some merely wrong because society has seen fit to prohibit them. We have also seen that the Constitution provides a number of procedural safeguards for those accused of crime.

The importance of the role of government in criminal law cannot be overestimated. Of course, government is responsible for detecting and preventing crime, as well as for seeing that criminals are caught and punished. But more important, government prosecutes criminals. This statement, while hardly revealing, is significant because of its implications. At one time, perhaps in philosopher John Locke's "state of nature," each person was individually responsible for his or her own protection, or else relied upon a family or clan for protection. When someone was injured, it was the duty of the individual to seek revenge; if the victim was unable to do so, the responsibility fell upon the family or clan. In our civilized society, we consider a crime to be an injury not only to a particular individual, but also to society as a whole, and it is society's responsibility to seek retribution on behalf of the victim. Instead of permitting blood feuds and vendettas to disrupt society, the government assumes the responsibility for prosecuting and punishing persons charged with crimes. Thus, criminal cases are typically entitled *State v. Jones* or *The State of Texas v. Jones* to indicate the state's active role as prosecutor. It was a significant step in the advancement of law in society when people began to permit government to seek retribution on their behalf. It is because of this awesome power that government has over our lives and liberties that we impose the procedural safeguards discussed in the previous section. Without significant checks on the power of government, our freedom would soon be lost.

Civil law governs the relationships between individuals in the course of their private affairs. It deals with such matters as contracts, property, wills, and torts. When two or more persons have a dispute, it is in the best interests of society as a whole to ensure that the dispute is resolved peacefully. Unlike criminal prosecutions, in which the government is an active participant, the government's main interest in civil cases is to provide a forum, a court of law, in which to resolve the dispute. The government itself does not care who wins the dispute as long as it is settled peacefully. Although the cost of providing courts to resolve these essentially private disputes is considerable, it is justified on the grounds of maintaining harmony in society. The fact that citizens are willing to submit their disputes to the courts and abide by the court's decision is in itself a tribute to the legitimacy of a society's judicial system.

One final point about criminal and civil law should be made. It is possible for both a criminal *and* a civil action to arise out of the same set of facts or the same incident. Two examples should clarify this point. Suppose Wilson runs a red light and collides with Johnson's car, causing considerable damage to it. The police will issue a traffic ticket to Wilson for running the light and he will be punished, probably by having to pay a fine. The state's interest is limited to punishing Wilson for disregarding one of its traffic laws. There is still the matter of Johnson's car, however. Wilson has damaged her property—which, in legal terminology, is called a **tort.** A **tort** is a legal injury one person has caused another. Let's further suppose that Wilson has no liability insurance (itself a crime in many states) to cover the damages, so Johnson decides to sue him in order to force him to pay for the damage he has caused. This suit is a **civil action,** and if Wilson loses the suit, he will be made to pay the cost of repairing the car. Thus, two legal actions, one criminal and one civil, arose from a single automobile accident.

Our second example is similar but a bit more complicated. Anderson starts a fight with Cooper. Anderson hits Cooper, breaking the latter's jaw. Anderson is arrested for assault, convicted, and given a year in prison as his punishment. Cooper has suffered a broken jaw, however, and has had to pay his own medical expenses. He decides to sue Anderson in order to force him to pay his medical bills. Again, the latter suit is civil in nature, and if Cooper wins, Anderson can be forced to pay. Someone might suggest that Anderson is being subjected to "double jeopardy" since he is being hauled into court twice for the same offense. But the prohibition against double jeopardy limits the number of times the *government* can prosecute a person for a *criminal offense* and does not protect Anderson from a civil action started by the person he has injured.

Constitutional Law.   In the United States and in each of the 50 states, the most basic fundamental law is a constitution. The national Constitution declares that "This Constitution, and the Laws of the United States which shall be made in Pursuance thereof; and all Treaties made, or which shall be made, under the Authority of the United States, shall be the supreme Law of the Land."[7] The Constitution adds that state judges must take an oath to uphold it and that state constitutions and state laws may not conflict with the national Constitution.[8]

Noted constitutional scholar C. Herman Pritchett has asserted that a good constitution should do four things: It should provide for the structure of government, place limitations on government, list the powers of government, and provide for an amending process.[9] The U.S. Constitution does all four, but with one small problem: The Framers had a tendency to write as if everyone understood exactly what they meant. The Eighth Amendment, for example, prohibits "cruel and unusual punishment" for criminal offenses, but we are given no clue as to just what is to be considered cruel or unusual. The executive power is vested in the president, but no attempt is made to define the scope of the executive power. The Framers probably figured that they had done the hard part, and it was up to future generations to do the rest.

Because the Constitution is so ambiguous and because it serves as our fundamental law, courts—especially the U.S. Supreme Court—have played an important role in our political, as well as legal, system. The Supreme Court has an opportunity to expand the meaning of the

Constitution each time it interprets it. With its power of judicial review—the power to invalidate laws or actions contrary to the Constitution—the Supreme Court effects changes never dreamed of by the Framers. Whether the Court is settling an ordinary dispute or the Watergate Case, defining the meaning of "interstate commerce" or the Establishment Clause, the Court breathes life into the words of the Constitution. *Constitutional law,* then, represents the sum of thousands of Supreme Court and lower court decisions which have been settled in nearly 200 years of constitutional development. We will say more about the role of the Supreme Court in subsequent chapters.

Statutory Law.   We have already noted that one of the major sources of positive law is statutes passed by elected representative bodies. Congress and state legislatures pass statutes on the national and state levels, while city and county governments pass ordinances on the local level. In most cases, statutes are passed by a simple majority vote of the legislative body, subject to a veto by the chief executive. The content of *statutory law* may serve any number of purposes. Statutes may be passed to create or abolish government programs, increase the penalty for a crime, make an appropriation from the treasury, or raise the salaries of government workers. Statutes can regulate business activities, create new judgeships, impose a new tax, or proclaim a new holiday. In short, statutes can do anything that does not conflict with the Constitution—including making everyone rise an hour earlier each morning during the summer months.

You will recall from our earlier discussion of natural law and positive law that there is an inherent conflict between constitutional and statutory law. Constitutional law deals with fundamental rights of citizens, such as freedom of speech and press. These are "natural rights" upon which no government, not even one based on the principle of majority rule, may infringe. Statutory law, on the other hand, reflects the collective will of the majority (at least insofar as we have faith in representative government). In exercising its power of *judicial review,* the Supreme Court must decide whether to adhere to the fundamental law or to a law that reflects current opinion on a particular subject. By their very nature, the kinds of issues the Court is asked to resolve (abortion, capital punishment, and so on) are ones that require tough choices to be made between two or more conflicting sets of values. Understanding this inherent conflict is crucial to understanding not only our legal system, but our political system as well.

Administrative Law.   Under the U.S. Constitution, it is the Congress which has the power to regulate various activities that affect our lives on a daily basis. Thus, it is within Congressional power to regulate railroads, telecommunications, labor activities, airlines, and many other aspects of business and industry. Given the structure and makeup of Congress, it is impossible for it to have the expertise needed to regulate highly technical industries like broadcasting or nuclear energy. Consequently, Congress has seen fit to delegate its authority to regulate business and industry to more specialized bodies it has created within the executive branch of government. Over the years it has created numerous executive departments (such as the Department of Transportation) and so-called independent regulatory agencies (such as the Federal Trade Commission) to perform the tasks Congress is incapable of doing itself. These executive agencies have been empowered to promulgate rules and regulations which have the force of law. For example, the Federal Aviation Administration (FAA) may promulgate a rule requiring commercial airlines to provide a no-smoking section on domestic flights. The Food and Drug Administration (FDA) may specify the procedures with which drug manufacturers must comply before they may market a new drug. Failure to comply with an agency's regulations may lead to a heavy fine or other penalty.

Lief Carter, a noted expert on administrative law, has pointed out that administrative law is often confused with regulatory law. What we have discussed thus far is technically **regulatory law**. Administrative law, by contrast, is the law that controls those whom Congress has empowered to regulate on its behalf. As Carter has noted, "Administrative law . . . governs the bureaucrats themselves."[10] Administrative agencies are not directly accountable to the people and yet, as we have seen, the rules they promulgate are just as binding as any statute passed by a legislative body. We have also seen that our political system seeks to reduce the potential for official abuse of power. Administrative law governs the bureaucrats to ensure that they will not act in an arbitrary manner or abuse their power. Although this area of law is of increasing importance, it still receives relatively little attention from scholars.

Case Law. There is an old maxim that says, "I will let you write the law if you will let me interpret it." The implication of this statement, of course, is that while a law may appear to be clear and unequivocal when written, it can be subjected to many different interpretations. In Mosaic law, the command "Thou shalt not kill" is precise and to the point. Yet questions about its meaning still arise. What about killing in self-defense? What about an accidental killing? Shouldn't the word *kill* actually be interpreted as "murder"? *Case law* develops when judges interpret the meaning of constitutions, statutes, or other forms of written law. It may also include interpretations of other cases that have previously been decided under the law. Instead of trying to write laws that attempt to cover every conceivable contingency, lawmakers prefer to write general laws subject to judicial interpretation. Then, as circumstances and real cases or controversies arise, the judge may interpret the law to resolve the conflict in question.

Whenever judges interpret a law in a particular way, they create a precedent, or rule of law. As we have seen with constitutional law, each time the Supreme Court interprets the Constitution, it breathes new meaning into it and may create a new precedent. In the classic case *Miranda v. Arizona*,[11] the Supreme Court ruled that persons accused of a crime must be given information about their constitutional rights to remain silent and to consult with an attorney. This case created a precedent that in future cases, not just in Miranda's case, any person subject to a custodial arrest must be given these same *"Miranda* warnings." The Court, in effect, created a new rule of law where one previously had not existed. Although the justices claim only to "find" law, it is decisions like *Miranda* that leave the Court open to charges that the justices are really "making law." We will have more to say about judicial lawmaking in a later chapter.

Common Law. It is customary to save the best for last. Anglo-American law is rooted in the tradition of the common law. In 1881, Justice Oliver Wendell Holmes, Jr., wrote, "The life of the law has not been logic: It has been experience."[12] What Holmes meant is that law is not so much a function of our ability to logically deduce solutions to every conceivable conflict as it is a response to what he called "the felt necessities of the time."[13] Common law developed as a response to the need to find solutions to the felt necessities of the time.

Common law originated during the period of English history when there were very few written laws. Beginning about the time of Henry II, English kings sent their judges throughout the country to dispense the King's justice with little or no statutory law to guide their decisions. When conflicts arose and no statute applied, judges still had to resolve them somehow. As a result, decisions were based on rules of law, which in turn were based on an individual judge's sense of equity or fairness. Like King Solomon, who had to decide which of the two women should be given the baby, English judges had to make on-the-spot decisions to resolve pressing disputes. Once a rule of law thus formulated was recognized as just and reasonable, other judges in other jurisdictions would adopt it and apply it in their own, similar cases. Eventually the rule would be written down and used by all judges in the realm. A rule of law became "common," not in the sense of being ordinary, but in the sense of being common to all parts of England.

The reader should note the close relationship between common law and case law. Both rely heavily on the rule of precedence and both allow the judge discretion in interpreting the law. Common law, like case law, is often described as "judge-made." One important difference exists: Unlike case law, which is a court's interpretation of an existing constitution or statute, common-law rules developed in the absence of any positive law. In addition, a common-law rule can be set aside by the enactment of a statute. For example, under the common-law doctrine of *caveat emptor* ("let the buyer beware"), the purchaser of an item was expected to examine the merchandise before buying it in order to avoid being cheated by the merchant. If the purchaser failed to do so, he was partly to blame for not being careful; that is, he should have taken care so that he would not be cheated. Today, most states have laws to protect consumers from fraudulent business practices, and the common-law doctrine of *caveat emptor* is no longer applicable. Thus the common-law doctrine may be superseded by the enactment of positive law.

BOB JONES UNIVERSITY V. UNITED STATES

Our approach to the discussion of the functions, sources, and kinds of law might lead one to believe that law can be neatly categorized. In reality, it is a bit more complicated. A recent Supreme Court decision, *Bob Jones University v. United States*, illustrates how a single case may involve several kinds of law and incorporates a number of the points made in this chapter.

   Background of the Case.[14]   Section 501 (C) (3) of the Internal Revenue Code contains a description of organizations that are granted tax-exempt status by the national government. Section 170 of the Code specifies that individual contributions to these organizations may qualify as charitable deductions on individual tax returns. Until 1970, Bob Jones University was granted tax-exempt status under Section 501 (C) (3) by the Internal Revenue Service (IRS). Due to its interpretation of a lower federal court ruling,[15] however, the IRS notified the University in November 1970 that it could no longer grant tax-exempt status to "private schools which practice racial discrimination," nor could contributions made to them be charitable deductions under Section 170. The IRS formalized this policy by promulgating Revenue Ruling 71–447.
   Bob Jones University is an institution dedicated to teaching fundamentalist Christian beliefs. Until 1971, it had completely excluded blacks. From 1971 to 1975 it accepted applications from blacks who were married within their own race. The University permitted the enrollment of unmarried blacks in 1975 but also enforced a strict policy banning interracial dating and marriage and expelling any student who espoused the idea. According to the IRS interpretation, an organization

qualifies for tax-exempt status only if it is a "charitable" institution within the common-law meaning of that term. Under the common law, an institution that pursues activities contrary to public policy is not charitable. The IRS ruled that by practicing racial discrimination, Bob Jones University was acting against a clear "national policy to discourage racial discrimination in education."[16]

Ruling in the Case. Bob Jones University challenged the revocation of its tax-exempt status on three grounds. First, it asserted that the IRS had no authority to promulgate Revenue Ruling 71–447. Second, the University challenged the IRS's interpretation of Section 501 (C) (3). According to the University's interpretation, the section grants tax-exempt status to organizations that operate exclusively for ". . . religious, charitable, scientific, . . . *or* educational purposes."[17] Because the word *or* separates "charitable" from "educational" purposes, the IRS's application of the common-law definition of *charitable* was inappropriate. Since the University clearly is organized for educational purposes, it should have qualified for the exemption. Finally, the University argued that the IRS's construction of Section 501 (C) (3) and Section 170 violated the Free Excercise Clause of the First Amendment because the University's racial policy was based upon sincerely held religious beliefs.

In an 8–1 decision, the Supreme Court rejected all three of the University's challenges in an opinion written by Chief Justice Warren E. Burger. The Court rejected the University's contention that the IRS had no authority to promulgate Revenue Ruling 71–447 without specific congressional authorization. Chief Justice Burger noted that since the inception of the tax code, Congress had granted broad authority to the IRS to interpret the tax laws. He wrote, "In an area as complex as the tax system, the agency Congress vests with administrative responsibility must be able to exercise its authority to meet changing conditions and new problems."[18] The Chief Justice then proceeded to note that any time after the promulgation of Revenue Ruling 71–447, Congress could have modified it; Congress had chosen not to do so, however, indicating tacit approval of the policy. Thus, if Congress felt that the IRS's ruling was arbitrary or constituted an abuse of its authority, Congress could have done something about it during the ensuing ten years and did not.

The Court also rejected the University's contention that the IRS misapplied the term *charitable* and that it should qualify for tax-exempt status solely because of its educational purposes. The Chief Justice stated that it was clearly the intent of Congress to exempt "charitable" organizations—that is, organizations that serve a public purpose, and not purposes contrary to established public policy. In a footnote to the opinion,[19] Chief Justice Burger pointed out that if the University's interpretation was accepted, then a school for training terrorists (clearly "educational" in purpose) would qualify for an exemption. He concluded that Congress surely did not intend for that to happen.

Finally, the Court rejected the University's First Amendment claim that the revocation of the tax exemption constituted a violation of the Free Exercise Clause. In previous cases[20] interpreting that clause, the Court has ruled that the government may justify a limitation on religious liberty by demonstrating "an overriding governmental interest." Chief Justice Burger concluded that the government's interest in eradicating racial discrimination in education was "compelling" and that it justified the burden on religious liberty. He noted that although the denial of tax benefits would have an impact on the University, it would not prevent the University from observing the tenets of its religion.[21]

Analysis of the Case. The *Bob Jones University* case illustrates several of the points previously made in this chapter. First, it involves several kinds of law: constitutional, statutory, regulatory, administrative, case law, and common law. The constitutional question raised was the free exercise claim made by the University. Statutory law was involved when the Court was called upon to interpret Section 501 (C) (3) and Section 170. The common law definition of *charitable* adopted by the IRS was a major issue in the case. The question of whether or not the IRS had the authority to promulgate Revenue Ruling 71–447 was one of administrative law, while the IRS's use of *charitable* in promulgating the Ruling was one of regulatory law. Finally, the Court cited numerous precedents, not included in our analysis, to substantiate its decision, thus illustrating the use of case law.

Second, *Bob Jones University* demonstrates the conflict between minority rights and majority rule. There is no reason to doubt that the officials of the University were sincere in their racial viewpoint or that their views were grounded in their religious beliefs. In following the course they chose, these officials undoubtedly believed that they were obeying a higher law, superior to the laws of the IRS or even the United States government. But the Supreme Court's opinion made it clear that the racial views of Bob Jones University were incompatible with a public policy endorsed by all three branches of the national government. The conflict was between the University's right to act upon its sincerely held religious beliefs and the majority's right to eradicate racial discrimination in the field of education.

Third, the case demonstrates the role of courts in supervising the government bureaucracy. The Supreme Court had to decide whether the IRS's application of the term *charitable* to the University was reasonable and within IRS's power. A ruling either that the IRS's application was unwarranted or that it had exceeded its authority would have resulted in a victory for the University.

Finally, the case illustrates how judges make decisions. Attorneys for the University offered some sound arguments that Congress intended to exempt organizations that are "charitable *or* educational" rather than "charitable *and* educational." Courts must often ascertain the intent of Congress when interpreting an ambiguous statute. Even when one or more interpretations are reasonable, courts must choose one over the other. In cases of far-reaching importance, such as *Bob Jones University*, the interpretation chosen will have a broad impact as a precedent in future cases. It is in this manner that law is an evolving concept that appears to be static but is actually constantly changing.

CONCLUSION

We began this chapter by asserting that there is a paradox of law in the United States. Americans possess ambivalent feelings about law. These feelings result from the fact that people disagree over what law is, where it comes from, and what it should do. We said that our ambivalence about law is related to the ambivalence we have about our society in general. We might all believe in "equality of opportunity" in principle, but disagree over the propriety of affirmative action programs. Likewise, we can agree with the ideal of the rule of law without agreeing on just what that means. There is no right or wrong, or even single, answer to the question, What is law? Our view of the law depends on what we consider to be the functions of law and the source of law. In the final analysis, we must decide for ourselves what law really is.

Understanding the major ideas in this chapter is important to understanding what will follow. Without a firm grasp of these basic concepts, it will be more difficult to fully appreciate much of the discussion of the material covered in the remaining chapters.

NOTES

[1] Harold Lasswell, *Politics: Who Gets What, When, How?* (New York: McGraw-Hill, 1936).

[2] Anthony G. Amsterdam, "The Void-for-Vagueness Doctrine in the Supreme Court," *Univ. of Pennsylvania Law Review*, Vol. 109 (1960), p. 67.

[3] *Ginzburg v. United States*, 383 U.S. 463 (1966) (Black, J., dissenting).

[4] cf. David Eliot Brody, *The American Legal System: Concepts and Principles* (Lexington, Mass.: Heath, 1978), pp. 4–7.

[5] Martin Luther King, Jr., "Letter from Birmingham Jail," in Fred R. Harris, *America's Democracy*, 2nd ed. (Glenview, Ill.: Scott, Foresman, 1983), pp. 117–118.

[6] *People v. DeFore*, 242 N.Y. 13, 150 N.E. 585 (1926) (Cardozo, J.).

[7] U.S. Constitution, Art. VI, sec. 1, para. 2.

[8] Ibid.

[9] C. Herman Pritchett, *The American Constitutional System*, 5th ed. (New York: McGraw-Hill, 1981), p. 2.

[10] Lief H. Carter, *Administrative Law and Politics: Cases and Comments* (Boston: Little, Brown, 1983), p. 38.

[11] *Miranda v. Arizona*, 384 U.S. 436 (1966).

[12] Oliver Wendell Holmes, Jr., *The Common Law* (Boston: Little, Brown, 1881), pp. 1–2.

[13] Ibid.

[14] The facts of this case are summarized from the majority opinion of Chief Justice Warren E. Burger, *Bob Jones University v. United States*, 461 U.S. 574 (1983).

[15] *Green v. Kennedy*, 309 F.Supp. 1127 (D.D.C., 1970).

[16] *Bob Jones University v. United States*, 461 U.S. 574 (1983), at 579.

[17] Ibid., p. 585.

[18] Ibid., p. 596.

[19] Ibid., footnote 18, pp. 591–592.

[20] *Sherbert v. Verner*, 374 U.S. 398 (1963); *Wisconsin v. Yoder*, 406 U.S. 205 (1972).

[21] *Bob Jones University v. United States*, 461 U.S. 574 (1983), at 603–604.

2

History and the Law

The life of the law has not been logic; it has been experience. . . . The law embodies the story of a nation's development through many centuries and it cannot be dealt with as if it contained only the axioms and corollaries of a book of mathematics. In order to know what it is, we must know what it has been, and what it tends to become.[1]

All societies develop methods of resolving conflicts among their members. Some are formally organized, such as the U.S. court system, while others are much more primitive; but it is imperative that the rules governing a society be enforced if chaos is to be prevented.

The need to maintain order in society is not recent. Ancient civilizations created laws and legal systems to control their members and to resolve conflicts. Remnants of these legal systems linger, and many of today's theories and practices may be traced to them. Cases such as *Roe v. Wade*, the abortion case, are replete with historical references to other, older systems of legal doctrine.

LAW THROUGH THE AGES

One of the earliest extant sets of laws is the Code of Hammurabi, developed by King Hammurabi of Babylon in about 2000 B.C. It set forth the rules of human behavior demanded by the gods. The code was harsh; for example, adulterers were punished by death.

Egyptian law, like the civilization itself, was highly developed. The law was enforced by priests, and its criminal provisions were more lenient. Although the death penalty existed, it was often commuted to penal servitude or slavery.[2]

Hebrew law blended characteristics of both systems. It was based on the premise that law is of divine origin (the Ten Commandments, for example)—that is, that God is the source of all law. It advanced the legal theory of revenge—"an eye for an eye"—a theory later mitigated by the idea of forgiveness, which was advanced in the New Testament. Early Hebrew law was based on the Pentateuch (the first five books of the Old Testament, or the Mosaic Code) and the Talmud (a legal encyclopedia and collection of traditions which governs many aspects of Jewish life). Ancient Hebrew law provided for some 36 capital crimes, which were punished by beheading, strangling, burning, and stoning, depending on the nature of the crime. Imprisonment was not initially used as a form of punishment; instead, the usual corporal punishment was flagellation, or whipping. Slavery was the punishment for theft. The Hebrew system had two striking features: (1) There were no advocates or lawyers involved, and the witnesses were the accusers and prosecutors; and (2) all courts had more than one judge—three at the lowest level, twenty-three at the next, and seventy-one at the highest court in Jerusalem.[3]

The Greeks also made major contributions to legal philosophy. The laws of Greece in the fourth and fifth centuries B.C. were flexible and could be tailored to fit the dispute when it was brought before the King, who relied on the gods for help in making his decisions. This individualization probably stemmed from the fact that Greek citizens could participate in government and were therefore influential.

Several prominent philosophers of the time considered the role of law in society. For example, Draco felt that all crimes were equal and should be punished alike; it was the violation of the law, the act against society, that was critical, and not the harm to the individual. Plato and Aristotle struggled with the question of whether the required conduct was fair and just by nature or merely required by convention or legislative enactment. For them, law was primarily a method of maintaining the status quo and the social order.[4]

Following the Greeks, the Romans became the dominant force in the development of law. Cicero, a noted Roman philosopher, defined three elements of law: legislation, administrative edicts, and judicial reasoning on the basis of legal tradition. Today, these same three dominate U.S. law. **Roman law** was highly developed, and it had spread throughout the far reaches of present-day Europe under the Empire's superb administrative system. Even after the fall of the western empire in 476, the eastern empire, led by the emperor at Constantinople, continued to develop the concepts of Roman law. In A.D. 528, the emperor Justinian collected the laws of the vast empire and published them as the Code of Justinian, or *Corpus Juris Civilis.* The authority and power of this collection is immense. Justinian's Code is a cornerstone of today's so-called *civil law* systems. Much of the *canon law* developed by the Catholic Church reflects Justinian's Codes, and its precepts can be found in common-law countries as well. Although the Code essentially disappeared during the Middle Ages, it was revived during the twelfth century by professors at the Italian universities, especially at Bologna. This initiated the growth of new law and the system of legal science; however, the process was a long and complex one, spurred on by changes in both the political and commercial spheres that accompanied the revitalization of trade and the emergence of Europe from the Dark Ages.[5]

In civil-law countries, the law is extensively codified, and decisions are based on the code as designed by the legislature, rather than on binding judicial precedent. The premise is that each case should be decided on its own merits within the parameters prescribed by the codes. "From the Anglo-American point of view, French legal reasoning appears to start with a highly generalized proposition of law to which the facts are then fitted, rather than to begin with a detailed examination of the facts followed by application of a narrowly formulated rule."[6] The same transactions and activities are governed or barred by the civil codes as by common law jurisdictions; it is the approach taken in legal reasoning and methodology which distinguishes them. Generally, judges in these systems are specially trained for their role; they are not elevated from among practicing lawyers. In France, virtually anyone can give legal advice or prepare legal documents, but specialists must be hired for litigation and presentation of oral argument.[7]

Today, the civil-law tradition dominates in Europe, South America, Scotland, Quebec, and Louisiana. Many of the former French colonies of Northern Africa adapted much of the Napoleonic Code and grafted it onto tribal and customary law. The Napoleonic Code, adopted in 1804, provided a unified system of law for the country as a whole, replacing a system of localized laws. The 1896 Germanic Code was later adopted by Japan and by precommunist China. Thus, the widespread use of the civil system has extended far beyond the boundaries of Europe.[8]

Nearly 100 years after Justinian codifed the Roman law, a new religion developed in the Middle East, the teachings of which have expanded into a major legal system with worldwide influence. "The sacred law of Islam is an all-embracing body of religious duties, the totality of Allah's commands that regulate the life of every Muslim in all its aspects. . . . Islamic law is the epitome of Islamic thought."[9]

Before Islam, the law in the area for both the Bedouins and the sedentary populations was the law of the ancient Arabian tribal systems, and the pattern of adhering to tradition and precedent continues. Islam supplied a uniform system of laws, a system that was not limited by national boundaries but encompassed all the followers of Allah. The schism among Muslim sects (which continues to this day) affected the interpretation of the law, but many of the basic precepts are adopted by all.[10] Modern nations in the Middle East often seek to synthesize Islamic laws and western legal systems. The religious law prevails with regard to family, inheritance, and criminal matters, while the western influence is frequently stronger in the area of commercial matters. The "most potent" western source is the Napoleonic Code, which is modified to meet the unique requirements of Islam.[11] One of the most obvious influences of Islamic law in the United States is in prisoners' rights cases in which incarcerated Black Muslims claimed the protection of the First Amendment's Free Exercise Clause.

Americans are known for their insular approach to many things, not the least of which is law. The English common law has so dominated our jurisprudence that we tend to overlook other systems; but that system was not created in a vacuum, nor was it the only highly developed one. For example, treatises describing the Chinese codes, which were developed as early as 220 B.C., are extant. In his work *Law and Society in Traditional China*, T'ung-Tsu Ch'u argues that Chinese society remained essentially static until the twentieth century, and that the prominent elements of the system—status by kinship and by social stratification—and the laws remained remarkably unaltered from the law codes of the Ch'in (221–207 B.C.) until this century.[12] Today there are three dominant legal systems: the common-law systems (which will be discussed in the next section), the civil-law systems, and the Russian system, which borrows heavily from the civil-law system and then superimposes the legal requirements of communism and its centrally planned economy.[13] All derive from common origins, and each system serves the same purposes. They cannot be wholly separated from one another in tracing the sources and effects, nor should they be.

THE ENGLISH HERITAGE

Development of the Common Law.   During the Dark Ages following the collapse of the Roman Empire, anarchy and confusion predominated. No one source of authority had the might to enforce order. Any restraints on antisocial behavior developed within tribes or within local areas, and most conflicts were resolved by violence. As society emerged from that period, the demand for order increased, and the primary source was the Roman civil law, especially Justinian's Code. In England, however, the pattern was broken. The first code in that country was a succinct collection of laws created by order of Aethelbert, Christian King of Kentings, in about A.D. 600. This brief code was expanded by Canute, who ruled from 1017 until 1035, and whose laws were written in English.[14]

By the early twelfth century, Anglo-Saxon England differed from other European realms in that there was an organized system of justice. The country was divided into vills, or townships, a number of which composed the hundred, while several hundreds formed the shire. The administration of justice was primarily local. There were public courts at both the hundred and shire levels, and there were courts headed by the lord of the manor, who resolved disputes among his own tenants.

Court procedure was fairly uniform. Each party appeared in court. The plaintiff would allege the improper activity in the form of an oath, and the defendant would enter a denial in the form of an oath. Generally, the defendant would then present a requisite number of character witnesses (frequently twelve) who would swear that the defendant was telling the truth; these witnesses did not testify as to the facts of the case, but merely as to the veracity of the defendant. The communities were small, and all the trial participants were known to each other. Those who swore falsely were subject not only to distrust from their peers, but also to punishment imposed by God.

In criminal cases, twelve freemen served as the accusers before the court and presented the names of those they believed to have committed crimes. Guilt or innocence would then be proven either by compurgation (the process, just described, of clearing a person by oaths of others as to his veracity) or by ordeal. Trial by ordeal frequently involved burning a person's hand or arm, binding the wound, and examining it after a short period. If the wound was clean, the accused was cleared of the crime. Another creative method of trial was to toss a bound person into a stream. If he sank, he was innocent; if he floated, he was guilty. Either result was quite unfortunate. The Anglo-Saxons also employed fines or a system of reparation for those found guilty. They used the system even for homicides; each person's life had a value, set according to his or her station, with the king's being the most valuable. The *wergild*, the fine, was divided among the king for the loss of a subject, the lord for the loss of a vassal, and the deceased's family. The Normans added the possibility of trial by combat, wherein one could either compete for oneself or hire a champion to engage in battle. Although the methods were crude, these courts provided a forum for grievances to be heard.

The Normans greatly strengthened the administrative organization of the country and tightened the control of the government in the hands of the monarch. In addition, feudalism, which had just begun to flourish in England, became the dominant social order. William the

Conqueror assumed ownership of land for himself as monarch, but he allowed his followers dominion over great tracts of it in exchange for certain services and goods, including military service or agricultural products. In turn, William's tenants subdivided the land and responsibilities until they had established an entire chain of reciprocal duties, reaching from the monarch to the lowliest serf.

William also maintained his own tribunal, the King's Court, both for the protection of royal interests and as an appellate court for those litigants who could travel to the royal court; however, the vast majority of cases were resolved in the hundred or shire courts or in the seignorial courts of the barons. It was a time of establishing new patterns in resolving conflicts, of turning from self-help methods of revenge to a quasi-formal means of adjudication; nevertheless, much of Anglo-Saxon law and customs continued relatively unchanged. William and his successors did not overturn the laws that they found, but instead supplemented them with a strong centralized judiciary and uniformity of decisions.

Henry II, the first Plantagenet, who ruled from 1154 until 1189, had a major influence on the development of English law and the centralization of the judicial system. His goals were two: The first was to ensure that the fees paid by litigants flowed into the royal coffers and not to the barons, and the second was to consolidate royal control. Crimes became wrongs against the king as well as against the individual, and more serious criminal matters came before the Curia Regis, an advisory body of the king's counselors who carried out judicial, executive, and administrative functions. Juries were employed in trial, supplanting the older systems of trial by compurgation, ordeal, and combat.

Henry II bolstered his control over local courts by vigorously applying the royal executive writ, which directed his subjects to perform or to refrain from certain actions; failure to obey the writ could result in punishment. A writ might very well order judges of the shire, hundred, or seignorial courts to find for a particular plaintiff, a usurpation of authority which contributed to the demise of the local courts. In addition, Henry II revived the practice, instituted by Henry I, of sending judges from the Curia Regis into the countryside to settle disputes, although their primary task was revenue collection. It was Edward I who, by the Statute of Westminster in 1285, institutionalized the practice of sending itinerant judges on circuits to render justice.

As these changes were occurring, other developments were also taking place. By the end of the thirteenth century, there were three law courts in the secular realm and a firmly entrenched system of ecclesiastical courts. The latter enforced canon law as handed down by the Catholic Church and had sole jurisdiction over matters of marital relationships and inheritance. The canon law was composed of papal decrees, writings of church scholars, and Scripture; it was heavily influenced by Italian law and by the training that the priests received in the traditions of Roman law. The domination of the ecclesiastical courts over marriages lasted until the mid-nineteenth century, although the Catholic Church was supplanted by the Church of England.

The three law courts were distinguished by function, although their jurisdictions often overlapped. The Court of Common Pleas, located in London, dealt with disputes that were essentially civil in nature. The Court of the King's Bench was mobile; it initially followed the king on his journeys across the countryside. It exercised appellate jurisdiction over the Court of Common Pleas and over matters, including criminal matters, involving the king. The third court, the Exchequer, dealt primarily with matters of revenue and taxation.

The outcome of the monarchs' centralization of the judicial system is the rejection of the civil-law tradition in England and the substitution of the common law. Strong kings who consolidated judicial power in their own hands, and who imposed a uniform system of tribunals over the entire country rather than allowing the local courts to remain viable, contributed mightily to the development of the common law, often termed *judge-made law.* Due to the paucity of statutes, the judges formalized the customs and mores of the times into court decisions and applied the same rules in whatever corner of the realm they happened to be. Consistency was facilitated by written reports of judicial decisions kept by the king's courts, collected by such authors as Henry of Bracton, and used as authority or precedent by subsequent judges.[15] Common law "describes that part of the law that is unenacted, non-statutory, that is common to the whole land and to all Englishmen."[16] It became the basis for the legal systems of the English-speaking nations of the world.

Development of Equity. The business of government in England during the thirteenth century was carried out by two governmental departments: the Exchequer, which handled fiscal matters, and the Chancery, which was the secretarial department. The Chancery was headed by an official called a chancellor, usually a cleric, who was responsible for handling the government's paperwork, including the writs for courts. The writs served three purposes: (1) as the document giving the plaintiff access to the courts in exchange for the payment of a fee; (2) as a method of designating which court would decide the case; and (3) as a tool for directing the sheriff to summon the defendant for the court appearance. The Chancery eventually developed standard writs for various legal wrongs, but by statute (the second Statute of Westminster in 1285) the Chancery was empowered to "let a writ be made by those learned in the law so that for the future it shall not befall that the court shall delay over-long in doing justice to complaints."[17]

Although the common-law courts were initially creative and flexible, they soon petrified, adopting rigid, harsh procedures. In addition, the courts could provide only one remedy—damages. The reservoir of justice remained the king, who was God's secular representative on earth. In those situations in which the remedy provided by the common-law courts was inadequate, or when the plaintiffs were impoverished and could not afford the court fees (or their opponents were influential and wealthy), the complainants petitioned the king to consider their causes. The king, in turn, transferred to the chancellor the laborious task of reading the numerous petitions, and soon the petitions were filed directly with the Chancery rather than with the monarch. But the plea remained the same: "to do what is right for the love of God and in the way of charity."[18] Remember that the chancellors were ecclesiastics who were trained in Roman and canon law, with its foundation of natural law. The appeal was to the conscience of the chancellor and a higher system of justice.[19] If the chancellor agreed with the petition, the defendant would be ordered to appear before the chancellor to respond to the allegations. At that time, the defendant would be placed under oath and questioned by the chancellor, who determined questions of both law and fact and then shaped a remedy.

It is for the formation of extraordinary relief that the Chancery achieved its greatest fame in jurisprudence. As pointed out earlier, the sole remedy in common-law courts was monetary damages; however, that is not always an adequate solution. Suppose that there is a building of substantial historic significance in your community, but over the years it has deteriorated; now the new owner of the property is determined to tear it down. The payment of monetary damages will neither reconstruct the building nor pay the community for the loss of a symbol of its past. Preservationists would seek an injunction to prevent the destruction of the building. The *injunction,* a court order directing a person to refrain from carrying out certain acts, could halt demolition of the building. If the property owner defied the injunction, he or she would be subject to certain legal penalties, such as fines and possibly even a jail sentence. The injunction is an example of the remedies created by the courts of *equity;* the common-law courts, on the other hand, as originally structured, would not intervene and would wait until the injury had occurred to award damages—a patent absurdity. Other equitable remedies included specific performance and trusts, both of which will be discussed in later chapters. The result of the Chancellor's activities was to forge parallel court systems, each with different remedies.

Thus, for some 400 years, England had two types of courts—the historic common-law courts and the more flexible courts of equity; in the late nineteenth century, the two were merged, and all courts were to apply the rules of both, with equity being dominant in case of conflict. The remedies fashioned by the English jurists during these centuries are basically the same as those used by courts today. The remedies provided for particular types of legal wrongs are discussed in connection with particular theories, but it is appropriate to describe the traditional forms of redress here also. Judges, whether in common-law or equity courts, adhered to the principle that "for every wrong there is a remedy," and they struggled to create the forms of judicial relief available today.

One approach to the study of remedies is to examine them from the perspective of both the plaintiff and the defendant. A court may award specific relief and substitutionary relief to a successful plaintiff. *Specific relief,* such as an injunction or an order for the defendant to perform his portion of a contract, is an equitable remedy and is directed to individuals and their activities. It has limited application and is not always the most appropriate nor the most desirable remedy. *Substitutionary relief,* the basic common-law remedy, generally refers to the award of money as compensation for a loss. The losing defendant may be imprisoned (for contempt of court, as an example), required to pay either compensatory or punitive damages or to transfer property to the plaintiff, or required to perform or to refrain from some act.

A second approach is to identify the type of legal wrong and the related remedial goals. Tort law deals with injuries sustained by individuals and with their lawsuits against those who injure them. There are three general remedial goals in tort law: restoration to the status quo, compensation or indemnification, and punishment. For example, assume that there has been an automobile accident with injuries sustained by the drivers and property damage to the cars. The repair work done to the vehicles to remove the dents and replace the headlights is an example of restoration to the status quo, or to the preaccident condition. The money paid to the injured party for his hospital bills and lost wages illustrates the principle of compensation or indemnification, whereby the party is reimbursed for pecuniary losses stemming from the accident. A money award may be assessed by the jury to punish the wrongdoer for egregious acts, such as driving while intoxicated and injuring a child. In contrast, the goals of contract remedies include the following: (1) putting the party in the position he or she would have been in if the contract been fulfilled; (2) restoring the parties to their original positions; (3) compensating the plaintiff for any detriment incurred in reliance of the contract (such as a painter purchasing paint in expectation of the homeowner fulfilling his portion of the contract); and (4) punishing the party breaching the contract. Obviously, some of the goals are similar in both areas (restoration of the plaintiff to his original position and punishment of the wrongdoer), but other remedies are tailored to rectify specific legal wrongs.[20]

Equity provided the flexibility to tailor remedies to situations in which the legal remedies were not adequate. It added a sense of a fairness, of an appeal to the conscience of the purveyors of justice, which greatly strengthened the system. Fredrick Maitland, one of the greatest English legal scholars and a noted expert on equity, described its place in jurisprudence:

> [W]e ought to think of equity as supplementary law, a sort of appendix added on to our code, or a sort of gloss written round our code, an appendix, a gloss. . . . The language which equity held to law, if we may personify the two, was not "No, that is not so, you make a mistake, your rule is an absurd, an obsolete one"; but "Yes, of course that is so, but it is not the whole truth." . . . We ought not to think of common law and equity as of two rival systems. Equity was not a self-sufficient system, at every point it presupposed the existence of common law. Common law was a self-sufficient system. . . .
>
> [I] do not think that any one has expounded or ever will expound equity as a single, consistent system, an articulate body of law. It is a collection of appendixes between which there is no very close connexion. If we suppose all our law put into a systematic order, we shall find that some chapters of it have been copiously glossed by equity, while others are quite free from equitable glosses.[21]

THE AMERICAN EXPERIENCE

The colonists who moved to the New World brought with them the legal traditions of their homelands. Vestiges of each system—Dutch, English, French, and Spanish—can be found in the laws of the various states.

> History of a system of law is largely a history of borrowings of legal materials from other legal systems and of assimilation of materials from outside the law. In the history of Anglo-American law there are successive borrowings and adaptations from Roman law (e.g. the rules as to title by occupation), from the canon law (e.g., our law and practice as to marriage and divorce and probate and administration), from the modern Roman law and Continental codes (e.g., in our law of riparian rights), and from the commercial law of Continental Europe . . .[22]

The dominant scheme was the common-law system of England. Formalistic in tenor and designed to deal with a highly structured society, it was inadequate for the demands of the colonists. They tempered the system and forged new precepts that more accurately reflected the social and economic realities of the New World. One hallmark of the new system was the merger of law and equity, and the power of a single judge to render both types of remedies in the appropriate cases (as opposed to the English scheme of parallel court systems). A second characteristic of the new system was the abolition of the common-law power of judges to define crimes, and the substitution of the legislature as the body to identify criminal activity and to determine the appropriate range of punishment. In the new land, there was increased emphasis on the individual, because of both the religious beliefs and the need to be self-sufficient in opening up new territory. The colonists adopted those portions of the common law that were appropriate and modified others, and each colony developed innovative approaches to conflict resolution. In sum, there was no abandonment of important principles or abrupt break with the English system, although adjustments were made to suit the new environment.

> Those who formed the Constitution struck out anew free of previous shackles in an effort to obtain a better order of government more congenial to human liberty and welfare. It cannot be seriously claimed that they intended to adopt the common law wholesale. They accepted those portions of it which were adapted to this country and conformed to the ideals of its citizens and rejected the remainder. In truth there was widespread hostility to the common law in general and profound opposition to its adoption into our jurisprudence from the commencement of the Revolutionary War until long after the Constitution was ratified.[23]

To illustrate the adaptation process, consider the incorporation of established elements of citizens' rights against government into the fundamental laws of the United States. The Magna Carta, signed by King John in 1215 and regarded as one of the most important documents in the history of the English-speaking world, constituted formal recognition by the monarch of certain rights held by citizens. It contains two provisions that were adopted into the U.S. Constitution. First, the section of the Magna Carta that stated that there should be no criminal "trial upon . . . simple accusation without producing credible witnesses to the truth therein" was the foundation of the rights guaranteed to criminal defendants in the Fifth and Sixth Amendments. Similarly, Section 39, which provides that "no freeman shall be taken, imprisoned or disseised, or outlawed, or banished, or in any other way destroyed, nor will we go upon him, nor send upon him, except by legal judgment of his peers or the law of the land," was the basis of the constitutional provisions preventing deprivation of life, liberty, or property without due process of law. Other basic guarantees found in the English Bill of Rights of 1689, such as the ones preventing the suspension of laws without the consent of Parliament and protecting the freedom of speech which "ought not to be impeached or questioned," were wholly adopted by the writers of the U.S. Constitution. Fundamental liberties available to the English were identified and guaranteed to the former colonists, but the influence of the English pattern extends to both substantive and procedural laws as well.

Following the Revolution, legislatures representing the will of the sovereign people came to supplant judges as the primary lawmakers.

This was due, in part, to several factors. First, the absolute governments in Europe had been successfully challenged by legislative bodies, as indicated by the victory of Parliament and Oliver Cromwell over the absolute monarchs in the English Revolution of 1688. Second, these entities represented the will of the sovereign people to have a democratic and representative government. Third, the Founding Fathers were familiar with the law on the Continent, with its strong tradition of the legislature as absolute lawgiver; in addition, English law and the king's judges were in some disrepute in this nation following the Revolution. Fourth, the legislature was the dominant branch of government during these formative days. Fifth, the Constitution of the United States, unlike that of Great Britain, carefully prescribes the responsibilities of each governmental branch; however, judges retain the option to approve new theories of recovery and to demand new procedures in accordance with their assigned constitutional duties.[24]

In addition, the legislatures began in the early 1800s to codify the various statutes within the states. Unfortunately, legislatures pass laws in a haphazard order and amend them at later dates, again with no particular attention paid to organization. The purpose of the codification movement in the United States was to collect the related statutes and arrange them coherently in order to facilitate their use. Although some advocates anticipated that these codes would be used as the continental codes were, that has not been the result; instead, courts retained much of their power to determine the constitutionality of the codes, and judges still rely more on precedent than on the code provisions. Today's practitioners, laypersons, and judges routinely use codes, such as the Internal Revenue Code or the Penal Code, but they use them primarily as references or collections of statutes; the interpretation of the statutes is left to the judicial and administrative branches. Some of the codes are merely reenactments of judicially established rules, such as the various codes of criminal or civil procedures and the Uniform Commercial Code. Both the uniform laws that are adopted by individual states and the Restatements (standard compilations of laws in various substantive areas) have contributed to the consistency of laws within a nation composed of 51 sovereign entities invested with the power to make law.

Nevertheless, judges remain the most potent and powerful component of the American legal systems. It is they who work daily with the law and who give it a unique twist to fit the situations confronting the courts. The reliance of judges on precedent and the doctrine of *stare decisis* remains as strong and viable as it was in the day of Henry II. **Stare decisis** refers to the policy of courts to follow the rules laid down in previous judicial decisions and to refrain from disturbing established points of law. The purpose is to ensure stability and certainty in the legal system. Litigants are aware of the results in similar prior cases and make their decisions in regard to the lawsuit accordingly; *stare decisis* enhances predictability. Judges are entrusted with great power and authority, not only in deciding specific cases but also as lawgivers.

THE AMERICAN LEGAL PROFESSION

As discussed in Chapter 3 on court organization, most American judges—although not all—are practicing attorneys at the time they assume the bench. Americans have a love-hate relationship with lawyers. On the one hand, lawyers are highly regarded and respected; on the other, many citizens share the feelings of Plato, Shakespeare, and others who have launched scathing attacks on the legal profession and its practitioners. For instance, King Ferdinand of Spain commented that, on the colonization of the West Indies, "no lawyers should be carried along, lest lawsuits should become ordinary occurrences in the New World."[25] Americans both appreciate and resent lawyers' specialized knowledge and the power that information carries.

Most lawyers in the United States today have at least a baccalaureate degree in addition to three years of law school. They must also be licensed by the state in which they practice and by the federal courts in which they try cases. This was not historically true. Attorneys lacked formal legal education; instead, they trained as apprentices by "reading" law with established practitioners. In fact, reading the learned treatises about the law, especially William Blackstone's *Commentaries on the Laws of England,* was the major method of legal education. Few reports of court cases were available, and Blackstone's comprehensive restatement of the law served as the principal collection for students for many years. His work was eventually supplemented by American scholarly writings, published reports of court cases, and formal legal training.

Modern legal education centers around universities, as has always been the case in civil-law countries. The usual educational model is for students to read cases, extract the general principles, and then submit to classroom interrogation by professors. Law classes rarely involve lectures; instead, they are conducted along the lines recommended by Socrates—that is, a continuous series of challenging questions to be answered by the students. The students are to apply to hypothetical situations the reasoning and rules of law they have abstracted from assigned cases. The procedure resembles that used by a judge in examining the pertinent precedent and applying it to the case at bar.

This format enables students to think in terms of plaintiffs and defendants and to consider only those facts relevant to the guiding principle of the case. It is an impersonal analysis. It obscures the reality that the cases involve real people with real injuries, a fact which has been frequently criticized. In his book *Persons and Masks of the Law,* John T. Noonan examines the treatment of one of the most famous of all tort cases, *Palsgraf v. Long Island Railroad Company.* In part, his purpose is to challenge impersonal, detached treatment and to advance the argument that scholars and lawyers "should be concerned with law not as a set of technical skills which may be put to any use but as a human activity affecting both those acting and those enduring their action."[26] The facts of the Palsgraf case, as described in the opinion, were that a railroad passenger carrying some fireworks was jostled by railroad employees who were trying to assist him. The passenger dropped the fireworks, which exploded, and the shock of the explosion knocked down some scales, which struck and injured the plaintiff. She sued the railroad company.

For law students, this meager description raises the question of whether the railroad should be held liable for damages since neither it nor its employees directly caused the injury. For Noonan, the description of the facts obscures as much as it reveals. The opinion does reveal that the plaintiff is a woman, but it says nothing about "her age, marital status, maternal responsibilities, employment or income. What injuries she had suffered, whether she had been almost decapitated or whether she had been mildly bruised . . . What compensation she had sought or what compensation she had been awarded."[27] (As an aside, Mrs. Palsgraf, age 43, had three children, two of whom were with her at the time of the accident. She was a janitor in the apartment building in which she lived and earned about $8 a week. She was struck on the arm, hip, and thigh, but the lingering effect was a stammer, which her physicians attributed to the trauma of the accident. She was awarded $6,000 from a company with assets valued at $1,700,000 in 1924, the year in which the accident occurred. In addition, the railroad industry had a dismal safety record, with 6,617 people killed and 143,739 injured that year.[28])

Interesting though these parenthetical facts might be, they are irrelevant to the law student because they do not add to the understanding of the legal principles of the case. Both the ability to sort through the various accounts in order to reduce the event to its barest legal bones and the resulting detachment are valued skills for most lawyers. They actively pursue detachment from the parties and their misery. The reason advanced is that the advocate must be able to accurately assess the situation and choose the appropriate legal tactics, a task hampered by the involvement of emotions. Yet Noonan challenges the accuracy of that premise:

> Focusing on the rules, [the professors] instilled in students a sense that
> the legal system was not the creature of individual caprice or the expression

of raw power, but tradition constantly refined by reason . . . . Their purpose, as is mine, was to increase the sense of responsibility of those who by their thought and action make the system exist. But, for me, the responsibility comes in the response to other persons.[29]

Litigants, who are emotionally involved with their lawsuits and usually care passionately about the outcomes, often have difficulty dealing with the impersonality of their attorneys and of the legal system, and might very well agree with Noonan. They seek revenge or justification and are frustrated with their advocates' lack of involvement. Watching the opposing lawyers talking and laughing together in the halls during breaks, they suspect collusion. Laypersons not familiar with courthouse proceedings fail to recognize the norms that bind the court personnel. "Courts are not an occasional assemblage of strangers who resolve a particular conflict and then dissolve, never to work together again. Courts are permanent organizations."[30] The judge, clerk, court reporter, and bailiff are a fairly static group. Attorneys work together and oppose each other on a fairly regular basis. Thus, group norms promote the establishment of friendly relations among the workgroup participants.

These same norms characterize every legal system. In the United States, the bench and bar are closely connected, not only as officers of the court but also by training. In the United States, as contrasted with continental nations, there is no specialized track for those who aspire to judicial positions; nor are there formal divisions between those who argue cases in court and those who do not, such as is found in France and Great Britain. The English distinguish between barristers, who are courtroom advocates, and solicitors, who are general practitioners who do not appear in higher courts. Barristers are specialists who seldom have the right of direct access to the lay client and whose referrals come from solicitors. Each of the branches is governed by professional organizations—the Law Society for solicitors and the four Inns of Court for barristers—which control membership and the discipline of its members. Again, the group is essentially closed, tied together by professional norms and education.

Bar associations at the local, state, and national levels help unify the legal profession in the United States. The American Bar Association (ABA), a voluntary organization, is generally dominated by the more conservative elements of the bar and plays an active role in the selection of federal judges, especially Supreme Court justices. State bar associations may be integrated; that is, all practitioners of law within the state must belong to the association. Integrated bars often govern the conduct of the lawyers within the state; otherwise, a state commission or court will consider grievances against lawyers. The ABA has formulated the Code of Professional Responsibility, a code of ethics by which the professional behavior of attorneys is judged. Violation of the code may lead to reprimands, temporary suspensions, or permanent disbarment of erring lawyers, depending on the severity of the breach.

Lawyers are both cursed and praised. They are criticized for their detachment and applauded for their honed analytical skills. They are reviled for feeding upon the sorrows of others and acclaimed for representing the downtrodden of our society. They are denounced as too powerful and too influential in government, but they are frequently elected to office. The bar is not a monolithic group, however. The members represent a wide spectrum of political philosophies and interests, as indicated by the varying approaches to their profession and its practice.

CONCLUSION

The American legal system is a hodgepodge of borrowed principles and homegrown theories. An adaptable system, it changes to meet the needs of the times. Its origins can be traced through 4,000 tumultuous years, and it owes an indelible debt of gratitude to the lawmakers (and lawbreakers) who have gone before. It represents the sometimes controversial efforts of society to provide justice and fair treatment in the resolution of conflicts and in the prescription of appropriate behavior.

NOTES

[1] Oliver Wendell Holmes, "The Place of History in Understanding the Law," in John Honnold, ed., *The Life of the Law* (London: Free Press, 1964), p. 3.

[2] Robert W. Ferguson and Allen N. Stokke, *Concepts of Criminal Law* (Boston: Holbrook Press, 1976), p. 26.

[3] Walter M. Chandler, *The Trial of Jesus from a Lawyer's Standpoint* (Norcross, Ga.: The Harrison Co., 1976), pp. 35–87.

[4] Ferguson and Stokke, p. 29.

[5] Arthur T. von Mehren, "The Civil Law System: An Historical Introduction," in John Honnold, ed., *The Life of the Law* (London: Free Press, 1964), pp. 486–493.

[6] Rene David and Henry D. deVries, "French Legal Tradition," in John Honnold, ed., *The Life of the Law* (London: Free Press, 1964), p. 520.

[7] Ibid., pp. 519–525.

[8] Rudolf B. Schlesinger, "The Code Systems," in John Honnold, ed., *The Life of the Law* (London: Free Press, 1964), pp. 494–509.

[9] Joseph Schacht, *An Introduction to Islamic Law* (Oxford: Clarendon Press, 1964), p. 1.

[10] Ibid., pp. 1–99.

[11] Schlesinger, pp. 506–507.

[12] T'ung-Tsu Ch'u, *Law and Society in Traditional China* (Paris: Mouton & Co., 1965).

[13] Harold J. Berman, *Justice in the U.S.S.R.: An Interpretation of Soviet Law* (Cambridge: Harvard University Press, 1963).

[14] F. W. Maitland, "History of English Law," in Helen M. Cam, comp., *Selected Historical Essays of F. W. Maitland* (Cambridge: Cambridge University Press, 1957), pp. 97–98.

[15] C. Gordon Post, *An Introduction to the Law* (Englewood Cliffs, N.J.: Prentice-Hall, 1963), pp. 18–61.

[16] F. W. Maitland, *Equity: A Course in Lectures,* rev. by John Brunyate, (Cambridge: The University Press, 1969), p. 2.

[17] Post, p. 40.

[18] Maitland, *Equity,* p. 5.

[19] S. F. C. Milsom, *Historical Foundations of the Common Law* (London: Butterworths, 1969), pp. 74–87.

[20] Kenneth H. York and John A. Bauman, *Cases and Materials on Remedies,* 2nd ed. (St. Paul, Minn.: West Publishing Company, 1973), pp. 1–10.

[21] Maitland, *Equity,* pp. 18–19.

[22] Roscoe Pound, *The Formative Era of American Law* (Boston: Little, Brown, 1938), pp. 94–95.

[23] *Green v. United States,* 356 U.S. 165 (1958) at 212.

[24] Pound, pp. 52–79.

[25] Chandler, p. 62.

[26] John T. Noonan, *Persons and Masks of the Law* (New York: Farrar, Straus & Giroux, 1976), p. xi.

[27] Ibid., p. 113.

[28] Ibid., pp. 113–139.

[29] Ibid., p. xi.

[30] James Eisenstein and Herbert Jacob, *Felony Justice: An Organizational Analysis of Criminal Courts* (Boston: Little, Brown, 1977), p. 20.

3

Court Organization

Court organization in the United States is complicated by our federal form of government. Instead of a single, unified court system such as exists in Great Britain or France, the United States actually has 51 court systems—the federal courts and the courts of the 50 individual states. This situation results in two very different consequences for the American legal system. First, Congress and the state legislatures are free to organize their respective court systems to meet their own needs. The results are that not only is the federal court structure different from those in the states, but there is also tremendous diversity among the individual states. A trial court might be called a district court in one state, a superior court in another, and a supreme court in yet another. Some states have a single supreme court; others, like Oklahoma and Texas, have two courts of last resort—one for civil appeals and one for criminal appeals. Such diversity makes it difficult to generalize about the "typical" state court system.

A second consequence of our federal form of government is its impact on substantive and procedural law. As will be noted in Chapter 7, each state is free to determine for itself what behavior is forbidden, and each is free to establish reasonable punishment for defined crimes. Consequently, two states may have entirely different definitions of the same criminal act and two entirely different penalties for it. Likewise, in the case of civil law, different states may have different grounds for divorce. For example, for many years Nevada had a liberal divorce law, which prompted many people from outside the state to establish residency in Nevada so that they could obtain a "quickie" divorce. When other states began to liberalize their own divorce laws, it became unnecessary for people to travel to Nevada. Federalism also impacts the role of precedent in the law. Since each state's substantive law is unique to that state, it follows that interpretations of state laws by state judges will also be unique. What is true for substantive law is also true for procedural law. Although rulings of the U.S. Supreme Court have tended to make criminal procedural law more uniform throughout the country, rules of civil procedure may vary slightly from state to state. As a result, a lawyer trained in the law of one state sometimes finds it necessary, upon moving to another state, to seek additional training in the substantive and procedural law of the new state. Indeed, many states require lawyers from other states to pass their own bar exams even though they were licensed to practice in their home states.

Such problems notwithstanding, this chapter will try to describe court organization in the United States. Since any attempt to describe all 50 state systems would be tedious and repetitious, no such attempt will be made. Although there are enough similarities among state court systems to allow some generalization, the reader should keep in mind that each state's system is truly unique. Since the federal court system offers a relatively simple introduction to court structure, we will begin with it and will return to state systems later in the chapter.

THE FEDERAL COURT SYSTEM

The federal court system is characterized by two types of courts: constitutional and legislative. **Constitutional courts** are sometimes referred to as *Article III courts* because they are created under Article III of the Constitution, which authorizes Congress to "ordain and establish" courts inferior to the Supreme Court.[1] The Constitution also states that judges of both the supreme and inferior courts "shall hold their Offices during good Behaviour,"[2] which is tantamount to a lifetime appointment, subject to removal only through the impeachment process. Finally, Congress may not reduce the salaries of constitutional court judges "during their Continuance in Office."[3] U.S. district courts, U.S. courts of appeal, and the U.S. Supreme Court are examples of constitutional courts.

Legislative courts are also created by Congress, pursuant to one of its other legislative powers. For example, Article I empowers Congress to make all laws ". . . for organizing, arming, and disciplining the Militia."[4] Under that authority, Congress may establish military tribunals for the purpose of disciplining soldiers. Similarly, Article IV empowers

Congress to make rules and regulations for U.S. territories.[5] The judges who serve in the legislative courts do not have lifetime appointments, nor are their salaries protected as are those of Article III judges. However, all federal judges are appointed by the president, subject to confirmation by the Senate. While it should be noted that these and other differences[6] between constitutional and legislative courts exist, the line is not always a clear one. For example, in 1956 Congress changed the status of the U.S. Customs Court from a legislative to a constitutional court.[7] Ultimately, Congress determines the status of federal courts. Let us now proceed to discuss each of the two types of federal courts separately.

Constitutional Courts.   Constitutional courts may be classified as either courts of general or specialized *jurisdiction.* Article III of the Constitution establishes federal jurisdiction over certain parties to a case and over certain subjects. For example, the federal judicial power extends "to all Cases affecting Ambassadors, other public Ministers and Consuls" and "to Controversies between two or more States."[8] Thus, if a foreign ambassador is a party to a case, federal courts have jurisdiction regardless of the subject matter of the case. Similarly, Article III gives federal courts jurisdiction over "Cases of admiralty and maritime Jurisdiction."[9] Consequently, if the subject matter of the case is admiralty or maritime, the federal courts have jurisdiction regardless of who the parties are. Finally, Article III states that "The judicial Power shall extend to all Cases, in Law and Equity, arising under this Constitution, the Laws of the United States, and Treaties made, or which shall be made, under their Authority."[10] This means that if a case raises what is called a federal question—an interpretation of the Constitution, a federal statute, or a U.S. treaty—federal courts may hear the case. Generally speaking, it is a constitutional court of general jurisdiction that will hear these kinds of cases.

As previously noted, under its delegated powers Congress may make uniform laws on the subject of bankruptcies,[11] may lay and collect taxes, and may impose duties on goods coming into the United States.[12] Because of the specialized subject matter of some areas of the law, Congress has created specialized courts with jurisdiction limited to specialized subject matter; these are the constitutional courts of specialized jurisdiction. Since most readers will be more familiar with the courts of general jurisdiction, we will begin our discussion of constitutional courts with them.

The federal courts of general jurisdiction are organized in three tiers, or levels. The first tier consists of the U.S. district courts. When Congress first created the lower federal courts in 1789, it merely created one for each state, or thirteen federal district courts. As the nation grew, it became apparent that some states needed more than one federal court, so Congress created new ones while maintaining the tradition that district courts should not cross state lines.[13] Today there are 90 federal district courts in the 50 states, one in the District of Columbia, and four in U.S. territories (Guam, the Virgin Islands, the Northern Marianas, and Puerto Rico), for a total of 95 federal district courts. States that have more than one federal district court use geographical designations to distinguish among them. For example, a court may be named the U.S. District Court for Eastern Oklahoma to distinguish it from the U.S. District Court for Western Oklahoma. The number of federal judges assigned to each federal district varies from a single judge, such as in the Northern District of West Virginia, to as many as 25 judges in the Southern District of New York.[14] It is common for each major city within each federal court district to have at least one judge assigned to it. In all there are 576 federal district court judges in the United States.[15]

The U.S. district courts, which are the main trial courts for the United States, have both criminal and civil jurisdiction. When our Constitution came into existence, the states already had fully functioning state court systems, and opponents of the Constitution feared that the newly created federal courts would supplant state courts. To alleviate this concern, the judicial power of the federal courts was limited so that most legal controversies would continue to be settled by state courts. Today, the vast majority of cases are still litigated in state courts. In 1983, for example, only 277,714 suits were filed in federal courts,[16] compared to over 15,000,000 filed in major state trial courts in 1978.[17] Approximately one-fourth of the federal cases in 1983 were either criminal prosecutions or petitions from prisoners, while the remaining cases were civil rights, labor, Social Security, tort, or contract cases.[18] Approximately 21 percent of the cases filed in 1983 were *diversity of citizenship suits*.[19] Because the Framers of the Constitution believed the state courts would favor their own citizens over citizens of another state, federal courts were given jurisdiction over cases involving citizens of different states. Today, in addition to involving citizens of different states, the amount in controversy in a diversity suit must be greater than $10,000.

U.S. district courts function like other trial courts in the country: A single judge presides, and a jury hears the evidence. Federal courts have their own unique rules of evidence, but evidence is submitted and a verdict is reached in the same manner as in state trial courts. Federal courts are no better or worse than state courts in many ways; they are just different because of the different jurisdiction, organization, and procedures. Nor are state courts necessarily inferior to federal courts. Unless a case raises a federal question or otherwise falls within the jurisdiction of the federal courts, the decisions of state courts are not reviewable by federal courts. Indeed, federal judges are required to respect the interpretations of state laws by state courts if there is not a federal question raised.

The second tier of federal courts with general jurisdiction consists of the U.S. courts of appeal. There are currently twelve U.S. courts of appeal, which are designated as numerical circuits. For example, the U.S. Court of Appeal for the Fifth Circuit includes Texas, Louisiana, and Mississippi, and any appeal from one of the district courts of those states will go to it. Eleven of the circuits cover the 50 states, and the twelfth, the U.S. Court of Appeals for the District of Columbia, also hears appeals from federal regulatory agencies, such as the Federal Trade Commission (FTC). Since U.S. courts of appeal hear only cases on appeal from U.S. district courts, they naturally have the same substantive jurisdiction.

The number of appeals court judges total 156, with the number of judges assigned to individual circuits varying from 6 for the First Circuit to 28 for the Ninth Circuit.[20] Normally appeals are heard by groups of 3 judges, called *panels.* When an appeal reaches the court, 3 judges are assigned to hear it, and the decision of a majority decides the case. Occasionally, the court of appeals will decide to hear a case *en banc,* which simply means that all of the judges assigned to that circuit will hear the case.[21] In a majority of federal cases, the court of appeals is the last stop. For a variety of reasons, including time, money, and the unlikely chance of Supreme Court review, the parties will abandon their fight, resulting in the decision of the court of appeals being the final one.

Contrary to what many people believe, appellate courts do not retry cases brought to them. Decisions of the trial court, as the trier of fact, are generally final. *Appellate courts* are concerned mainly with questions of law—that is, with whether or not the trial judge ruled correctly on questions of substantive and/or procedural law. For example, suppose the lawyer for a criminal defendant objects to the admission of some incriminating evidence that he believes was seized in violation of the Fourth Amendment. Suppose further that the trial judge overrules his objection and allows the evidence to be introduced. If the defendant is convicted, his appeal may be based on the grounds that the trial judge erred in admitting the evidence and that the error was a *reversible error* sufficient to warrant a new trial. Appellate court judges are not concerned with the guilt or innocence of the accused. Their sole concern is with legal issues—in this case, with whether the trial judge ruled correctly on the question of the admissibility of the seized evidence. If the court of appeals rules that the error was a reversible one, the accused is entitled to a new trial. However, if the appellate court rules that the error was a *harmless error,* the conviction will stand. Likewise, if the appellate court rules that the trial judge ruled correctly in the first place, the conviction will stand.

The third and highest tier is, of course, the U.S. Supreme Court, consisting of the Chief Justice of the United States and eight associate justices. Unlike the other federal courts discussed in this chapter, the Supreme Court was created by the Constitution. However, the Constitution is silent about the number of justices and other aspects of the Court's organization. For example, the first Supreme Court had only six members, and right after the Civil War it had ten members. In 1869 Congress set the number at nine, where it remains today. President Franklin D. Roosevelt's famous court-packing attempt in 1937 has been the only really serious attempt to alter the Court's membership since 1869. Roosevelt tried to expand the number of justices to as many as fifteen, but the attempt failed. It appears that the number will remain at nine for some time to come.

The Supreme Court has both original and appellate jurisdiction, but as a practical matter it functions almost entirely as an appellate court. For example, in 1983 there were 5,079 cases on the Court's dockets, of which only 17 were cases coming to it under its original jurisdiction.[22] There are three ways in which a case may reach the Supreme Court under its appellate jurisdiction. The first is an appeal as a matter of right. Congress has stipulated that under certain conditions a party has an absolute right to have a case heard by the Court. For example, if a state law has been declared unconstitutional because it conflicts with a U.S. statute or treaty, or with the Constitution itself, the state may appeal to the Supreme Court. In reality, however, the Court may refuse further considerations of the merits of the case by dismissing it for "lack of a substantial federal question." Just what constitutes a "substantial" federal question is known only to the justices themselves.

The second avenue of appeal is through the *writ of certiorari.* A writ of *certiorari* is an order from a higher court to a lower court to send up the record of a case so that the higher court may review it. Since 1925 the Supreme Court has had complete discretion in deciding whether or not to issue *certiorari* in specific cases. The Court operates under the *rule of four,* which states that at least four of the nine justices must agree that a case merits the Court's attention before it will issue the writ.

The final way in which a case may reach the Supreme Court is through *certification.* Certification is used when a lower court seeks clarification on a question of law before it can make a ruling in a case. For example, President Franklin D. Roosevelt once dismissed a man named Humphrey from the FTC. Humphrey sued the government for lost wages. The lower court, before it could decide if Humphrey was entitled to his lost wages, first had to decide if his dismissal had been legal. In *Humphrey's Executor v. United States*,[23] the Supreme Court ruled that the dismissal was not legal. Cases that reach the Court through certification are relatively rare since the Court seems to prefer that the lower court make a ruling, which it may then later review if it chooses to do so.

Once the Supreme Court has agreed to hear a case, both parties are required to submit written briefs stating the exact nature of the controversy, their side's position, the legal precedents upon which they are relying, and arguments justifying why the Court should rule in their favor. In addition, all transcripts and other court papers from the proceedings of the lower courts are submitted to the Court. *Oral argument* is next; here the attorneys for both parties appear in person before the justices to argue the case. Each side is given 30 minutes to present its case, with the understanding that any justice may interrupt to question the lawyers. Oral argument is not just a rehash of the written briefs; it is designed to allow the justices to clarify issues presented by the case before the Court.

The actual outcome of the case is decided during the Supreme Court's conference. By tradition, each justice shakes the hand of the other eight justices upon entering the conference room. This is to ensure that the conference begins on a friendly note. The Chief Justice presides over the discussion of the case, and then a tentative vote is taken. At least six of the nine justices must participate in order to decide a case, and a simple majority determines the outcome. If, for example, one justice fails to participate in a case and the others are deadlocked 4–4, the decision of the highest court below the Supreme Court will stand. In such instances, a similar case that raises the same issue will have to come before the Court before there will be resolution.

After the case has been discussed and voted upon in conference, the next stage is the opinion writing. If the Chief Justice is in the majority, he assigns the task of writing the *majority opinion* to one of the justices in the majority, which includes, of course, himself. If the Chief Justice is not in the majority, the job of assigning the majority opinion goes to the senior associate justice in the majority. The majority opinion is important for several reasons. First, it explains to the parties directly involved in the case why each side won or lost. Second, it establishes a precedent for future cases that raise the same substantive issue. Third, it provides cues for court-watchers as to how the Court might decide similar issues in future cases.

Although there is no official "minority opinion," the justices in the minority may informally decide that one of them should write the main *dissenting opinion* setting forth the reasons for the minority's disagreement with the majority. However, any of the justices in the minority is free to write a separate dissent or to join another's dissent, or both. In addition to being critical of the majority's legal reasoning or analysis of a case, dissenting opinions can provide the opponents of a particular decision with powerful arguments for opposing that decision. Also, a well-argued dissent may even convince enough members of the majority to change their minds, turning a minority into a majority; a justice may change his or her mind at any time prior to the actual announcement of the decision in the case.

There are instances in which a majority of the Court may agree on the outcome of a case—that is, on who should win the case—but cannot agree on the reasons why the party should win. For example, a justice may agree that one side should prevail but cannot agree with the legal reasoning given in the majority opinion. In such instances a justice may choose to write a separate *concurring opinion.* A concurring opinion is one in which the justice agrees with the outcome of the case but not with the legal grounds relied upon by the majority. In a concurring opinion, a justice sets forth his own rationale for reaching the same result as the majority. Concurring opinions often do little more than provide additional grounds for reaching the Court's decision. However, there are situations in which the consequences of a concurrence could be significant. Suppose, for example, the Court were divided 5–4 in a particular case and one of the justices in the majority refused to sign the majority opinion, preferring to write a separate concurring opinion. In this case there would be no majority opinion. Instead, the opinion of the four remaining justices in the majority becomes what is known as a *plurality opinion.* The outcome of the case would not be changed in this situation, but the case would have no value as a precedent because a majority of the Court could not agree on the legal grounds for the case. This is another situation in which the issue will probably have to come before the Court again for final resolution.

Written opinions of the Court are products of much compromise. The justice assigned to write the majority opinion drafts a copy of the opinion and circulates it among the other eight justices for comments and criticisms. At the same time, any justice writing a separate dissenting or concurring opinion does the same. In this manner, each justice knows exactly what arguments the others plan to use in their opinions and may use that information in writing subsequent drafts of his or her own opinion. A justice may incorporate any comments suggested by another justice in the final draft of the opinion. The author of the majority opinion must be especially careful in drafting that opinion, since failure to take into account the suggestions of the other justices in the majority could lead to one or more concurring opinions—a situation that should be avoided if possible. Obviously, authors of dissenting and concurring opinions, while sensitive to the criticisms of the other justices, do not have to worry about keeping a majority together. Consequently, they are freer to express their own views in their opinions.

When all of the opinions have been written and rewritten, the Court is ready to announce its decision. The justices assemble in the courtroom, and the Chief Justice announces that the Court's decision has been made. The author of the majority opinion summarizes the Court's decision, and any other justices who have written separately may summarize their opinions. The process of Supreme Court decision making is now complete.

As previously noted, Congress has created some constitutional courts that have specialized jurisdiction. Among these are the U.S. Court of International Trade and the Court of Appeals for the Federal Circuit. The Court of International Trade was created by Congress in 1980 to be the successor of the old U.S. Customs Court. Its jurisdiction covers disputes over goods imported into and exported out of the United States. Such disputes include controversies over the admissibility of goods and the duties owed on them.[24] A second specialized constitutional court is the U.S. Court of Appeals for the Federal Circuit, created in 1981. This court was given jurisdiction which formerly belonged to the U.S. Court of Custom and Patent Appeals. It also hears appeals from the Court of International Trade, the Patent and Trademark Office, the Merit System Protection Board, and the U.S. Claims Court.[25] Other courts that are of questionable constitutional status include the Rail Reorganization Court, the Foreign Intelligence Surveillance Court, the Foreign Intelligence Surveillance Court of Review, and the Temporary Emergency Court of Review. These last four courts use federal judges borrowed from other federal courts.[26]

It should be apparent by now that the federal court system is a hodgepodge of courts created by Congress in a piecemeal fashion to deal with cases arising under federal jurisdiction. As two noted experts on the federal court system have observed, ". . . the distinction between a constitutional and a legislative court is of the type that would have delighted those meticulous medieval scholastics who argued about how many angels would fit on the head of a pin."[27] With that caveat in mind, we now turn our attention to the legislative, or Article I, courts.

Legislative Courts.　As discussed earlier, Article I courts are created by Congress to implement one of its legislative powers. Although confusion exists about the exact status of some federal courts, two major distinctions generally differentiate legislative courts from constitutional courts. First, judges of legislative courts do not have lifetime appointments, but instead serve fixed terms of office. The length of the term designated by Congress is often a long one in order to ensure judicial independence, but it is a fixed term nonetheless. The second distinction is that a legislative court judge's salary is not protected, as in the case of constitutional court judges. The Constitution stipulates that the compensation of Article III judges "shall not be diminished during their Continuance in Office."[28] Congress has recently tried to clarify the status of individual federal courts by designating whether they are to be legislative or constitutional, but, as we have seen, it has not been entirely successful.

Three courts that bridge the legislative–constitutional court gap are the U.S. District Courts in three American territories: Guam, the Virgin Islands, and the Northern Marianas.[29] These three courts hear the same kinds of cases heard in regular federal district courts, but they also hear cases involving local laws.[30] This would be analogous to a single court being authorized to hear cases involving both state and federal law. Congress governs the territories of the United States under Article IV of the Constitution and may make laws for them much the same as a state legislature does for a state. The judges on these courts do not enjoy life tenure, but serve four- to eight-year terms.[31]

Another example of a legislative court is the U.S. Claims Court (formerly the U.S. Court of Claims), which has jurisdiction over claims against the U.S. government involving alleged violations of public contracts.[32] These claims arise because the federal government does business with thousands of private businesses and contractors. Any dispute over the terms of government contracts is handled by this court. The U.S. Tax Court, created by Congress in 1924, is also a legislative court. It consists of nineteen judges who serve 15-year terms. Although the U.S. Claims Court and the regular district courts also have jurisdiction over tax cases, the Tax Court is the only court the taxpayer can appeal to before the payment of the disputed tax. In the Claims Court and in district courts, the taxpayer must first pay the tax and then try to recover it later.[33] Finally, bankruptcy-court judges serve as adjuncts to the district courts. Until 1978, bankruptcy-court judges served six-year terms and were appointed by the district court judge. In 1978 Congress lengthened their terms to 14 years and made them presidential appointees. When the Bankruptcy Reform Act of 1978 was declared unconstitutional by the Supreme Court,[34] Congress passed new legislation retaining the 14-year term but leaving the selection of bankruptcy judges to the courts of appeals.[35] For the time being at least, it appears that bankruptcy judges will remain in the "twilight zone" of the federal judiciary.

The final legislative court is the U.S. Court of Military Appeals. This court consists of three civilian judges who are appointed for 15-year, staggered terms. As its name implies, the Court of Military Appeals reviews the decisions of courts martial. Its caseload consists mainly of cases involving military personnel discharged for bad conduct or sentenced to prison under the Uniform Code of Military Justice. In most instances the decisions of the Court of Military Appeals are not reviewable by the Supreme Court. The exceptions are cases in which there is a question about the jurisdiction of the military court over the defendant and cases involving military personnel in nonservice-related offenses.[36]

In conclusion, the federal court system is composed of courts created by Congress under either its Article I or Article III powers. The federal courts are not "superior" to state courts; rather, they exist alongside state courts. The vast majority of cases are tried in state courts, and it follows that they will resolve many important cases. Nevertheless, the federal courts remain an alternative forum that citizens can turn to for relief if state courts prove unresponsive. It is no surprise to discover that Southern blacks preferred to file their civil rights cases in federal rather than state courts, since Southern judges were notoriously unsympathetic to black claims. It is quite possible that, with the appointment of conservatives to the federal bench by President Reagan, blacks may begin to press their claims in state courts. Despite the confusion caused by federalism, a dual court system provides additional guarantees that justice will eventually prevail.

STATE COURT SYSTEMS

As we have noted, there is no "typical" state court system because federalism allows each state to adopt a court system fitted to its individual needs. Consequently, the most that can be done is to describe state courts in general, without being too specific about any particular state's courts. The following section describes the structure and jurisdiction of courts that are found in some form or fashion in each of the fifty states.

Courts of Limited Jurisdiction.   All state courts have had their jurisdiction limited in some way. The jurisdiction of any court comes from the state constitution or from statutes passed by the state legislature, or both. Some state constitutions spell out the jurisdiction of the courts in great detail, while others leave the details of court jurisdiction to the discretion of the legislature. In either case, courts are dependent upon others for the source of their jurisdiction. Similarly, the organization and number of state courts will also be determined by the constitution or by state statutes. Courts of limited jurisdiction, as their name implies, are created to handle cases of a limited or specialized nature. In this section we will examine some of the more common courts of limited jurisdiction found in the states.

One of the most common courts of limited jurisdiction is the municipal court. Municipal courts are often, although not always, limited to minor offenses or misdemeanors. Municipal courts are often referred to as "traffic courts" because their main function is to hear cases involving traffic violations within the city limits. Municipal courts frequently have jurisdiction over cases involving violations of city ordinances. Cities possess **ordinance power**—that is, the power to enact laws enforceable within the city limits. Such laws include prohibitions against discharging firearms, burning trash, and letting animals run loose within the city limits. Persons who receive traffic citations or citations for other offenses may have their cases heard in municipal court.

The phrase "You can't fight city hall" must have been coined by someone after an experience in municipal court. Typically, the defendant's cause is a lost one. That is because it is usually the defendant's word against the word of the arresting officer, and judges tend to believe the latter. That is also why most people simply pay the fine and save themselves the trouble of going to court even if they believe themselves to be innocent. Those who do choose to fight a ticket often discover that municipal court is not what they expected. First, attorneys are infrequently used in municipal court because their fees often exceed the fine. The defendant normally opts to "tell it to the judge" in his or her own words without benefit of counsel. A second difference is that there is often no jury. Although some states give the defendant the right to a jury trial, most of the matters that come before a municipal court are relatively trivial, and most defendants prefer a bench trial, in which the judge decides the outcome. A third, and somewhat surprising, difference is that in some cases the judge may not even be a lawyer. Although many municipal court judges are laywers, some states allow city officials, such as the mayor, to double as municipal court judge, especially in small towns. Finally, although appeals are allowed, like jury trials, they do not occur very often. Again, considering the fine involved, the time and trouble associated with an appeal are seldom worth the effort. If the average citizen ever encounters a courtroom situation as a party to a case, however, it is quite likely to be in a municipal court.

A second common type of court of limited jurisdiction is the justice of the peace court. JP courts, as they are commonly called, have a variety of functions, not all of which are judicial in nature. Justices of the peace in some states are still permitted to perform marriages, and in some states they serve as coroner in cases in which foul play is suspected in someone's death. Most justices of the peace also have minor administrative duties, such as preparing the court's yearly budget and hiring court personnel.

JP courts usually have both criminal and civil jurisdiction. Their criminal jurisdiction extends to misdemeanor offenses that occur within the limits of their geographic boundaries. Crimes such as petty larceny, simple battery, and juvenile offenses are the kinds that are most likely to be tried in JP court. Most states limit the amount of punishment a JP court can hand out. For example, a JP court's criminal jurisdiction may be limited to offenses in which the maximum penalty is six months in the county jail or a $500 fine. In addition to hearing trials, justices of the peace often conduct arraignments for persons accused of more serious crimes.

The civil jurisdiction of a JP court is limited to small monetary amounts—$2,000, for example. That is, the amount involved in the lawsuit cannot exceed $2,000 if the JP court is to have jurisdiction. This is why JP courts are frequently called *small claims courts.* Although lawyers are allowed to appear in JP courts in most states, the litigants often just represent themselves and let the judge decide the case without a jury. The popular television show "The People's Court" has done much to familiarize the general public with the operation of small claims court.

As can be seen, the kinds of cases handled by the typical JP court are more varied than those of a municipal court. However, many states still do not require justices of the peace to be licensed attorneys, a common criticism of the JP system. The JP system is a holdover from an era when people believed that anyone with a little common sense could fairly apply the law in simple cases. Whether that remains true today is debatable. However, justices of the peace, through strong and effective lobbying of state legislatures, have retained their essential functions and character despite repeated attempts to reorganize them out of existence. It appears that the office, though accused of being antiquated, will be with us for some time to come.

A third category of courts of limited jurisdiction includes county courts. Like municipal courts, which are limited to exercising their jurisdiction within city limits, county courts' jurisdiction is limited to county lines. County courts typically have a greater expanse of jurisdiction than either municipal or JP courts. In criminal cases, for example, county courts may have jurisdiction over offenses with penalties as great as one year in prison and relatively high fines. For civil cases, the amount in controversy may be as high as several thousand dollars. County courts may also function as courts of appeal for lower courts of limited jurisdiction. County courts are frequently *courts of record* (which means that a transcript is made of the proceedings), whereas municipal and JP courts are not. When an appeal is made to a county court from a lower court, it is not an "appeal" in the usual sense of the word. In actuality, since no record exists in the lower court, the county court conducts a *trial de novo*. A trial *de novo* is, in effect, an entirely new trial, or a trial from the beginning.

Like other judges in courts of limited jurisdiction, the judges of county courts are not required to be licensed attorneys in some states. However, states that have attempted to modernize their judicial systems are requiring judges at all levels to have law degrees. Many states retain the tradition of the county judge as the political leader of the county. In such states, county judges are as much administrative officials as judicial ones. A county judge may be responsible for duties such as budget preparation and the county welfare system. County judges probate wills, take responsibility for wards of the county, commit persons to mental institutions, and serve as juvenile court judges in some states. It is at this level that we see a fusion of judicial, executive, and legislative functions that is not as evident at the national level, with its stricter adherence to the system of separation of powers. For this reason, characterizing the office of county judge as a purely judicial one is misleading.

Courts of General Jurisdiction. A second level of courts in most state judicial systems consists of courts of general jurisdiction. A court of general jurisdiction has the power to hear any case that falls within the general judicial power of the state. That is, a court of general jurisdiction has the authority to render a verdict in any case capable of judicial resolution under the constitution and laws of the state. Cases involving the state's criminal laws, civil code, or state constitution fall within the judicial power of the state. Laws regulating marriage, corporations, real estate, insurance, and education are just a few of the categories of law within the state's authority. It will be recalled that the Framers of the Constitution intended that most lawsuits would fall within the judicial power of the states, thus ensuring the continued importance of state courts.

Courts of general jurisdiction are the major trial courts of the state. As noted in the chapter's introduction, they may be called superior courts, district courts, circuit courts, or, as in the case of New York, supreme courts. For the sake of simplicity, we will refer to this type of court as a district court. Despite the general nature of the district court's jurisdiction, they too are limited by geography. The state legislature typically divides the state into well-defined and numbered judicial districts that have definite boundaries. These boundaries may coincide with county lines, consist of several counties, or even overlap and disregard county lines. Although most judicial districts will have only a single judge assigned to each, others will be multijudge districts. Finally, the boundaries of the districts may overlap, in which case two or more judges will exercise concurrent jurisdiction over suits. In these instances, the judges may agree to specialize by allowing one judge to hear exclusively criminal cases while the other hears only civil cases. Such specialization is common in large metropolitan areas because of the workload faced by urban courts.

Courts of general jurisdiction have both criminal and civil jurisdiction but may, as just noted, specialize out of necessity. Some judges may prefer to handle divorces, while others concentrate on juvenile cases. The criminal jurisdiction of these courts includes felony offenses. Most states adhere to the definition of a felony as any offense for which the penalty exceeds one year of imprisonment or imprisonment at the state penitentiary as opposed to a county jail. Felony cases, then, include more serious crimes, such as burglary and murder. The civil jurisdiction of district courts have no upper limit as to the amount in controversy. Lawsuits may run into the millions or hundreds of millions of dollars. The kinds of cases range from the typical divorce case to multimillion-dollar tort or breach of contract cases. This point illustrates again the importance of state courts: When the stakes are high, state courts do not play second fiddle to federal courts. The operation of trial courts will be examined more closely in Chapter 4.

Appellate Courts.   All states have some kind of appeals mechanism available for litigants who were unsuccessful at the trial-court level. Most states have created an intermediate appeals court between the trial courts and the state's highest court of appeal. Like the U.S. courts of appeal, the purpose of intermediate appeals courts is to guarantee the litigants the right to at least one appeal while preventing the state's highest court from having to hear "routine" appeals. The intermediate appellate courts screen out the routine cases so that only the most important cases reach the state's highest court. However, this screening process does not mean that intermediate appellate courts are totally lacking in discretion in selecting cases. Like all appellate courts, intermediate courts of appeal are limited to deciding questions of laws raised during the trial, decide cases in panels or *en banc,* and rely upon written decisions in making their rulings.

Every state has a *court of last resort,* usually called the state supreme court.[37] As the name implies, a court of last resort is a litigant's last chance to have his or her case decided favorably once the case has exhausted all other appellate avenues. Most states have a single court of last resort which handles both civil and criminal appeals, but two states, Oklahoma and Texas, have two courts of last resort. In Texas, for example, the state supreme court hears only civil cases while criminal cases are handled by the Court of Criminal Appeals. Many states have chosen to pattern their state's highest court after the U.S. Supreme Court in the number of justices, procedures, and so forth. But, as we have seen, states have shown considerable independence in creating their court systems, and state supreme courts should not be viewed as merely "little Supreme Courts."

The duties of state supreme courts are identical to those of other appellate courts except that their decisions are final unless an appeal is made to the U.S. Supreme Court. As previously noted, when a state's highest court makes a ruling involving the interpretation of the state constitution, a state statute, or a precedent in an earlier state case, that ruling is final. The exception is when the case raises a federal question; such a matter may be taken to the U.S. Supreme Court. Another duty of state supreme courts includes ruling on opinions of the state's attorney general. Some states permit the attorney general to make preliminary interpretations of state laws, which are binding unless overturned by a state court. Finally, state supreme court justices, especially the chief justice, are often given additional duties by the state. For example, the state's chief justice is usually given the task of presiding over impeachment trials. In addition, other justices may have to serve on various state boards or commissions dealing with the judiciary. A common practice is to have several supreme court justices serve on the state's judicial conduct board.

The coexistence of state and federal court systems adds an element of complexity not present in nations without federalism. Nevertheless, it is the possibility that each state may approach court organization in its own unique fashion that makes federalism an attractive form of government. There is much to criticize about state courts. There are too many judges and courts, delays in coming to trial are too long, the procedures are antiquated and overly complex, and so forth. Lawyers, like most of us, are loath to change a system with which they have become familiar, and judges see plans to unify, modernize, or reorganize the court structure as threats to their power and prestige. But change does come, albeit slowly, to court systems, just as it does to all areas of the law. As in most cases, those with patience will eventually prevail.

JUDICIAL SELECTION

Once when New York Yankee manager Casey Stengel was reminiscing about his own career as a major league ballplayer, Mickey Mantle expressed surprise that Stengel had once been a major leaguer. Stengel reportedly replied, "Do you think I was born 60 years old and manager of the New York Yankees?" Although this story may be apocryphal, it does serve to remind us that judges are not born judges at any age. The selection of judges at both the state and federal level is a complex and political process. The selection method as well as the criteria for selection will have much to do with the kinds of persons chosen for the bench. The selection process is not only political, but also highly partisan and heavily influenced by the organized bar. In this section we will examine in detail the selection of federal judges of the three major constitutional courts and then describe the process used to select judges in the states.

Selection of Federal Judges.   The selection of federal judges is a deceptively simple process: The Constitution authorizes the president to nominate Supreme Court justices with the consent of the Senate, and Congress has extended the practice by statute to other federal judges. Surprisingly, there are no constitutional or legal qualifications for appointment to the federal bench. Theoretically, the president could appoint anyone reading this book to a federal judgeship as long as the Senate concurs. In reality, of course, there are informal qualifications to be met, and each president may add to or subtract from the list of qualifications. A general qualification is that the nominee be a lawyer, preferably a graduate of one of the nation's prestigious law schools. The nominee need not have previous judicial experience, but some presidents prefer that their nominees do have prior experience on a state court. Some presidents require a certain number of years of legal experience, a minimum or maximum age limit, and even a clean bill of health before they will consider a person for nomination.

Although most presidents are loath to admit it, they also consider such factors as sex, race, religion, ethnicity, and even geography when choosing nominees. Despite protests that he was seeking the most qualified person for the job, President Richard Nixon in 1970 consciously tried to place a Southerner on the Supreme Court. When his two Southern nominees, Clement Haynesworth and G. Harrold Carswell, were rejected by the Senate, Nixon nominated Harry Blackmun of Minnesota to fill the vacancy. President Jimmy Carter promised to nominate qualified blacks and women to the federal bench. Even partisan politics come into play, as evidenced by the fact that approximately 90 percent of all federal judges belong to the same political party as the president who appointed them.

Finally, a president may require some general ideological qualifications of his nominees. For example, it is no secret that President Ronald Reagan has chosen to appoint only persons of conservative ideology to the federal bench. The extent to which a president weighs professional competence, past judicial experience, age, ideology, and partisanship will vary with each president. A president normally determines the general criteria for his nominees and then allows the other significant actors in the process, such as the attorney general and the deputy attorney general, to recruit candidates who conform to his standards. Just how the process of choosing particular individuals occurs will be discussed later in this chapter. At this point it is preferable to have a general overview of the entire selection process.

Once a nominee for the federal bench has been determined, the Federal Bureau of Investigation (FBI) is called upon to do a background check. In the past, the FBI background investigations were conducted only on the nominee actually selected. Since the Nixon Administration, however, background checks have been run on all serious contenders.[38] The purpose of the background check is to ensure that there is nothing in the candidate's background that might prove embarrassing to the president. It would not do if the president's nominee turned out to be a spouse abuser or to have a history of drunken driving. Even past and present political and social affiliations are checked out; membership in a racially segregated club, a restrictive covenant in a property deed, or some ill-considered remarks in a speech may come back to haunt a candidate for the federal bench.

The next step, the rating of the nominee's qualifications by the ABA, is not a part of the formal selection process. The ABA has created the Committee on the Federal Judiciary to serve as a kind of watchdog over the federal judiciary. The Committee is composed of prominent attorneys from each of the federal circuits. Their job is to review the qualifications of the president's nominee according to "judicial temperament, age, trial experience, character, and intelligence."[39] Once evaluated, the nominee is rated "exceptionally well-qualified," "well-qualified," "qualified," or "not qualified." Although every president would like all of his nominees to receive the highest rating, the weight given to the ABA rating will depend on the individual president. During the Eisenhower administration, for example, the President refused to appoint anyone rated "not qualified." This, in effect, gave the ABA a virtual veto over nominations to the federal bench. President Nixon followed a similar policy early in his administration, but later began to submit his nominees' names to the ABA only after he had announced them publicly.[40] Other presidents, notably Kennedy and Johnson, have given less weight to ABA ratings by proceeding with the nominations of persons even rated "not qualified." The influence of the ABA seems to have waned in recent years, as evidenced by the fact that President Reagan failed to consult with the Committee when he nominated Sandra Day O'Connor to the Supreme Court.[41]

After the various clearances have taken place, the nominee's name is formally submitted to the Senate Judiciary Committee for confirmation hearings. The Judiciary Committee handles judicial nominations in much the same way as it handles regular legislation within its jurisdiction. That is, formal hearings are held on the nomination and testimony is taken. The nominee is "invited" to testify, of course, but it is really a command performance. In general, the Committee hearings are fairly routine. If a nominee for district judge who has the blessing of his home state's senators is being considered, most of the members of the Judiciary Committee are not interested in the nomination. After all, if the nominee is incompetent, the damage will be confined to a single federal district court in someone else's home state. As we shall see, however, nominees for the courts of appeals and the Supreme Court are subject to much greater scrutiny.

If the nominee, regardless of the court level, is noncontroversial, the witnesses before the Committee are usually a parade of supporters who have come to sing the praises of the nominee. On the other hand, a nominee who is controversial because of past judicial decisions, public statements, or political philosophy may come under fire from interest groups. Interest-group opposition, especially when the Supreme Court is involved, can be intense. Civil rights groups, women's groups, labor organizations, pro- and antiabortion groups all may wish to testify for or against the nominee. Coalitions of interest groups did successfully defeat the Carswell and Haynesworth nominations of President Nixon in the early 1970s and President Reagan's nomination of Robert Bork in 1987. Interest groups may uncover information about the nominee's background that was overlooked or ignored by the FBI and the ABA. Interest-group activity, even if ineffective, serves to remind us of the political nature of the judicial selection process.

Finally, after all the testimony has been given and all the witnesses heard, the Judiciary Committee votes to recommend approval or rejection of the nomination to the full Senate. If the nomination is approved by the Committee, approval by the Senate is almost assured. Very little, if any, debate takes place unless the nominee is controversial. A vote is taken, and if it is approved by a simple majority, the nominee is confirmed. Upon being sworn in, the president's nominee is a federal judge for life.

Although the process of FBI investigation, ABA scrutiny, Judiciary Committee hearings, and Senate confirmation is the same for the appointment of all federal judges, the process by which the selection is narrowed from a large pool of candidates to a single individual differs according to the level of federal court involved. Selection of district court judges is heavily influenced by state politics and the state's U.S. senators. Selection of court of appeals and Supreme Court judges tends to be influenced more by the president and national politics. We shall examine the selection process at each level and compare all three.

There is an old saying that a federal judge is just a lawyer who knows a president. At the district-court level, however, it is more accurate to say that a federal judge is a lawyer who knows a U.S. senator. That is because at the district-court level, the selection process is heavily influenced by the state's senators. It will be recalled that the boundaries of U.S. district courts are entirely within the boundaries of a single state. U.S. senators have traditionally felt that the appointment of federal officials within their states should be their prerogative; that is, the president should clear any federal appointment in a state with the senators of the president's party. This tradition is known as **senatorial** *courtesy.* Should a president attempt to nominate someone to the federal bench without the senator's blessing, the senator in question would merely ask his or her colleagues in the Senate to defeat the nomination and, except under unusual circumstances, the Senate would reject the president's nominee. In the past, a senator merely had to state that the president's nominee was "personally obnoxious" to him, and that was sufficient justification. Today, senators are expected to provide more substantive grounds for invoking senatorial courtesy.[42]

Because of senatorial courtesy, the actual selection process works like this: Let us assume that there is a Republican president in the White House. When a vacancy occurs on the federal bench, the attorney general will contact the Republican senators concerned for input into the selection. If there is only one Republican senator, the choice of a nominee is essentially made by him or her. In some cases the senator may have in mind a specific candidate who generally meets the president's criteria for nomination. In such a case, if the person is not totally objectionable to the president (and in some cases even if he is), the president will nominate the senator's candidate. Senators often use federal judgeships to reward political supporters in their home states for past political support. Another possibility is that the senator may have several qualified candidates for the position but is reluctant to alienate the others by actively promoting one over the others. In that case the senator may merely send a list of acceptable candidates to the attorney general and let the president make the final choice. This removes the onus from the senator of offending the persons not selected. A variation of this approach is for the senator to establish his own merit-selection process. The senator may ask a committee of judges, lawyers, law professors, and the like to screen the applicants and select the person best qualified. This approach also takes the pressure off the senator who does not want to offend his or her supporters. Finally, a senator may choose to stay out of the process by allowing the president to make the choice. The senator would merely retain the option of exercising a veto over the final choice in the event that the president selects a Democrat or someone from a rival faction of the party. This latter strategy keeps the senator from being obligated to the president.

If there are two Republican senators in the state, both might be consulted and asked to agree on a single candidate. What is more likely to happen, however, is that one senator will fill the current vacancy and the other senator will get to fill the next one, alternating the choice between the two senators. If the state has no Republican senators, the attorney general may consult with state Republican officials, party leaders, or Republican members of the House of Representatives. Under these circumstances, the president is freer to choose whomever he pleases for the judgeship. Finally, in some unusual circumstances, a strong Democratic supporter of the president might be consulted as a courtesy, especially if that senator's vote may be needed on a crucial upcoming vote in the Senate. Generally speaking, however, the selection of district court judges is a partisan process left to the party faithful.

The selection of persons to fill vacancies on the courts of appeals is less sensitive to the pressures of senatorial courtesy that is selection at the district court level for two reasons. First, the federal circuits consist of several states, unlike district courts, which are located entirely within a single state. Since, by tradition, the president is free to nominate anyone from the circuit, no single senator can claim the appointment as a personal prerogative. Custom dictates that court of appeals judge-ships be fairly evenly divided among the states within the circuit so that all of the judges do not come from the same state. For example, if a judge from Texas retires from the Fifth U.S. Court of Appeals, the expectation is that another Texan will be named to the bench and that the state's senators will be consulted if they belong to the president's party. However, the senators from Texas are not in a position to force a particular candidate on the president, as they are at the district-court level. If they try to "muscle" the president with the threat of senatorial courtesy, he can merely nominate a candidate from either Louisiana or Mississippi, the two other states in the Fifth Circuit. Still, the president may need the support of the senators from Texas and may therefore allow them considerable influence over the nomination.

A second reason for the decreased influence of senatorial courtesy at the court-of-appeals level is the perception that these positions are more important than district-court judgeships. A district-court judge's influence is confined to a single state or part of a state. If a district-court judge is lazy, incompetent, or corrupt, the damage is limited to one court. However, the decisions of appeals-court judges serve as precedents for every district court in the circuit. Because only a small fraction of federal cases move on to the Supreme Court, the decisions of the courts of appeals are often final. The decisions of a court of appeals may never be reviewed or overturned by the Supreme Court, so the precedents set by them are the law within that circuit. Conse-quently, more emphasis is placed on the professional competence of candidates for the courts of appeals. For these reasons, politics is not allowed to play as great a role as in the selection of federal district judges.

Senatorial courtesy is virtually nonexistent where the nomination of a Supreme Court justice is involved. This does not mean, of course, that a president may totally disregard the Senate when making a nom-ination. Historically, around 20 percent of the presidents' nominees have been rejected by the Senate, which indicates that its members do not take their obligation to give "advice and consent" lightly. A Supreme

Court justice is in a position to influence public policy in America for many years; the nominee must therefore be chosen carefully. Justice William O. Douglas, appointed by Franklin D. Roosevelt in 1939, served until 1975, some 30 years after Roosevelt's death. Every president knows that the person he names may have an impact on constitutional law in the United States long after he has left the White House. For this reason, presidents are keenly aware of the importance of each nomination to the Court.

Despite the importance of nominations to the Supreme Court, it does not necessarily follow that politics plays no role in the selection process. Indeed, it is because the stakes are so high that we might guess that politics plays an even greater role in the selection of Supreme Court justices. Generally speaking, nominees are chosen for their ideology, their representational qualities, and their professional competence, in roughly that order of importance. Let us examine all three areas in order to ascertain how each influences the president's decision to select a particular individual to serve on the Supreme Court.

As will be discussed in Chapter 6, the Constitution, like the Bible, is open to a variety of interpretations. This means that two individuals can read the same section of the Constitution and arrive at two totally different interpretations. And since judges, like major-league managers, are not born 60-year-old judges, each person who comes to the Supreme Court arrives with his or her "bags packed." That is, each justice comes to the Court with preconceived ideas about such issues as abortion, the death penalty, law and order, civil rights, and civil liberties. Although it is not uncommon for a justice to change views once on the Court, a majority come with their views set. In making his nomination to the Supreme Court, a president seeks to nominate a person whose views are similar to his own. Whether he is a liberal or a conservative, a loose or strict constructionist, pro- or antiabortion, the president wants a nominee who will decide constitutional issues as he would if he were on the Court. Presidents have had their share of disappointments: Theodore Roosevelt was disappointed with Oliver Wendell Holmes, Jr., and Dwight D. Eisenhower regretted his nomination of Earl Warren as Chief Justice. Consequently, the better informed he is about the political and judicial philosophies of his nominee, the less likely it is that a president will be stuck with a justice he does not like.

Even more revealing of the political nature of the Supreme Court selection process are the representational qualities that presidents seek in their nominees. Presidents are reluctant to admit that politics influences their choices for the Court, but that is indeed the case. That is because the judiciary is suppose to be "above" politics. In a nation that stresses equality before the law, it is incongruent to admit that political considerations influence the selection process. But just as the nominee's political philosophy is taken into consideration, so are the nominee's representational qualities. The Supreme Court is a very important political symbol in our system of government. Because of the significance of the Court's symbolism, it is important to certain groups in our society that they be represented on the Supreme Court. As a result, there has developed the tradition of reserving certain "seats" on the Supreme Court for representatives of prominent groups. For example, Catholics, as a significant religious minority, feel that at least one member of the Court should be a Catholic—hence the creation of the "Catholic seat" on the Court. In 1916, President Woodrow Wilson created the "Jewish seat" by making Louis Brandeis the first Jew to serve on the Court. Similarly, the "Black seat" was created by President Lyndon Johnson in 1967, and President Ronald Reagan nominated the first woman to the Court in 1981. When Sandra Day O'Connor eventually leaves the Court, there will be tremendous pressure on whomever is president to replace her with another female justice. Although presidents profess to seek the best-qualified person regardless of race, religion, or sex, the reality of the process is that these factors cannot be ignored.

The influence of representational qualities on a Supreme Court nomination can be illustrated with several examples. In one situation a president might wish to use a Supreme Court nomination to reward a group that has helped him politically. For example, every Jewish Supreme Court justice has been nominated by a Democratic president (Brandeis by Wilson, Cardozo and Frankfurter by Roosevelt, Goldberg by Kennedy, and Fortas by Johnson)—this because Jewish voters constitute a consistently loyal and significant part of the Democratic party's coalition. When the last Jewish justice, Abe Fortas, resigned from the Court, President Johnson's Republican successor, Richard Nixon, felt no obligation to nominate a Jew to the Court. The reason was simple: Most Jews vote for Democrats. Consequently, Fortas was replaced with a non-Jew, Harry Blackmun. Since Democrat Jimmy Carter had no opportunity to name someone to the Court, there is currently no occupant of the "Jewish seat." Similarly, when President Johnson nominated to the Court Thurgood Marshall, the first black justice, he did so in appreciation for the support of black voters in his 1964 election victory, and in anticipation of continued black support in 1968 (although Johnson ultimately did not seek reelection in 1968).

A second instance in which the president might use a nomination to the Supreme Court for political purposes is when he is trying to curry the favor of an important political group. We have already mentioned the nominations and Senate rejections of Clement Haynesworth and G. Harrold Carswell. In 1968, Richard Nixon had devised his so-called Southern Strategy for winning the presidency. The Southern Strategy called on Republicans to appeal to disgruntled conservative

Democrats in the South who were opposed to the liberal policies of the national Democrat party. Nixon hoped to establish a Republican base in the South from which to launch his 1972 reelection bid. As part of the Southern Strategy, Nixon promised to nominate a Southerner to the Supreme Court. (President Nixon apparently did not consider Justice Hugo Black of Alabama a Southerner.) Thus, when Justice Abe Fortas resigned, Nixon chose to nominate not a Jew but a Southerner, Clement Haynesworth. When the Senate rejected the Haynesworth nomination, Nixon nominated another Southerner, G. Harrold Carswell. After the Senate rejected Carswell, Nixon accused the Senate of prejudice against Southerners. Even in defeat Nixon won: He could point out to Southerners that he had twice tried to place one of their own on the High Court but had been thwarted in his attempts by the Northern liberal Democrats in the Senate.

Finally, a president might nominate a particular person to the Supreme Court as a means of bolstering his support among a key political group. Voting studies indicated that in the election of 1980, President Reagan had not done as well among women voters as men voters. This was probably due in part to Reagan's opposition to the Equal Rights Amendment (ERA). When Justice Potter Stewart announced his resignation in 1981, it gave Reagan an opportunity to mend his fences with an important bloc of voters. Reagan's nomination of Sandra Day O'-Connor helped put to rest criticisms that he was "anti-women."

The last area of qualifications presidents consider in their choice of Supreme Court nominees is professional competence. As previously noted, presidents would like their nominees to receive the highest possible ABA approval rating and overwhelming Senate approval. Naturally, the president seeks persons of high intellect, character, and integrity for the Court. The public expects and the Senate demands that Supreme Court justices be of the highest caliber. What, then, does the president seek by way of professional competence? Some presidents want their nominees to have previous judicial experience on either a lower federal court or a prominent state court. Judicial experience does not guarantee that a person will be a great, or even good, Supreme Court justice. There are some indications that political experience is more important than judicial experience. Chief Justice John Marshall was Secretary of State when he was nominated to the Court by President John Adams. Chief Justice Earl Warren was a former governor of California, Hugo Black was a senator from Alabama, and William O. Douglas was chairman of the Securities and Exchange Commission when nominated. With the exception of Black, who had only minor judicial experience, none had been a judge prior to his appointment. Yet each, in his own way, left an indelible mark on our constitutional law. The common thread seems to be a history of public service in often highly political positions. That is not to say that justices with judicial experience have all been failures; it simply means that judicial experience does not ensure judicial greatness.

Some presidents consider prominence in the legal profession an important qualification for a Supreme Court nomination. Lewis Powell was a former president of the ABA when named to the Court by President Nixon. Overall, judicial experience and professional competence, although important, take a back seat to ideological and representational qualifications. That is because there are enough outstanding judges and lawyers in the country to give the president the luxury of basing his choice on nonprofessional criteria.

Selection of State Judges.   The selection of judges for state courts varies according to several factors. First, due to federalism, states may vary the selection method according to their individual wishes and needs. Basically, there are three selection methods from which to choose: election, appointment, and merit selection. States may use a combination of selection methods; they may choose, for example, to elect lower-court judges and to appoint appellate and supreme-court judges. Another factor is the influence of the state bar association. State bars have promoted merit selection in the past because it is believed to increase their influence in the selection of judges. Still another factor is the political environment of the state. Some states look upon judgeships as just another political office, to be controlled by election or patronage. Other "reform" states have tried to remove the judiciary from politics as much as possible. In this section we will examine each of the three methods of judicial selection used by the states, indicating the strengths and weaknesses of each.

One method, used in approximately half the states, is to elect judges by a popular vote of the people. Candidates for judgeships run on either a partisan or a nonpartisan basis. If the state has partisan elections, the judicial candidate vies for the nomination in the primary, campaigns just as any other candidate would, and wins if he or she receives a majority (or plurality) of the vote. The election method became popular in the states during the period known as Jacksonian Democracy. Jacksonian Democracy held that if it was a good idea to elect some officials to government office, it was a good idea to elect all of them, including judges. Judges, after all, make political decisions (abortion, busing, prayer in schools, for example), so the people should be able to hold them accountable for those decisions. The election of judges would guarantee that judges would not become judicial tyrants. The fact that a judge must periodically face the voters and run on his or her record ensures that the judge will not stray too far from local community standards when applying the law. It also guarantees that judges will not abuse their power, as federal judges are often accused of doing.

Those who oppose the election method do so for several reasons. First, elections undermine judicial independence. If we are to have a nation of laws, not men, we must allow judges to apply the law as they see it without fear of political reprisals at the next election. Subjecting them to election tempts judges to make rulings that are popular but not necessarily legally or even morally correct. Second, the election method does not guarantee that the most qualified person will be elected to the bench. Studies indicate that elections favor white, male, middle class, and professional candidates. The possibility of qualified minorities becoming judges is reduced with the election method. A third criticism is that most voters are not qualified to evaluate candidates for judicial office. The average voter is simply not equipped to assess the professional competence or judicial temperament of candidates for the bench. Even if there is an incumbent, who has a record on which to run, the average voter is unfamiliar with the decisions a judge has made. The exception, of course, is when the judge has made a controversial ruling resulting in a move to unseat the judge at the next election. The voters may never hear of the many good rulings the judge has made, but may hear of only the controversial one. Finally, critics of judicial elections argue that the election method demeans the judicial system by forcing candidates for the bench to campaign for office. Candidates often must solicit campaign contributions from the same lawyers who will later come before them in court. It is unreasonable, critics argue, to assume that a judge will be able to treat impartially the lawyer who gave him $5,000 during the last campaign. Similarly, a judge might be biased against a lawyer who supported the judge's opponent in the last election. For these reasons, critics argue that election injects politics into the judicial system in ways that undermine the integrity of the process.

Regardless of the relative merits of electing judges, a little-known phenomenon occurs in some states that use elections, and that is the practice of appointing persons to fill the unexpired term of retiring or resigning judges. The process works like this: An incumbent judge who is ready to resign or retire announces his intentions a year or so before his term expires. This allows the governor to name a replacement to serve out the rest of the unexpired term. The newly appointed judge now has the advantage of seeking reelection as the incumbent. In most cases, any other lawyer who was considering making a bid for the judgeship will back off for fear of offending the new judge, whom he may later have to face in court. Since most incumbents are reelected, challengers are difficult to find and the incumbent usually runs unopposed. The voters, instead of choosing among several qualified candidates, find that they have little choice but to ratify the governor's preselected candidate. In Texas, for example, a survey revealed that nearly two-thirds of the judges had initially reached the bench by appointment and not by winning an election.[43] In such cases, judges are lawyers who know a governor.

The second method of judicial selection used in the states is the appointment method. The appointment of state judges often parallels that of federal judges. Candidates are nominated by the governor with the consent of the state senate, or perhaps with the consent of both the senate and the house of representatives. Confirmation by one or more chambers of the state legislature prevents the governor from merely appointing his friends to office.

Its supporters argue that the appointment method allows the governor to choose judges on the basis of their qualifications. As previously noted, the average voter is unqualified to evaluate the qualifications of judges. The governor and his advisers, on the other hand, are in a better position to make such evaluations. The governor, with the advice of the state bar association and other judges, is better able to ensure that the most qualified persons are chosen. Another argument is that well-qualified persons are more willing to serve if appointed rather than elected. This argument asserts that the onerous task of running a political campaign for election discourages otherwise qualified applicants from seeking judicial office. A third argument is that the appointment process allows a governor to name well-qualified minority group members to bench. Proponents of the appointment method argue that minority representation on the bench influences how other minority members perceive the judicial system. Finally, supporters of the appointment method point to the high caliber of federal judges who were selected by appointment.

Opponents of the appointment method make an equally strong case against it. They argue that lifetime appointments encourage arbitrariness in the courts. Judges should be held accountable for their decisions to the people. Second, the appointment process leads to cronyism. The governor is inclined to use judicial appointments to reward his friends with public office, regardless of their qualifications; this injects an element of partisan politics into the selection process as well. Finally, while it is true that the quality of federal judges is high, it is not the appointment method that has produced that quality. Federal judgeships pay more and are more prestigious than many state judgeships; hence the federal bench attracts a higher quality of applicants from the outset.[44]

The third method of judicial selection is merit selection, often called the **Missouri Plan** because the state of Missouri pioneered its use. Merit selection is an attempt to combine the best features of the election and appointment methods. One of the key features of merit selection is the presence of a judicial nominating committee. The judicial nominating committee is usually composed of a combination of lawyers, laypersons, and incumbent judges. When a vacancy occurs in a judicial post, it is the job of the judicial nominating committee to serve as a screening committee. Persons wishing to be considered for the judgeship may submit their own credentials or they may be nominated by someone else. The judicial nominating committee screens the applications and reduces the choices to three candidates. The names of the three candidates are then submitted to the governor, who must appoint one of the three to the judgeship. The person appointed then begins his or her tenure on the court.

A second key feature of the Missouri Plan is the use of a retention election. After the newly appointed judge has served a probationary period of at least one year, he or she must go before the voters for their approval. The judge has no opponents, however. The voters are simply asked, "Shall Judge X of the state [Supreme Court] court be retained in office?" The voter votes either yes or no. If the voters approve, the judge begins a full term of office. Terms of office for judges under the Missouri Plan are generally long—from 8 to 12 years— in order to ensure judicial independence. At the end of the term, a judge must stand for retention again, with the voters being asked the same question. If the voters approve once again, the judge serves another full term. A judge may continue to serve as long as he or she wishes and as long as the people vote to keep the judge in office. If a judge loses the retention election, the position is declared vacant and the judicial nominating committee must begin the process of filling it.

Supporters of merit selection are generally enthusiastic about the method. The Missouri Plan, like the appointment method, gives a greater role to those most knowledgeable about judicial qualifications. As is the case with election method, judges are periodically held accountable to the voters; judicial tyranny is thereby discouraged. At the same time, lengthy terms of office offer the judge a certain amount of judicial independence. A judge may make a controversial ruling with less fear that the voters will punish him for it at the next election, especially if the ruling is made early in the judge's term. Supporters argue that merit selection combines the positive features of the election and appointment methods with few, if any, of their drawbacks.

Critics of merit selection are not convinced that the method is as effective as its supporters claim. First, they point out that merit selection gives inordinate influence to the organized bar. The lawyer-members of the judicial nominating committee are usually chosen by the state bar, and the judge-members are also lawyers. This means that even if there are nonlawyers on the committee, they are outnumbered by the lawyers. Another problem is that the lay members are at a disadvantage in evaluating judicial qualifications. They may allow the lawyers on the committee to unduly influence them in the screening process. Another criticism is that merit selection does not eliminate politics from judicial selection as its supporters claim. The political struggle shifts from partisan politics to the politics of the state bar. State bars usually have factions which try to control the selection of lawyer-members to the judicial nominating committee. Partisan politics may also enter the picture: A Republican governor who is given the choice of two Democrats and one Republican by the judicial nominating committee may conclude that the lone Republican is the "best" candidate. Even after a judge has reached the bench, partisan politics may enter into the retention election. For example, Chief Justice Rose Bird of the California Supreme Court was a frequent target of conservative Republicans, who disapproved of her liberal judicial philosophy. Finally, critics of merit selection argue that there is simply no conclusive evidence that merit selection actually produces a higher caliber of judges than either election or appointment. Given the subjective nature of evaluating judicial qualifications, it is unlikely to be proven that merit selection provides better judges.

REMOVAL OF JUDGES

The office of judge is one of the most prestigious in American society; yet judges, like other humans, are prone to the vices of corruption, abuse of power, alcoholism, and so on. Consequently, we hear every year of cases of judges being removed from the bench for various offenses. Judicial removal involves three very different kinds of situations. The first is the case of the judge who has committed an illegal act either before or after taking office. Judges have been accused of soliciting murder, accepting bribes, and committing perjury, among other crimes. In a sense, the case of a judge who commits a crime is the easiest to deal with because the judge is treated like any other criminal defendant and is therefore entitled to due process of law.

The second kind of situation occurs when a judge has abused his or her power but has not necessarily committed a crime or an impeachable offense. For example, William Perry, a Long Island traffic court judge, had a coffee vendor brought before him in handcuffs so that he could berate the vendor for selling him a bad cup of coffee.[45]

The third situation occurs when a judge is either incompetent or senile. In some ways, this is the most difficult of the three situations to deal with. For example, a judge who may have served with distinction for many years may simply have stayed too long on the bench. Most states have mandatory retirement for judges at age 70, but senility does not always wait until then to strike. A judge, regardless of age, may simply be incompetent. Since there is no formal training for judges in the United States, virtually every lawyer is a potential judge. Yet lawyers have different talents and temperaments, so it is possible that a well-meaning judge may just be in over his or her head. Removal of the senile or incompetent judge must be handled carefully. Friends of the judge will usually suggest privately that it is time to resign or retire, but if the judge refuses, forced removal may be necessary.

Removal of Federal Judges. There is only one formal method of removing Article III judges and that, of course, is impeachment. The Constitution specifies that impeachment is by a majority vote of the House of Representatives, followed by a trial in the Senate. Conviction is by a two-thirds vote of the Senate, and the penalty may not extend beyond removal from office and disqualification from holding further offices under the authority of the United States. There have been eleven impeachment proceedings against federal judges: Five were acquitted by the Senate, five were convicted, and one resigned from the bench before articles of impeachment could pass the House. The five who were convicted by the Senate were John Pickering of New Hampshire, West H. Humphreys of Tennessee, Robert W. Archbald of the United States Commerce Court, Halsted L. Ritter of Florida, and Harry E. Claiborne of Nevada. Pickering was removed in 1804 because of insanity and chronic alcoholism; Humphreys was removed in 1862 for supporting the Confederacy. Archbald, in 1913, and Ritter, in 1936, were convicted of various types of misconduct in office. Of the four, Humphreys and Archbald were barred from holding further office under the authority of the United States.[46]

A recent impeachment of a federal judge involved Judge Harry E. Claiborne of Nevada. Judge Claiborne was convicted of income tax evasion on August 10, 1984, was sentenced to serve two years in federal prison, and was fined $10,000. But Claiborne refused to resign from the bench following his conviction and continued to draw his yearly salary of $78,800 while in prison. The House of Representatives finally voted to impeach Claiborne on July 22, 1986, by a vote of 406-0.[47] On October 9, 1986, Claiborne was found guilty on three of the four articles of impeachment by the Senate.[48]

The federal removal process illustrates the problem with impeachment as the only means of removing federal judges. First, the impeachment process is cumbersome, especially the trial stage in the Senate. The Senate, in effect, may be forced to delay other legislative matters pending the outcome of the impeachment trial. A second problem is that impeachment must cover a variety of judicial removal situations. John Pickering, the judge impeached for insanity and alcoholism, undoubtedly deserved to be removed from the bench, but he probably did not deserve the ignominious distinction of being the first federal judge to be removed from office. George W. English was impeached by the House in 1926 for "partiality, tyranny, and oppression."[49] The question raised by English's impeachment (he resigned before conviction by the Senate) was whether "partiality, tyranny, and oppression" constitute "Treason, Bribery, or other high crimes and misdemeanors," the grounds for impeachment specified by the Constitution. In other words, the impeachment process must cover activities ranging from "partiality" to murder, with the same punishment for both. Finally, as the Claiborne case illustrates, even a judge who has been convicted of a felony may continue to draw his or her salary until the long impeachment process has run its course. In recognition of this problem, Congress passed the Judicial Councils and Reform and Judicial Conduct and Disability Act in 1980. The Act establishes a procedure for investigating complaints against federal judges. If the allegations merit action, a committee composed of federal judges may investigate. Possible disciplinary actions include "private or public reprimand or censure, certification of disability, request for voluntary resignation, or prohibition against further case assignments."[50]

Removal of State Judges. Just as in other areas of court organization, the states have addressed the problems of judicial removal in a variety of ways. Forty-five states allow their state legislatures to impeach state judges.[51] The impeachment process in the states parallels the federal model with some modifications, such as the size of the majority needed to impeach in the house or to convict in the senate.

Another method of removal is *legislative address.* Legislative address, unlike impeachment, is not reserved for high crimes and misdemeanors but may be used in cases of incompetency, senility, or partiality. The judge in question does not have to commit an indictable offense to warrant removal. Under legislative address, the unfortunate Pickering could have been spared the indignity of impeachment.

A third method of removal that is popular in some states is the *recall.* Recall is a method of removing officials, not only judges, from public office before the expiration of the official's term. Recall begins with the circulation of a recall petition. Suppose a judge was deemed deserving of removal from office. A group of citizens could start a recall campaign by securing a specified number of signatures on a recall petition. In some states the petition must be signed by a specified percentage—for example, 5 or 10 percent—of the voters. If enough valid signatures are collected, the judge in question must face a retention election similar to that used under the Missouri Plan. However, the question before the voters would be, "Shall Judge X of the state [Supreme Court] court be removed from office?" The voters answer either yes or no. Other states allow alternative candidates to run against the incumbent judge in the recall election. This permits the voters to show their discontent with the incumbent by electing someone else to the position. In 1977, a Wisconsin judge named Archie Simonson made some inappropriate remarks about the "provocative clothing" worn by the young victim during a rape trial he was conducting. The remarks so angered women's groups in Madison that they mounted a successful recall campaign against Simonson.[52]

Finally, a fourth device used by some states to discipline judges is the *judicial conduct board/commission.* As we have seen, the severity of alleged offenses against judges ranges from the trivial to the very serious. Some allegations made against judges prove to be no more than the unfounded complaints of disgruntled litigants who lost a case over which the judge presided. Still other complaints are more serious and deserve some disciplinary action. Similarly, the punishment should fit the offense. For this reason, some states have created judicial conduct boards to investigate allegations made against judges to determine whether disciplinary action is warranted. If a judge is found guilty of misconduct, the board is empowered to discipline the offender. Such discipline could be a private or public reprimand, censure, suspension, or a recommendation of removal from office by impeachment or legislative address. State judicial conduct boards thus possess a variety of punishments that are appropriate to the seriousness of the offense.

CONCLUSION

In this chapter we have examined court organization in the United States. Because of our federal form of government, we have a federal court system superimposed on the 50 state court systems. In addition, federalism results in considerable variation among the states in the organization of their courts as well as in their substantive and procedural law. Federalism has resulted in different approaches to the selection and removal of judges. In short, our federal form of government adds complexity to our courts, but it also adds an element of diversity so that each state may deal with judicial organization, selection, and removal in its own way. For better or worse, federalism has had a remarkable impact on our judicial system.

NOTES

[1] U.S. Constitution, Art. III, sec. 1.

[2] Ibid.

[3] Ibid.

[4] Ibid., Art. I, sec. 8, clause 16.

[5] Ibid., Art. IV, sec. 3, clause 2.

[6] See Henry J. Abraham, *The Judiciary: The Supreme Court in the Governmental Process,* 4th ed. (Boston: Allyn & Bacon, 1977), pp. 8–9.

[7] Ibid., p. 12.

[8] U.S. Constitution, Art. III, sec. 2.

[9] Ibid.

[10] Ibid.

[11] Ibid., Art. I, sec. 8, clause 4.

[12] Ibid., Art. I, sec. 8, clause 1.

[13] The one exception to this rule today is the District Court for Wyoming, which covers the Montana and Idaho parts of Yellowstone National Park. See Stephen L. Wasby, *The Supreme Court in the Federal Judicial System,* 2nd ed. (New York: Holt, Rinehart and Winston, 1984), p. 33.

[14] Ibid.

[15] Lawrence Baum, *American Courts: Process and Policy* (Boston: Houghton Mifflin Company, 1986), p. 26.

[16] Ibid., p. 27.

[17] Ibid., p. 43.

[18] Ibid., p. 27.

[19] Ibid.

[20] Sheldon Goldman and Thomas P. Jahnige, *The Federal Courts as a Political System,* 3rd ed. (New York: Harper & Row, Pub., 1985), pp. 21–23.

[21] Because of its size (28 judgeships), not all of the judges of the Ninth Circuit sit *en banc.* See Wasby, pp. 42–43.

[22] Robert A. Carp and Ronald Stidham, *The Federal Courts* (Washington, D.C.: Congressional Quarterly Press, 1985), p. 43.

[23] *Humphrey's Executor v. United States,* 295 U.S. 602 (1935).

[24] Wasby, p. 41.

[25] Ibid., pp. 45–46.

[26] Baum, p. 36.

[27] Goldman and Jahnige, p. 18.

[28] U.S. Constitution, Art. III, sec. 1.

[29] Until 1982, the federal district court for the Canal Zone was included in this group, but that court was abolished after the ratification of the Panama Canal Treaty.

[30] Wasby, p. 36.

[31] Ibid.

[32] Howard Ball, *Courts and Politics: The Federal Judicial System* (Englewood Cliffs, N.J.: Prentice-Hall, 1980), pp. 73–74.

[33] Wasby, p. 40.

[34] *Northern Pipeline Construction Co. v. Marathon Pipe Line Co.,* 102 S. Ct. 2858 (1982).

[35] Carp and Stidham, p. 30.

[36] Wasby, pp. 46–47.

[37] In New York, trial courts are called *supreme courts;* therefore, the highest appellate court is simply called the *Court of Appeals.* See Baum, p. 47.

[38] Wasby, p. 75.

[39] Carp and Stidham, p. 107.

[40] Ibid., pp. 107–108.

[41] Ibid., p. 108.

[42] Wasby, p. 77.

43 Richard H. Kraemer and Charldean Newell, *Texas Politics*, 2nd ed. (St. Paul, Minn.: West Publishing Company, 1984), p. 243.

44 Robert S. Lorch, *State and Local Politics: The Great Entanglement* (Englewood Cliffs, N.J.: Prentice-Hall, 1983), p. 220.

45 Nicholas Henry, *Governing at the Grassroots: State and Local Politics*, 2nd ed. (Englewood Cliffs, N.J.: Prentice-Hall, 1984), p. 208.

46 Henry J. Abraham, *The Judicial Process*, 3rd ed., (New York: Oxford University Press, 1975), pp. 43–44.

47 "House Votes 406–0 to Impeach Federal Judge," *Congressional Quarterly*, Vol. 44, No. 30, July 26, 1986, pp. 1683–1684.

48 "Senate Finds Claiborne Guilty, Strips Him of Federal Judgeship," *Congressional Quarterly*, Vol. 44, No. 41, October 11, 1986, pp. 2569–2570.

49 Abraham, p. 43.

50 Carp and Stidham, p. 127.

51 Richard D. Bingham, *State and Local Government in an Urban Society* (New York: Random House, 1986), p. 223.

52 Henry, p. 209.

4

Procedure and Evidence

The difference between substantive and procedural law was first introduced in Chapter 1. Substantive law was defined as that which is concerned with the content or substance of the law. Legal definitions of crimes are examples of the law's substantive content. Procedural law was defined as governing the *process* of the law. Later chapters will deal with civil and criminal substantive law in greater detail. In this chapter we will elaborate on procedural law by examining it in both civil and criminal contexts. Before we begin the discussion of the actual civil procedure, it is important to review the reasons for our insistence upon strict rules of procedure. In Chapter 1 we stated that most Americans want to prevent government from acting toward them in an arbitrary manner. We are so concerned with the problem of arbitrary government that we have adopted an elaborate system of criminal procedural safeguards to ensure that the innocent person is not wrongfully convicted of a crime. We even accept the inevitability that some guilty persons will go free if "the constable blunders." That is the price we pay to protect our civil liberties.

Our desire to check government capriciousness in criminal cases does not tell us why we also have such elaborate procedural requirements in civil cases, in which, by definition, the government is unconcerned about the outcome. The answer lies in the fact that government, by passing laws, sets up the "rules of the game." No one would even begin to play a board game without some prior knowledge of its rules; likewise, before a person will risk his time, energy, and money in a lawsuit, he wants to know the rules that govern the process. Common sense, therefore, dictates that the rules of civil procedure be known beforehand.

There is, however, another important reason for studying the rules of procedure in civil cases that does directly involve the government. It was an extremely important step in the advancement of civilization when people began relying on government or some other societal institution to resolve disputes. In prehistoric times it may have been a clan or tribal leader who was responsible for settling disputes among people. In later times it may have been a king or a council. Regardless of who the dispute-settler was, the willingness of individuals to submit their disputes to some neutral third party was a vital characteristic of an advanced society. One important aspect of the willingness to submit disputes for peaceful resolution is the perception by all parties that the dispute-settler is fair. Two teams willingly allow a neutral umpire to apply neutral rules of play to their game of baseball if both teams perceive the umpire and the rules to be fair. Then, if a call should go against them, they accept it even if they do not agree with it. Similarly, if courts of law designated to settle disputes among citizens are perceived by all to apply neutral rules of procedure fairly, the losing party will more readily accept the bitter pill he must swallow. In societies in which courts are not perceived as fair and just, people will often resort to illegal or extralegal means to ensure that they receive justice.[1] Consequently, the government has a tremendous stake in maintaining the appearance (and the reality) of its system of justice even though it seldom cares about the outcome of a particular case. Its main interest is in ensuring that the appearance of justice is preserved.

With this background in mind, we turn our attention to the discussion of the rules of civil procedure. In order to avoid confusion and for the purposes of instruction, we have simplified the process as much as possible. In addition, since there are several types of civil actions, we have chosen to use a tort case to illustrate the civil legal process. We hope that this will help the reader to become generally familiar with civil procedure.

CIVIL PROCEDURE

Every tort case begins with a dispute or controversy that cannot be resolved in a less formal manner. A person who feels that he has been injured by another may begin a civil action against him. The person filing the suit is called the *plaintiff,* and the person against whom the suit has been filed is called the *defendant.* Prior to actually filing a suit, the plaintiff will usually consult a lawyer, who will advise him about the soundness of his case. If the lawyer feels her prospective client has a good case, she may either agree to handle it personally or refer him to someone else who specializes in the kind of case in question. Lawyers often agree to work on the basis of a *contingency fee,* which means the lawyer is paid only if the client's claim is successful. The contingency fee is typically from 30 to 40 percent of the award. Should he lose, the client pays only for court fees and other expenses involved in pursuing the case.

Often the plaintiff's lawyer will initially suggest an informal resolution of the conflict. She may call or write to the defendant to convey her client's intent to sue, in the hope that the defendant will see that the plaintiff "means business" and will thus be persuaded to settle out of court. The defendant, in turn, may have retained his own lawyer in anticipation of the plaintiff's action. It is quite possible that after the lawyers for both sides confer, an informal agreement can be worked out, thus avoiding the formal legal process. A majority of cases are resolved after some informal negotiating by the lawyers involved.

When informal methods fail, the next step is the filing of the *complaint.* In the complaint, the plaintiff relates the injury he has received at the hands of the defendant, alleges negligence and liability on the defendant's part, and states what remedy he seeks from the court. In the case of a tort, for example, the complaint will describe the injury; allege that the defendant's negligence caused the injury, thus making him liable; and seek relief, usually in the form of a monetary award for damages. The plaintiff may seek *general damages* to cover items like hospital bills, lost income, and damage to his property. The purpose of general damages is to compensate the plaintiff and to return him, as nearly as possible, to his condition prior to the alleged injury. In addition, if the defendant's behavior has been especially wanton, reckless, or reprehensible, the plaintiff may seek *punitive damages.* Punitive damages are designed to impose monetary punishment upon persons who act in a reckless manner toward fellow human beings. Its purpose is to make an example of the defendant and warn others that society will not tolerate that type of behavior. Movie stars frequently ask for punitive damages against newspaper tabloids that exhibit "reckless disregard for the truth" when publishing stories about the private lives of celebrities.

After the complaint has been filed in the court with the appropriate jurisdiction, the next step is to notify the defendant formally that a legal action has been brought against him by the plaintiff. This is called the *service.* The defendant is served a copy of the complaint listing the allegations made against him by the plaintiff. Along with the copy of the complaint, the court clerk also issues a *summons* to the defendant.

The summons directs the defendant to submit what is called an *answer* within a certain number of days. The answer is the defendant's written account of what happened. The defendant's answer, prepared by his attorney, will deny the facts as alleged in the complaint or deny liability or both. Often the defendant will file a *demurrer,* or motion to dismiss the complaint; however, the motion is infrequently granted. It is extremely important that the defendant respond to the summons because failure to do so could result in a *default judgment* being given to the plaintiff. Failure to respond is tantamount to an admission of liability, and the plaintiff would become entitled to the damages sought in his complaint.

After the pleadings have been completed, the process known as *discovery* begins. Despite the tendency of movie and television scriptwriters to create situations in which a surprise witness drops a bombshell, real-life court cases seldom happen that way. In fact, the general tendency is for both sides to lay all their cards out on the table. This is done for a number of reasons. First, going through the formal trial process is expensive and time-consuming. Second, putting the decision in the hands of a jury may be risky. A case may seem airtight to everyone but the jurors, and strange verdicts and awards are possible. A third reason for laying the cards on the table is to determine if some facts of the dispute can be agreed upon beforehand, thus saving the need to establish them at the trial. Fourth, once the cards are on the table, one side or the other may decide it cannot win, and serious negotiations about a settlement may begin. Lawyers often find that their clients have not been totally candid with them. As a result, certain facts left out of the client's version of the events may come to the lawyer's attention during discovery. Either lawyer may then advise the client to settle the case out of court. Finally, both sides will know exactly what they are up against and can plan their courtroom strategies accordingly.

Discovery can take a number of forms. One of the more common ones is a *deposition,* which can be taken in either of two ways. One way is to have a *witness* appear at the office of one of the lawyers in the case and answer questions put to him by the lawyer. The witness is under oath, and a stenographer records the questions and responses verbatim. Or a witness may be questioned in the presence of both lawyers and subjected to direct questioning by one and cross-examination by the other. As in the first instance, everything said is recorded. Like all forms of discovery, a witness's testimony may be so devasting to one party's case that the lawyer may urge him to reach a settlement with the other party.

An *interrogatory* is a second form of discovery. An interrogatory is a written question directed to one of the *parties* to the case by the other party. Unless questions are answered, the person may be cited for contempt. For example, if the case involved an automobile accident, a lawyer might ask, "Were you drinking?" "Had you been drinking?" "How much?" "How fast were you driving?" Truthful answers must be given because the same questions may be asked at the trial while the party is under oath.

The last form of discovery involves the production of physical evidence in the possession of one of the parties. The judge may issue a *subpoena duces tecum,* which is a court order requiring a person to appear in court and to produce specified documents pertinent to the case. In a debt-collection case, for example, the defendant might be required to produce a receipt or a cancelled check as proof of payment of the debt. In a personal-injury case, the plaintiff might have to produce copies of a medical exam and of hospital and doctor bills to establish the extent of the injury.

Discovery is designed to expedite the legal process. If certain facts can be agreed upon by both parties before the trial, these facts will only need to be recorded as having been stipulated as true by both sides. In a personal-injury case, for example, the extent of the plaintiff's injury might be agreed upon by both sides because the real issue is not whether the plaintiff was injured, but whether the defendant was liable for the injury. This simplifies the case for the jury, thus enabling them to concentrate solely on the issue of liability.

Remainder of the Pretrial Process.   After the discovery process has been completed, the parties can make a pretrial motion requesting a *summary judgment.* In a personal-injury suit, for example, if there is no dispute over the facts but only over the legal question of liability, the plaintiff may request that the judge grant a summary judgment in his favor. That is, the plaintiff is asking the judge to settle the legal question of the defendant's liability in favor of the plaintiff. If it is clear that the defendant's negligence caused the injury, the judge will grant the plaintiff's motion. In most cases, however, the defendant's negligence is not clear cut, and the plaintiff's motion is denied. The defendant may also request a summary judgment. According to the rules of civil procedure, the plaintiff must make what is called a *prima facie case.* This term means that at first glance, or "first face," the plaintiff's version of the facts are credible. If the plaintiff has failed to make a prima facie case, the defendant may ask the judge to rule that he was not negligent and to dismiss the plaintiff's case. As already noted, most cases are not easily settled if they have gone this far, and the motion is usually denied.

Selection of the Jury.   Once the preliminary maneuvering is over, the focus turns to the actual resolution of the conflict at trial. The first order of business is the selection of the jury, if a jury is to be used.

The parties to the case, if both are agreeable, may choose to have a **bench trial,** in which the judge becomes the **trier of fact** while simultaneously acting as the interpreter of the law. After submission of the evidence, the judge alone will decide the outcome of the case. In highly complex or technical cases, the parties often prefer to let the judge decide the case since laypersons, who compose juries, frequently lack the expertise to make a learned decision. In other instances—personal injury cases, for example—the parties prefer to let the judge decide simply because juries are unpredictable, sometimes allowing irrelevant factors, such as the wealth of the defendant, to be considered in awarding damages.

If a jury is used, its members are selected from a pool of prospective persons, called a **venire.** Although we generally think of juries as comprising twelve persons, the number can be less than twelve, even as few as five, in civil cases. Each prospective juror, or **venireman,** takes the stand to be asked a few questions by each attorney and perhaps the judge. The initial questions are generally simple ones, designed more to put the person at ease than to elicit information. Lawyers want to know if the prospective juror has any prejudices concerning the client's case. For example, a lawyer representing an insurance company will try to ascertain the venireman's attitude toward insurance companies. If the venireman appears hostile to insurance companies, the lawyer will try to prevent his selection.

A venireman may be struck from a jury in two ways: challenge for cause and peremptory challenge. If, as we have seen, the lawyer's questioning reveals prejudice on the part of the venireman, the lawyer may cite that as a reason for excluding the person. This is known as a **challenge for cause,** and the judge must agree that the reason given is sufficient to exclude the person. The use of challenge for cause is unlimited. The second type of challenge is called a **peremptory challenge;** if a lawyer feels that a venireman's presence on the jury would harm her client's chances of winning but she cannot specify a cause sufficient to satisfy the judge, the lawyer may strike the person without giving any reason. The rules of civil procedure limit the number of peremptory challenges for each side to a specified number, usually around six. This process of questioning prospective jurors and striking some from the jury is called **voir dire,** which means "to speak truth."

After the jury has been selected, they are sworn in and said to be **impanelled.** The jury's major function is to serve as the trier of fact. They are to listen to the evidence presented in the case and decide who is telling the truth and which party deserves to win. In a sense, the jury serves as the conscience of the community. Although the jurors are not personally concerned with the outcome of the case, they are interested in seeing that the case is resolved in a peaceful, fair manner.

For that reason, it is important that the jury be selected from a representative cross-section of the community. The parties to the case are more inclined to accept the final verdict if they perceive the jury to be fair and impartial. As we have noted, this acceptance by the parties is crucial to the acceptance of the legitimacy of the entire judicial system.

Submission of Evidence.   After the jury has been impanelled, the trial begins. Each lawyer is allowed to make an *opening statement* to the jury, in which he or she outlines his or her case. Generally speaking, the opening statement will inform the jury as to exactly what the lawyer intends to prove and how he or she plans to prove it. After both lawyers have made their opening statements, the plaintiff's lawyer calls her first witness. In civil law, since the plaintiff is the complaining party—that is, the one who initiated the lawsuit—he bears the burden of proof. The standard of proof in civil law is the *preponderance of the evidence* standard; that is, a preponderance, or a majority, of the evidence must support the plaintiff's allegations against the defendant. If the plaintiff fails to meet this standard, the defendant will win the case. Therefore, the plaintiff begins the trial by presenting his case to the jury.

The plaintiff's lawyer calls her first witness and proceeds to question him. This is known as *direct examination.* When the plaintiff's lawyer has finished, the defendant's lawyer may *cross-examine* the plaintiff's witness. On cross-examination, the defendant's lawyer is free either to limit his questions to topics raised by the plaintiff's lawyer or to open a new line of questioning. When the defendant's lawyer has finished, the plaintiff's lawyer may *redirect,* or ask additional questions of the same witness. On redirect examination, however, the plaintiff's lawyer may ask only questions raised by the defendant's lawyer on cross examination; she may not open a new line of questioning. Upon completion of redirect, the defendant's lawyer may *recross-examine* but he also is limited to questions raised on redirect. When both lawyers have asked all of their questions, the witness is excused.

Strict rules of procedure govern the questioning of witnesses and the admission of evidence. The hearsay rule, for example, forbids witnesses from testifying about facts of which they have no direct knowledge or information. Lawyers are forbidden to ask *leading questions* of their own witness. A question such as "Did you see the defendant strike the plaintiff on the evening of May 1?" would be improper. However, the question "What did you see on or about 6:00 PM on the evening of May 1?" would be acceptable. During the questioning of a witness, a lawyer may note his objection to either the other lawyer's question or the witness's response. The judge must make a ruling to either sustain the objection as valid or overrule it as invalid. These objections, and the judge's subsequent rulings, may provide the losing party with the legal grounds on which to base a future appeal. Objections to a judge's ruling must be "timely"; after-the-fact objections when the trial is over usually do not provide grounds for an appeal.

During the examination of witnesses, the lawyers will submit physical evidence to substantiate their cases. For example, while questioning the attending physician in a personal-injury suit, the lawyer may introduce into evidence a copy of the written medical report on the plaintiff's injury. As with testimony, the defendant's lawyer may object to the introduction of the medical report, forcing the judge to make a ruling on its admissibility. The judge's ruling may also serve as grounds for an appeal if the ruling is incorrect. Any incorrect ruling may be considered a reversible error by an appeals court at some later date. Reversible error results in a new trial for the losing party.

As we can easily see, the presentation of evidence is the heart of the trial. Because the evidentiary stage of the trial proceeding is so important, we will return to it later in this chapter in order to examine in greater depth the rules of evidence as they apply to both civil and criminal cases. For now, let us continue with our overview of civil procedure.

After the plaintiff's lawyer has called all of her witnesses and submitted all of her physical evidence, the defense may present its side of the case. The defense calls its rebuttal witnesses and the same procedure of questioning is followed, except this time it is the defendant's lawyer who conducts direct examination and the plaintiff's lawyer who cross-examines. The main strategy of the defense is to rebut as much of the plaintiff's damaging evidence as possible. One way to rebut a plaintiff's tort case is to show **contributory negligence** on the part of the plaintiff. If the defendant's lawyer can show that the plaintiff was wholly responsible for his own injuries, the defendant is not liable. The theory is that the plaintiff should come before the court with "clean hands"; that is, he should be able to show that he did not contribute to his own injury through his own negligence. Another defense strategy is to show **comparative negligence** on the part of the plaintiff. Unlike contributory negligence, which removes the defendant's liability, comparative negligence assumes that both parties are partially to blame for the plaintiff's injury. The plaintiff will not be allowed to recover for that portion of his injury for which he himself was responsible. A showing of even partial negligence on the plaintiff's part will at least reduce the amount of damages the defendant will have to pay. Thus, a good offense becomes a good defense.

Following the submission of all the oral and physical evidence, the two lawyers will address the jury a final time in their **closing statements.** The plaintiff's lawyer will summarize her case to the jury with the assertion that a preponderance of the evidence supports her client's claims against the defendant. The defendant's lawyer will summarize his own rebuttal evidence and ask the jury to rule in favor of his client.

Final Actions.   Once the evidentiary stage of the trial is complete, some additional legal maneuvering is possible before the case is actually submitted to the jury. Either side may request a **directed verdict.** A motion for a directed verdict is a lawyer's request that the judge direct the jury to bring in a verdict favorable to his client. If, for example, the plaintiff has failed to carry the burden of proof in the case, the judge might well grant the defense lawyer's motion for a directed verdict. Similarly, if the defendant has failed to rebut successfully the plaintiff's allegations and evidence, the judge might grant the plaintiff's motion. Generally, however, few judges are willing to take the decision out of the hands of the jury, and so these motions are routinely denied. Like all denied motions, the judge's refusal to order a directed verdict can be appealed.

Once all the formal pleadings have ceased, the judge charges the jury. In his **charge to the jury,** the judge explains the applicable law as it relates to the case and describes what the jury must decide if they are to rule in favor of the plaintiff. The judge also explains what the jury must find if they are to rule for the defendant. After the charge has been completed, the case is formally submitted to the jury.

Jury Deliberation and Verdict.   Once the jurors have the case, the fate of both parties is in their hands.[2] In a tort case, such as the one we have been discussing, the jury is called upon to render one of two types of verdicts. The first type is called a **general verdict.** Under a general verdict, the jury could find the defendant liable and award the plaintiff the monetary damages he sought, less than what he sought, or more than what he sought. The jury could also find that the defendant was not liable; the plaintiff would then not be entitled to damages. A second type of verdict, called a **special-issues verdict,** presents the jury with a series of questions that it must answer. For example, in a comparative-negligence case, the first question might be, "Do you find the defendant not liable for plaintiff's injury?" If the answer is No, the next question might be, "Do you find the defendant 10 percent liable?" The percentage—20 percent, 30 percent, and so forth—is increased incrementally until the jury reaches the appropriate degree of comparative liability for each party. Damages would then be awarded to the plaintiff on the basis of the percentage of comparative liability. If, for example, the total amount of damages sought by the plaintiff was $50,000 but the jury found the defendant only 60 percent liable, then the defendant would pay the plaintiff only $30,000 in damages. Of course, should the jury rule that the defendant was not liable for the plaintiff's injuries, there is no other decision to be made and the jury's job is over.

After the jury has reached its verdict, the foreman informs the bailiff, who in turn notifies the judge. Court is reconvened and the jury's verdict is formally read. Verdicts in civil cases, unlike many criminal cases, need not be unanimous. The judge may poll each individual juror to make sure there is no mistake about the decision. The judge then thanks the jurors for their service and dismisses them. The trial stage of this particular civil case is now over.

Appellate Procedure.   The person who loses the case at trial has the right to appeal the decision. The grounds for the appeal may vary but generally fall into two categories. The first alleges that the judge made an error or errors regarding questions of law. Recall our previous discussion of the need for attorneys to make timely objections to the judge's rulings on points of law. When an attorney makes such an objection and the judge overrules it, there is a disagreement over a point of law. That disagreement provides the legal grounds upon which the appeal may be based. The appellate court must first decide whether the trial judge was correct in his ruling. If the trial judge is ruled to have been incorrect, the appellate court must next determine whether the error was serious enough to warrant a new trial. In the case of a reversible error, the appellate court concludes that the error was so serious that it might have adversely affected the outcome of the trial. In that instance, a new trial will be ordered. If the error is found to be a harmless error, however, the judgment of the trial court will be affirmed. An appellate court will frequently refuse to overrule the trial judge if the alleged error falls into an area committed to the trial judge's discretion. In such an instance, the trial judge is presumed to be correct and the appellate court is precluded from overruling him.

The second category of appeals, known as **remittitur,** occurs in cases in which money damages have been awarded. Such appeals are often based on the grounds that the award was excessive. Juries find it difficult to determine the proper monetary damages to be awarded. In a libel suit, for example, how much is a person's reputation worth, and how can money compensate the victim for damage to his reputation? These are difficult questions to answer, and juries sometimes get carried away and award more in damages than is warranted. An appellate court may reduce the award if, in its judgment, the award was excessive.

Strict rules of procedure also govern the appellate process. The losing party, or **appellant,** has a specified time limit, usually 30 days, in which to file a motion for an appeal. Failure to do so constitutes a waiver of the right to appeal, and the judgment of the trial court will be carried out. The appellant's "right" to appeal is a limited one. A motion for an appeal merely asks the appellate court to review the case for possible legal errors. Should the appellate court find the basis for the appeal to be frivolous, however, the motion for an appeal can be denied since the granting of such appeals is discretionary. In a technical sense, the appellant's case *has* been reviewed by the appellate court but has simply been judged to be frivolous. The appellate court will not address itself to the merits of the case in that situation.

If the motion for an appeal is granted, the appellant's lawyer must file the appropriate **brief** with the appellate court, making sure every *t* is crossed and every *i* is dotted. A brief is a summary of the case, a list of the alleged errors on questions of laws that were made at trial, legal arguments and precedents in support of the appellant's position, and a request for the appropriate judicial relief, usually in the form of a reversal. The winner at trial, or **appellee,** must direct his lawyer to file a brief denying that errors were made, or that if they were made they were harmless errors, and asserting that the appellate court should affirm the decision of the trial court.

Once all appeals have been exhausted and a final judgment entered, the civil case is over except for the execution of the trial court's decision. In a negligence case such as we have been using to illustrate the civil process, the defendant will have to pay the damages awarded at the trial. This may require the defendant to sell his property or to borrow the needed money, but it usually means the defendant's insurance company will pay off. Should a defendant refuse to pay the damages, the plaintiff may resort to two alternatives to get what is due to him. First, the plaintiff may ask the court for a **writ of execution.** This writ authorizes a sheriff or other law enforcement officer to seize the property or bank accounts of the defendant. If property is seized, the sheriff may sell it at auction. The plaintiff's award plus any additional expenses are deducted from the proceeds, and the remainder is returned to the defendant. The second course of action is **garnishment.** In some states the defendant's salary may be garnished to pay the plaintiff. This means that a certain percentage of defendant's salary is withheld from his paycheck until the plaintiff's award is paid in full. The drastic measures described here are necessary to enforce the court's authority. The victorious party, in this case the plaintiff, must be able to rely upon the power of government to enforce the judgment. Otherwise, as suggested at the beginning of this chapter, few persons would be willing to go to the trouble of bringing a lawsuit, and many would resort to extralegal or illegal methods to resolve conflicts.

CRIMINAL PROCEDURE

Criminal and civil processes are similar enough that it is unnecessary to repeat every step of the procedure in detail. However, the reader should keep in mind the major difference between the two procedures.

The defendant who loses a civil suit may be forced, as we have just seen, to pay damages to the plaintiff and perhaps even have his property confiscated in the process. As serious as that penalty may be, it hardly compares to the loss of life or liberty that the criminal defendant faces upon conviction for a crime. It is because the consequences of a criminal conviction are so serious that the U.S. system of justice goes to great (some say excessive) lengths to ensure that the innocent go free and only the guilty are punished.

Another important distinction about the criminal justice system also must be understood. A person who is *factually* guilty—that is, one who really committed the crime of which he is accused—must be found to be *legally* guilty as well.[3] Unless the determination of legal guilt is accompanied by strict adherence to the rules of criminal procedure, there is denial of due process of law. No matter how firmly convinced we may be that the accused actually committed the crime, the full coercive power of the State cannot be imposed until legal guilt has been proven "beyond a reasonable doubt." Our belief that a person is innocent until proven guilty reflects the difference between factual and legal guilt. With these two distinctions in mind, we begin our discussion of criminal procedure.

Pretrial Procedures. The process of criminal justice begins with the arrest of the defendant. The defendant's arrest may result from a complaint sworn out by the victim of the crime, who is called the **complaining witness.** The complaint is sworn out before a magistrate, who then issues an **arrest warrant.** If the crime was committed in the presence of a police officer, the officer is the complaining witness and will secure the arrest warrant from the magistrate if the defendant is not already in custody. The arrest warrant authorizes the police to take the accused into custody and to bring the accused before the magistrate.

When the accused is taken into custody, he is brought before the magistrate "without undue delay" for what is termed the **initial appearance.** Prior to the famous *Miranda v. Arizona*[4] decision, the major purpose of the initial appearance was to allow the magistrate to inform the accused of his constitutional rights to remain silent and to have the assistance of counsel. At one time, the police, in their eagerness to secure confessions, unfortunately often delayed presenting the accused before a magistrate until after he had been subjected to lengthy periods of questioning. In *Mallory v. United States,*[5] the accused, Andrew Mallory, was arrested in the early afternoon and was questioned throughout the day until he confessed. Mallory was not brought before a magistrate and informed of his constitutional right to remain silent until the next day. The Supreme Court overturned Mallory's conviction on the grounds that the police had acted improperly in delaying Mallory's initial appearance. In addition, according to the Court, the fact that Mallory was of fairly low intelligence made it even more imperative that he have the assistance of counsel.

As a result of the *Mallory* and *Miranda* decisions, the police are obliged to inform the accused of his constitutional rights whenever a custodial arrest is made, thus lessening the importance of the initial appearance. The initial appearance remains significant, however, because the magistrate will inform the accused of his right to a **preliminary hearing** and will set **bond** for him. Bond is money or property left as security to ensure that the accused will not flee from the jurisdiction of the court. If the magistrate feels that the accused is reliable, has ties to the community, or is unlikely to flee, he may release the accused on his own **recognizance.**

Unless the accused waives it, the next step is the preliminary hearing. The purpose of the preliminary hearing is to determine whether there is **probable cause** to believe a crime has been committed and whether there exists sufficient evidence that the accused committed it. The preliminary hearing is largely one-sided, with the prosecutor offering enough evidence to convince the judge that there is sufficient probable cause to continue proceedings against the accused. Should the judge decide that sufficient probable cause exists, the accused is **bound over.** If probable cause is insufficient, the accused is released but may be rearrested and recharged at some future time. As indicated, accused persons often waive their right to a preliminary hearing on the advice of counsel since in most cases the police will have enough evidence to have the accused bound over.

The next stage of the criminal justice process is the formal accusation, called the **indictment.** About half the states and the federal government have indictment by **grand jury.** A grand jury is a body of from twelve to twenty-three persons who decide whether the accused should be tried for a crime. The grand jury passes a **true bill,** which declares that there is sufficient evidence to require the accused to stand trial. The passage of the true bill by a majority of the grand jury constitutes the indictment. If the grand jurors decide that there is insufficient evidence, they return a **no bill.** Critics of the grand jury maintain that it is little more than a rubber stamp for the prosecutor since a grand jury rarely fails to follow the prosecutor's recommendation in a case.[6] Defenders of the grand-jury system maintain that it serves to protect accused persons from malicious prosecution and harrassment by unscrupulous prosecutors. As is often the case, one's perspective is based on one's view of the criminal justice system.

The remaining states have chosen to use what is called indictment by **information.** Under this method, the indictment is made at the discretion of the prosecuting attorney. Indictment by information is preferred by those who seek greater efficiency in criminal justice since it is less troublesome than the grand-jury system. Although subject to possible abuse by overzealous prosecutors, the states that use indictment by information seem to be satisfied with it.

Following the indictment, the accused is brought before a judge for **arraignment.** At the arraignment, the accused is formally notified of the charges and is asked to enter a plea. The accused may plead not guilty, in which case a trial will be scheduled. A second option is for the accused to plead guilty. If the defendant's lawyer and the prosecutor have worked out a **plea bargain,** the defendant may agree to plead guilty in exchange for leniency or some other consideration on the part of the judge. Plea bargains, therefore, are arrangements by which the defendant exchanges a guilty plea for a reduced sentence, a lesser offense, or dismissal of other charges.[7]

Finally, the defendant may choose to plead **nolo contendere** to the charges, which literally means "no contest." A *nolo contendere* plea is tantamount to a plea of guilty, and the judge is free to impose any sentence allowable after either a guilty plea or a conviction at trial. The major difference is that a *nolo* plea is a denial of culpability on the part of the defendant. In effect, the defendant denies any moral wrongdoing. A *nolo* plea also serves as a "face-saving" device for a person like Spiro T. Agnew, who was allowed to plead *nolo contendere* to bribery and corruption charges in Maryland in exchange for his resignation from the vice presidency in October 1973. If for any reason the defendant should refuse to enter a plea, the judge will merely enter a not-guilty plea on his behalf.

The discovery process in the criminal process is different from the one we saw in the civil process. Recall that in a civil proceeding, either party may request a deposition or send questions, in the form of interrogatories, to the other party. In a criminal case, on the other hand, the accused may not be forced to answer interrogatories or give a deposition because the Fifth Amendment protects him against self-incrimination. The accused does not have to prove his innocence, nor may he be forced to assist the state in proving its case against him. The accused is entitled to know what evidence of his guilt the prosecutor has, however, so that his lawyer can prepare an adequate defense. This is another example of how the rules of criminal procedure are tilted in favor of the defendant. Given the resources that the state may bring to bear to secure the defendant's conviction, this small advantage is somewhat justified.

The pretrial conference in a criminal case is similar to that in a civil suit. The defendant's lawyer and the prosecutor hammer out with the judge the basic issues of the case and any facts that can be agreed upon beforehand. If, for example, the defendant is pleading not guilty by reason of insanity in a murder case, the defense may be willing to stipulate that the accused killed the victim. The real issue is the question of the defendant's sanity, and the trial will revolve primarily around that issue. Once these ground rules have been agreed upon, the trial stage begins.

Criminal Trial Stage.   The trial process for civil and criminal cases is very similar, so we will highlight only significant differences between the two. One such difference is in jury selection. Criminal procedure usually allows more peremptory challenges than are allowed in civil cases. In Texas, for example, each side is allowed fifteen peremptory challenges in a capital case and ten in a noncapital case.[8] Once the *voir dire* process is completed and the jury is impanelled, the defendant is said to be in **jeopardy.** The significance of being placed in jeopardy is that the Fifth Amendment to the U.S. Constitution declares that no person shall "be twice put in jeopardy of life or limb." In other words, if the defendant is acquitted or the charges are subsequently dropped, he may not be tried again for the same offense.

Another important difference between a civil trial and a criminal trial is the standard of proof required for each. Under the rules of civil procedure, in order for the plaintiff to prevail, he must show that the weight, or preponderance, of evidence favors his version of the facts. In a criminal case, however, the State, as the plaintiff, must meet a higher standard—beyond a reasonable doubt. One way to think of the beyond-a-reasonable-doubt standard is to consider and then reject all other possible explanations for the crime except the conclusion that the defendant did indeed commit the crime for which he is being tried. All alternative or feasible explanations as to who might have committed the crime other than the defendant are considered and discarded. In presenting evidence, the prosecutor seeks to establish that the conclusion that the defendant is guilty of committing the crime is the only conclusion a reasonable person could reach. The job of the defendant's lawyer is to create a reasonable doubt in the minds of the jurors in order to avoid a guilty verdict. If state law requires a unanimous verdict, a single juror may cause a **hung jury.** In the event of a hung jury, the State retains the right to either retry the defendant on the same charge or on a lesser (but not greater) charge without violating the double jeopardy clause. Finally, the prosecutor may decide that a new trial will not result in a conviction and drop the charges against the defendant.

A third difference between the civil and criminal processes involves the directed verdict. After each side has presented its case, the defense may request a directed verdict from the judge. While the defense may ask the judge to direct the jury to return a not-guilty verdict, the State may not request a directed guilty verdict. This is another example of how the rules of criminal procedure tend to favor the defendant. The presumption is that the defendant, who is without the vast resources possessed by the State, must be given some advantages to offset the power that the State is capable of marshalling against him.

After the closing statements and the charge, the men and women of the jury begin their deliberations. In routine cases, the jury will reach a verdict in a relatively short period of time. In highly publicized cases, the judge may order the jury *sequestered.* The jury is then isolated until they either reach a verdict or inform the judge that they are hopelessly deadlocked. The judge must be very careful about how long he allows a deadlocked jury to deliberate. Naturally, the judge (and perhaps the parties) would prefer a definite verdict in order to avoid another trial. However, the jury may not be pressured to bring in a verdict, especially if it turns out to be a guilty verdict. The defendant, on appeal, could argue that the lengthy deliberation indicated reasonable doubt among some of the jurors and that these "holdouts" were pressured to change their votes to "guilty" in order to avoid prolonging their ordeal. Such undue pressure could constitute reversible error, resulting in a new trial for the defendant.

A final way in which criminal and civil cases differ is in the right of appeal. The defendant, of course, is free to appeal his conviction based on errors made during the trial. The State, however, can appeal an acquittal only on rare occasions. Generally speaking, the State may appeal an acquittal only to clarify a matter of law. That is, if the prosecutor believes that the judge has rendered an incorrect legal ruling, the State may appeal the ruling to clarify the point of law for future reference. The defendant actually tried in the case involving the disputed ruling cannot be retried without violating the double-jeopardy clause.

The appellate process in a criminal case can be long and arduous if the defendant is willing to pursue it. Conviction for a crime in a state court allows the defendant to avail himself of the state's appellate procedure. If unsuccessful at the state level, the defendant may seek further review in a federal court under federal *habeas corpus* procedures. Habeas corpus review, in effect, allows federal courts to reopen a case on the grounds that a right secured by the U.S. Constitution has been abridged by the State. There is some evidence, however, that in the mid-1970s Burger Court became increasingly reluctant to allow federal courts to review challenges to violations of constitutional rights when those challenges have been repeatedly reviewed by state courts.[9]

RULES OF EVIDENCE

As previously noted, the submission of evidence is the most crucial part of a legal proceeding. In this section we will examine the rules of evidence in greater detail, providing examples from both civil and criminal cases. Specifically, we will discuss the types and forms of evidence, the hearsay rule, and the exclusionary rule. We begin our discussion with some general observations about evidence.

Trials are perhaps the ultimate contests in our competitive society. Even the names of cases, such as *Smith v. Jones,* reflect the adversarial nature of our judicial system. Each party bears the responsibility of persuading the trier of fact, whether judge or jury, to accept its version of the case, in much the same manner that it is the responsibility of a baseball team to move the batters around the bases in order to score runs and win. Each party is charged with structuring the facts it presents to persuade the fact-finder, although certain "rules of the game" govern the introduction of evidence in legal proceedings.

The umpire of the match is the judge. He or she decides whether a particular piece of evidence is relevant—that is, whether it tends to establish a material fact in the case.[10] The parties involved in the trial elect to have either a judge alone or a jury act as the fact-finder and render the decision in the case. The fact-finder hears the statements of the witnesses, observes their demeanor, and examines the physical evidence. They decide the credibility of each witness and assess the weight of the evidence. Suppose that X testifies that she saw the accused assault Y, but the defense produces other witnesses who say that X was not present at the scene. The jury may choose to disbelieve X, and therefore not rely on her testimony, while giving full weight to the testimony of the defense witnesses. In other words, the "weight" of the evidence depends on the credibility of the statement in the fact-finder's mind as well as on the amount of influence the evidence has on the final verdict.[11]

Everyone is familiar with the concept of evidence, whether the exposure comes from television dramas, media coverage of sensational trials, or actual involvement in a hearing. Evidence introduced at trials includes not only physical evidence but also the statements of witnesses who testify on the stand. It ranges from simple declarations, such as "I saw the yellow car run the light and smash into the other car," to sophisticated scientific evidence relating to design weaknesses in product-liability cases. Evidence that was once considered exotic—bitemarks, various body fluids (blood, saliva, semen), and fabric fibers—is becoming commonplace in criminal trials and often forms the basis for a conviction.

Direct and Circumstantial Evidence.   Evidence may be classified as either direct or circumstantial, depending on the nature of the facts. **Direct evidence** is derived from one's five senses—taste, touch, smell, sight, and hearing. The following statements are examples of direct evidence: "I smelled alcohol on her breath," or "I saw the accident." Direct evidence proves the facts without the introduction of additional testimony. Although direct evidence may stand alone as proof, the fact-finder may decide to give little weight to it for a variety of reasons, such as the unreliability of the witness or contradictory testimony from another witness.

In contrast, **circumstantial evidence** requires the fact-finder to fit pieces of evidence together to complete the picture, just as one might fit a jigsaw puzzle together. The lawyer carefully provides the necessary pieces of evidence to construct a credible and viable case.[12] To illustrate, suppose the State presents a series of witnesses who testify to the following: (1) Sebastian and Osborn had a disagreement at a party; (2) the two of them went alone into a windowless room with only one exit and locked the door behind them; (3) eavesdroppers loitering outside the room heard a loud bang and decided to investigate; and (4) upon breaking down the door, they found Sebastian holding a revolver and Osborn stretched out on the floor with a neat, circular wound in his arm. Although none of the witnesses actually saw Sebastian shoot Osborn, the fact-finder at Sebastian's trial can easily use the building blocks of testimony provided by the State to infer Sebastian's guilt and convict him.

Forms of Evidence. Evidence may be presented in the form of tangible evidence (physical exhibits such as weapons or charts), evidence that comes under **judicial notice** (facts that are commonly known or are verifiable by referring to some widely accepted reference book), or **oral testimony.** First, **tangible evidence** is evidence that the fact-finder can touch or observe in the courtroom. This category is subdivided into two groups: real evidence and demonstrative evidence. Real evidence is a physical object that is involved in the case, such as a murder weapon or the cocaine allegedly sold by the defendant to an undercover police officer. Demonstrative evidence is a visual or audiovisual aid, such as a chart of the intersection where an automobile accident occurred, a skeleton in a personal injury case, or a videotape of the incident.[13] Lawyers are becoming increasingly creative in the use of these visual aids. For example, a fairly common practice is to present a videotape of an average day in the life of a person who is paralyzed because of the defendant's negligence.

A second form of evidence is judicial notice, which allows the judge to recognize that certain facts are commonly known within the community (it is very cold in the Arctic) or can be ascertained by reference to a highly reliable source such as a calendar (December 25, 1983, was a Sunday). The parties are then relieved of the obligation to provide formal proof through witnesses or exhibits.[14] Judicial notice is particularly useful when the case involves the law of several jurisdictions. For example, several states claimed Howard Hughes, the extremely wealthy recluse, as their resident in order to enrich their state treasuries through the inheritance tax. The crux of the case was an interpretation of the laws of the various states regarding the definition of legal residency. In such a case, the court could accept the statutes into evidence by judicial notice without calling the state official who is charged with publishing the official version of the laws to testify.

The third and most common form of evidence is oral testimony, which is given by a witness on the stand in open court or in a deposition under oath. Each party has the opportunity to question the witness and to test his veracity, either on direct examination or on cross-examination. This right to observe the witnesses and their demeanor is guaranteed in criminal trials by the Sixth Amendment to the U.S. Constitution, which states that "the accused shall enjoy the right . . . to be confronted with the witnesses against him; to have compulsory process for obtaining witnesses in his favor." The opportunity to cross-examine opposing witnesses and to present one's own witnesses is entrenched just as firmly in criminal law as it is in civil law. A *subpoena,* a written order from the court, may be served on a prospective witness demanding that he either appear in court to testify or be subject to a penalty, often contempt of court. As previously noted, a *subpoena duces tecum* requires the witness to bring to court any records in his possession that relate to the case. These legal tools are available in civil and criminal cases to both parties in order to enable them to command the presence of witnesses.[15]

Presentation of Evidence.   Evidence is presented to the fact-finder through the testimony of witnesses. Generally, one of the first orders of business in a trial is to segregate the witnesses from the courtroom proceedings in order to prevent them from tailoring their testimony to fit the evidence that has already been presented. Obviously, this procedure is not followed for party-witnesses, who have a right to be present throughout the proceeding.[16] Witnesses may also be sequestered for the duration of the trial, although this is rather rare. During the trial, the attorney identifies the person to be called to testify and the oath is administered.

Information is elicited from the witness through a series of questions and answers. The lawyer calling the witness first questions the person in direct examination, and then the opposing lawyer cross-examines the same witness. The process continues until one or the other counsel informs the judge that there are no more questions for this witness. The successive questions are limited to topics in the previous statements and thus are narrowed on each round of questioning.[17]

As previously noted, an attorney may not lead his own witness. However, leading questions may be used during cross-examination for such purposes as impeaching a witness. To impeach a witness is to put his credibility at issue in the minds of the trier of fact. Many methods are used to implant doubts about the witness's testimony. One is to show that the witness is biased or has a monetary interest in the case. (Expert witnesses are often challenged on the basis that they are being paid for their testimony. In fact, they are selling their time and knowledge to one party or the other, but in a perfectly acceptable manner.) Another method is to show that the person has a poor reputation for truth and veracity in the community. A third way is to present conflicting testimony from other witnesses.[18] Finally, an attorney may not impeach a witness he has called to the stand unless he has previously identified that person as an *adverse witness.*

Even tangible evidence is introduced into the trial through oral testimony. In other words, a witness on the stand must identify the tangible evidence and explain its significance to the case. However, the parties may agree on certain evidence (such as the statutes mentioned in the Howard Hughes case) beforehand, and it is then presented to the fact-finder by the attorneys. To present tangible evidence of all types requires that *foundation,* or basic information, be provided about the item before the court will admit it into evidence; this is called *laying a predicate.*[19] Assume, for example, that a contract case involves the records of the XYZ Corporation and that these records are essential to the plaintiff's case. The custodian of the corporation's records is called to the stand and is required to testify to the following before the records are admissible: (1) that the record was made during the regular course of business; (2) that the record was made at or near the time of the event in question; and (3) that the record was made by an employee with personal knowledge or as a regular part of business activities based on information from someone who did have personal knowledge. Different requirements are set forth for items such as photographs, weapons, and other pieces of tangible evidence.[20]

The judge is the umpire who decides on the admissibility of evidence. The opposing party has the opportunity to object to the testimony or tangible evidence as it is introduced, and the party who introduced the evidence then has to explain why the evidence should be admitted. Failure to enter a timely objection often constitutes a waiver of the objection for purposes of appeal.[21] Evidence that might be inflammatory, such as gory pictures of a murder victim, or otherwise prejudicial might be the subject of a *motion in limine.* Such a motion is filed and considered before trial or outside the presence of the jury. The judge may forbid the introduction of such evidence and even prevent the attorneys from referring to such evidence.[22] Many jurisdictions allow the parties to exclude evidence that the defendant's insurance company will actually pay the damages if the defendant is found to be at fault.[23] The obvious intent is to prevent juries from assessing heavier or lighter damages because of the ultimate source of funds.

Rule Against Hearsay.   When a witness is testifying about information based on his own sensory perceptions, the jury and the parties to the lawsuit have the opportunity to observe the witness's demeanor. This is not the case when the witness quotes someone else, however. For example, statements like "I know he forged the check because he told me he did," or "Dick said that the defendant admitted it was all his fault" are deemed *hearsay* because the person who initially made the statement is not in the courtroom and cannot be cross-examined. Courts have therefore, developed the *rule against hearsay*, which prevents such statements from being admitted as evidence.

Hearsay includes not only spoken and written comments but also conduct. To illustrate, suppose a police officer testifies that he conducted a lineup of suspects and that the victim pointed out the defendant as the perpetrator of the crime. The victim did not orally identify the defendant, but the officer is relaying her nonverbal assertion that the defendant is the one who committed the crime. The definition of hearsay is three-pronged: (1) it is an assertion (by verbal, written, or assertive conduct), (2) made by someone other than the testifying witness, which (3) is offered to prove the truth of the matter stated. If an assertion meets all three of these conditions, it is hearsay and *must be excluded from trial*.[24] Not all out-of-court statements are offered to prove the truth of the matter stated, however. For example, an ambulance driver's testimony that "Henry told me that the driver of the green car ran the light and was at fault" is not admissible to show which driver was at fault, but it is admissible to show that Henry was conscious following the accident.

The most celebrated case of a conviction based on hearsay, and one which contributed to the development of the rule against hearsay, is that of Sir Walter Raleigh. Raleigh, founder of the American colony of Roanoke, is famous for swirling his cloak to the ground to prevent Queen Elizabeth I from stepping into the mud. He was later charged with treason on the basis of two out-of-court statements. A ship's pilot told the court that a Portugese gentleman reported to him that Raleigh had expressed an intention of cutting the queen's throat. Lord Cobham declared in his sworn statement that Raleigh and he had plotted to dethrone Elizabeth and put Arabella Stuart in her place. Although Cobham was imprisoned only a few feet away from the site of the trial, he did not appear in person at the proceedings. Thus, Raleigh was convicted on the accusations of two people who did not appear in court and whose veracity was never questioned by the trier of fact. In fact,

Cobham later recanted his allegations. Public disgust with the decision spurred the development of a new rule of law—hearsay evidence should be excluded from trials.[25]

There are three primary reasons for the exclusion of hearsay evidence. First, it is very possible that the statement has not been repeated accurately. A popular party game called "gossip" illustrates this possibility. The first person whispers a comment to the next person and so on until everyone in the group has heard the statement. The final statement often does not even resemble the beginning comment. The same may be true for a statement that is being offered as evidence. Second, the person who has made the statement is not in court and therefore is not subject to cross-examination. As we have already discussed, the right to confront witnesses is one of the mainstays of our legal tradition. In addition, the trier of fact, whether judge or jury, is not given the opportunity to observe the declarant and his demeanor in order to determine his veracity. Nor can the fact-finder determine the basis of the declarant's information, whether personal observation or casual rumor. The third reason for excluding hearsay, and perhaps the most obvious, is that the declarant was not under oath when he made the original statement and was therefore not compelled to tell the truth.[26]

Over the years the courts have backed away from the absolute stand that hearsay is never admissible, and certain exceptions have developed. The most familiar one is the exception that permits dying declarations to be admitted as evidence on the questionable theory that a person who is dying will be truthful because he will soon be facing his Maker. Four basic requirements must be met before such a statement will be admitted: (1) the declarant was aware of his pending death; (2) the declarant had direct and accurate knowledge; (3) the statement contains facts, and not opinions or guesses; and (4) the person must actually be deceased at the time of the trial. There are other exceptions, each of which carries its own requirements that must be met before the statement can be admitted into evidence. Among these other exceptions are declarations against one's own interest, such as admissions, excited utterances, and descriptions of physical conditions to prove injury.[27]

The Witness. One of the main issues at any trial is the credibility of the witnesses. In other words, can and will the trier of fact believe the witness's statements? The chief method of presenting a case in our adversarial system is through the witnesses. The party calling the witness to the stand claims the witness as his own and cannot impeach his own witness unless he designates the witness as a hostile or adverse witness from the beginning. It is therefore imperative that the attorneys have an accurate picture of what the witness will say before calling him to the stand.

People who observe the same event do not always perceive it in the same way. A fan of one football team may deem an interception by his team as a great defensive play, while the other team's fans might call it a horrible offensive play. A husband and wife are both parties to the same marriage and the same events. When each is called to the witness stand in a divorce action, however, the testimony often sounds as if they are talking about two different marriages and totally different people. The spouses are not intentionally distorting the truth, but one's perceptions color the testimony given. Police reports abound with eye-witnesses giving conflicting information about a crime. It is the responsibility of the fact-finder to sort through the information in order to arrive at an accurate assessment of the situation.

The first question about any witness is his competency to testify. Adults are presumed to have the necessary attributes of competency: the ability to perceive and understand what they are testifying about, the ability to remember the event, and the ability to communicate their knowledge to the fact-finder. This presumption may be challenged for a variety of reasons; the witness's having been intoxicated or hard-of-hearing are two examples. Even a witness who has been adjusted insane may be a competent witness if the court finds that he is able to give an accurate description of the event and that he understands the consequences of lying on the stand.[28] The latter requirement is the same for infant witnesses. The question for children is whether they understand the difference between right and wrong and whether they know what it means to lie. The trial judge has a great deal of discretion in deciding whether a child is competent to testify.[29]

An issue similar to competency is that of qualifying someone as an expert witness. The general rule prevents the opinions and conclusions of laypersons from being admitted as evidence. There are two reasons for this rule. The first is that the jurors themselves, given the same facts, can form a conclusion just as well as the witness can (and it is their job to do so). The second reason is that the witness lacks the necessary training, skill, or experience necessary to be considered an expert and is therefore unqualified. On the other hand, experts are permitted, and even encouraged, to testify as to their conclusions. The main criteria are (1) that the opinions to which the expert is testifying were formed because of special knowledge, skills, or training that is not within the ordinary experiences of jurors and (2) that the witness is truly an expert. Qualification as an expert does not require formal training.[30] For example, a mechanic who has worked in his field for 20 years may be qualified as an expert just as easily as would a mechanical engineer.

Although a witness may be competent, she may not be credible. The judge or the jury has the opportunity to observe the witness to detect any telltale signs that she is lying. They are assisted in this task by the opposing counsel, who may try to impeach the other party's witnesses. Four primary tactics are used in impeaching witnesses: (1) showing bias or prejudice, (2) using prior inconsistent statements, (3) proving a sensory deficiency, and (4) providing evidence of prior behavior that casts doubt on the witness's veracity.

A lawyer can show a witness to be biased by eliciting information that the other party is paying him for his testimony or that his expenses are being paid during the trial (a frequent and proper arrangement for expert witnesses). A second method of impeachment is through the use of prior inconsistent statements. Suppose that Smith testifies on the stand that it was foggy on the day of the accident, but she had said in her deposition that it was clear. Another method is to challenge the witness's ability to perceive the event. For example, Pasternacki testifies that his glasses were broken but that he clearly saw the accident from two blocks away, while his optometrist testifies that Pasternacki's vision would have been blurry and that he could not possibly have seen the accident clearly. A fourth way to cast doubt on veracity is to show prior felony convictions or a bad reputation in the community for truthfulness. For example, Sam admits on cross-examination that he has previously been convicted for perjury; this admission would certainly hurt his credibility with the jury.[31]

Privileges.   Certain communications are considered privileged; that is, the witness does not have to reveal the contents of the conversation. The **privilege** is based on the relationship of those having the discussion. As a society, we have decided that maintaining confidentiality in certain relationships is more important than having the relevant information in a particular trial. Examples of privileges are those between attorneys and clients, physicians and patients, and clergy and penitents. The states are split with regard to the marital privilege; some states treat it as a privilege of one spouse not to have the other testify against him, while other states treat it as a privilege of the spouse not to give testimony against the other. In other words, some states treat it as a privilege belonging to the defendant to prevent the spouse from testifying against him, while others treat it as a privilege of the witness-spouse to elect not to testify. Obviously, government officials do not have to reveal military or state secrets if they can show that disclosure would be harmful to national defense; there is also a privilege that allows police officers to refuse to reveal the name of an informer. Some states are enacting limited statutory privileges to journalists in regard to their sources.[32] These statutes, called *shield laws,* are discussed more fully in Chapter 6.

The Exclusionary Rule. As we have repeatedly discussed, our legal system places a premium on due process and the fairness of the procedures used for conviction. The courts have outlined procedures to be followed in the course of gathering evidence and preparing for trial. Just as we are aware of the rules we must obey in order to avoid entanglement in the legal system, so the police are aware of the rules that govern the gathering of evidence. When the police violate those rules, the courts decline to accept the improperly collected evidence into the trial. This refusal to accept such "tainted" evidence is called the **exclusionary rule.**

The exclusionary rule was established in the case of *Weeks v. United States,*[33] wherein the Supreme Court argued that if there were no exclusionary rule, "the protection of the Fourth Amendment . . . might as well be stricken from the Constitution." Although the *Weeks* rule initially applied only to cases in federal courts, the Supreme Court extended the rule to state cases in *Mapp v. Ohio.*[34] Evidence uncovered as a result of improper police conduct, called "the fruit of the poisonous tree," is inadmissible at trial. The Supreme Court, under former Chief Justice Warren Burger, has somewhat eroded the strong protection of the rule through the enunciation of limited exceptions in recent cases. The exclusionary rule continues to be controversial, and we will say more about it in Chapter 7.

Scientific Evidence in Criminal Trials. Technological advances have been made in every societal endeavor, and police work is no exception. For years, courts have given credibility to certain pieces of scientific evidence, such as firearms identifications through ballistics tests, chemical tests for intoxication, fingerprints, handwriting samples, and photographs, just to name a few. However, courts still do not routinely accept the use of evidence gathered through hypnosis, and the results of polygraph tests usually come in as evidence only if both parties agree to the admission.[35] Courts do not rush to endorse technological advances, but today cases are decided by microanalysis of fibers, analysis of bitemarks, and neutron activation analysis of evidence. As in civil cases, the credibility of this evidence depends on the party's ability to show the fact-finder that the test was conducted in a fair manner by a qualified person.

Each party in a lawsuit has the responsibility to convince either the judge or the jury to accept its version of the case. They do so through the presentation of evidence. Evidence is classified by types: real evidence, evidence admitted by judicial notice, and oral testimony. All evidence is presented by witnesses who testify under oath either in open court or in depositions about the matters within their personal knowledge or by stipulation by the parties. Statements that fall under the hearsay rule or improperly seized evidence in criminal trials will not be admitted at trial.

CONCLUSION

Procedural due process of law, whether civil or criminal, is fundamental to American law. As we have seen, the rules of civil procedure provide the standard by which essentially private disputes are settled in a just and orderly fashion. Before a person is willing to put his case before a court of law for resolution, he must believe that the ground rules are fair to both sides and that the dispute settler will be impartial. The rules must be spelled out clearly and in advance. All of this is necessary so that citizens will accept the legitimacy of the judicial process.

Procedural due process in the area of criminal law presents an additional problem. There is little doubt that government possesses awesome power to deprive individuals of life, liberty, or property. Consequently, due process places strict procedural requirements on government to ensure that public officials do not abuse their power. Although sometimes criticized for favoring the accused, procedural due process is necessary for liberty in a free society. The requirement that government obtain the deprivation of a person's life or liberty "by the book" is considered by many to be an essential safeguard of freedom. Even a cursory examination of repressive and totalitarian governments reveals that denial of fundamental principles of due process is a common element. In a democratic society, *how* the government deprives a person of life, liberty, or property is every bit as important as *why* it does so.

NOTES

[1] The opening scene in the film *The Godfather* illustrates this point. The undertaker, whose daughter has been brutally beaten, seeks "justice" from the Godfather when his daughter's attackers receive only a suspended sentence.

[2] In rare instances, the disputing parties might be able to work out a last-minute negotiated settlement before the jury returns its verdict. However, such a settlement is highly unlikely.

[3] Herbert L. Packer, "Two Models of the Criminal Process," in George F. Cole, *Criminal Justice: Law and Politics*, 4th ed. (Monterey, Calif.: Brooks/Cole, 1984), pp. 15–29.

[4] *Miranda v. Arizona*, 384 U.S. 436 (1966).

[5] *Mallory v. United States*, 354 U.S. 449 (1957).

[6] Herbert Jacob, *Justice in America: Courts, Lawyers, and the Judicial Process*, 4th ed. (Boston: Little, Brown, 1984), p. 188.

[7] James V. Calvi, "Plea Bargaining: An Empirical Study of Participant Perspectives" (unpublished PhD dissertation, University of Missouri, 1977), pp. 2–3.

[8] *Texas Code of Criminal Procedure*, Art. 35.15.

⁹ *Stone v. Powell,* 428 U.S. 465 (1976).

¹⁰ Edmund Morris Morgan, *Some Problems of Proof under the Anglo-American System of Litigation* (Westport, Conn.: Greenwood Press, 1975), p. 86.

¹¹ Milton D. Green, *Basic Civil Procedures* (Mineola, N.Y.: Foundation Press, 1972), pp. 164–165.

¹² Paul B. Weston and Kenneth M. Wells, *Criminal Evidence for Police,* 2nd ed. (Englewood Cliffs, N.J.: Prentice-Hall, 1976), pp. 185–186.

¹³ Jon R. Waltz, *Introduction to Criminal Evidence* (Chicago: Nelson-Hall, 1983), pp. 14–15.

¹⁴ William Farnum White, *Winning in Court on the Law of Facts* (Englewood Cliffs, N.J.: Prentice-Hall, 1972), pp. 122–125.

¹⁵ Weston and Wells, pp. 55–56.

¹⁶ Fed. R. Evid. 615.

¹⁷ Edward W. Cleary, ed., *McCormick's Handbook on the Law of Evidence,* 2nd ed. (St. Paul, Minn.: West Publishing Company, 1972), p. 6.

¹⁸ Weston and Wells, pp. 64–66.

¹⁹ Waltz, pp. 30–35.

²⁰ Rolando del Carmen, *Criminal Procedure and Evidence* (New York: Harcourt Brace Jovanovich, 1978), pp. 117–118.

²¹ Morgan, pp. 86–88.

²² Fed. R. Evid. 403.

²³ Cleary, p. 479; Fed. R. Evid. 411.

²⁴ Ibid., p. 584.

²⁵ Sir Walter Raleigh's Case as cited in David W. Louisell, John Kaplan, and Jon R. Waltz, *Cases and Materials on Evidence* (Mineola, N.Y.: Foundation Press, 1972), pp. 51–52.

²⁶ Morgan, p. 112.

²⁷ del Carmen, pp. 113–114.

²⁸ Waltz, pp. 303–305.

²⁹ Weston and Wells, p. 57.

³⁰ Andre A. Moenssens, Ray Edward Moses, and Fred E. Inbau, *Scientific Evidence in Criminal Cases* (Mineola, N.Y.: Foundation Press, 1973), pp. 1–4.

³¹ Waltz, pp. 105–133.

³² del Carmen, pp. 105–110.

³³ *Weeks v. United States,* 232 U.S. 383 (1914).

³⁴ *Mapp v. Ohio,* 367 U.S. 643 (1961).

³⁵ Waltz, pp. 337–432.

Limitations

The judicial branch of government, although immensely influential, is not unrestrained. The powers of courts and judges are circumscribed by barriers emanating from a variety of sources, including the judicial system itself. The doctrine of *stare decisis*, or following the precedent of prior court decisions, evolved through judicial custom. Courts are confined by constitutional provisions and the procedural guarantees of the Bill of Rights. Although statutes are often merely legislative enactments of established court procedure, they serve to establish boundaries for courts. The procedure for selecting judges, particularly election, also acts to constrain the power of the judicial branch. This chapter will further describe some of the limitations on the power of courts; other limitations, both substantive and procedural, will be discussed elsewhere in this book.

JUDICIAL RESTRAINT

Despite the widely held belief that judges, like fools, rush in "where angels fear to tread," courts have established rules of procedure that allow them to avoid many of the hard cases that lawyers claim make bad law. Courts, especially appellate courts, have considerable discretion over the cases they hear and use that discretion to engage in what is

often referred to as *judicial gatekeeping.* As Alexis de Toqueville observed in *Democracy in America,* virtually every issue of public policy
comes before the courts sooner or later. The reason usually given for
this propensity to litigate is the legalistic nature of the American people.
Americans tend to have strong feelings about their rights, and courts
of law are the logical forums for vindicating those rights. Consequently,
every schoolchild kicked off the football team or dismissed from the
cheerleading squad seeks judicial protection of what is perceived to be,
at the very least, a God-given right.

While there is much disagreement among judges, lawyers, and legal
scholars about the degree to which courts should intervene in such
disputes, the heart of the debate centers around the question of *access*
to courts as appropriate forums for the resolution of societal conflict.
One school of thought holds that the formal adjudication of conflict
should be limited to those issues that are important and worthy of a
court's time. Issues such as those raised by our football player and
cheerleader are too trivial to warrant a court's time and are a waste of
taxpayers' money. Other issues are viewed by this school of thought as
inappropriate for judicial resolution. This argument holds that courts
are ill-equipped to resolve some issues and that other political bodies,
usually legislatures, should handle them. Finally, some believe that courts
should not allow themselves to become embroiled in issues that might
bring the stature of the courts into disrepute. Those who take the
positions just listed wish to close the judicial gates—that is, to limit
access to the courts as forums for the resolution of certain conflicts.

Another school of thought would prefer to see the judicial gates
opened wider. Proponents of this position argue that the courts are
often the last resort for persons whose rights have been violated. Courts
are frequently the last hope of the poor, the elderly, or any other group
unable to achieve its goals in the larger political system. If courts are
established to ensure that justice is done, then every issue, no matter
how seemingly trivial, is worthy of judicial resolution. Proponents of
opening the judicial gates concede that there are limits to the courts'
ability to resolve every societal conflict. They also concede that certain
issues are best resolved by the more traditionally political branches of
our government. However, proponents of greater judicial involvement
argue that courts have a constitutional duty "to say what the law is,"
and that to avoid thorny issues entirely is a dereliction of judicial duty.

In this section we will examine a number of judicial doctrines relied
upon by courts to either open or close their judicial gates to conflict.
Although there are numerous examples illustrating both of these doctrines, we will focus on those aspects of each doctrine that reveal the
political nature of judicial gatekeeping. Let us begin our discussion with
the issue of standing.

Standing.   The term **standing** refers to the right of a litigant to "stand" before a court. In general, standing refers to the litigant's right to bring a cause of action before a court for judicial resolution. Issues of standing often turn on whether or not the party bringing the case before the court is the appropriate one to do so. For example, in most cases one cannot sue to protect the rights of another because only the party who has actually been injured may bring a lawsuit.[1] A court may close the judicial gates by denying standing to persons wishing to raise issues that the court would prefer to avoid.

Standing is the major bar to so-called **taxpayer's suits.** A taxpayer's suit is a suit filed by someone claiming standing solely on the basis of status as a taxpayer. Taxpayer's suits often involve government programs or policies that a taxpayer, or even a group of taxpayers, disapproves of as a waste of money. In other words, the taxpayer claims that a continuation of the government program being challenged is injurious to the taxpayer because it increases the tax burden. Someone might conclude, for example, that the space program is a waste of taxpayers' money and ask a court to enjoin the government from continuing to finance it. Since there is hardly a government program that does not offend someone, acceptance of the right of a taxpayer *qua* taxpayer to sue would open a big can of worms, requiring courts to review virtually every government program enacted. Such a prospect has caused courts to bar taxpayer's suits in all but a few limited instances.

The first case to raise the issue of taxpayer's suits was *Frothingham v. Mellon.*[2] Congress had enacted the Maternity Act of 1921, which encouraged states to create special health programs for mothers and infants in an attempt to reduce the infant mortality rate. The Act provided federal funds as an incentive to states that created such programs. Frothingham, a taxpayer, claimed that the Act increased her tax burden and deprived her of her property without due process of law. The Supreme Court ruled against Mrs. Frothingham, stating that the amount of tax an individual taxpayer contributes to the program is so small that it is indeterminable. In addition, the Court realized that to permit Frothingham to challenge the expenditures under the Maternity Act would conceivably allow every disgruntled taxpayer to challenge every program of which he disapproved. Because the injury to the individual was so slight and the consequences so potentially damaging, *Frothingham* barred most taxpayer's suits for over 40 years.

In 1968, however, the Supreme Court opened the judicial gates to taxpayer's suits just a crack in the case of *Flast v. Cohen.*[3] Conventional wisdom held that *Frothingham* served as an absolute bar to taxpayer's suits; in *Flast,* however, the Court held that although a taxpayer could not challenge federal spending solely on the basis of status as a taxpayer, neither could a taxpayer be barred from showing sufficient personal stake in the outcome of a case to meet the requirement of adversariness that courts demand. If such a showing could be demonstrated, standing could be granted.[4] *Flast* held that the taxpayer must first establish a link, or nexus, between taxpayer's status and exercises of congressional taxing and spending powers *only*. Second, the taxpayer must establish a link between taxpayer's status and a specific constitutional limitation on the taxing and spending powers of Congress. In *Flast*, the petitioners filed suit to enjoin the expenditure of federal funds for parochial schools as a violation of the Establishment Clause of the First Amendment. Consequently, the Court ruled that the petitioners in *Flast* had met both conditions. Mrs. Frothingham had met only the first condition; she merely alleged that the Maternity Act exceeded the general powers of the national government without linking the Act and expenditures to a specific constitutional limitation, thus failing to meet the second condition set forth in *Flast*.

Subsequent cases[5] involving the war in Vietnam, the secret budget of the Central Intelligence Agency, and other controversial government spending programs have retreated from *Flast* somewhat, leaving the exact status of taxpayer's suits in limbo. Such a situation does illustrate the political nature of the standing issue, however. If a court, especially the Supreme Court, wishes to open the gate to litigants or their claims, *Flast* may serve as a precedent for granting standing. If, on the other hand, a court wishes to dodge a controversial issue, it can merely rule that the litigants have not demonstrated the links outlined in *Flast*. As mentioned at the beginning of this section, this leaves the courts free to exercise their discretion to open or close the judicial gates on issues of standing.

Mootness and Ripeness.   Two judicial doctrines that also permit courts to avoid controversial issues, at least in the short run, are **mootness** and **ripeness**. One requirement that American courts insist upon is that a case be a "real case or controversy" within the meaning of Article III of the Constitution. Because American law is based upon the adversary system, courts will refuse to hear cases in which one party lacks a personal stake in the outcome or in which the controversy originally at issue has somehow resolved itself. The question of mootness involves both situations. If a situation that gave rise to the lawsuit in the first place somehow resolves itself, then a court will rule that the issue is moot. A case is rendered moot not only because the problem is no longer a problem, but also because the party who brought the suit has lost the personal stake in the outcome that the adversary system demands.

Perhaps the best illustration of the Supreme Court's use of mootness to avoid a controversial issue is *DeFunis v. Odegaard*,[6] a case which involved affirmative action. Marco DeFunis applied to law school in the state of Washington but was denied admission. The law school to which DeFunis applied had an affirmative action program which admitted members of certain minority groups, some of whom had lower grades and Law School Admissions Test (LSAT) scores than did DeFunis. DeFunis brought suit, alleging "reverse discrimination," and won in the lower court. The trial court granted DeFunis temporary admission to the law school pending the outcome of the school's appeal. By the time the case reached the Supreme Court, DeFunis was enrolled in his last quarter of law school. Officials of the law school indicated that regardless of the Court's decision, DeFunis would be allowed to finish the current quarter in which he was enrolled. The Court ruled that, inasmuch as DeFunis had won what he had set out to win and since whatever the Court ruled would have no bearing on DeFunis's rights, the case was now moot.

The dissenting justices in *DeFunis* argued that the case should not have been declared moot. They pointed out that even though DeFunis was in his last quarter, he could become ill, flunk out, or otherwise fail to complete his final quarter. Should that happen, DeFunis might be barred from re-enrolling and completing his law degree. More important, the dissenters believed that the Court should address the issue of affirmative action raised by the case. They argued that it was inevitable that the Court would have to rule on the constitutionality of affirmative action programs and that to delay resolution of the issue would only result in further waste of time and money. In fact, the dissenters proved to be correct. Four years later the Supreme Court faced the issue again in *Regents of the University of California v. Bakke.*[7] As the dissenters had predicted, the Court had merely succeeded in postponing the inevitable. On the other hand, the Court had four more years to reflect on one of the most controversial issues to come before it in recent years. Use of a doctrine like mootness can provide the Court with the time it needs to prepare itself for difficult and controversial issues.

The Supreme Court cannot always demand strict adherence to the mootness requirement. One quick example will illustrate why. Except under the most unusual circumstances, it takes about three years for a case to reach the Supreme Court. Recall that DeFunis was in his third year of law school before his case reached the High Court. A pregnant woman wishing to challenge the constitutionality of a state's abortion law would be unable to do so because the gestation period of humans is only nine months; the issue would thus be moot before it could ever reach the Court. Naturally, the Court could not be expected to adhere to the mootness doctrine since the woman would either have to have the baby or have an illegal abortion. In *Roe v. Wade,*[8] the Court said as much by agreeing to hear the case notwithstanding the issue of mootness.

Whereas mootness involves a situation in which an issue has waited too long before reaching a court, ripeness involves a situation in which an issue reaches a court too soon. A case is said to be "not ripe for review" when a court feels that judicial resolution of the controversy would be premature. The Supreme Court, for example, requires litigants to exhaust all of their lower remedies before bringing a case before it. If the issue is at all capable of being resolved below, the Court wants it to be. Since the nine justices can review only a small percentage of the total number of cases the Court is asked to review, it wishes to handle only those difficult questions incapable of being resolved by the lower courts.

The requirement for ripeness can postpone the necessity of resolving a difficult issue for the Court. The Court can sit back, wait, and hope that, in effect, the problem will go away. Although we saw with the case of affirmative action that some issues just will not go away, the requirement that an issue be ripe for review may, like mootness did in *DeFunis,* buy the Court enough time to reflect on how to resolve a difficult issue.

Political Questions.   Perhaps the clearest indication of the unwillingness of courts to become embroiled in controversial issues is the **political question** doctrine. The exact nature of what constitutes a legitimate political question is open to debate. For example, the Supreme Court has agreed to hear cases involving such highly charged issues as busing, abortion, school prayer, reverse discrimination, and Watergate. These are certainly "political" questions within any ordinary meaning of that word. Why, then, does the Court choose to label some issues "political questions," thereby avoiding them, while agreeing to hear cases involving some of the most political issues imaginable? The answer, as we have already suggested, is that the "political question" label is a convenient way for courts to avoid issues they would rather not address. Unlike standing, mootness, and ripeness, however, political questions tend to put courts on a collision course with one of the other branches of government, and those are confrontations that courts have a tendency to lose. Consequently, courts, preferring discretion over valor, defer (some say surrender) the resolution of controversial issues to Congress or the president.

An early example of the use of the political question doctrine is *Luther v. Borden.*[9] In that case, Chief Justice Taney refused to decide which of two competing governments in Rhode Island was the legitimate one. Taney ruled that either Congress or the president should decide whether a state has a "republican form of government" within the meaning of Article IV of the Constitution. In *Luther,* since Congress had not refused to seat the members of the House elected from Rhode

Island under the Charter Government and since President Tyler had promised to send federal troops to support the Charter Government, the Supreme Court did not believe that its decision could or should countermand the decisions of the two political branches of government.

In reaching its decision in *Luther,* the Court did not necessarily remain neutral. Indeed, by refusing to decide the issue, the Court implicitly backed the Charter Government. By adopting a hands-off policy, the Court may actually be supporting the status quo, as the case of *Colegrove v. Green*[10] demonstrates. After many years of failure to redraw the lines of congressional districts, Illinois was severely malapportioned. Some Illinois congressional districts had as much as eight times as many people as others. This left the people in the large districts severely underrepresented. Colegrove, living in one of the disfavored districts, sought an injunction against further congressional elections in Illinois until the district lines had been redrawn to reflect equal populations. The Supreme Court ruled against Colegrove for several reasons. First, the Court was unsure about whether it could provide an appropriate judicial remedy. If the Court did rule that the existing lines were unconstitutional, it could do nothing if the state still refused to redraw them. Second, if the Illinois delegation was elected in violation of the Constitution, Congress could refuse to seat the state's representatives. Third, if malapportionment was a problem in Illinois, it was not for the Court, but for the people—through the ballot box—to correct it. Finally, the Court took note of the highly partisan nature of reapportionment and ruled that courts ought not to enter this "political thicket."

Colegrove did not put an end to the issue of reapportionment as a political question. In 1962 the Court was faced with the issue again, except this time the case involved the malapportionment of *state* legislative districts. In *Baker v. Carr,*[11] the Supreme Court ruled that federal courts could take jurisdiction in reapportionment cases. In reversing itself on whether reapportionment was a "political question," the Court outlined six criteria for determining whether an issue raises a political question. The Court ruled that a case raises a political question (1) if the issue has clearly been left to a coequal branch of the national government by the Constitution; (2) if a judicial decision would embarrass the nation in its foreign relations; (3) if the Court lacks manageable judicial standards by which to decide the case; (4) if the Court's decision would demonstrate a lack of respect for a coequal branch of government; (5) if there is a need to adhere to a decision already made; or (6) if the issue involves a policy determination clearly left to nonjudicial policymakers.[12] In ruling that reapportionment cases were not political questions, the Court opened the door to numerous challenges of legislative and nonlegislative districts that did not conform to the "one person, one vote" standard of equal population.

The most recent applications of the political-question doctrine have involved some of the most controversial issues of our times. In *United States v. Nixon*,[13] lawyers for former President Richard Nixon argued that the use of "executive privilege" was a political question left to the president's discretion. The Supreme Court disagreed, ordered the Watergate Tapes released, and the rest is history. In *Massachusetts v. Laird*,[14] the Court refused to hear a case on the constitutionality of the war in Vietnam. Finally, in *Powell v. McCormack*,[15] the Court was asked to decide whether the refusal by Congress to seat a member of the House was a political question. The Court agreed to hear the case despite arguments that the decision to seat members was clearly left to the Congress by the Constitution.

In this section we have attempted to demonstrate how courts can use doctrines such as standing, mootness, ripeness, and political questions as tools of judicial policymaking. If the Supreme Court wishes to enter a particular "political thicket," it seldom has trouble finding a way to do so. On the other hand, these doctrines serve as a convenient excuse for the Court if it wishes to avoid controversy. An important point to remember is that the decision *not* to get involved in a controversy can have as many policy implications as the decision *to* get involved. By not involving itself, the Court supports the status quo. Similarly, a decision to rush in where angels fear to tread can put the Court in the forefront of policymaking in the United States. The decision as to which road to take is itself a highly charged political question.

LEGAL LIMITATIONS

The previous section dealt with political limitations that are invoked by judges to avoid having to resolve certain questions. Those same limitations may also be regarded as legalistic in nature. To illustrate, standing may be employed to restrict access to courts, but it may also be used to prevent those without a stake in the matter from meddling in a lawsuit while allowing those with an interest to participate in the proceedings. For example, you cannot intercede in a lawsuit brought by a creditor against your best friend merely because the debtor is such a good person and you think it is harsh that she must pay the debt. On the other hand, a statute might grant standing to grandparents to intervene in their child's divorce (a lawsuit in which the grandparents would otherwise not have standing) in order to protect visitation rights with their grandchildren. Just because we arbitrarily categorize these limitations on judicial power as either political or legalistic does not imply that they are exclusively one or the other.

Jurisdiction. The threshold question in any lawsuit is to determine which court or courts have jurisdiction in the matter. Judicial *jurisdiction* can be defined as the power or authority of a court to decide a particular case. As discussed in Chapter 3, jurisdiction stems from constitutional or legislative provisions, and the boundaries of each court's jurisdiction is carefully delineated. The concept of jurisdiction appears fairly simple in its initial definition but is infinitely complex in its application.

Jurisdiction has three facets: (1) geographic limitations, (2) subject matter limitations, and (3) personal or *in rem* jurisdiction. All three requirements must be met before a court may decide a case. Every tribunal in our system is limited by geographic boundaries. Decisions of the U.S. Supreme Court are operative everywhere in the United States, but they are both irrelevant and ineffective in Brazil. The same principle holds true for state and local courts as well; municipal courts lack power to decide cases that arise outside the city boundaries and that do not involve city ordinances. The Supreme Court succinctly explained the principle in the following excerpt:

> The authority of every tribunal is necessarily restricted by the territorial limits of the State in which it is established. Any attempt to exercise authority beyond those limits would be deemed in every other forum . . . an illegitimate assumption of power.[16]

In addition, jurisdiction is defined topically. Courts are assigned particular types of lawsuits to handle. Misdemeanors are generally heard by courts of limited jurisdiction, while felonies are heard by trial courts of general jurisdiction in the state systems. In civil matters such as tort or contract litigation, jurisdiction is commonly determined by the amount in controversy or the monetary damages sought by the parties. Cases involving relatively smaller amounts, perhaps less than $1,000, can be heard by county or JP courts, while suits involving $5,000 or more can be heard in superior courts. As you may remember from Chapter 3, the amount in controversy must be at least $10,000 in order for federal courts to consider diversity suits.[17]

The third element is that the court must have either *in personum* or *in rem* jurisdiction. "Every state possesses exclusive jurisdiction and sovereignty over persons and property within its territory."[18] **In rem jurisdiction,** which arises in suits affecting property interests, stems from the physical location of the property inside state boundaries and under the control of the court. Technically, suits *in rem* are filed against the property itself—for example, a suit to seize an obscene film or to determine ownership of an abandoned cache of jewels—but the term is also used generically to describe suits affecting the property interests of the parties. Probate proceedings or suits to partition land would fall into this category.

In personum jurisdiction is the power of the court to "determine the personal rights and obligations of the defendants."[19] Personal jurisdiction may be founded on presence, domicile, consent, and certain activities within the state. Those who reside in a state or who are physically present within the territorial limits of a state are subject to the *in personum* jurisdiction of the state's courts; however, a caveat must be added in that the other prerequisites must be met for a court to have jurisdiction to render an effective decree. Out-of-state residents come under the jurisdiction of the court either by voluntarily consenting to be sued in that state (a common provision in contracts) or because of jurisdictional statutes. Specific legislative enactments, commonly referred to as **long-arm statutes,** extend the power of state courts over nonresident parties. The long-arm statutes are based on a form of implied consent; that is, if one is doing business in the state or commits a tort therein, one is deemed to have consented to be sued in the state courts.

> Due process requires only that in order to subject a defendant to a judgment in personum, if he be not present within the territory of the forum, he have certain *minimum contacts* [emphasis added] with it such that the maintenance of the suit does not offend "traditional notions of fair play and substantial justice."[20]

Remember that the defendant, whether a natural person or a corporation, must receive adequate notice of the proceedings and an opportunity to be heard. That notice may be in the form of either personal or substituted service. Personal service occurs when the party is officially notified of the pending litigation in accordance with the statutory requirements, generally by mail or by personal delivery of the petition by the process server. **Substituted service** frequently occurs through publication in the local newspaper. **Personal service** is the preferred method of advising the defendant of the pending litigation, and substituted service is ineffective in certain instances. These are rather technical rules, and reference to applicable state rules would be needed to determine whether substituted service is acceptable in a given lawsuit.[21]

Quasi-in-rem jurisdiction allows the court to exercise judicial jurisdiction over land, chattels, and intangibles to satisfy a personal obligation such as a debt of the owner, even if the owner is not personally subject to the court's jurisdiction.[22] For example, a state statute may allow a nonresident to be sued in the state's courts, even if the accident occurred elsewhere, on the basis that his insurance company is incorporated in that state. This type of jurisdiction is not employed as frequently. A defendant who wishes to challenge the jurisdiction of the court generally must either do so in the initial pleading or forfeit the right to question the authority of the court. Similarly, any effort to change the location of a trial must be filed as a pretrial motion.[23]

Venue. Venue must be distinguished from jurisdiction, or the power to adjudicate. **Venue** refers to the site or geographic location where a trial takes place. A court may have jurisdiction to hear a particular case, but venue may not be proper with the particular court. District courts may have the prerequisites of jurisdiction to hear felony cases, but the venue statute will limit the venue to the county in which the crime occurred. Venue is thus a further limitation on the power of the court.[24]

Venue provisions are deemed so important that they appear in the U.S. Constitution: "The trial of all crimes . . . shall be held in the State where the said crimes shall have been committed."[25] The social policy is that the parties to a lawsuit, whether civil or criminal in nature, should not be hauled into far distant forums and forced to defend lawsuits in a place inconvenient for them and for their witnesses. Such inconvenience might seriously prejudice the case in that the witnesses might be unable to travel to the new location; in addition, transporting and lodging the necessary personnel can be expensive. A particular concern in criminal cases is that the defendant be tried in the community in which the crime was committed for at least two reasons: (1) the defendant is entitled to be tried before peers who are applying contemporary community standards; and (2) the community has a vested interest in the trials of those accused of committing crimes in their neighborhoods.

Venue is generally governed by statutory provisions and may based on the issues involved in the lawsuit. In litigation concerning land, for example, venue is proper in the county in which the land is located. Litigants have a limited opportunity to modify the venue of the proceeding, but such a move requires court approval. The most common ground for transfer in a civil case is *forum non conveniens,* a doctrine which allows the court to decline jurisdiction if in the interest of justice and for the convenience of the parties the case should be moved.[26] Much more frequent, however, is the motion in a criminal case to change venue because of prejudice and bias in the community that would prevent a fair trial. This perceived prejudice or bias is often attributed to pretrial publicity in a particularly newsworthy case.[27] The issue for the court and potential jurors is not whether they have heard about the case, but rather whether they have already formed an opinion about the matter to the extent that they would be unable to listen to the evidence and render a fair and impartial verdict. In other words, the jurors do not have to be recluses who know nothing about community events, but they must have open minds about the guilt or innocence of the accused despite having heard the pretrial publicity.[28] Courts are hesitant to grant motions to move trials because of the community's interest in resolving local matters and because it may be a very expensive proposition. Moving may be especially costly in criminal cases, in which the original forum has to pay all travel and lodging expenses for court personnel, attorneys, and witnesses.

Statutes of Limitation.   An additional legislative restriction on the court's power to hear a particular matter is statutes of limitation. **Statutes of limitation** are temporal in nature and prescribe the time periods in which actions must be brought. The plaintiff must file within the time limit or be forever barred from seeking relief; violation of the statute of limitations is a defense to the suit.[29] The purpose is to ensure that the action is brought within a reasonable time and while the evidence is still fresh. As time proceeds, valuable information could be lost or destroyed, and witnesses' memories of the event fade.[30]

Again, statutes of limitation vary according to the type of lawsuit. The basic rule in civil cases is that the statute begins to run when the cause of action accrues—at the time of injury, for example.[31] However, determining the time of injury is not always as easy as it might first appear. A medical condition caused by an automobile accident or by malpractice might not manifest itself immediately; similarly, a psychological problem caused by a traumatic event such as child molestation may surface years after the event. Some statutes allow tort victims leeway by extending the limit from the date of injury to the date that the injury was discovered or should have been discovered; the latter provision protects a defendant from perennial potential for suit. Criminal laws also include statutes of limitation. The limits for misdemeanors are usually shorter than those for felonies, whereas there is rarely a statute of limitations for the crime of murder.

To mitigate the possible harshness of the statute of limitations, there are provisions allowing the statute to be tolled, or suspended.[32] Conditions such as infancy or insanity might cause the statute to be tolled. It is the time of filing the petition, and not the time of judgment, which is critical. In other words, the statute is tolled with the initiation of the legal action.

Conflict of Laws.   Americans live in a mobile and interconnected society. For business or for pleasure, we frequently cross state lines or even cross the country, and we think nothing of entering into contracts with companies located across the continent from us. We often change our domiciles from one state to another. We seek assistance from experts in cities and institutions far from home. We purchase goods produced in factories in other regions of the country. We do all of these things without fully appreciating the ease with which we do them and the legal safeguards that are afforded to us as we move around the nation.

This mobility poses special legal problems. If our extraordinary communications and transportation systems failed and we were isolated within our own states, an entire subfield of law would be eradicated. But we are not confined and unable to communicate, and conflict of laws is therefore a flourishing branch of law. The area of conflict of laws involves three subsidiary issues: (1) selection of the court with the correct jurisdiction; (2) choice-of-law questions; and (3) effect of judgments under the Full Faith and Credit clause of the U.S. Constitution. The former was discussed in the section on jurisdiction, and the latter two are the topics here.

Each of the 50 states and the national government is a sovereign entity with its own unique laws and procedures. Plaintiffs naturally gravitate to the forum in which the laws are likely to be most beneficial and in which they are likely to be most successful. Jurisdiction and choice-of-law rules limit plaintiffs' ability to "forum shop" in order to find the best deal. *Choice-of-law* questions arise in ascertaining which law the forum will apply when some or all of the operative events occurred in a jurisdiction other than the forum state. To illustrate, assume that Roberts and Golden, both Michigan residents, are involved in an automobile accident in Santa Fe. The other driver, Ellison, is from California. Due to diversity jurisdiction, Roberts and Golden could file suit in their home state of Michigan, in New Mexico, in Ellison's home state of California, or in federal court in any of the three states if the amount of controversy exceeds $10,000. It would certainly be more convenient for the pair to pursue the lawsuit on their home ground, but Ellison can make the same argument about California. The witnesses are in New Mexico. (This may be the ideal time for using the discovery techniques discussed in Chapter 4.) It appears, then, that there is no one place that is truly convenient for all.

The choice of the forum in which to pursue this matter is very important. Like all good bargain hunters, the plaintiffs are seeking the best deal. Such situations also generate "races to the courthouse" because as long as all other prerequisites are met, the party who files first (and in our example it could be Ellison) typically determines the location. If the plaintiff seeks relief in federal courts, the federal court is obligated to enforce the law of the state in which it is located, unless the matter is governed by the U.S. Constitution or by federal statutes.[33] Our accident case involves neither, and the applicable law will be that of one of the states.

If the suit is filed in either Michigan or California, we have the classical choice-of-law problem, in which the operative facts occurred elsewhere. Generally, when a state applies the law of a sister state (foreign law), it applies the *internal* law, or the law that the sister state would use if there were no conflicts issue. The theory that would allow the use of the sister state's *whole* law, including choice-of-law rules, is **renvoi;** renvoi is seldom used in this country because it often exacerbates the problem of determining which law applies. Procedural matters, such as pleading and venue, are normally governed by the local law of the forum, whereas substantive matters, loosely interpreted to mean any matter determinative of outcome, are governed by the appropriate foreign law. Again, however, classifying a particular aspect of a case as one or the other can be rather complex.[34] Foreign law must be proven at trial, and in the absence of proof, it is presumed to be the same as the law of the forum.[35] Most states allow judicial notice of foreign law or provide some method to facilitate its introduction and proof.

There are fairly standard rules for determining which state law will be applied in choice-of-law questions; like many other legal standards, however, they are riddled with exceptions. In a tort case, the place of injury determines the applicable law, although many courts are applying a more flexible significant-relationship rule; that is, the court determines which state has the most significant contacts and then applys that state's rules.[36] Questions involving title or interest in land are governed by the laws of the state in which the land is located.[37] The most confused area is that of contract law, and a number of approaches have been used by courts. These include the place of making; the place of performance; the intention of the parties, which may be expressed in a specific contractual clause; and the newer balancing approach of applying the law of the state with which the parties and the contract have the greatest relationship or most significant contacts.[38]

The concept of **domicile** is important because the law to be applied in many controversies is the law of the party's domicile, or home. Domicile involves more than mere physical presence; it requires intent to retain permanent ties with the locale. Nonresident college students living in dormitories are classic examples of those whose residence may not coincide with their domicile. Domicile is likely to be the controlling factor in the following areas: (1) probate matters; (2) divorce, including child custody and property matters; (3) political rights and privileges, such as voting; (4) federal diversity jurisdiction; and (5) in personum jurisdiction, which automatically accrues to the state courts of the party's domicile.

The mobility of our society and the complexity of our transactions complicate the courts' job of resolving conflicts. The Framers of the Constitution were concerned about the orderly flow of commerce and business among the various states and about state courts discriminating against residents of other states, as exemplified by the inclusion of diversity jurisdiction, which provides a neutral forum in federal courts.

In addition, Article IV, Section 1 provides that "Full faith and credit shall be given in each State to the public acts, records, and judicial proceedings of every other state." Remember that state law, standing alone, has no force outside the state's geographic boundaries, but the Full Faith and Credit Clause expands the effective reach of state law. This does not mandate automatic and immediate acceptance. Before it will be recognized by the receiving state,[39] the party wishing to enforce the court order must file suit in the new state and prove the foreign judgment which is presumed to be valid and final. Equity decrees apparently do not fall under the Full Faith and Credit Clause, but they may be recognized on a *comity,* or courtesy, basis. The same holds true for international judgments and decrees, although there may be special treaty provisions relating to the reciprocal recognition of court judgments among sovereign nations.

Stare decisis. Another precept which limits the judges' power in resolving cases is *stare decisis,* which, as you remember, is the doctrine of applying precedents from previous case law to the case at bar. Precedent is developed from examining the facts and applying the appropriate law to reach the decision. It adds stability and predictability, in that cases are decided in the same way when the material facts are the same.[40] In part, it is a result of the itinerant justices who travelled England and employed the same principles to decide similar cases, thereby developing the common law.

The general rule is that *stare decisis* is mandatory, and judges are bound to follow precedent. However, the same judicial innovators who developed the doctrine also determined how to circumvent it. One of those ways is to distinguish the present case from the prior one. This is usually done on the basis that the material facts in the current case are not the same as those in the preceding case. To illustrate, let us examine two dog-bite cases. The first case, or the precedent, occurred when a casual passerby was bitten by the dog, and the owner was held fully responsible and ordered to pay all damages. The second situation varied in that the person who was bitten had been beating the dog. The injuries are the same: The dog, under the control of his owner, bit the passerby. Employing the legal formula of precedent, the results should also be the same; that is, the owner should pay in both instances. In the second case, however, the court could consider that the provocation offered the dog was a material fact, differentiate the two cases on that basis, and relieve the owner of all or partial liability.

Decisions rendered by the highest courts within the same state are binding on lower courts; that is, the lower court must follow the precedent. In order to avoid that obligation, however, the court may determine that the relevant section of the precedent was ***obiter dictum—***

statements by the judge that were not essential to the resolution of the particular case and are therefore ineffective as precedent. Those points and the reasoning critical to the case are known as **ratio decidendi**, which is binding.[41] In addition, a certain hierarchy exists in the organization of U.S. court systems, and judges are exempt from complying with orders of courts not in their particular hierarchy. Every court must follow the decisions of the Supreme Court and their own state's highest courts. In regard to intermediate courts of appeals, which generally have only regional jurisdiction, judges are bound only by the decisions of their own regional courts, and opinions of other courts are only persuasive, not mandatory.[42]

CONCLUSION

Courts are extremely powerful institutions; however, they are not unencumbered by restrictions. Some of these restraints are judicially created and serve to protect the integrity of the judicial branch by providing mechanisms for the court to avoid confrontations with the more "political" branches. Others stem from constitutional provisions or statutes ratifying long-standing judicial practices and are rather technical in application. Both the "gatekeeping" aspects and the legalistic rules affect access to the courts and the availability of relief for those seeking assistance from the judicial branch.

NOTES

[1] As is the case with most rules, there are exceptions, such as those for minors and the mentally incompetent.

[2] *Frothingham v. Mellon*, 262 U.S. 447 (1923).

[3] *Flast v. Cohen*, 392 U.S. 83 (1968).

[4] Peter Woll, *Constitutional Law: Cases and Comments* (Englewood Cliffs, N.J.: Prentice-Hall, 1981), pp. 40–42.

[5] See *U.S. v. Richardson*, 418 U.S. 166 (1974); *Schlesinger v. Reservists' Committee to Stop the War*, 418 U.S. 208 (1974); *Warth v. Seldin*, 422 U.S. 490 (1975); and *Simon v. Eastern Kentucky Welfare Rights Organization*, 426 U.S. 26 (1976).

[6] *DeFunis v. Odegaard*, 416 U.S. 312 (1974).

[7] *Regents of the University of California v. Bakke*, 438 U.S. 265 (1978).

[8] *Roe v. Wade*, 410 U.S. 113 (1973).

[9] *Luther v. Borden*, 7 Howard 1 (1849).

[10] *Colegrove v. Green*, 328 U.S. 549 (1946).

[11] *Baker v. Carr*, 369 U.S. 186 (1962).

[12] Otis H. Stephens and Gregory J. Rathjen, *The Supreme Court and the Allocation of Constitutional Power: Introductory Essays and Selected Cases* (San Francisco: W. H. Freeman & Company Publishers, 1980), p. 90.

[13] *U.S. v. Nixon,* 418 U.S. 683 (1974).

[14] *Massachusetts v. Laird,* 400 U.S. 886 (1970).

[15] *Powell v. McCormack,* 395 U.S. 486 (1969).

[16] *Pennoyer v. Neff,* 95 S. Ct. 565 (1877), at 573.

[17] 28 U.S.C. Sec. 1332.

[18] *Pennoyer v. Neff,* 95 S. Ct. 565 (1877), at 568.

[19] Ibid., p. 570.

[20] *International Shoe Co. v. Washington,* 326 U.S. 310 (1945), at 316.

[21] Fed. R. Civ. P. 4.

[22] *Freeman v. Alderson,* 119 U.S. 185 (1886).

[23] Fed. R. Civ. P. 12.

[24] Milton D. Green, *Basic Civil Procedure* (Mineola, N.Y.: Foundation Press, 1972), pp. 50–51.

[25] U.S. Constitution, Art. III, sec. 2.

[26] Green, pp. 51–55.

[27] *Sheppard v. Maxwell,* 384 U.S. 333 (1966).

[28] *Murphy v. Florida,* 421 U.S. 794 (1975).

[29] *Christmas v. Russell,* 5 Wall. 290 (1866).

[30] *Weber v. State Harbor Commissioners,* 18 Wall. 57 (1873).

[31] *Maytin v. Vela,* 216 U.S. 598 (1909).

[32] *Amy v. Watertown,* 130 U.S. 320 (1889).

[33] *Erie R. Co. v. Tompkins,* 304 U.S. 64 (1938).

[34] 16 Am. Jur. 2d *Conflict of Laws* Sec. 4.

[35] *Loebig v. Larucci,* 572 F.2d 81 (2nd Cir. 1978).

[36] *Guillory on Behalf of Guillory v. United States,* 699 F.2d 781 (5th Cir. 1983).

[37] *Sunderland v. United States,* 266 U.S. 226 (1924).

[38] *Duncan v. Cessna Aircraft Co.,* 665 S.W.2d 414 (Tex. 1984).

[39] *Christmas v. Russell,* 5 Wall. 290 (1866).

[40] Lief H. Carter, *Reason in Law,* 2nd ed. (Boston: Little, Brown, 1984), pp. 40–42.

[41] Mark W. Cannon and David M. O'Brien, eds., *Views From the Bench* (Chatham, N.J.: Chatham House Publishers, 1985), pp. 123–124.

[42] Carter, p. 40.

6

Constitutional Law

In Chapter 1 we introduced constitutional law, along with case law, statutory law, and several others, as one of the many kinds of law comprised by the American legal system. We noted that the U.S. Constitution and the laws and treaties of the United States are the supreme law of the land. However, we also noted in Chapter 1 that the language of the Constitution tends to be ambiguous, employing such phrases as "due process of law," "equal protection of the law," and "cruel and unusual punishment" without clearly defining them. This ambiguity presents a problem: How can the Constitution be our supreme law if we don't know what it means? Also, how can we ever learn the meaning of the Constitution when those who wrote it have long since died? The answer lies in judicial interpretation of the Constitution, which is the main, but not exclusive, responsibility of the U.S. Supreme Court. As Chief Justice John Marshall wrote in the famous case of *Marbury v. Madison*, "It is emphatically the province and duty of the judicial department to say what the law is."[1] Chief Justice Charles Evans Hughes, in the same vein, remarked, "We are under a constitution but the constitution is what the judges say it is."[2]

This ability to be the final arbiter of the meaning of the Constitution has given the Supreme Court tremendous power to affect not only the laws of the nation, but its politics as well. As the final interpreter of the Constitution, the Supreme Court has the ability to rule on the constitutionality of the actions of the other two branches of government as well as those of the states and other governmental entities. Through judicial elaboration of the meaning of the Constitution, the Court can broaden or limit the powers of the President and the Congress. In so doing, the Court breathes life into the Constitution, making it a "living" document that changes as the nation changes, and giving it as much relevance in the twentieth century as it had when it was written in 1787.

The study of constitutional law, then, becomes a study of the development of a nation. In a sense, constitutional law is a political history of the United States. While it is not possible in an introductory text to afford extensive coverage to any kind of law, we will attempt to provide our readers with sufficient background to acquaint them with at least one of the major areas of interest to constitutional law scholars. To that end, this chapter has two major objectives. First, we will discuss judicial review and its importance to constitutional law. Second, we will examine one area of constitutional law—First Amendment freedoms— in greater detail in order to better understand this important area of the law. Any understanding of constitutional law must begin with judicial review, to which we now turn our attention.

JUDICIAL REVIEW

Judicial review is the power of a court to review the actions of other government bodies in order to determine whether or not those actions are consistent with the Constitution. If, in the opinion of the court, an act is not consistent with the Constitution, the court will declare the act invalid. Judicial review is usually associated with the court's determination that a law passed by Congress or a state legislature is unconstitutional, but judicial review is much broader than that. It extends to all actions taken by the president, administrative agencies, or any other government body. Justice Owen Roberts, in *United States v. Butler,* wrote the following famous passage describing judicial review:

> The Constitution is the supreme law of the land ordained and established by the people. All legislation must conform to the principles it lays down. When an act of Congress is appropriately challenged in the courts as not conforming to the constitutional mandate the judicial branch of the Government has only one duty—to lay the article of the Constitution which is invoked beside the statute which is challenged and to decide whether the latter squares with the former.[3]

Although many constitutional scholars view Justice Roberts's description of the process as overly simplistic, it does capture the essence of judicial review.

Having defined judicial review as a court's ability to declare unconstitutional the actions of government bodies, we need to understand how the courts acquired this important power. To do so we must understand the case of *Marbury v. Madison,* in which the Supreme Court, in effect, gave itself the power of judicial review.

Marbury v. Madison. Constitutional scholar Craig R. Ducat has written, "There is scarcely a casebook on constitutional law that does not begin with *Marbury v. Madison.*"[4] Ducat's observation underscores the importance of *Marbury,* for without the power of judicial review, the Supreme Court would be unable to transform the Constitution into a living document. Understanding *Marbury* is therefore essential to understanding not only judicial review, but also our entire constitutional development. We will begin our discussion of this important case with some historical background.

Marbury v. Madison really begins with the election of 1800. The two dominant political parties of that era were the Federalists, led by President John Adams and Alexander Hamilton, and the Democratic-Republicans, led by Thomas Jefferson and James Madison. In the election of 1800, the Federalists suffered a tremendous defeat. Jefferson, in an election which was eventually decided by the House of Representatives, defeated Adams for the Presidency. At the same time the Jeffersonians, as the Democratic-Republicans were called, had also won control of both houses of Congress. The Jeffersonians had dealt the Federalists a defeat from which the latter would never recover. In those days, however, a new president was not inaugurated until March 4 of the following year, so Adams remained in office as a "lame duck" president from late 1800, when the election was held, until March 4, 1801, when Jefferson was inaugurated.[5] During the same period, the "lame duck" Congress was also controlled by the Federalists.

The Federalists realized that they were on the ropes politically, but they did not intend to take their defeat lying down. Instead, they devised a plan to entrench themselves in the one branch of government they still controlled—the federal judiciary. On February 3, 1801, the Federalist Congress passed a law creating 16 new circuit-court judgeships, and a few weeks later it passed another law creating 42 new justice-of-the-peace positions for Washington, D.C. President Adams promptly nominated, and the Federalist Senate confirmed, the individuals chosen to fill the positions. The Jeffersonians were outraged at this blatant attempt by the Federalists to entrench themselves in the judicial branch, but there was nothing they could do about it until they came to power.

At this point the events that led to the *Marbury* case began to unfold. Because of the hurried manner in which the judgeships were created and in which the judges were nominated and confirmed, the

Adams administration was actually still trying to complete the appointment process late on the evening of March 3, 1801.[6] The person responsible for delivering the judicial commissions to the appointees was Adams's secretary of state, John Marshall. Since Secretary Marshall was too busy to deliver the commissions personally, he asked his brother James to deliver them for him. James was unable to deliver twelve of the commissions, so he merely placed the undelivered commissions (including William Marbury's) on the secretary of state's desk. The next day, however, Jefferson's secretary of state, James Madison, took office, and the undelivered commissions came into his possession. Because of the blatantly partisan way in which the judgeships had been created and because he believed the positions were unnecessary, President Jefferson ordered Secretary Madison not to deliver the twelve commissions. The stage was now set for a dramatic confrontation between Jefferson and the Federalist-dominated Supreme Court.

William Marbury and three others decided to sue to recover their commissions. In 1789, Congress had passed the Judiciary Act, which established the federal court system for the United States. Section 13 of the Act authorized the Supreme Court "to issue . . . writs of *mandamus* . . . to . . . persons holding office under the authority of the United States."[7] A writ of *mandamus* is a court order directing a government official to perform a nondiscretionary act. Therefore, under Section 13 of the Judiciary Act of 1789, Marbury had the right to bring an original action suit in the Supreme Court against James Madison. Marbury's suit asked the Supreme Court to order Madison to deliver his commission since Madison had no legal authority to withhold it from him. Because of some retaliatory legislation on the part of the Jeffersonians once they took power, the case was not decided until the 1803 term of the Court.

The Chief Justice of the United States in 1803 was none other than John Marshall. The *Marbury* case presented Chief Justice Marshall with a number of problems. First, as the person responsible for the failure of Marbury to receive his commission, Marshall probably should have recused himself in the case. Second, Marshall's own appointment to the Supreme Court was under a cloud. As part of the Federalist "court-packing" scheme, the previous chief justice, Oliver Ellsworth, had been persuaded to resign so that President Adams could appoint the younger Marshall to be chief justice. Third, the highly partisan case threatened the integrity of the Supreme Court itself. If the Court denied the writ, the public might question the validity of all of the Federalist appointments to the federal bench. If the Court ruled in favor of Marbury, it would leave itself open to charges that it had based its decision solely on partisan issues. Finally, President Jefferson had made it clear that he would not comply with a writ of *mandamus* coming from the High Court. He would instead defy a direct order from the Supreme Court, and, given Jefferson's popularity, the Chief Justice knew that the Court would be unable to do anything about the defiance. Marshall appeared to be in a classic no-win situation, which is why *Marbury v. Madison* is a masterpiece of judicial decision-making.

Chief Justice Marshall's decision revolved around the answers to three questions posed by the Court. The first question was, "Has Marbury a legal right to the commission he demands?" Marshall answered that Marbury was indeed entitled to the commission since the positions had been legally created by the Congress and Marbury had been nominated by the president and confirmed by the Senate in accordance with the law. Marbury, the Chief Justice ruled, unquestionably had a legal right to the commission. (At this point one could imagine a smile forming on William Marbury's face.)

The second question was, "If Marbury has a legal right to the commission and if that right has been violated, does the law afford him a legal remedy?" Again, Marshall answered affirmatively by indicating that a legal right is useless if it is without a legal remedy. Marshall proceeded to discuss the writ of *mandamus* and concluded that the delivery of a judicial commission was not a discretionary power of the secretary of state; that is, the secretary had no authority to refuse to perform what is essentially a ministerial or clerical task. Therefore, the writ of *mandamus* was the appropriate legal remedy in this case. (The smile on William Marbury's face broadened as victory seemed ever more apparent.)

It was with the third question, however, that Chief Justice Marshall dropped his bombshell. The question was, "If the law affords Marbury a legal remedy, is it a *mandamus issuing from the Supreme Court?*" To this Marshall answered no. The key to Marshall's negative answer is the phrase "issuing from the Supreme Court." Marshall, in effect, threw out Marbury's suit on a technicality: The Supreme Court, according to Marshall, lacked jurisdiction to hear Marbury's case. But did not Section 13 of the Judiciary Act of 1789 specifically authorize the Supreme Court to issue writs of *mandamus* to persons holding office under the authority of the United States? Yes, Marshall conceded, but Section 13 was unconstitutional and therefore invalid. According to the Constitution, the Supreme Court has only two types of jurisdiction: original and appellate. Any case that comes before the Court must do so under either its original or appellate jurisdiction. But the Constitution limits the Supreme Court's original jurisdiction to cases involving foreign ambassadors and cases involving states. By enacting Section 13, Congress had created, whether intentionally or not, a third category of original jurisdiction— that is, suits involving the writ of *mandamus.* This, Marshall ruled, Congress could not do. The only way to either increase or diminish the original jurisdiction of the Supreme Court was to amend the Constitution in the manner prescribed in the Constitution itself. To allow Congress to change the Court's original jurisdiction by ordinary statute (as Section 13 was) would defeat the purpose of having a written constitution as fundamental law. Since the law under which Marbury brought his suit was invalid, the Supreme Court had no authority to hear the case, and Marbury's suit was dismissed.

With the decision in *Marbury v. Madison,* Chief Justice Marshall appropriated for the Supreme Court (and all courts) the power of judicial review. We must remember that there is no specific reference to judicial review in the Constitution. Marshall used a logical reasoning process first to deduce that the power to invalidate unconstitutional legislation actually exists, and second to conclude that the power to decide when and if legislation conflicts with the Constitution belongs to the judiciary. Marshall accomplished his first goal by arguing that a written constitution must be considered to be superior to ordinary legislative acts; otherwise, having a written constitution would be senseless. Next, he argued that the Constitution implicitly recognizes that Congress could inadvertently pass a law that conflicts with the Constitution. Article VI declares that the Constitution and the laws of the United States *made in pursuance of the Constitution* are the supreme law of the land. Marshall argued that laws *not* made in pursuance of the Constitution were *not* the supreme law of the land. Someone or some group, then, must determine which laws are and which laws are not made in pursuance of the Constitution.

Having established the fact that laws passed in violation of the Constitution were invalid, Marshall next appropriated the power to determine their invalidity for the judiciary. With a sweep of the pen, Marshall declared, "It is emphatically the province and duty of the judicial department to say what the law is." Marshall argued that judges take an oath to uphold the Constitution and that it was their duty, when confronted with a law that clearly violated the Constitution, to declare that law null and void.

Chief Justice Marshall accomplished a number of goals with his decision in *Marbury.* First, he extricated himself from a serious dilemma that he, through his failure to deliver the commissions personally, had created. The Federalist Supreme Court could not be accused of partisan politics since it had not ruled in Marbury's favor. In addition, the Court had avoided a potentially dangerous confrontation with President Jefferson. The president could hardly refuse to obey an order the Court had declined to issue; thus the president had no need to openly defy the Court's authority. Second, Marshall, in answering the first two questions he posed, scolded the president for refusing to deliver to Marbury that which was legally his. Third, the Court increased its own prestige by showing that it was "above politics." Fourth, and most important, Marshall secured for his Court and future courts the power of judicial review. Since the federal judiciary was heavily dominated by the Federalists, the Jeffersonians were put on notice that laws passed by them in Congress might someday be subjected to Federalist scrutiny. Despite this veiled threat, having once acquired the power of judicial review, the Supreme Court would not use it again for another 54 years.[8]

Judicial Review and Constitutional Law.   The Supreme Court's power of judicial review enables it to interpret the meaning of the Constitution and, in so doing, give substance to the Constitution's ambiguous phrases. But the Supreme Court is not free to roam at will, handing down constitutional decisions like some self-proclaimed prophet interpreting the meaning of the stars. There are real limits to the Court's use of judicial review, some of which are self-imposed[9] and some of which are political.[10] Our primary concern, however, is in understanding how the Supreme Court has used its power to interpret the Constitution and has thereby shaped what we have called constitutional law.

As we have noted, the Supreme Court is not free to issue constitutional pronouncements on its own. It cannot, in other words, issue what are commonly called "advisory opinions." If the president proposed to take an action of dubious constitutionality and wanted to clear it with the Court first, the justices would simply refuse to do so. That is because the Court will rule on the constitutionality of acts only if there is a real "case or controversy." If the president proceeded to take the same action, and if his action were later challenged in court by a person with proper standing, the Court could properly hear the case. Other reasons that the Court might refuse to hear certain cases are because they raise "political questions," because a controversy has become moot, or because the Court feels that the issue is not "ripe" for judicial review.[11] It is important to remember that the availability of judicial review does not mean that the justices will always use their power "to say what the Constitution is."

A second important aspect of constitutional law is that it tends to be evolutionary. Recall that in Chapter 1 we defined case law as law that develops when judges make interpretations of the meaning of constitutions, statutes, or other forms of written law.[12] Case law develops over a long period of time and tends to be an ongoing process. Let us look at the right to counsel as an example.

The right to counsel was included in the Bill of Rights because of the British practice of refusing the accused the right to have an attorney in certain cases, even if the accused could afford one. Throughout most of our constitutional history, the Sixth Amendment's guarantee of the right to counsel meant only that the accused was entitled to an attorney *if he could pay for one.* Beginning in 1932, the Supreme Court began to change the meaning of the right. In the Scottsboro Boys Case,[13] a number of black youths were accused of raping two white women near Scottsboro, Alabama, in March 1931. Because of what the Court termed an atmosphere of "great hostility," the local sheriff had to call in the state militia to protect the defendants. At the trial the judge appointed the entire Scottsboro bar as the defendants' counsel and, to no one's surprise, all the youths were convicted. The Supreme Court overturned the convictions on the grounds that the defendants had been denied effective counsel. In addition, because of their youth, their illiteracy, and the hostile environment, the defendants had been denied due process of law as a result of their lack of effective counsel. With the Scottsboro Boys Case, the Supreme Court began the "special circumstances" rule, which stated that when special circumstances were present (youth, illiteracy, low mentality), the state had an affirmative duty to provide counsel for persons accused of serious crimes.

For the next 10 years, the Supreme Court wrestled with the problem of which "special circumstances" required the state to appoint counsel for indigent defendants. In 1942, the Court ruled that indigency alone was insufficient grounds for requiring court-appointed counsel. In that case, *Betts v. Brady*,[14] an indigent defendant named Betts was forced to defend himself and was convicted. The Supreme Court said that Betts was a man of average education and intelligence, capable of understanding the proceedings and protecting his own interests. They allowed Betts's conviction to stand, ruling that indigency alone did not constitute a "special circumstance."

The next major step in the development of the right to counsel was the *Gideon v. Wainwright*[15] case. Gideon was charged with a felony in Florida, and because he was indigent, he asked for court appointed counsel. Under Florida law, a judge was permitted to appoint counsel for indigent defendants only in capital cases, so the trial judge denied Gideon's request. Gideon proceeded to defend himself but was convicted and sent to prison. Gideon appealed his case to the U.S. Supreme Court *in forma pauperis,* and in a rare occurrence, the Court agreed to hear his case. The Court ruled 9–0 that the due process clause of the Fourteenth Amendment requires states to provide free counsel to indigent defendants in all noncapital felony cases. At his new trial, this time with the assistance of court-appointed counsel, Gideon was found not guilty. A few years later the Court extended its ruling to include misdemeanor cases in which the possibility of a jail term exists.[16] By its interpretation of the meaning of the Sixth Amendment and due process of law, the Supreme Court changed the meaning of the right to counsel. Instead of merely denying a defendant who can afford to hire a lawyer the right to have that lawyer with him in court, the state has an affirmative duty to provide counsel to those who cannot afford to hire their own.

Later cases, such as the *Escobedo*[17] and *Miranda*[18] decisions, addressed the question of when a person accused of a crime has the right to consult with an attorney, and even today the Supreme Court continues to struggle with the problem of right to counsel.

The final aspect of the nature of constitutional law is related to the one just discussed. If constitutional law has an evolutionary character, then it is also true that the resolution of constitutional issues is seldom final. Recall that in Chapter 1 we discussed the sociological theory of law, which holds that law changes as a society changes. As a society's view of what constitutes fairness or justice changes, those views will slowly be incorporated into its system of law. The previously discussed issue of the right to counsel illustrates this point. Prior to the 1963 *Gideon* decision, many well-intentioned people saw nothing unfair about requiring an indigent defendant to argue his own case without the assistance of a lawyer. But in 1988, a majority of people would probably agree with Justice Hugo Black, author of the *Gideon* decision, who wrote that "lawyers in criminal courts are necessities, not luxuries."[19] Yet as our society continues to change and the makeup of the Supreme Court changes, "settled" issues such as the right to counsel are raised again and again. Although unlikely, it is possible that a future generation will return to the pre-*Gideon* view of the right to counsel. As unfortunate as that may be, that is a fundamental characteristic of the American legal system.

The changing face of constitutional law is even more apparent in the area of civil liberties. The times and circumstances have much to do with how much liberty we enjoy at a given moment. Controversial questions of abortion, school prayer, freedom of press, and freedom of expression are constantly seeking resolution before the Supreme Court. It is to some of those questions that we now turn our attention in the hope of increasing our understanding of constitutional law.

CIVIL LIBERTIES

The field of civil liberties concerns one of the most controversial areas of constitutional law because it involves the fundamental question of the rights of the individual versus the rights of society. Most people recognize that order and stability are necessary for personal freedom to exist and that individuals must therefore sacrifice some freedom for the good of society. At the same time, we do not wish to sacrifice more freedom than is absolutely necessary to achieve the desired stability. But how much is enough and how much is too much? Unfortunately, there is no easy answer. It is an especially difficult question in a democratic society that simultaneously values individual freedom and majority rule.

The tension between the rights of the individual and the rights of a democratic society as manifested by majority rule is not easily reconciled. In the American political system it is the Supreme Court's job to try to reconcile the tension by attempting to strike a balance between the two. As noted in the previous section, the times and circumstances of our society will determine the extent of personal liberty, so that civil liberties are in a constant state of fluctuation. The amount of freedom we enjoy may depend on the willingness of society and the Supreme Court to tolerate our exercise of freedom.

The field of civil liberties is traditionally divided by constitutional scholars into two major areas: First Amendment freedoms and the rights of the accused. First Amendment freedoms can be broken down into the following categories: freedom of religion, freedom of speech and assembly, and freedom of press. The rights of the accused include, but are not limited to, the right to counsel, the protection against self-incrimination, and the right to a fair trial. In the following sections we must limit our discussion to only those topics associated with First Amendment freedoms. The reader is reminded, however, that civil liberties is a vast area of constitutional law encompassing many interesting topics. We begin our discussion with freedom of religion.

Freedom of Religion. There are actually two clauses in the First Amendment that pertain to freedom of religion: the Establishment Clause and the Free Exercise Clause. As we will soon discover, a basic conflict between the two clauses adds another dimension to the question of religious liberty. For example, does a Sunday Closing law simultaneously "establish" the Christian religion and interfere with the rights of Jews and others who celebrate the Sabbath on Saturdays? This question and others will be explored as we learn more about freedom of religion.

The Establishment Clause reads, "Congress shall make no law respecting an establishment of religion . . ." In an early case that required the Supreme Court to interpret the meaning of "an establishment of religion," Justice Hugo Black wrote:

> The "establishment of religion" clause of the First Amendment means at least this: Neither a state nor the Federal Government can set up a church. Neither can pass laws which aid one religion, aid all religions, or prefer one religion over another. Neither can force or influence a person to go to or to remain away from church against his will or force him to profess a belief or disbelief in any religion. No person can be punished for entertaining or professing religious beliefs or disbeliefs, for church attendance or non-attendance. No tax in an amount, large or small, can be levied to support any religious activities or institutions, whatever they may be called, or whatever form they may adopt to teach or practice religion. Neither a state nor the Federal Government can, openly or secretly, participate in the affairs of any religious organizations or groups and vice

versa. In the words of Jefferson, the clause against the establishment of religion by law was intended to erect "a wall of separation between church and State."[20]

Among the issues raised by the Establishment Clause is the question of government aid to education. In the *Everson* case, just quoted, the issue was a New Jersey law which allowed local school boards to reimburse the parents of parochial school students for bus fares on public buses to parochial schools. Everson believed that the law made it easier for parents of parochial school children to send their children to religious schools, thus aiding the religious organizations operating the schools at the taxpayers' expense. After building what appears to be an extremely high wall of separation between church and state, Justice Black concluded that the New Jersey law did not violate the Establishment Clause by announcing the so-called Child Benefit Theory. The Court reasoned that the safety of its children was what concerned the State in enacting the law and that any benefit derived goes to the child and his parents, not the schools. Any benefit to the school, Black reasoned, would be indirect at best. Justice Black concluded that the Establishment Clause requires the state to be neutral toward religion, but not hostile toward it. The Child Benefit Theory left unanswered the question of where the line between a direct and indirect benefit to religion was to be drawn. Consequently, in a series of cases the Court had to rule on the constitutionality of providing parochial schools with secular textbooks,[21] supplementing teachers' salaries in parochial schools,[22] providing testing services for parochial-school children,[23] and granting tax credits for tuition paid by parents of students attending private schools.[24]

A second area of Establishment Clause cases centers around the general topic of religion in public schools. *McCollum v. Board of Education*[25] raised the issue of whether religious instruction could be given on school property during class time. The Supreme Court ruled that it could not. Another case concerned the practice in New York of releasing children during normal class hours to enable them to receive religious instruction off-campus. The Supreme Court ruled that such "time release" programs did not violate the Establishment Clause.[26] Recent cases have dealt with the use of facilities at public schools and universities by religious organizations. These religious groups have argued that they should be allowed the use of facilities just like any other student organization, and the Supreme Court agreed, although as much on free speech grounds as free exercise grounds.[27]

Prayer in public schools is one of the most heated issues of constitutional law in American history. In 1962, in *Engel v. Vitale*,[28] the Supreme Court was asked to rule on the constitutionality of the so-called Regents' Prayer. The New York State Board of Regents had approved a nondenominational prayer that was to be recited at the beginning of the school day. The practice was challenged as a violation of the Establishment Clause, and the Supreme Court agreed by striking down the practice. With Justice Hugo Black again writing for the majority, the Supreme Court stated:

> . . . we think that the constitutional prohibition against laws respecting an establishment of religion must at least mean that in this country it is no part of the business of government to compose official prayers for any group of the American people to recite as a part of a religious program carried on by government.[29]

The next major school prayer case was decided the following year. A Pennsylvania law required the reading of at least ten verses from the Bible at the beginning of each public school day. The King James and Douay versions of the Bible were alternated with the Jewish Holy Scriptures. Edward L. Schempp challenged the act on behalf of his children as an unconstitutional establishment of religion, and the Supreme Court agreed. Despite the fact that students were allowed to absent themselves from the classroom during the Bible reading, the Court found that the law violated the constitutional requirement of neutrality toward religion. The Court rejected claims that the refusal to permit Bible reading and the recitation of the Lord's Prayer denied religious believers their right to practice their religion. Justice Clark wrote, "While the Free Exercise Clause clearly prohibits the use of state action to deny the rights of free exercise to *anyone,* it has never meant that a majority could use the machinery of the State to practice its beliefs."[30]

The Supreme Court's decision in *Abington School District v. Schempp* did not put an end to the issue of religion in public school. Some states, determined to circumvent the Supreme Court's decision, tried new ways to introduce religion into the classroom while still passing judicial scrutiny. Kentucky passed a law requiring that a copy of the Ten Commandments be posted on the wall of each public classroom in the state. The Supreme Court struck down the act on establishment grounds.[31] The State of Alabama passed a law authorizing a period of silence "for meditation or voluntary prayer."[32] After examining the legislative history of the law, the Court concluded that its sole purpose was to "put prayer back in public schools." The Court felt compelled to strike down the law as violative of the Establishment Clause. Finally, the issue of creationism, the study of the Biblical account of the origin of humans, has been introduced into the public schools. In *Epperson v. Arkansas,*[33] the Court ruled that a state law forbidding the teaching of evolution in public schools was unconstitutional. Recent efforts by proponents of creationism have centered on requiring that creationism be given equal time in classrooms in which evolution is taught. The Supreme Court will eventually rule on the constitutionality of such laws.

Not all of the cases requiring an interpretation of the Establishment Clause have pertained to education. In 1961, the Supreme Court was asked to rule on the constitutionality of Sunday Closing laws. Among the arguments brought forth by opponents of the laws was the establishment question. The Court ruled in *McGowan v. Maryland*[34] that although the laws originally had a religious purpose, providing citizens with a uniform day of rest also has a secular purpose. The Court especially noted that entertainment activities were exempt from closing, thus adding a secular or nonreligious cast to the law. Other recent noneducational establishment cases have included the constitutionality of granting tax-exempt status to religious organizations,[35] the practice of allowing a state-paid chaplain to open each session of the Nebraska legislature with a prayer,[36] and the right of a Rhode Island municipality to include a Nativity scene in its annual Christmas display.[37] In all three cases, the Supreme Court ruled that the challenged practice did not violate the Establishment Clause.

It may at first appear that there is no rhyme or reason to the Supreme Court's application of the Establishment Clause. In actuality, however, the Court has been fairly consistent in applying what it calls the "three-pronged test" to establishment cases. Chief Justice Warren Burger spelled out the three criteria in *Lemon v. Kurtzman,* writing:

> First, the statute must have a secular legislative purpose; second, its principal or primary effect must be one that neither advances nor inhibits religion . . .; finally, the statute must not foster "an excessive government entanglement" with religion.[38]

If a statute can pass all three criteria, it is constitutional. Although the components of the test are easily stated, it is the application of the test to particular factual situations that determines what does or does not constitute an establishment of religion. As we have already noted, the makeup of the Supreme Court and the general political climate will influence those determinations.

The second great clause of the First Amendment that deals with religion is, of course, the Free Exercise Clause. After admonishing Congress not to establish a religion, the Constitution forbids it to prohibit "the free exercise thereof." The Free Exercise Clause presents society with a number of difficult questions, such as, what is a religion? Is there any way to tell a "real" religion from a "false" one? Who or what will decide which religions are genuine and which are not? Is that a proper decision for government to make? What happens when the freedom of individuals to exercise their religion interferes with other norms or values of society? The constitutional problems surrounding the Free Exercise Clause are just as troublesome as any we encountered with the Establishment Clause.

A common thread that runs throughout the free exercise cases is this fundamental question: Should an individual or group be exempted from some general law or obligation for religious reasons? The Supreme Court was first confronted with this very question in the case of *Reynolds v. United States*,[39] better known as the Mormon Polygamy Case. Congress had passed a law making bigamy a crime in Utah Territory. Reynolds challenged the law on the grounds that the Mormon religion imposed polygamy upon males as a religious duty and that practicing Mormons should be exempt from the law on religious grounds. Chief Justice Waite, writing for the Court, declined to allow the exemption. The Chief Justice noted that while Congress may neither forbid nor punish the belief in polygamy, it may forbid and punish individual actions based on that belief. "Suppose," the Chief Justice asked, "one believed that human sacrifices were a necessary part of religious worship, would it be seriously contended that the civil government [could] not interfere to prevent a sacrifice?"[40] With the *Reynolds* decision, the belief–action distinction became a test by which free exercise cases were judged. One's religious beliefs are sacrosanct and beyond the reach of government interference. But if someone, on religious grounds, takes action that violates the norms of society, the State does not have to stand idly by. Chief Justice Waite reasoned that, "To permit [polygamy in the face of a bigamy law] would be to make the professed doctrines of religious beliefs superior to the law of the land, and in effect to permit every citizen to become a law unto himself. Government could exist only in name under such circumstances."[41]

The Supreme Court had occasion to modify the *Reynolds* decision in *Cantwell v. Connecticut*,[42] one of the so-called Jehovah's Witness cases. Newton Cantwell and his two sons were proselytizing in a largely Roman Catholic neighborhood in New Haven, Connecticut. They asked passersby to listen to a phonograph recording that vilified the Pope, which offended some of the residents. They also distributed books and pamphlets, for which they solicited contributions. Under Connecticut law, a permit was required to solicit funds for religious or charitable organizations. The Cantwells were charged with breach of the peace and with failure to have a permit. Although the Court overturned their convictions, largely on the basis of freedom of speech issues, it struck down the ordinance requiring the permit on the grounds that it afforded public officials too much discretion in determining which religions were bona fide ones and which were not. Similarly, in *Murdock v. Pennsylvania*,[43] the Court struck down a city ordinance that required persons soliciting for religious purposes to purchase a license to go door-to-door. In each of these cases the Court recognized, in the words of Justice Owen Roberts, that "[Free exercise] embraces two concepts,—freedom to believe and freedom to act."[44]

Cantwell and *Murdock*, while sustaining the belief–action distinction, also make it clear that the freedom to take action based on one's religious beliefs is not limited to attending church on Sunday. On the other hand, the freedom to act on one's religious beliefs still must be tempered by public policy demands. For example, the Supreme Court has upheld laws requiring mandatory vaccinations for smallpox, despite religious objections,[45] laws prohibiting the selling of religious tracts by minor children,[46] and laws restricting the distribution of religious literature at a state fair.[47]

Thus far we have discussed the right to act on one's religious beliefs. But what about the right *not* to act or to do something because of one's religious beliefs? This question was raised in the Flag Salute Cases,[48] which again involved the Jehovah's Witness religion. As a means of instilling patriotism in public-school children, many states passed laws requiring the recitation of the Pledge of Allegiance at the beginning of the school day. Jehovah's Witnesses, a fundamentalist sect, interprets the Bible's condemnation of worshipping "graven images" literally. They believed that forcing their children to salute the flag violated their religious beliefs, so they sought a ruling from the Supreme Court exempting their children from the flag-salute exercise. In the first case to reach the Court, the *Gobitis* case, the justices refused to grant the exemption on the grounds that instilling patriotism in school children was a legitimate concern of the state and in no way interfered with the rights of Jehovah's Witnesses to practice their religion. Surprisingly, however, just three years later the Supreme Court reversed itself in *West Virginia State Board of Education v. Barnette.* In striking down a West Virginia law virtually identical to the Pennsylvania law previously upheld in *Gobitis,* Justice Robert Jackson wrote for the new majority:

> If there is any fixed star in our constitutional constellation, it is that no official, high or petty, can prescribe what shall be orthodox in politics, nationalism, religion, or other matters of opinion or force citizens to confess by word or act their faith therein. If there are any circumstances which permit an exception, they do not now occur to us.[49]

Another case that illustrates the refusal of a person to express a belief contrary to his or her religious convictions is *Wooley v. Maynard.*[50] New Hampshire license plates bear the state motto, "Live Free or Die." George Maynard, a Jehovah's Witness, considered the motto repugnant to his religious and political beliefs and so placed tape over the motto to cover it. Maynard was fined under a state law prohibiting the concealment of license plates, and he appealed his conviction. The Supreme Court struck down Maynard's conviction on the grounds that the First Amendment prohibits the state from making an individual the unwilling courier of a particular point of view. While Maynard's objections to displaying the motto may seem trivial to most, Justice Robert Jackson has written, "The test of its [freedom's] substance is the right to differ as to things that touch the heart of the existing order."[51]

We have not exhausted all the issues related to the Free Exercise Clause, nor could we do them all justice in an introductory text. Suffice it to say that the issues surrounding the free exercise of religion are many and varied. As previously noted, "old" issues of constitutional law are seldom resolved with finality, and new ones are constantly appearing. How we treat the religious dissenter says quite a bit about not only our legal system but our entire political system as well.

FREEDOM OF SPEECH

If one assumes that the Framers of the Constitution listed the First Amendment freedoms in order of their importance, then freedom of speech was the second most valued civil liberty. Freedom of speech, like all of our liberties, poses problems for a democratic society. It is a peculiar characteristic of the human species that when its members disagree with what they hear, they try to silence the speaker. Not all humans react that way, of course, but most of us have wanted, at one time or another, to silence a speaker who espouses an idea with which we disagree. Tolerance of another person's viewpoint, regardless of how repugnant it is to our own beliefs, is the essence of freedom of speech. "Freedom for the thought we hate" is how Justice Holmes once described freedom of speech.[52] In a democratic society, the tolerance of the views of others is not just some idle commitment to fairness. Because all persons are created equal, each person's worth is equal to another's, and therefore each person's views are equally deserving of our respect. Although we may ultimately reject the views of another as wrongheaded (the authors do so quite regularly), we respect the right of all to express different points of view.

Another reason for tolerance in a democratic society is the belief that truth can be ascertained only through an exchange of ideas. Justice Holmes called this concept "the marketplace of ideas."[53] In a capitalistic system such as ours, new products are introduced each day. Some are new, and others are merely "new and improved." The point is that each product must compete with other, similar products for acceptance and for its share of the market. Justice Holmes believed that every idea, however hateful it may have been to him personally, deserved a chance to enter the marketplace and to "sell" itself to the people. If the idea is a good one, people will accept it, and if not, they will reject it. Justice Holmes believed that the American people have enough sense to reject false doctrines because anything less would mean a lack of faith in democratic government. If one does not believe that the people will be able to see through false doctrines and reject them, then one does not have faith in democratic government.

A final reason to protect freedom of speech is to avoid having the United States become like those countries in which liberty is not allowed. There is an old saying, "If you sleep with pigs, you wake up smelling like garbage." If we allow our government to silence dissenters and to punish people for their political beliefs, how is our government different from that of the Soviet Union or Nazi Germany? Although our government's abridgment of freedom of speech may seem trivial when compared to the Soviet Union's, we would do well to remember the words of Justice Wiley Rutledge, who wrote, "If the restraint were smaller than it is, it is from petty tyrannies that large ones take root and grow."[54] What Justice Rutledge realized is that once the first step that reduces liberty is taken, the next step is easier to take, until one day we may awaken to find our own liberty gone.

Despite our defense of freedom of speech as an essential ingredient of a democratic society, the fact remains that none of the First Amendment freedoms has ever been regarded as an absolute right by a majority of the justices of the Supreme Court.[55] Freedom of speech, like other liberties, requires the Supreme Court to balance the rights of the speaker and the rights of society. For our purposes, we will examine the issues of freedom of speech in the following areas: pure speech, symbolic speech, and speech plus action.

A noted constitutional scholar, C. Herman Pritchett, has defined pure speech as "communication taking place by the spoken word in face-to-face contacts, addresses, or remarks at meetings. . . . Pure speech can range from dull expositions to the most emotional harangues."[56] One of the problems with pure speech develops when the speaker urges someone to do something illegal. In *Schenck v. United States,*[57] the Supreme Court was asked to rule on whether Congress could constitutionally pass a law punishing speech. Schenck, a Socialist, published and distributed a pamphlet opposing entry of the United States into World War I, attacked the draft as a form of involuntary servitude, and encouraged young men to resist induction. Schenck was convicted under the Espionage Act of 1917, and his defense was that the law violated the First

Amendment. Justice Oliver Wendell Holmes, writing for the Court, admitted that in peacetime, Schenck would have been within his rights to say what he did in the pamphlet.[58] But, Holmes said, an act must be viewed in terms of its circumstances; "When a nation is at war many things that might be said in time of peace are such a hindrance to its effort that their utterance will not be endured."[59] Holmes went on to outline his "clear and present danger test":

> The question in every case is whether the words used are used in such circumstances and are of such a nature as to create a clear and present danger that they will bring about the substantive evils that Congress has a right to prevent.[60]

On the basis of this rationale, the Court upheld Schenck's conviction and the constitutionality of the Espionage Act.

It quickly became apparent that the "clear and present danger test" was not very clear. In *Abrams v. United States*[61] and *Gitlow v. New York*,[62] Holmes dissented because he believed that the majority misapplied his clear and present danger test. In *Abrams,* over Holmes's objections, the Court upheld the conviction of Abrams for distributing pamphlets condemning U.S. involvement in the Russian Revolution. Holmes argued that the "silly leaflet" could not possibly create a clear and present danger to the government and that the 20-year sentence imposed was excessive. Holmes clearly believed that Abrams was being persecuted for his leftist political views.

In *Gitlow,* the defendant was accused of violating the New York Criminal Anarchy Act, which made it a crime to advocate the overthrow of government through force and violence. Justice Edward T. Sanford, writing for the Court, argued that the State does not have to wait until the revolution has actually begun to protect itself from violent overthrow. Justice Sanford wrote that "A single revolutionary spark may kindle a fire that, smouldering for a time, may burst into a sweeping and destructive conflagration."[63] Holmes again disagreed that Gitlow's actions constituted a clear and present danger to the government.

The pure speech cases make it clear that prosecution is more likely when the speaker advocates an unpopular idea, whether of the political left or right. In *Thomas v. Collins,*[64] the Court struck down a Texas law requiring a union organizer to secure a speaking permit before addressing an audience on unionism. In *Hartzel v. United States,*[65] the Court reversed the conviction of a Nazi sympathizer who espoused Hitler's racial theories. In *Dennis v. United States*[66] and *Yates v. United States,*[67] the Court ruled on the constitutionality of convicting organizers of the American Communist Party. Indeed, as we have seen, the Court has overturned the convictions of religious advocates on the grounds of freedom of speech as much as on religious grounds.[68]

Another area in which pure speech has raised problems is in the category of "fighting words." In *Chaplinsky v. New Hampshire,*[69] the defendant called a city fire marshall a "God damned racketeer and a damned fascist" and was convicted under a New Hampshire law that made it illegal to call another person "by any offensive or derisive name."[70] The Court upheld the state's statute, calling the speech "fighting words" or "what men of common intelligence would understand would be words likely to cause an average addressee to fight."[71] In *Feiner v. New York,*[72] the Court upheld Feiner's disorderly conduct conviction after he referred to President Truman as a "bum" and called for blacks in his audience to "rise up in arms." The police arrested Feiner only after it became clear that his audience's hostile reaction created a danger of a public disturbance. Next, in *Cohen v. California,*[73] the Supreme Court overturned the conviction of a man seen in a municipal courthouse wearing a jacket that read, "Fuck the Draft." The Court rejected, among other things, the argument that the phrase constituted "fighting words." Justice John M. Harlan wrote, "No individual actually or likely to be present could reasonably have regarded the words on appellant's jacket as a direct personal insult."[74] Finally, in *Gooding v. Wilson,*[75] the Court upheld a Georgia statute that prohibited "opprobrious or abusive language tending to cause a breach of the peace." Wilson, the defendant, had yelled at one police officer during a demonstration, "White son of a bitch, I'll kill you." The Court ruled that the Georgia statute was neither overbroad nor too vague. *Gooding* does raise the issue, however, of whether police officers must endure a more restricted version of "fighting words," given their occupation and their likelihood of encountering abusive language.

A second major area of freedom of speech involves the issue of symbolic speech. Symbolic speech, unlike pure speech, may be characterized by the old saying that "actions speak louder than words." Symbolic speech involves the nonverbal conveyance of an idea or opinion; burning of an American flag or of a draft card are examples. Although not the first case to raise the issue of symbolic speech, *Tinker v. Des Moines Independent School District*[76] is perhaps the best known. Students opposed to the war in Vietnam wore black armbands as a means of protesting. School administrators had banned the display as disruptive and threatened punishment against violators. Despite the school policy, John F. Tinker, then 15 years old, and others wore the armbands and were suspended. The Supreme Court, through Justice Abe Fortas, noted that, had school officials banned all discussion of the Vietnam conflict, such a ban would clearly have been unconstitutional on its face. The ban on the armbands, Fortas wrote, "is no less offensive to the Constitution's guarantees."[77] In addition, Justice Fortas said that it was obvious the armbands had been unconstitutionally singled out because other political symbols, such as campaign buttons, were not similarly banned. Since the wearing of the armbands had not been disruptive, and since school officials could offer no valid reason for their action, the students were, the Court ruled, entitled to freedom of expression. Note that Justice Fortas substituted freedom of *expression* for *speech*, since pure speech was not at issue in this case.

Another series of cases involved the problem of disrespect for the American flag. In *Street v. New York*,[78] the defendant, Street, upon learning that civil rights activist James Meredith had been shot, took an American flag to a street corner, burned it, and said, "We don't need no damn flag." Street was arrested and convicted under a New York statute that made it a misdemeanor to burn an American flag "or cast contempt upon [any flag of the United States] by words . . ."[79] Although the case appeared to present the Court with a clear test of the constitutionality of flag burning as symbolic speech, the Court sidestepped the issue. The Court ruled that the statute punished both action (the actual burning) and speech (the words of contempt). The "speech" itself was constitutionally protected but since it was impossible to determine whether Street's conviction rested wholly or partially on the basis of his speech, the Court felt compelled to overturn the conviction entirely, including his actions related to the flag burning. Similar attempts to get a definitive ruling on flag desecration have also been unsuccessful. In *Smith v. Goguen*,[80] the Court overturned the conviction of a young man who had sewn a flag on the seat of his pants; in *Spence v. Washington*,[81] the Court also overturned the conviction of a man who had taped a peace symbol on a flag and then had hung it from his window upside down. Subsequent attempts to secure Supreme Court review of the flag-desecration issue have failed.[82]

A final issue of symbolic speech has involved draft-card burning. During the war in Vietnam, students and others opposed to that war demonstrated their opposition by burning their draft cards. After David O'Brien and three others publicly burned their draft cards on the steps of a Boston courthouse, they were arrested and convicted under a federal statute making it illegal to knowingly destroy one's draft card. O'Brien believed that the law had no legitimate legislative purpose and that it abridged his freedom of speech. In *United States v. O'Brien*,[83] the Supreme Court disagreed. Speaking through Chief Justice Earl Warren, the Court ruled that the government did have a legitimate interest in requiring draft-age men to carry their cards. Information such as the registrant's draft board, selective service number, and address were needed for the efficient administration of the draft law. The ruling in *O'Brien* makes clear that freedom of expression does not protect every act of symbolic speech if there is a legitimate governmental interest involved.

FREEDOM OF ASSEMBLY

Freedom of speech is often closely linked with another right guaranteed by the First Amendment—freedom of assembly. Congress and the states may not abridge "the right of the people peaceably to assemble and to petition the Government for redress of grievances." The events surrounding the famous Boston Massacre were undoubtedly on the minds of the Framers of the First Amendment as they included this protection. Disputes involving freedom of assembly have frequently centered around three groups: labor organizers, religious workers, and civil rights activists. These groups often come into conflict with government officials over the requirement of having a permit to conduct a march or protest demonstration. City officials, usually concerned about the possibility of violence or counterdemonstrations, seek to restrict or deny the use of public streets and parks to controversial groups, citing public safety as grounds for denial of permission. But what if the denial is based on some unconstitutional reason? Suppose a city official who has been given the discretion to deny parade permits does so because he is unsympathetic to the aims of the protesting group? Suppose "public safety" is used as a mere pretext for denying an unpopular group a public forum for its views? Is the right to assemble and to petition the government absolute, or may government impose reasonable restrictions on freedom of assembly? As we will see in reviewing the following cases, the Supreme Court has approached the problem by trying to strike a balance between the needs of government and the exercise of legitimate First Amendment rights.

One of the earliest cases to raise a challenge to the requirement of a parade permit was *Hague v. CIO*[84] in 1939. A Jersey City ordinance prohibited assemblies "in or upon public streets, highways, public parks or public buildings." In accordance with this ordinance, city officials prohibited the distribution of leaflets and circulars passed by CIO workers who were trying to organize in the city. The Supreme Court ruled the ordinance unconstitutional on First and Fourteenth Amendment grounds. Justice Owen Roberts wrote as follows:

> Wherever the title of streets and parks may rest, they have immemorially been held in trust for use of the public and, time out of mind, have been used for purposes of assembly, communicating thoughts between citizens, and discussing public questions.[85]

The Jersey City ordinance required the permit to be obtained from the Director of Public Safety, who could deny the permit "for the purpose of preventing riots, disturbances or disorderly assemblage."[86] The Court found this broad discretion inconsistent with the First and Fourteenth Amendments.

The Court's decision in *Hague* did not entirely preclude the use of parade permits by city governments. In *Cox v. New Hampshire*,[87] the Supreme Court unanimously upheld a statute creating a licensing system as a means of regulating traffic congestion. Cox, a Jehovah's Witness, failed to obtain a permit on the theory that, because his group was marching to advertise a religious meeting, a permit would abridge the free exercise of religion. The Court ruled, however, that the permit requirement was neutral and was not used discriminately to suppress a particular religious point of view. The state has a right to regulate the lawful use of its thoroughfares as a part of its police power.

Two cases, *Walker v. Birmingham*[88] and *Shuttlesworth v. Birmingham*,[89] also challenged the constitutionality of parade permits. Both cases arose out of a planned peaceful demonstration to protest the racial segregation practices in Birmingham, Alabama. In *Walker*, after repeated denials of requests for a parade permit and in the face of official hostility, the march leaders announced plans to proceed with the march without the permit. City officials quickly secured an *ex parte injunction* banning the march until a judicial hearing could be held. March leaders decided to ignore the injunction as unconstitutional and held the march anyway. Walker and others were arrested and cited for contempt for ignoring the injunction. The Supreme Court, in a 5–4 decision, ruled that although the original ordinance was of dubious constitutionality, the marchers should nevertheless have complied with the injunction until the question of the ordinance's constitutionality could be fully litigated in court. That is, the marchers should have challenged the injunction itself instead of ignoring it and marching in defiance of it. Due process, the Court ruled, required the affected parties to follow prescribed procedures for challenging the allegedly unconstitutional injunction. The marchers, by ignoring the injunction, had, in effect, taken the law into their own hands. Consequently, the Court upheld the convictions (over strong dissents) for contempt.

Oddly enough, in *Shuttlesworth*, the Supreme Court ruled that the Birmingham ordinance (the same one involved in *Walker*) was unconstitutional. Unlike Walker, who had been cited for contempt, Shuttlesworth was convicted of parading without a permit. This enabled Shuttlesworth to challenge directly the constitutionality of the Birmingham ordinance. Using reasoning somewhat similar to that in *Hague*, the Court overturned Shuttlesworth's conviction and ruled that the ordinance gave city officials "virtually unbridled and absolute power"[90] to grant or withhold the permit. Testimony in the case made it clear that city officials did not intend to grant the marchers a permit under any circumstances. Faced with that dilemma, the marchers were within their constitutional rights to defy the ordinance and challenge its constitutionality in court, which they did.

One final case that is used to illustrate the problem of parade permits is *Nationalist Socialist Party v. Skokie.*[91] The American Nazi Party announced plans to hold a demonstration in Skokie, Illinois, a suburb of Chicago. Skokie had a large Jewish population, many of whom were survivors of Nazi concentration camps. A state trial court issued an injunction against the demonstration, and the Illinois State Court of Appeals refused to stay the injunction. The Illinois State Supreme Court refused to grant an expedited appeal. Party leaders appealed to the U.S. Supreme Court, and in a 5–4 decision, the Court ruled that when a state court issues an injunction in a case such as this, the state must provide prompt judicial review of any challenge—which Illinois did not do. Ultimately, the Illinois courts ruled that the injunction was unconstitutional.[92] A subsequent compromise succeeded in avoiding a serious confrontation between the Nazis and the citizens of Skokie.

Although the previous cases, especially the *Skokie* case, indirectly raised the issue of *where* a demonstration may be held, the Supreme Court has addressed the issue more directly in another series of cases involving freedom of assembly. In *Edwards v. South Carolina,*[93] a group of black civil rights demonstrators conducted a peaceful march to the South Carolina State House, where they protested the state's racial segregation policies. The evidence indicated that, although 200 to 300 onlookers gathered, the crowd was peaceful and mostly just curious. The police ordered the demonstrators to disperse, whereupon they began to sing religious and patriotic songs. They were arrested and convicted for breach of the peace. In reversing the convictions, Justice Potter Stewart noted that by all accounts the demonstration was peaceful, the crowd was not belligerent, and the police were in control. In addition, the Court noted that the grounds of the South Carolina State House were generally open to the public. Justice Stewart noted:

> The circumstances in this case reflect an exercise of these basic constitutional rights in their most pristine and classic form. The petitioners felt aggrieved by laws of South Carolina which allegedly "prohibited Negro privileges in this State." They peaceably *assembled at the site of State Government and there peaceably expressed their grievances* . . .[94] [Emphasis added]

In other words, if a group cannot assemble at the seat of government to petition for redress of grievances, where can it assemble? The Court's ruling in *Edwards* makes clear that a state legislature's grounds is an appropriate place as long as the demonstration remains peaceful.

The Supreme Court's ruling in *Edwards* did not mean that protestors have the right to use public property to air their grievances in every instance. In *Cox v. Louisiana*,[95] the Court had the opportunity to rule on whether a courthouse was an appropriate place to engage in protest. Cox, a civil rights worker, led a group of students to a courthouse in Baton Rouge to protest the arrest of another group of students who had been arrested the previous day in yet another protest demonstration. A Louisiana statute made it unlawful to parade or picket near a state court "with the intent of interfering with, obstructing or impeding the administration of justice."[96] Although the Supreme Court upheld the constitutionality of the statute, it reversed Cox's conviction on the grounds that his protest had taken place on a sidewalk across the street from the courthouse itself and that police had previously given the demonstrators permission to use the sidewalk as long as they were peaceful. When white onlookers became agitated, the police withdrew their permission. This, the Court said, resulted in "convicting a citizen for exercising a privilege which the State had clearly told him was available to him."[97]

The Court ruled in *Cox* that a state may prohibit protests at its courthouses; but does the same logic apply to its jails? In *Adderley v. Florida*,[98] petitioner Adderley, like Cox, was arrested for protesting the arrests of other students. She was convicted of trespassing on the premises of the county jail. In addition to protesting the arrests of the other students, Adderley and 31 others were protesting the fact that the jail itself was segregated. Justice Hugo Black, writing for a sharply divided Court, upheld the convictions on the grounds that, "The State, no less than a private owner of property, has the power to preserve the property under its control for the use to which it is lawfully dedicated."[99] Justice Black noted that this was not a case in which the trespass law was used as a pretext for denying blacks their constitutional rights. Blacks as a group were not being discriminated against; other groups were also forbidden to use the jailhouse as a focus of their protest. There was no evidence that the trespass law was being used against the demonstrators simply because public officials were unsympathetic to their cause.

Several other cases that raise the issue of where persons have the right to assemble and to protest are worth mentioning. In *Brown v. Louisiana*,[100] five black students staged a "sit-in" at a branch of the public library that did not serve blacks. When they refused a request to leave, all five were arrested for breach of peace. The Court, noting that the sit-in was orderly, reversed the convictions. The Court "found no disturbance of others, no disruption of library activities and no violation of library regulations."[101] In *Greer v. Spock*,[102] the Court upheld an injunction against famous pediatrician Benjamin Spock, who had sought to pass out political leaflets at Fort Dix in violation of base regulations. Even though Fort Dix is accessible to the public, the Court rejected the notion that it became a public forum for First Amendment purposes.[103] Finally, the Supreme Court itself is not immune from picketing. In *United States v. Grace*,[104] the Court ruled that a congressional law banning all picketing on public sidewalks around the Supreme Court building was unconstitutional.

FREEDOM OF PRESS

To some extent, freedom of press is of less concern to individuals as a civil liberty than are freedom of speech and religion. Freedom of press is, or should be, a major concern of all people who value democratic principles. One inherently human characteristic is dislike of criticism, and the individuals who run a government, democratic or otherwise, are no exception. Because of this distaste for criticism, governments, almost since the invention of the printing press, have tried to control the press in one of two ways. One method of controlling the press is through suppression, or government censorship—that is, forbidding the press to print articles or editorials critical of those in power. Censorship can take the form of licensing; that is, the government can require newspapers to have government permission to publish within the country. If a publisher becomes overly critical of the existing government, the license may be revoked. Publishers who publish without a license may be subject to criminal penalties or worse. Censorship may also take the form of what is called *prior restraint.* Under a system of prior restraint, the government requires the press to submit to a preclearance procedure whereby officials can check a publication for criticism and eliminate it before the publication reaches its audience. It is the latter form that most people think of as censorship.

Propaganda is the second method used by governments to control the press. Propaganda is common when the press is actually owned, operated, or otherwise controlled by those in power. The government allows only favorable information to be printed, leaving readers the impression that the country is running smoothly, when in reality it may not be. Most people associate propaganda with lying, but there is really more to it than that. Propaganda can be half-truths as well. For example, a laundry soap manufacturer might not be lying when it boasts that its detergent beat Brands A, B, and C in "laboratory tests." However, the manufacturer might fail to tell you that its detergent did not perform as well as Brands X, Y, and Z. Propaganda, then, can be false or misleading information. A government engages in propaganda when it prints false or misleading information in order to deceive or mislead its people about conditions in the country.

Freedom of press is essential to a democratic society because the people, in order to effectively evaluate government performance, must have an accurate picture of the state of affairs. If government is inefficient, inept, or corrupt, the people have a right to know so that they can change political leaders. At the same time, however, freedom of press is subject to abuse, so once again we see the need to balance freedom of press with other important values in our society. In this section we will examine freedom of press in three areas: governmental interference with the press, obscenity, and libel. As in previous sections, we will rely on Supreme Court cases to illustrate the scope and complexity of freedom of press issues. Fortunately, there have been relatively few attempts in American history on the part of the government to suppress, or "muzzle," the press. In 1798, the Federalists passed the Alien and Sedition Acts, which made it illegal to criticize government officials. It was the public outcry over these acts that led to the defeat of President Adams in the previously discussed election of 1800.

The first real test of government suppression of the press was *Near v. Minnesota*.[105] A 1925 Minnesota law made it a crime to publish "malicious, scandalous and defamatory" articles and allowed judges to issue court orders to stop such publications as a public nuisance. Near published a weekly newspaper that, among other things, made accusations of corruption against the mayor of Minneapolis and other city officials. A local prosecutor successfully sought an injunction against the publication, and the injunction was upheld by the Minnesota courts. The Supreme Court struck down the Minnesota law, however, on the grounds that it allowed prior restraint, in violation of the First Amendment. Chief Justice Hughes, the author of the Court's opinion, noted that the law did not seek to protect individuals from private wrongs. That is, any person libeled by Near could sue him after the fact under Minnesota's existing libel laws. In addition, the fact that a publisher had to satisfy the enjoining judge that the charges were true and were published with good motives presented the judge with the opportunity to censor the publisher. The Court made it clear that its ruling did not give Near a license to libel public officials with impunity. The Court ruled merely that Near could not be prevented from publishing his libelous remarks by statute, but it did not rule that he could not be sued for libel by his victims.

The next major case to deal with government suppression of the press was *New York Times Co. v. United States*,[106] the Pentagon Papers Case. Daniel Ellsberg, a Defense Department employee, copied a secret study depicting how the United States became involved in Vietnam. Ellsberg leaked the Pentagon Papers to the *New York Times* and the *Washington Post*, which began to serialize the Papers. Because the Papers might have proved damaging to national security and to relations with our allies in Southeast Asia, the Nixon administration sought an injunction against the newspapers ordering them to cease further publication of the Pentagon Papers. Because of the extraordinary nature of the case, the Supreme Court ruled on the case just 15 days after a lower federal court had issued the injunction. Although the justices were unable to agree on a single majority opinion, the Court's *per curiam decision* was simple: Any attempt to impose prior restraint imposes on the government the heavy burden of proof in justifying the restraint, and the Nixon administration had failed to prove just how the publication of the Papers would damage national security. Several concurring opinions made it clear that the Court was not saying that the government could never censor the press. The classic example of press censorship is the publication of departure times of troop ships during a war. Obviously, the government should be free to impose restraints in the name of national security in some instances. The Nixon administration had not shown, however, that the publication of the Pentagon Papers created a "clear and present danger" to national security.

Perhaps the most perplexing problem of freedom of press occurs when it conflicts with some other freedom that is highly valued in our constitutional system. The most common area of conflict has been the free press–fair trial controversy and the problem of prejudicial pretrial publicity. One of the leading cases is *Sheppard v. Maxwell*,[107] a spectacular murder case in which a prominent Cleveland doctor was accused of killing his wife. Although Dr. Sheppard was not initially a suspect in the case, newspaper editorials implying special treatment prompted police officials to focus on him. Sheppard was eventually indicted, and during his trial the courtroom had what Justice Tom Clark later described as a "carnival atmosphere." Newspaper accounts of "evidence" never actually introduced at trial were made available to jurors, reporters were allowed to be inside the bar (an area normally restricted to lawyers and participants), and the trial judge made no effort to control the press. The Supreme Court, after severely criticizing the trial judge, reversed Sheppard's conviction, noting, "Due process requires that the accused receive a trial by an impartial jury free from outside influences."[108] On retrial, in a calmer atmosphere, Sheppard was acquitted of the murder charge.

Sheppard v. Maxwell implies a need for a balance between the right of the press to cover sensational trials and the right of the accused to a fair trial. *Sheppard* was one of the cases that began marking the parameters of the free press–fair trial dilemma. For example, in *Gannett Co. Inc. v. DePasquale*,[109] the defense made a motion to exclude the press in a pretrial preliminary hearing in which the trial judge would decide whether or not to exclude certain evidence in a murder case. The trial judge granted the motion, and the newspaper company quickly challenged its exclusion. The Supreme Court upheld the trial judge's decision on the grounds that the public (and therefore the press as part of the public) "have no constitutional right under the Sixth and Fourteenth Amendments to attend criminal trials."[110] The Court ruled that although the press does have a *First* Amendment right of access to trials, the trial judge correctly decided that the defendant's right to a fair trial outweighed the newspaper's right in this case.[111]

The Supreme Court's ruling in *DePasquale* that the public has no right to attend a criminal trial did not settle the issue. *DePasquale* involved the exclusion of the press/public from a *pretrial* hearing. In *Richmond Newspapers Inc. v. Virginia*,[112] the Court was asked to rule on whether or not the press/public could be excluded from the actual trial. After three previously unsuccessful attempts to try a defendant on a murder charge, a Virginia trial judge granted the defense lawyer's motion to exclude the public, including two reporters, from the courtroom. The Supreme Court, in a divided opinion, ruled that the public does have a First Amendment right to attend criminal trials. The Court ruled that the trial judge should have resorted to less restrictive measures to guarantee the defendant a fair trial. However, public access to criminal trials may be limited in cases involving juveniles and in certain rape and child abuse cases. The issue of public access to criminal trials is far from settled, since new cases with different circumstances are sure to arise.

One other issue associated with the public's right to know is that of television broadcasts of criminal trials. In *Estes v. Texas*,[113] the Supreme Court ruled that the bright lights and heavy equipment used in broadcasting disrupted criminal trials. In *Chandler v. Florida*,[114] however, the Court reversed itself, stating that *Estes* was not intended to impose an absolute ban on televised trials. Chief Justice Warren Burger noted that changes in television technology and greater sensitivity on the part of judges to the need for precautionary measures have made television less intrusive than it once was. *Estes* and *Chandler* illustrate how changes in technology can also affect changes in constitutional law.

Thus far we have discussed government interference with the press in terms of outright censorship and judicial control of pretrial publicity. One final area of tension between government and press is over disclosure of news reporters' confidential sources. The leading case in this area is *Branzburg v. Hayes*.[115] Branzburg wrote a newspaper article in which he described two young men making hashish from marijuana. He was subpoenaed by a local grand jury but refused to identify the two men because he had promised them confidentiality. A state court judge ordered Branzburg to answer the questions, but still he refused. Branzburg appealed to the Supreme Court on the grounds that the First

Amendment gave news reporters immunity from forced disclosure of confidential sources of information. The Supreme Court disagreed. Justice Byron White argued that Branzburg was being neither subjected to prior restraint nor prevented from gathering and printing the news. White rejected the idea that reporters' confidential sources would "dry up" once it became known to informants that their identities might be made known to law enforcement officials. The Court ruled that even if some sources did dry up, the public interest in prosecuting crimes outweighs any need to protect confidential sources. The dissenting justices accused the majority of "attempting to annex the journalistic profession as an investigative arm of government."[116] In other words, if Branzburg can infiltrate a hashish operation, undercover police should be able to do so as well. The decision in *Branzburg* prompted some states to pass "shield laws," which, by statute, granted news reporters the same immunity the Court denied to Branzburg. It is worth noting here that even though the Court ruled that there is nothing implicit in the First Amendment that requires granting news reporters this immunity, states are free to grant or withhold the immunity as they wish.

Two other cases involving the privilege of news reporters are worthy of note. In *Zurcher v. Stanford Daily*,[117] the Court upheld the use of a search warrant to search the files of a student newspaper for photographs of a student riot in which police officers were injured. In a case involving a New Jersey shield law, the Supreme Court refused to review the case of Myron A. Faber, a *New York Times* reporter, who spent 39 days in jail for refusing to reveal his sources in a murder case. The New Jersey court ruled that the state's shield law notwithstanding, the reporter's privilege must give way to a criminal defendant's Sixth Amendment right to a fair trial.[118] These cases indicate that the Burger Court was unwilling to extend special privileges to the press under the First Amendment.

The second major area of conflict involving freedom of press is by far the most perplexing: the problem of obscenity. Perhaps most of us would agree with Justice Potter Stewart, who would not try to define obscenity, but who asserted, "I know it when I see it."[119] That is the crux of the problem: Obscenity, like beauty, is in the eye of the beholder, and consequently defies definition. Although most people have a point at which they would say that a book or movie "goes too far," that "obscenity breaking point" varies from person to person: "One person's trash is another person's treasure," as the old saying goes. Because obscenity has so many perplexing facets, we will limit our attention to a single aspect of it: the efforts of the Supreme Court to formulate a legal definition of obscene material.

In *Roth v. United States*,[120] the Supreme Court made a crucial decision by asserting that "implicit in the history of the First Amendment is the rejection of obscenity as utterly without redeeming social importance."[121] That decision was crucial because once the Court took the position that obscene materials were not protected, it became incumbent upon the Court to fashion a definition to separate the permissible materials from the impermissible materials. In other words, the Court had to develop a definition by which lower court judges could determine whether a particular book or movie fell into the protected or unprotected category. The *Roth* test, as the Court's first attempt at a definition was called, was "whether to the average person, applying contemporary community standards, the dominant theme of the material taken as a whole appeals to prurient interest."[122] Critics of the test immediately began to assail it. Who is the "average person"? How are "community standards" ascertained? What is "prurient interest"? Another problem was that persons selling pornographic materials might not discover until it is too late that their materials are also obscene. They could be fined or jailed for selling materials that, while admittedly pornographic, are *later* declared to be obscene by a court. Fundamental to the concept of due process is the belief that the lawbreaker must know that his actions are illegal, but a vendor of pornographic materials might discover that what he thought was perfectly legal to sell was really obscene and illegal to sell. Prosecution under such circumstances begins to take on the appearance of an ***ex post facto*** law, expressly forbidden by the Constitution. It was clear that additional guidance would be needed.

The next major attempt to define obscenity came in the Fanny Hill Case.[123] A lower Massachusetts court found *Memoirs of a Woman of Pleasure*, by John Cleland, to be obscene. The Supreme Court, with *Roth* author Justice William Brennan again writing for the Court, ruled that the state courts had misapplied the *Roth* test. Justice Brennan restated the tripartite test, writing:

> Under this [*Roth*] definition, as elaborated in subsequent cases, three elements must coalesce: it must be established that (a) the dominant theme of the material taken as a whole appeals to prurient interest in sex; (b) the material is patently offensive because it affronts contemporary community standards relating to the description or representation of sexual matters; and (c) the material is utterly without redeeming social value.[124]

The Court ruled that under these criteria a work must be "*utterly* without redeeming social value" before it can be proscribed. In addition, all three criteria, each applied independently, must be present to make a work obscene. Under that test, the Court ruled, *Memoirs* could not be held to be obscene. The *Memoirs* test, as it was called, made it exceedingly difficult to get an obscenity conviction because it was virtually impossible to show that a particular work was "utterly without redeeming social value."

The *Memoirs* test was formulated during the last years of the liberal Warren Court. Beginning with the appointment of Warren E. Burger as Chief Justice, President Richard Nixon was able to name a total of four justices to the Court who were much more conservative on the obscenity question. Court-watchers knew that it would not be long before the Nixon/Burger Court would address the issue yet a third time, and this occurred in *Miller v. California.*[125] *Miller* rejected the "utterly without redeeming social value" standard of *Memoirs* and replaced it with "whether the work, taken as a whole, lacks serious literary, artistic, political, or scientific value." Prosecutors found that they now had a lesser standard to meet in order to win a conviction than was previously required under the *Memoirs* test. In addition, the *Miller* decision made it clear that local, not national, community standards were to determine whether materials violate the community-standards part of the test. Local community standards were to be determined by the use of local juries in obscenity cases.

The weakness of the *Miller* test became apparent almost immediately in *Jenkins v. Georgia.*[126] Jenkins, a movie-theater owner in Albany, Georgia, was found guilty of distributing obscene material for showing *Carnal Knowledge,* a critically acclaimed motion picture. The Supreme Court had to decide whether the local jury's determination that the movie was obscene should prevail. After viewing the film, the Court ruled that *Carnal Knowledge* was not obscene and that the state courts had misapplied the *Miller* test. Just where that leaves local juries in the determination of obscene materials remains a mystery, since the Court has not attempted to modify or clarify the *Miller* test. Recent Supreme Court decisions dealing with the regulation of pornographic material have shown a not-so-subtle desire to steer clear of any further attempts at a definition. Doubtless, however, the issue of obscenity has not been laid to rest.

We will conclude our survey of civil liberties with a discussion of libel. Libel is a form of the tort of defamation, which in turn may be defined as the act "of injuring a person's character, fame, or reputation by false and malicious statements."[127] Libel, then, is "a method of defamation expressed by print, writing, pictures, or signs."[128] Like obscenity, libel has been considered by the Supreme Court to be outside the protection of the First Amendment. Recall that in *Near v. Minnesota,* the Court struck down the law in question partly because the officials whom Near had maligned could have resorted to Minnesota's libel laws for relief. The question remains, to what extent do libel laws protect public officials from libelous attacks? Another problem: To what extent does the First Amendment protect the press from libel suits filed by persons who are not public officials?

The question of libel of public officials was answered by the Supreme Court in *New York Times Co. v. Sullivan.*[129] Civil rights activists had purchased an ad in the *Times* describing the civil rights situation in Montgomery, Alabama. A number of allegations were made against Montgomery city officials, including the city commissioner in charge of the police department. Some of the statements were either false or misleading, so Sullivan sued the *Times* and the persons who placed the ad, even though the ad did not mention Sullivan by name. The Alabama trial court awarded Sullivan $500,000 in damages, and the Alabama Supreme Court sustained the award. The *Times* appealed the decision on First Amendment grounds.

Justice William Brennan, author of the Court's opinion, reversed the Alabama courts. Brennan noted that "debate on public issues should be uninhibited, robust, and wide-open."[130] Public officials were expected to be "men of fortitude, able to thrive in a hardy climate."[131] The Court also noted that although Alabama had a criminal libel law, the judgment in this case was one thousand times the maximum fine allowed by the criminal libel statute. Observing that a newspaper could be hit by a number of libel judgments, Brennan wrote:

> Whether or not a newspaper can survive a succession of such judgments, the pall of fear and timidity imposed upon those who would give voice to public criticism is an atmosphere in which First Amendment freedoms cannot survive.[132]

The Court concluded that the evidence failed to show proof of actual malice either on the part of the purchasers of the ad or the *Times* itself, and that malice must be proven in cases involving the criticism of public officials. Later, the Court extended the *Times* rule to include candidates for public office as well as public officials.[133]

While *New York Times Co. v. Sullivan* made libel suits by public officials much more difficult, the press still had to contend with libel suits brought by persons who were not public officials but who were in the public eye. In two cases, *Curtis Publishing Co. v. Butts*[134] and a companion case, *Associated Press v. Walker*,[135] the Court extended the *Times* rule to include public figures. In a concurring opinion in *Walker*, Chief Justice Earl Warren defined public figures as persons "who do not hold public office at the moment [but] are nevertheless intimately involved in the resolution of important public questions or, by reason of their fame, shape events in areas of concern to society at large."[136] In libel suits involving public figures, plaintiffs must show actual malice just as if they were public officials.

Once it was established that public figures were to be treated like public officials for purposes of libel cases, the Court heard a series of cases in which it had to decide who was and who was not a public figure, with a number of strange results. The Court ruled that a man referred to as a "smut-peddler" could not win a libel judgment since concern over obscenity was a "public issue" under the *Sullivan* decision.[137] Three years later, however, the Court ruled that a lawyer defending a person accused of killing a police officer was not a public figure, even though killing a police officer is undoubtedly a public issue.[138] In *Time Inc. v. Firestone*,[139] the Court ruled that Mrs. Firestone was not a public figure even though she paid a company to clip out newspaper and magazine articles about her. Finally, in *Hutchinson v. Proxmire*,[140] the Court ruled that a scientist, the recipient of Senator William Proxmire's "Golden Fleece Award," was not a public figure, nor did the Speech and Debate Clause of the Constitution give the Senator immunity from a libel suit.

CONCLUSION

In this chapter we have focused on First Amendment freedoms as an introduction to the vast area of constitutional law. In so doing, we have barely touched the surface of this multifaceted and always fascinating subfield of law. We hope that this survey has made the reader aware of the variety of issues that are covered by this part of constitutional law. We also hope that it has conveyed some idea of the complexity of the issues that arise under our constitutional system and of the unique role of the Supreme Court in interpreting the Constitution. Finally, we hope that we have whet the appetites of our readers so that they will want to learn even more about their rights under our Constitution.

NOTES

[1] *Marbury v. Madison*, 1 Cranch 137 (1803).

[2] Arthur A. North, *The Supreme Court: Judicial Process and Judicial Politics* (New York: Appleton-Century-Crofts, 1966), p. 3.

[3] *United States v. Butler*, 297 U.S. 1 (1936), at 62.

[4] Craig R. Ducat, *Modes of Constitutional Interpretation* (St. Paul, Minn.: West Publishing Company, 1978), p. 1.

[5] The date of the president's inauguration was not changed to the twentieth of January until the passage of the Twentieth Amendment in 1933.

[6] This is why those appointed came to be known as the "Midnight Judges."

[7] Alfred H. Kelly, Winfred A. Harbison, and Herman Belz, *The American Constitution: Its Origins and Development*, 6th ed. (New York: W. W. Norton & Co., Inc., 1983), p. 180.

[8] In 1857, the Supreme Court invalidated the Missouri Compromise in the *Dred Scott* Case.

[9] See, for example, Henry J. Abraham, *The Judicial Process*, 3rd ed. (New York: Oxford University Press, 1975), pp. 354–376.

[10] See, for example, Sheldon Goldman and Thomas P. Jahnige, *The Federal Courts as a Political System*, 3rd ed. (New York: Harper & Row, Pub., 1985), pp. 224–229.

[11] See Howard Ball, *Courts and Politics: The Federal Judicial System* (Englewood Cliffs, N.J.: Prentice-Hall, 1980), Chapter 4.

[12] Chapter 1, p. 12.

[13] *Powell v. Alabama*, 287 U.S. 45 (1932).

[14] *Betts v. Brady*, 316 U.S. 455 (1942).

[15] *Gideon v. Wainwright*, 372 U.S. 335 (1963).

[16] *Argersinger v. Hamlin*, 407 U.S. 25 (1972).

[17] *Escobedo v. Illinois*, 378 U.S. 478 (1964).

[18] *Miranda v. Arizona*, 384 U.S. 436 (1966).

[19] *Gideon v. Wainwright*, 372 U.S. 335 (1963), at 344.

[20] *Everson v. Board of Education*, 330 U.S. 1 (1947), at 15–16.

[21] *Board of Education v. Allen*, 392 U.S. 236 (1968).

[22] *Lemon v. Kurtzman*, 403 U.S. 602 (1971).

[23] *Meek v. Pittenger*, 421 U.S. 349 (1975); *Wolman v. Walter*, 433 U.S. 229 (1977); and *Committee for Public Education and Religious Liberty v. Regan*, 444 U.S. 646 (1980).

[24] *Committee for Public Education and Religious Liberty v. Nyquist*, 413 U.S. 756 (1973) and *Muller v. Allen*, 103 S. Ct. 3062 (1983).

[25] *McCollum v. Board of Education*, 333 U.S. 203 (1948).

[26] *Zorach v. Clauson*, 343 U.S. 306 (1952).

[27] *Widmar v. Vincent*, 454 U.S. 263 (1981).

[28] *Engel v. Vitale*, 370 U.S. 421 (1962).

[29] *Ibid.*, at 425.

[30] *Abington School District v. Schempp*, 374 U.S. 203 (1963), at 226.

[31] *Stone v. Graham*, 449 U.S. 39 (1980).

[32] *Wallace v. Jaffree*, 472 U.S. 38 (1985).

[33] *Epperson v. Arkansas*, 393 U.S. 97 (1968).

[34] *McGowan v. Maryland*, 366 U.S. 420 (1961) and *Braunfeld v. Brown*, 366 U.S. 599 (1961).

[35] *Walz v. Tax Commission*, 397 U.S. 664 (1970) and *Bob Jones University v. United States*, 461 U.S. 574 (1983).

[36] *Marsh v. Chambers*, 463 U.S. 783 (1983).

[37] *Lynch v. Donnelly*, 465 U.S. 668 (1984).

[38] *Lemon v. Kurtzman*, 403 U.S. 602 (1971), at 612–613.

[39] *Reynolds v. United States*, 98 U.S. 145 (1879).

[40] Quoted in Gerald Gunther, *Constitutional Law: Cases and Materials*, 10th ed. (Mineola, N.Y.: Foundation Press, 1980), p. 1582.

[41] *Ibid.*

[42] *Cantwell v. Connecticut*, 310 U.S. 296 (1940).

[43] *Murdock v. Pennsylvania*, 319 U.S. 105 (1943) and *Martin v. City of Struthers*, 319 U.S. 141 (1943).

[44] Gunther, *Constitutional Law*, 10th ed., p. 1582.

[45] *Jacobson v. Massachusetts*, 197 U.S. 11 (1905).

[46] *Prince v. Massachusetts*, 321 U.S. 158 (1944).

[47] *Heffron v. International Society for Krishna Consciousness*, 452 U.S. 640 (1981).

[48] *Minersville School District v. Gobitis*, 310 U.S. 586 (1940) and *West Virginia State Board of Education v. Barnette*, 319 U.S. 624 (1943).

[49] *West Virginia State Board of Education v. Barnette*, 319 U.S. 624 (1943) at 642.

⁵⁰ *Wooley v. Maynard,* 430 U.S. 705 (1977).

⁵¹ *West Virginia State Board of Education v. Barnette,* 319 U.S. 624 (1943) at 642.

⁵² *United States v. Schwimmer,* 279 U.S. 644 (1929) (Holmes, J., dissenting).

⁵³ *Abrams v. United States,* 250 U.S. 616 (1919) (Holmes, J., dissenting).

⁵⁴ *Thomas v. Collins,* 323 U.S. 516 (1945).

⁵⁵ For a description of the absolutist position of Justice Hugo Black, see Ducat, pp. 64–78.

⁵⁶ C. Herman Pritchett, *Constitutional Civil Liberties* (Englewood Cliffs, N.J.: Prentice-Hall, 1984), p. 36.

⁵⁷ *Schenck v. United States,* 249 U.S. 47 (1919).

⁵⁸ Although technically the pamphlet was at issue, the Court treated *Schenck* as a freedom of speech case, not a freedom of press case.

⁵⁹ *Schenck v. United States,* 249 U.S. 47 (1919), at 52.

⁶⁰ Ibid., p. 52.

⁶¹ *Abrams v. United States,* 250 U.S. 616 (1919).

⁶² *Gitlow v. New York,* 268 U.S. 652 (1925).

⁶³ Ibid., at 669.

⁶⁴ *Thomas v. Collins,* 323 U.S. 516 (1944).

⁶⁵ *Hartzel v. United States,* 322 U.S. 680 (1944).

⁶⁶ *Dennis v. United States,* 341 U.S. 494 (1951).

⁶⁷ *Yates v. United States,* 354 U.S. 298 (1957).

⁶⁸ For example, see *Cantwell v. Connecticut,* 310 U.S. 296 (1940) and *Murdock v. Pennsylvania,* 319 U.S. 105 (1943).

⁶⁹ *Chaplinsky v. New Hampshire,* 315 U.S. 568 (1942).

⁷⁰ Ibid., p. 569.

⁷¹ Ibid., p. 573.

⁷² *Feiner v. New York,* 340 U.S. 315 (1951).

⁷³ *Cohen v. California,* 403 U.S. 15 (1971).

⁷⁴ Ibid., p. 20.

⁷⁵ *Gooding v. Wilson,* 405 U.S. 518 (1972).

⁷⁶ *Tinker v. Des Moines Independent School District,* 393 U.S. 503 (1969).

⁷⁷ Ibid., p. 514.

⁷⁸ *Street v. New York,* 394 U.S. 576 (1969).

⁷⁹ Ibid., p. 578.

⁸⁰ *Smith v. Goguen,* 415 U.S. 566 (1974).

⁸¹ *Spence v. Washington,* 418 U.S. 405 (1974).

⁸² For example, see *Sutherland v. Illinois,* 425 U.S. 947 (1976), appeal denied.

⁸³ *United States v. O'Brien,* 391 U.S. 367 (1968).

⁸⁴ *Hague v. CIO,* 307 U.S. 496 (1939).

⁸⁵ Ibid., p. 515.

⁸⁶ Ibid., p. 502.

⁸⁷ *Cox v. New Hampshire,* 312 U.S. 569 (1941).

⁸⁸ *Walker v. Birmingham,* 388 U.S. 307 (1967).

⁸⁹ *Shuttlesworth v. Birmingham,* 394 U.S. 147 (1969).

⁹⁰ Ibid., p. 150.

⁹¹ *Nationalist Socialist Party v. Skokie,* 432 U.S. 43 (1977).

⁹² Gerald Gunther, *Constitutional Law,* 11th ed. (Mineola, N.Y.: Foundation Press, 1985), p. 1239.

⁹³ *Edwards v. South Carolina,* 372 U.S. 229 (1963).

[94] Ibid., p. 235.

[95] *Cox v. Louisiana,* 379 U.S. 559 (1965).

[96] Ibid., p. 560.

[97] Quoted in M. Glenn Abernathy, *Civil Liberties Under the Constitution,* 4th ed. (Columbia, S.C.: The University of South Carolina Press, 1985), p. 396.

[98] *Adderley v. Florida,* 385 U.S. 39 (1966).

[99] Ibid., p. 47.

[100] *Brown v. Louisiana,* 383 U.S. 131 (1966).

[101] Quoted in Gunther, 11th ed., p. 1242.

[102] *Greer v. Spock,* 424 U.S. 828 (1976).

[103] Edward L. Barnett, Jr., and William Cohen, *Constitutional Law: Cases and Materials,* 7th ed. (Mineola, N.Y.: Foundation Press, 1985), p. 1193.

[104] *United States v. Grace,* 461 U.S. 171 (1983).

[105] *Near v. Minnesota,* 283 U.S. 697 (1931).

[106] *New York Times Co. v. United States,* 403 U.S. 713 (1971).

[107] *Sheppard v. Maxwell,* 384 U.S. 333 (1966).

[108] Ibid., p. 362.

[109] *Gannett Co. v. DePasquale,* 443 U.S. 368 (1979).

[110] Quoted in Sheldon Goldman, *Constitutional Law and Supreme Court Decision-Making: Cases and Essays* (New York: Harper & Row, Inc., 1982), p. 583.

[111] Ibid.

[112] *Richmond Newspapers Inc. v. Virginia,* 448 U.S. 555 (1980).

[113] *Estes v. Texas,* 381 U.S. 532 (1965).

[114] *Chandler v. Florida,* 449 U.S. 560 (1981).

[115] *Branzburg v. Hayes,* 408 U.S. 665 (1972).

[116] Ibid., p. 725.

[117] *Zurcher v. Stanford Daily,* 436 U.S. 547 (1978).

[118] Pritchett, p. 70.

[119] *Jacobellis v. Ohio,* 378 U.S. 184 (1964) (Stewart, J., concurring).

[120] *Roth v. United States,* 354 U.S. 476 (1957).

[121] Ibid., p. 484.

[122] Ibid., p. 489.

[123] *A Book Named "John Cleland's Memoirs of a Woman of Pleasure" v. Attorney General of Massachusetts,* 383 U.S. 413 (1966).

[124] Ibid., p. 418.

[125] *Miller v. California,* 413 U.S. 15 (1973).

[126] *Jenkins v. Georgia,* 418 U.S. 153 (1974).

[127] Henry C. Black, *Black's Law Dictionary,* 4th ed. (St. Paul, Minn.: West Publishing Company, 1968), p. 505.

[128] Ibid., p. 1060.

[129] *New York Times Co. v. Sullivan,* 376 U.S. 254 (1964).

[130] Ibid., p. 270.

[131] Ibid., p. 273.

[132] Ibid., p. 278.

[133] *Monitor Patriot Co. v. Roy,* 401 U.S. 265 (1971).

[134] *Curtis Publishing Co. v. Butts,* 388 U.S. 130 (1967).

[135] *Associated Press v. Walker,* 388 U.S. 130 (1967).

[136] Ronald D. Rotunda, *Modern Constitutional Law: Cases and Notes,* 2nd ed. (St. Paul, Minn.: West Publishing Company, 1985), pp. 795–796.

[137] *Rosenbloom v. Metromedia,* 403 U.S. 29 (1971).
[138] *Gertz v. Robert Welch Inc.,* 418 U.S. 323 (1974).
[139] *Time Inc. v. Firestone,* 424 U.S. 448 (1976).
[140] *Hutchinson v. Proxmire,* 443 U.S. 111 (1979).

7

Criminal Law

Of all the subfields of American law, criminal law is perhaps the most controversial. As we noted in Chapter 1, criminal law deals with activities that have been formally forbidden in a society by its government.[1] The controversy surrounding criminal law centers around both the substance or content of criminal law and the procedures by which we deprive accused persons of their life, liberty, and property. Substantive criminal law asks questions such as what should be made a crime, what is the appropriate punishment for committing a particular crime, and what specific behavior constitutes a crime. The first question focuses on the kinds of activities that may or should be forbidden by government. Certain actions, like murder, are inherently evil and universally condemned as criminal behavior. Other activities, such as gambling, are questionable as "criminal" since there is not universal consensus on their immorality, as there is with crimes like murder and rape.

Even if there is general agreement within a society that a certain activity should be banned, there is often disagreement over how severe the punishment should be. For example, some states impose long sentences on persons convicted of possessing marijuana. Many people, while still believing that marijuana use should be forbidden, believe that the penalty is excessive for the crime. Making the punishment fit the crime, then, is an important concern of criminal law.

As controversial as substantive criminal law is, it pales in comparison with the controversy generated by procedural law. Procedural criminal

151

law is closely associated with the concept of due process of law. Due process of law refers to the process or procedures that must be followed before a person can legally be deprived of "life, liberty, or property." In criminal law, procedural due process sets forth the procedures that government must observe before it can execute, imprison, or fine an individual. Although not really a game, procedural due process can be thought of as the "rules of the game" that the State must adhere to before it imposes punishment. Some people argue that government has "gone too far" in protecting the rights of those accused of crimes, while totally ignoring the rights of their victims. Critics of procedural due process argue that most persons accused of crimes are indeed guilty and that they should not be allowed to escape punishment because of a "technicality" in the law. Justice, after all, requires that persons committing crimes be punished.

Defenders of procedural due process offer a number of rationales for supporting the rights of persons accused of crimes. First, our system of justice is based upon the assumption that a person is innocent until proven guilty; thus the State bears the burden of proof in a criminal case. Under our legal system, the accused is not required to assist the State in securing his own conviction. Consequently, safeguards, such as protection against self-incrimination, ensure that the State has evidence other than the accused's own testimony to secure a conviction.

A second reason for procedural safeguards is the possibility of unjustly convicting an innocent person. No system of justice is infallible, so we believe that we should take whatever precautions are needed to ensure that, ideally, the innocent person is always freed and the guilty person is always convicted. Overall, most defenders of procedural due process would argue that it is better for ten guilty persons to go free than for one innocent person to be imprisoned.

A final rationale for protecting the rights of the accused is political. Since time immemorial, governments have used their criminal justice systems as a means of repressing certain groups in society. Governments have used the criminal justice system against religious, racial, and political dissidents throughout history. The argument, then, is that if government can use the law against one unpopular group today, it may very well use it against a group to which I belong tomorrow. Therefore, citizens must remain vigilant to ensure that punishment for criminal activity is never used as a pretext for persecuting an individual or a group for its religious or political beliefs. Only by guaranteeing that government obeys "the rules of the game" can we be certain that religious or political persecution does not occur under the pretext of law and order.

This chapter will focus on both the substance and procedures of criminal law. First, it will discuss the characteristics of criminal law and the elements of a crime. Second, it will examine the parties to a crime.

Third, it will examine three areas of criminal procedures to highlight our previous discussion of this controversial topic. Finally, we will look at two case studies, one substantive and one procedural, to illustrate the complexities of criminal law.

CHARACTERISTICS OF CRIMINAL LAW

What is the nature of criminal law? In Chapter 1, we noted that one of the functions of law is to proscribe certain activities. In so doing, a society is defining exactly what is and what is not acceptable behavior. In a democratic society, it is the function of legislative bodies, as the elected representatives of the people, to decide what behavior will be made criminal and what penalties will be attached to violations of the law. In this section, we will attempt to define the nature of criminal behavior more precisely, with an emphasis on how criminal law reflects the society that creates it.

In Chapter 1 we introduced two terms: *malum in se* and *malum prohibitum*. *Malum in se* means "wrong in itself" and is applied to behavior that could be considered inherently wrong or evil. Murder and rape are two examples of acts that are criminal because they are inherently wrong in themselves. Murder (as opposed to killing in self-defense, for example) is inherently wrong because there can be no legitimate justification for it. Rape is another example: What possible justification could exist for a man to force himself sexually on a woman? Crimes that are considered *malum in se* have two primary characteristics: They tend to have highly moral overtones, and there is nearly universal consensus that the type of behavior involved cannot be tolerated in a civilized society. The latter characteristic does not mean that every person agrees that rape should be a crime; obviously, the rapist may not think so. It means that acts of murder and rape have been universally condemned by most civilized societies throughout history. In a sense, then, crimes that are *malum in se* are the easiest to define because they are universally condemned.

A much more complex problem surrounds the second category of crimes—those defined as *malum prohibitum*. Some behavior has been labelled "criminal" not so much because it is inherently wrong or universally condemned, but merely because a legislative body has deemed it undesirable. As we noted in Chapter 1, parking in a "No Parking" zone is not the kind of behavior that arouses moral condemnation or social ostracization, but it is a crime, albeit a minor one. It is a crime because a city council has chosen to make it one. Crimes defined as *malum prohibitum* may have rational justifications, such as public safety or traffic control, but they are hardly inherently evil. What, then, makes the classification of *malum prohibitum* so complex? It is the fact that society is sometimes in disagreement over whether an activity is criminal because it is immoral or because it is just undesirable. In this chapter's introduction, we used gambling to illustrate this problem. Why is gambling a crime? Is it because it is a morally reprehensible activity? If so, then why do millions of presumably moral people bet on the Super Bowl? Is it because the compulsive gambler may gamble away his family's grocery money? Is it because gambling is an activity that brings "the wrong element" into a community? Any or all of these could be reasons that a legislature might choose to prohibit gambling. However, the success of places like Las Vegas and Atlantic City indicates that some people see no harm in it.

In addition to gambling, activities such as prostitution, illegal use of drugs, and even homosexuality have been declared criminal partly because they are considered immoral and partly because they are offensive to the majority. The prohibition of these activities is sometimes justified on the grounds that while morally debatable, they lead to other serious crimes or create other problems. Prostitution, for example, can spread venereal disease, exploit women, lead to drug addiction, and result in violence against women. Drug addiction may lead its victims to commit crimes, such as burglary, to feed their habit. Finally, prohibiting so-called victimless crimes is justified on the grounds that the State has the right to safeguard the quality of life in a community. Prostitution, gambling, and drug addiction rely on baser human needs. The State should uplift the human spirit by prohibiting activities that debase it and society. In the final analysis, then, activities labelled *malum prohibitum* may be considered immoral or just a nuisance, but either way, in a democratic society, legislatures may make them criminal.

One final aspect of the *malum prohibitum* category is worth mentioning. Given the debatable nature of the morality of such activities as gambling, what is the appropriate penalty? At one time some states allowed sentences of 10 or more years for mere possession of marijuana, regardless of the amount. Many people believed that such penalties were excessive given the nature of the crime. Still others argue that only a "get-tough" policy will eradicate the undesirable activity. Today, many of the crimes we have been discussing are classified as misdemeanors. Prostitution, possession of small amounts of marijuana, and so forth receive small fines and light sentences. Laws dealing with the purveyors of crime are harsher. Selling marijuana will result in a stiffer sentence than mere possession, and acting as a pimp is generally considered more serious than prostitution itself. In attempting to get at the source of the crime, the law has made the drug dealer, the pimp, and the bookmaker more criminally liable and therefore more susceptible to harsher penalties. Whether such tactics are effective in the "war on crime" is another matter.

As may already be apparent from the foregoing discussion of *malum in se* and *malum prohibitum*, criminal law is a reflection of the society that produces it. In an Islamic theocracy, such as Iran, criminal law will reflect the religious teachings of the Koran; in a Catholic country, it will reflect the tenets of Catholicism. In addition, the law will change to reflect changes in society, especially attitude changes. As noted, use of marijuana was once considered a serious crime with harsh penalties, whereas today the penalties in most states are relatively light. As public tolerance of marijuana use grew, the severity of the penalties were reduced. As a society advances, its judgments about crime and punishment change. Thomas Gardner has written:

> The criminal punishments used 200 years ago in England and Europe were severe. In England alone, more than 200 offenses were punishable by death. Condemned criminals were usually hanged, although occasionally they were beheaded, quartered, or drawn (dragged along the ground at the tail of a horse).[2]

Obviously, both the number of capital offenses and the penalties have been changed in modern England. The point is that attitudes about what should be made a crime and what penalty should be assessed vary from one society to another and from one historical era to another. In 1903, the first Justice John Marshall Harlan, quoting an earlier case, wrote of lotteries:

> ". . . [they] infest[s] the whole community; it enters every dwelling; it reaches every class; it preys upon the hard earnings of the poor; it plunders the ignorant and the simple."[3]

Today, many states are turning to lotteries as a means of relieving their financial problems. Law does and should change with the needs and attitudes of the society it serves.

ELEMENTS OF A CRIME

In this section we will examine a very important aspect of substantive criminal law: the elements of a crime. Specifically, we will focus upon the type of behavior that an individual must engage in to be guilty of a crime. Obviously, different crimes require different behavior, but there are common elements necessary for proving all crimes, and identifying these common elements will be our primary concern.

The first element of a crime is the **actus reus.** *Black's Law Dictionary* defines *actus* as "an act or action"[4] and *reus* as "a person judicially accused of a crime."[5] Therefore, *actus reus* is literally the action of a person accused of a crime. David W. Neubauer has defined *actus reus* simply as "the guilty act."[6] All this means is that a criminal statute must clearly define exactly what act is deemed "guilty"—that is, the exact behavior that is being prohibited. This is done so that all persons are put on notice that if they perform the guilty act, they will be liable for criminal punishment. Courts will occasionally nullify a law that is "void for vagueness." Justice William Brennan, quoting an earlier case, defined an unconstitutionally vague law as "a statute which forbids or requires the doing of an act in terms so vague that men of common intelligence must necessarily guess at its meaning and differ as to its application."[7] Unless the *actus reus* is clearly defined, one might not know whether or not one's behavior is illegal.

In addition to adequate notice of the proscribed behavior, another characteristic of *actus reus* needs clarification. The guilty act might not just be what one does; it might also be what one fails to do. Criminal laws not only prohibit certain behavior; in some cases they require action. That is, a person can be held criminally liable for failure to act. Thomas J. Gardner has listed examples of when failure to act is a crime, including failure to come to the aid of a police officer when requested to do so and failure to submit to a breathalyzer test when requested to do so.[8] Gardner cites two famous examples of when failure to act might have constituted a crime. In 1964, a young woman was brutally murdered on a New York street in an attack that lasted 35 minutes. Despite her repeated cries for help, no one called the police. In 1983, a woman was gang raped in a Boston bar while onlookers watched and cheered. No one came to her aid or called the police.[9] These are but two examples of when the failure to act is, or should be, a crime. Such crimes are crimes of omission as opposed to crimes of commission, but both may be considered morally reprehensible under the circumstances.

Finally, *actus reus* should be understood to mean that in order to be guilty of a crime, a person must do or not do something rather than just *be* something. The State may choose to make homosexual acts illegal, but it may not make being a homosexual a crime. Homosexuals have not committed a crime unless or until they engage in the specific behavior the State has forbidden. As commonsensical as that might seem, some states have passed laws making one's status a crime. In *Robinson v. California*,[10] the Supreme Court struck down a California law that made the status of narcotics addiction a crime. Under the law there was no need to provide evidence that Robinson had actually used narcotics in California—only that at some time he had been addicted to narcotics. In contrast, in *Powell v. Texas*,[11] the Court ruled that a chronic alcoholic could be punished even though the alcoholism was a disease. Powell had been convicted for being drunk in public, not for being an alcoholic.

Mens Rea.   A second element of a crime is **mens rea.** Black defines *mens rea* as "a guilty mind; a guilty or wrongful purpose; a criminal intent."[12] *Mens rea,* then, refers to an individual's state of mind when a crime is committed. Criminal statutes employ terms such as *knowingly, wilfully, intentionally,* and *purposely* to describe the state of mind one must have in order to possess "a guilty mind." While the *actus reus* is proven by physical or eyewitness evidence, *mens rea* is more difficult to ascertain. The jury must determine for itself whether the accused had the necessary intent to commit the act, and that raises a number of difficult problems.

Mens rea requires the accused to have the requisite intent to commit an illegal act. Some crimes require proof of *specific intent.* As indicated, specific-intent acts must be carried out "knowingly" and "wilfully." Under coercion, an individual might "knowingly" commit an illegal act without doing so "wilfully." Patty Hearst, for example, claimed that she was coerced into robbing banks by her kidnappers, but the jury refused to believe her.

Another type of intent is *general intent.* General intent "is sufficient for crimes for which a voluntary performance of the prohibited act constitutes an offense, regardless of whether the person intended to violate the law."[13] In other words, the prosecutor does not have to prove that a motorist "wilfully" ran a red light, only that the act itself was voluntarily performed and witnessed by a police officer. Otherwise, every motorist would argue that he ran the light inadvertently, thus not having the necessary "guilty mind."

Finally, *mens rea* includes an element called *scienter,* which refers to the degree of knowledge one must have to be guilty of a particular crime. One aspect of scienter is simply the knowledge that a certain activity is illegal. People of common intelligence know that murder, burglary, and arson are illegal. But certain crimes require additional knowledge on the part of the accused. In Texas, for example, the murder of a police officer is a capital offense, but the prosecutor must prove that the defendant knew that his victim was a police officer. The crime of receiving stolen property requires that the buyer know the property has been stolen.[14] These crimes require additional proof beyond the fact that the accused knew his actions were illegal.

The requirement of *mens rea* is one reason that insanity is a legal defense for some persons accused of crimes. In an insanity defense, the accused typically does not deny that he performed the *actus reus,* but merely asserts that because of his insanity he was incapable of distinguishing right from wrong. Under U.S. law, persons cannot be punished for a crime unless they are able to distinguish right from wrong. A similar rationale applies to children below a certain age: The law assumes that children are incapable of understanding that their acts are wrong and therefore they cannot be punished. Even if someone is found not guilty by reason of insanity, the law may require that he be institutionalized until such time as psychiatrists deem him mentally competent. John W. Hinckley's assassination attempt on the life of President Ronald

Reagan in March 1981, and the verdict in that case, has reopened the debate on the insanity plea in our legal system, illustrating once again that controversial legal issues are seldom, if ever, settled for good.

Causation.   The next element of a crime is *causation.* To *cause* an event is to bring it about or to make it happen. Often the phrase "but for" is used to determine whether causation has occurred. For example, we might say "Cain killed Abel," by which we really mean "Cain caused Abel's death." In other words, "But for Cain's act, Abel would still be alive." Causation, then, means that "but for" the actions of A, B would not have been harmed. In criminal law, causation is an element that must be proven beyond a reasonable doubt.

One type of causation is **direct causation,** which means that nothing intervenes between cause and effect. In a modern version of the Biblical story, let's say Cain shoots Abel, causing Abel's immediate death. Cain is clearly the direct cause of Abel's death. But suppose Cain shoots Abel, inflicting what is normally a nonfatal wound. Then, Abel is dropped by the ambulance attendants as he is being loaded into the ambulance, receives an infection from an unsterile blood-transfusion needle, and ultimately dies. Did Cain kill Abel? May Cain be charged with murder? Certainly Cain caused the bullet wound that necessitated the ambulance call and the blood transfusion that ultimately resulted in Abel's death, but did Cain "cause" Abel's death, or did other factors cause it? What, if any, is the extent of Cain's criminal liability in the death of Abel?

The foregoing example illustrates what is known as **proximate cause.** We see a chain of events that leads to Abel's death, but can Cain be held legally responsible? Cain is undoubtedly guilty of *something,* but is it the crime of murder? One might argue that but for the gunshot wound, Abel would not have been taken to the hospital, where he received the fatal blood transfusion. But can Cain be held responsible for the unsterile needle? Obviously, an intervening variable (the needle) has entered the equation contributing to Abel's death. In order to prove murder or even manslaughter, the prosecution must prove that Cain's actions were the proximate cause of Abel's death; otherwise, a lesser offense, such as assault with a deadly weapon, must be charged. The determination of causation under circumstances much more complex than those we have described is one of the most difficult tasks in criminal law.

Standard of Proof.   Under the U.S. system of law, the person who brings the cause of action before the court bears the burden of proof. That is, the plaintiff is responsible for proving the truthfulness of his allegations. Under the rules of civil law, the plaintiff must meet only the *preponderance-of-evidence* standard in order to win. Under that standard, the weight of evidence, however slight, must favor the plaintiff's version of the dispute. If the plaintiff fails to meet this standard of proof, the defendant will prevail. In criminal law, a different standard of proof, called *beyond a reasonable doubt*, is required. This standard places a greater burden on the State, which is the plaintiff, in a criminal case. "Beyond a reasonable doubt" essentially means that all possible alternative explanations for what happened have been considered and rejected except one—the one that concludes that the accused committed the crime for which he is charged. Note that the standard means not beyond all doubt, but only beyond "reasonable" doubt. Courts employ the "reasonable person" standard, which holds that if twelve reasonable persons, after hearing the relevant evidence, conclude beyond a reasonable doubt that the accused committed the crime, the burden of proof has been met.

The law requires a higher standard of proof in criminal cases than in civil cases for a number of reasons. One is that the stakes are much higher in a criminal case. A person convicted of a crime may be stripped of his liberty or even his life. The taking of a person's life or liberty is so serious that it may be done only if there is a high degree of certainty that the person committed the crime. Imagine the case of a person wrongfully convicted of a crime who serves five years in prison before the error is discovered. Now consider the mental anguish of such a person, who alone knows that he is innocent. How can such a person or his family ever be compensated for those five years of mental anguish? How can the State give back five years of a person's life? The beyond-a-reasonable-doubt standard seeks to minimize the chances of the innocent person's conviction, but even then we know that some innocent people are still convicted.

A second reason for the greater standard of proof in criminal cases is the relative strength of the two parties involved. The criminal defendant is usually David to the State's Goliath. The State has tremendous human and financial resources at its disposal to try to prove the defendant's guilt. Even with the requirement of court-appointed counsel, the poor person is at a distinct disadvantage. Since most defendants are poor, the higher standard of proof evens the odds somewhat.

A third reason for the higher standard is one mentioned earlier in this chapter. Since the criminal justice system is capable of becoming a means of repressing persons who hold unpopular political views, the higher standard of proof guarantees that the State will not use its awesome power to "railroad" an innocent person simply because she holds unpopular views. Although it is impossible to absolutely guarantee that the criminal justice system will not be used as a tool of repression, the higher standard of proof reduces the risk that it will be.

The beyond-a-reasonable-doubt standard places a heavy burden on the State in a criminal case. It is important to remember that the accused does not have to prove anything. The defendant does not have to take the stand in his own defense, call any witnesses to testify, or present any evidence in his own behalf. The defendant may do nothing, and if the State has failed to prove its case beyond a reasonable doubt, the defendant must be acquitted. That is why, in the technical sense, an accused is not found "innocent." Innocence implies that the defendant is blameless. The accused may be *factually* guilty of the crime, but unless the State proves its case, the accused is not *legally* guilty. Therefore, a verdict of not guilty may mean that the State was unable to prove its case to the satisfaction of the jury, not that the defendant was innocent or morally blameless.

Let us now summarize the elements of a crime. First, the prohibited behavior designated as a crime must be clearly defined so that a reasonable person can be forewarned that engaging in that behavior is illegal. There are also common law crimes. Each criminal statute has certain elements that distinguish that crime, and the state must prove each element. Second, the accused must be shown to have possessed the requisite intent to commit the crime. Third, the State must prove causation. Finally, the State must prove beyond a reasonable doubt that the defendant committed the crime. Understanding these essential elements of a crime can provide added insight into the substantive and procedural nature of criminal law discussed later in the chapter.

PARTIES TO A CRIME

Culpability is another important characteristic of criminal law. Culpability is the degree of blame involved in the commission of a crime— that is, how much legal responsibility a person bears for the commission of a crime. In most jurisdictions, two categories of persons—principals and accessories—are considered to be parties to a crime and, as a result, criminally liable for their actions. In this section we will define and differentiate principals and accessories and discuss the degree of culpability of each. We begin with the principals in a crime.

Principals. The law recognizes two types of principals: **principals in the first degree** and **principals in the second degree.** A first degree principal can be defined as "the person who actually perpetrates the deed either by his own hand or through an innocent agent."[15] A principal in the first degree, then, is the perpetrator of the crime, the person who actually commits the murder, rape, or arson. The principal in the first degree does not have to be physically present when a crime is committed. An example would be a case in which someone plants a bomb with a timing device set to go off later. Nor must the principal necessarily commit the deed personally. A person who uses an insane person or a child to plant the bomb is still the principal in the first degree.[16]

A principal in the second degree is a person who "is actually or constructively present, aiding and abetting another in the commission of the deed."[17] *Actual presence* is easily defined: The individual is physically present when the crime is committed, as in the case of the person who holds a gun on the customers while another robs the bank. *Constructive presence* means that a person is near enough to assist in the crime; examples are a lookout or the driver of a getaway car. The key to a second-degree principal's culpability is that such a person aids and abets the perpetrator.[18] In most jurisdictions, both types of principals are equally guilty, even if an unintended crime is committed. For example, if the intended crime is robbery of a liquor store and the perpetrator kills the owner, the driver of the getaway car is equally guilty of felony murder even though murder was never intended.[19] Under such circumstances, both perpetrator and abettor are equally culpable in the eyes of the law.

Accessories. Just as with principals, the law recognizes two categories of accessories: before and after the fact. An ***accessory before the fact*** is "one who, although absent at the time and place of the crime, procured, counseled, commanded, or encouraged its commission."[20] Accessory before the fact is intended to cover the "mastermind" of a crime, the person who plans the crime but does not actually take part in its commission. The key difference between an accessory before the fact and a second degree principal is the person's presence or absence. An accessory before the fact is just as culpable as the perpetrator as long as the perpetrator commits the act he was counseled to commit. If an accessory counsels a perpetrator to commit arson and the latter burglarizes the house before burning it, the accessory is culpable only for the arson, not the burglary.[21] Many jurisdictions have done away with the distinction between an accessory before the fact and a second-degree principal, preferring to treat both parties as principals.[22]

An ***accessory after the fact*** is "one who receives, relieves, comforts, or assists another knowing that he has committed a felony."[23] An accessory after the fact must know that another person has committed a felony and must have personally assisted the felon. The basis for condemning someone as an accessory after the fact is obstruction of justice.[24] Actions commonly attributed to an accessory after the fact include hiding a felon, lying to police officers about a felon's whereabouts, and helping a felon cover up his criminal activity.

Under the common law, it was the rule that an accessory could not be prosecuted until the principal had been convicted. Most jurisdictions today allow an accessory before the fact to be prosecuted even if the principal has not been convicted and even if the principal is acquitted.[25] Accessories after the fact may be prosecuted in some jurisdictions without a conviction of the principal, but in other jurisdictions the common-law rule prevails. Accessories may be subjected to the same punishment as principals. Although an accessory is as legally culpable as the principal, the sentencing authority, whether judge or jury, frequently assesses lighter sentences upon accessories after the fact.

PROCEDURAL CRIMINAL LAW

In Chapter 4 we discussed criminal procedures primarily from what might be termed a "cookbook" approach; that is, we followed the steps of the criminal process from arrest to appeal, much as one might follow the steps of a recipe. Our purpose in Chapter 4 was to provide the reader with an overview of criminal procedures without getting bogged down in details. In this section we wish to discuss in greater detail some of the procedural safeguards guaranteed by the Constitution. We will look at three controversial areas of constitutional law: search and seizure, the right to counsel, and the protection against self-incrimination. Our purposes in focusing on these three topics is to provide the reader with an understanding of the history of these procedural safeguards, the philosophical basis of each, and the complexity of the issues involved with each. As noted in the introduction to this chapter, our concern about procedural due process is motivated by our desire to ensure that government "plays by the rules," by our anxiety about convicting the innocent, and by our fear that government may use the criminal justice system to prosecute unpopular individuals or groups. With these considerations in mind, we turn our attention to the first topic: search and seizure.

Search and Seizure. "A man's home is his castle" is a common adage. Although this adage fails to inform us of the status of a *woman's* home, we will proceed on the premise that under the English common law, even the humblest home in the realm was to be a haven from the outside world. The lowest of the king's subjects was entitled to the sanctuary of his own home. It is with this understanding that the Fourth Amendment was included in our Bill of Rights. The Fourth Amendment reads as follows:

> The right of the people to be secure in their persons, houses, papers, and effects, against unreasonable searches and seizures, shall not be violated, and no warrants shall issue, but upon probable cause, supported by oath

or affirmation, and particularly describing the place to be searched, and the persons or things to be seized.[26]

Several things should be noted from the text of the Fourth Amendment. First, the amendment prohibits only "unreasonable" searches and seizures, thus implying that reasonable ones are permitted. What is reasonable and what is not ultimately becomes a question for the courts to decide. Second, search warrants are to be issued only "upon probable cause," another rather vague notion. Third, the warrant, if issued, must describe the place to be searched and the things to be seized. All three of these stipulations are of sufficient ambiguity to cause problems for the Supreme Court in interpreting the Fourth Amendment.

One might wonder why the Framers of the Constitution, and especially those who wrote the Fourth Amendment, were so concerned about the rights of criminal defendants. Were they a bunch of "knee-jerk" liberals who were "soft on crime"? On the contrary, we sometimes forget that the Framers were revolutionaries who had firsthand experience with a tyrannical government. They knew what can happen when government begins to ignore the rights of its citizens, and they were certainly familiar with the general warrants of George III authorizing British troops to search the homes of suspected patriots for powder and shot that might be used by the rebels. In other words, the Framers were not glassy-eyed idealists who failed to foresee the consequences of their actions. Instead they were pragmatists who, in balancing the rights of individuals against the need for law and order, made an initial determination that, in a free society, the former was more important. But, as noted in Chapter 6, constitutional law is constantly changing to meet the needs of new generations of Americans. The values underlying the protection against unreasonable searches and seizures, although important to our Founding Fathers, might not be shared by Americans in the late twentieth century. Or are they? Perhaps we should ask ourselves that question as we study the Fourth Amendment.

Historically, the items subject to seizure by government in a criminal case fell into three categories: contraband, fruits of the crime, and instrumentalities of the crime. *Contraband* is something the government has forbidden to be in a person's possession, such as illegal drugs, explosives, or obscene materials. *Fruits of the crime* include stolen goods or money. *Instrumentalities* of the crime are tools or weapons used in the commission of a crime. Even a getaway car could be classified as an instrumentality subject to seizure. In 1969, in *Warden v. Hayden*,[27] the Supreme Court created a fourth category it labelled "mere evidence." In *Hayden*, a jacket and a pair of trousers identified as being similar to those worn by the robber of a taxi company were found in Hayden's home after a warrantless search. After first deciding that the search was reasonable, the Court turned to the issue of whether the jacket and trousers were subject to lawful seizure. Rather than continue the legal fiction that the clothes were subject to seizure as "instrumentalities" of the crime, the Court ruled that the clothes, as "mere evidence," were also subject to seizure. The Court ruled that the purpose of the Fourth Amendment is the protection of privacy, not property, and noted, "Privacy is disturbed no more by a search directed to a purely evidentiary object than it is by a search directed to an instrumentality, fruit, or contraband."[28]

Besides the question of what may be seized as evidence, another issue is how evidence is obtained by the police. Under the common law, courts did not concern themselves about the methods used to obtain evidence, but only with the reliability of that evidence. That is, if the evidence was "good," it mattered not how the police acquired it. That common-law rule was changed for federal courts in *Weeks v. United States*.[29] Weeks was accused of running an illegal lottery through the mails. Local police and, later, a federal marshal conducted an illegal search and seized letters and papers as evidence. Weeks made a motion for the return of his property, which the trial court denied. The Supreme Court, in overturning Weeks's conviction, ruled:

> . . . If letters and private documents can thus be seized and held and used in evidence against a citizen accused of an offense, the protection of the 4th Amendment, declaring his right to be secure against such searches and seizures, is of no value, and, so far as those thus placed are concerned, might as well be stricken from the Constitution.[30]

Thus was born the exclusionary rule. The exclusionary rule states that evidence obtained in violation of a person's constitutional rights must be excluded from the trial of the accused person. Since Weeks's papers were seized by an illegal search and seizure, they could not be used as evidence against him. The *Weeks* rule initially applied only to the exclusion of evidence in cases in federal courts, but in 1961 the Supreme Court made the rule applicable to the states in the case of *Mapp v. Ohio*.[31] Although the exclusionary rule developed in the context of search and seizure, it was later extended to include other violations of a defendant's constitutional rights.

There has probably never been a more controversial issue in criminal law than the exclusionary rule. Proponents of the rule argue that there are a number of important justifications for its existence. First, proponents argue that the exclusionary rule preserves the integrity of the judicial system by excluding evidence "tainted" by illegal police activities. Most would agree that a confession extracted through torture is an improper way to obtain evidence even if the person is factually guilty. The argument, then, is that in accepting the "reliable" but coerced confession, the courts are aiding and abetting improper police tactics. Justice Louis Brandeis has written:

> If the Government becomes a lawbreaker, it breeds contempt for law; it invites every man to become a law unto himself; it invites anarchy. To declare that in the administration of the criminal law the end justifies the means—to declare that the Government may commit crimes in order to secure the conviction of a private criminal—would bring terrible retribution. Against that pernicious doctrine this Court should resolutely set its face.[32]

Courts, according to Brandeis, should not close their eyes to the methods used to obtain evidence, but should see that law enforcers also obey the law.

A second justification for the exclusionary rule is one mentioned by Justice Day, author of the *Weeks* opinion. If evidence seized in violation of the Fourth Amendment is admitted, then the Amendment has no meaning. Why should a police officer obey the Amendment's command to secure a search warrant when it is easier to obtain evidence without one? As long as the courts close their eyes to police methods, the police will continue to collect evidence without warrants.

A third justification is the deterrent effect of the exclusionary rule. The assumption is made that what police want most is to secure convictions. If evidence seized illegally is excluded, resulting in the accused getting off, the police will no longer have an incentive to engage in unconstitutional practices. That is, if an officer knows that the evidence he obtains from an illegal search will be excluded from the trial, he is less likely to conduct illegal searches. As a practical matter, the officer's work will be for nothing, and the criminal defendant will go free in some cases. Thus, the police will take greater pains to secure proper search warrants rather than risk letting a guilty person go free.

A fourth justification for the exclusionary rule is that it is the only viable solution to the problem of abuses of constitutional rights. Unless the police are to be "above the law," they too must obey the Constitution. According to proponents, the exclusion of illegally obtained evidence is the only realistic solution. Other solutions, such as making the offending officer liable in a civil suit for violating the constitutional rights of the accused, are simply impractical. Suppose, for example, an officer conducts an illegal search that produces reliable evidence which is then used to secure the defendant's conviction. The defendant may sue the officer for violating his constitutional rights, but what jury is going to rule in favor of a convicted criminal under such circumstances? Suggestions that officers be fined or suspended for violating the rights of accused persons also raise problems. Would the police be afraid to make an arrest or search a car for fear of being fined or suspended later? Proponents argue that the exclusionary rule is the only effective way to deal with violations of constitutional rights.

Finally, proponents of the exclusionary rule argue that it is more important to keep the police in check than to worry about guilty persons being set free. This argument is similar to the "integrity of the judicial system" argument discussed earlier. Police must be made to understand that they too must obey the Constitution, the supreme law of the land. Those in authority must understand that the ends (convictions) do not always justify the means (illegal searches). As Justice Tom Clark wrote in *Mapp*, "The criminal goes free, if he must, but it is the law that sets him free."[33] If we are truly to be a nation of laws, not men, then we must make sure that those who enforce the law also obey the law.

The opponents of the exclusionary rule advance a number of valid counterarguments. First, they reject the "integrity of the judicial system" argument by pointing out that the purpose of a trial is to arrive at the truth. If illegally seized evidence is reliable, then what difference does it make how it was obtained? Only in extreme cases of police over-zealousness—cases that "shock the conscience"[34] of the community—should the exclusionary rule be employed.

A second objection is that if the purpose of the Fourth Amendment is to protect privacy, then the exclusionary rule is a totally inadequate solution. The person's privacy has already been violated, so how does excluding the otherwise reliable evidence further any Fourth Amendment values? The damage to privacy interests has been done, so what purpose is served by perhaps letting a factually guilty person go free? Even if the State could get a conviction without the illegally seized evidence, why take the chance?

A third objection questions the deterrent effect of the exclusionary rule. Suppose a police officer makes what he believes to be a legal search, and the search is later ruled invalid. How could the officer have been deterred in his conduct? He made a "good-faith" error in conducting the search in the first place, so how could he have been deterred in making a search he believed to be valid?

A fourth objection is that the exclusionary rule punishes the wrong people. It is society that is being punished by the enforcement of the exclusionary rule because it allows some factually guilty defendants to go free just because "the constable blunders." The offending officers are not punished (except that they lose their "bust"), and the criminal reaps a bonus by getting away with no punishment in some cases.

Finally, opponents of the rule argue that the exclusionary rule itself "breeds contempt for the law." This argument holds that when law-abiding citizens see criminals set free on "technicalities," they become contemptuous of the law. Instead of protecting law-abiding citizens, the law seems to protect the lawless. For these reasons and others, the exclusionary rule continues to be the single most controversial issue of criminal law.

In the remainder of this section we will focus on the instances of reasonable and unreasonable searches. We begin by asking, When is a search reasonable? Obviously, a search made pursuant to a valid search warrant falls within this category. The police officer goes before a judge or magistrate with sufficient evidence to establish probable cause, and the latter will decide if a search warrant is justified. This allows a neutral third party to independently decide whether the warrant should be issued. A second type of reasonable search is one that is made pursuant to a lawful arrest. The Supreme Court has recognized that searches made pursuant to lawful arrests are valid because of the need for the officer to uncover any weapons the suspect might have that could harm others or aid in his escape. In *Chimel v. California*,[35] however, the Court also made it clear that the search could only extend to the area within the immediate reach of the suspect. In *Chimel,* the police, while serving an arrest warrant, searched Chimel's entire house despite his objections. The Court ruled that since Chimel was already in custody, a warrantless search of the house was not "pursuant" to the arrest and therefore was unreasonable. The police should have secured a warrant and returned later to conduct the search.

A third category of reasonable searches are those in which permission to make the search is granted. This can lead to a number of problem situations. For example, what constitutes an "intelligent waiver" of one's constitutional rights? A police officer's *request,* such as, "Do you mind if I look in your trunk?" becomes a *command* to most people. When the teacher says to Johnny, "Will you please go to the blackboard?" no one in the class believes Johnny really has the right to refuse. Similarly, a polite request from a police officer takes on the air of an order one may not refuse. Is "permission" under such circumstances an intelligent waiver of constitutional rights?

Another problem concerns the question of who may give permission to police to conduct a search. In *Warden v. Hayden,* the "mere evidence" case, the Supreme Court ruled the search valid because Mrs. Hayden had given the police permission to enter her home (although one might question whether her waiver was an intelligent one). The general rule is that "The person giving the consent must have the capacity to consent."[36] The Supreme Court has ruled that if a person has authority over the area to be searched, that person's consent is valid.[37]

A fourth area of controversy is so-called stop-and-frisk searches, which by their nature are warrantless. The leading case in this category is *Terry v. Ohio.*[38] McFadden, a plainclothes police officer with 39 years' experience, observed Terry and two other men acting in a suspicious manner. The men repeatedly walked past a store window, peered in, then conferred with one another on a street corner. After observing the ritual for approximately 10 minutes, McFadden concluded that Terry and the others were "casing" the store for a robbery. McFadden approached the men, identified himself as a police officer, and patted them down. When he discovered a revolver in Terry's coat pocket, he arrested him for carrying a concealed weapon. Terry was convicted and appealed on grounds of an unreasonable search and seizure. The Supreme Court, aware of the potential abuse of stop-and-frisk searches by police, nevertheless ruled that Officer McFadden had sufficient probable cause to believe a crime was about to be committed and was therefore justified in conducting his limited "pat-down" search. The Supreme Court has recognized that probable cause must be more than "a hunch." In *Terry,* the Court ruled that "in justifying the particular intrusion the police officer must be able to point to specific and articulable facts, which taken together with rational inferences from those facts reasonably warrant the intrusion."[39] Thus, probable cause requires "specific and articulable facts" along with "rational inferences" before a warrantless search is valid.

Another category of search and seizure that has caused problems is the search of automobiles and other movable vehicles. It is obvious that, in requirements for search warrants, an automobile cannot be treated like a house or a building since an automobile can be moved before the warrant can be obtained. The Supreme Court first recognized this problem in *Carroll v. United States.*[40] Since *Carroll,* many of the search-and-seizure cases involving automobiles have concerned the questions of whether police had enough probable cause to stop and search particular automobiles,[41] searches pursuant to an arrest for traffic violations,[42] and inventory searches of automobiles that have been impounded.[43]

Two final areas of search and seizure are cases involving the "plain-view" doctrine and wiretaps. The plain-view doctrine holds that police may seize evidence in plain view without a search warrant if the police are where they legally have a right to be. For example, in *Harris v. United States,*[44] the police searched Harris's apartment pursuant to a valid *arrest* warrant. Harris was suspected of forgery, and the police were looking for two cancelled checks. In the course of the search they found fake draft cards, which they seized and used as evidence against Harris. The Court ruled that the search was made pursuant to a lawful arrest (overturned by *Chimel*) and that the draft cards were subject to seizure as contraband. The Court reasoned that "the police are not required to close their eyes and need not walk out and leave the article where they saw it. Any other principle might lead to an absurd result and at times perhaps even defeat the ends of justice."[45] The discovery of evidence in "plain view" often turns on whether or not the police officer is where he has a right to be, for "if the officer does become a trespasser . . . his action then amounts to an illegal search and seizure. He cannot use information so obtained to procure a warrant, nor can he seize the evidence without a warrant."[46]

Wiretapping illustrates how advances in technology can affect the application of the Fourth Amendment. Is a wiretap a "search" or "seizure" within the meaning of the Fourth Amendment? It is obvious that the Court cannot rely on the intent of the Framers in such cases since telephones did not exist when the Constitution was written. The Supreme Court confronted the issue in *Olmstead v. United States*,[47] in which it ruled that a wiretap was not a "search" because there was no physical invasion of Olmstead's residence. In *Goldman v. United States*,[48] authorities used a listening device in an adjacent office to hear Goldman's conversations through the walls. Relying on *Olmstead*, the Court ruled again that the search and seizure of Goldman's conversations was valid since no physical intrusion had occurred. In *Katz v. United States*,[49] however, the Supreme Court ruled that a wiretap on a public telephone booth did constitute an illegal search and seizure, thus overruling *Olmstead*. Today, wiretaps are permitted only with a court order upon a showing of probable cause.

Olmstead, *Goldman*, and *Katz* raise the question of the underlying purpose of the Fourth Amendment. If one assumes that the Amendment protects *property*, then the *Olmstead-Goldman* position is defensible. If, on the other hand, the purpose of the Amendment is to protect people's *privacy*, then the *Katz* position is preferred. As technology provides new ways to invade our privacy, the courts must be vigilant that law enforcement officers, in their eagerness to fight crime, do not adopt a "Big Brother" mentality. The question of privacy or property will no doubt be a recurring one in the future.

Right to Counsel.   Much of the background of the right to counsel was discussed in Chapter 6, so only a brief summary is needed here. Suffice it to say that the right to counsel was intended to guarantee the services of a lawyer for those accused who could afford to pay for one. In Chapter 6 we chronicled how the Supreme Court extended the privilege in *Powell v. Alabama, Gideon v. Wainwright,* and *Argersinger v. Hamlin.* As a result of these cases, no person must face a serious criminal offense without the presence of an attorney, either retained or court appointed.

Despite the fact that the right to counsel has been clearly established at trial, a more perplexing problem is *when* the accused has the right to counsel. An early federal case illustrates the problem of what can happen if the accused does not have access to an attorney in the early stages of the criminal justice process. Andrew Mallory was a young man of "limited intelligence" accused of raping a woman in a Washington, D.C., laundromat. Although Mallory was arrested early in the afternoon, he was detained and questioned by the police throughout the rest of the day. During the interrogation, Mallory confessed to the crime. The next day he was taken before a U.S. magistrate for arraignment, at which time he was informed of his right to remain silent and his right to an attorney. But it was too late for Andrew Mallory. Any advice an attorney could have given him was useless in light of his confession. Mallory was convicted of rape and sentenced to die for his crime. Attorneys for Mallory decided to appeal his case, however, on the grounds that police had delayed too long before bringing Mallory before the magistrate. To inform Mallory of his constitutional rights after his confession was a classic case of closing the barn door after the horse is gone. In *Mallory v. United States*,[50] the Supreme Court agreed. The Court noted that the magistrate was located in the same building where Mallory was being interrogated, and it would have been a simple task to bring him before the magistrate before intense questioning began. The Court considered the delay between Mallory's arrest and his arraignment unreasonable and overturned his conviction. In *Mallory*, the Supreme Court recognized that the exercise of constitutional rights, such as the right to counsel, can be critical long before the accused is brought to trial. Knowledge and understanding of one's constitutional rights are needed early in the process, especially in the case of someone like Mallory, who had a limited capacity to understand what was happening to him.

The Supreme Court continued to develop the question of when the accused has the right to counsel in the case of *Escobedo v. Illinois*.[51] Danny Escobedo was accused of murdering his brother-in-law. He was arrested, interrogated, and later released by the police even though he remained the prime suspect. When additional evidence implicating Escobedo turned up, he was arrested again. In the meantime, his family had retained a lawyer who went to the jailhouse to see Escobedo, but the police purposely kept Escobedo from seeing his lawyer. When Escobedo asked to see his lawyer, he was told that his lawyer did not want to see him. At the same time, Escobedo's lawyer was being told that he could not see his client until the police were finished interrogating him. Escobedo subsequently confessed, and his confession was used to convict him of murder. In overturning Escobedo's conviction, the Court stressed the importance of the "guiding hand of counsel"[52] noting that "The right to counsel would be hollow indeed if it began at a period when few confessions were obtained."[53] In other words, the advice of an attorney is needed most during the period between arrest and arraignment, when most confessions are made. The Court ruled that when the focus had shifted from a general inquiry into an unsolved crime to a particular suspect, that suspect must be informed of his right to remain silent. Otherwise, he has been denied the assistance of counsel guaranteed by the Sixth Amendment.[54]

In the controversial *Miranda v. Arizona*[55] decision, the Warren Court reaffirmed *Escobedo* and explicitly stated what police must do when making an arrest. The Court ruled that when a person is taken into custody or otherwise denied freedom of movement, the police must inform the accused of his constitutional rights before questioning. These rights include the right to remain silent, the right to an attorney either appointed or retained, and the right to know that anything he says may be used against him in court. The *Miranda* decision is perhaps the most controversial decision in criminal justice since the imposition of the exclusionary rule. The police argued that the decision would make it virtually impossible to gain confessions from criminals, and that because confessions are a major source of evidence, convictions would be more difficult to obtain. Studies have indicated that the worst fears of the police have not been realized.[56] The major reason that police still obtain confessions from accused persons is plea bargaining. Guilty persons are still willing to trade their confessions for a charge reduction or lighter sentence. Since confessions are seldom the only evidence the police have, criminal defendants prefer to plea bargain rather than take chances at trial. Despite its limited impact, *Miranda* remains controversial even 20 years after it was handed down and even though the predicted consequences never materialized.

The issues surrounding the right to counsel in *Miranda* have focused on when the *Miranda* warnings are required and what constitutes an intelligent waiver of one's rights. One of the first cases to decide when the *Miranda* warnings are required was *Mathis v. United States.*[57] While in prison for an unrelated offense, Mathis was "routinely" questioned by IRS agents about his 1960 and 1961 tax returns. The agents failed to give Mathis the *Miranda* warnings, and evidence elicited from Mathis was used to convict him of tax fraud. The Supreme Court ruled that because tax investigations can lead to criminal charges, the *Miranda* warnings are required.

Similarly, in *Orozco v. Texas,*[58] the Court ruled that suspects must be given the *Miranda* warnings when they are under arrest, even if the questioning is not in a "coercive environment." The police arrested Orozco at his boardinghouse and questioned him, without the *Miranda* warnings, while he sat on his bed. The Court ruled that Orozco had been deprived of his freedom of action in a significant way and therefore the warnings were required. In contrast to *Mathis* and *Orozco,* however, the Court ruled in *Beckwith v. United States*[59] that an interrogation by IRS agents in the home of the accused was not a custodial arrest requiring the specific *Miranda* warnings. It should be noted, however, that the

IRS agents did advise Beckwith of his right to remain silent and his right to an attorney.

In *Oregon v. Mathiason*,[60] the Court ruled that a confession by a person who voluntarily appears at police headquarters and who is not under arrest may be used even though the *Miranda* warnings were not given. Although the interrogation of Mathiason took place in a "coercive environment," the Court ruled that he was not denied his freedom of action in any significant way. Finally, in *Estelle v. Smith*,[61] the Court extended the *Miranda* requirements to include pretrial psychiatric examinations in which the psychiatrist is permitted to testify in the punishment stage of a capital case.

A second area of concern in right-to-counsel cases involves the intelligent waiver of constitutional rights after *Miranda* warnings have been given. Police may not rely on "trickery and deceit" nor do anything to overbear the defendant's will. For example, in *Brewer v. Williams*[62] (one of our case studies at the end of this chapter), police, after being warned not to question Williams, made statements designed to elicit incriminating information from him. Police, knowing of Williams's religious beliefs, talked of allowing the parents of his 10-year-old victim to give her a "Christian burial." The Supreme Court held that the "Christian burial" speech was psychologically calculated to coerce Williams into identifying the location of the girl's body, which he did. The *Brewer v. Williams* case and its aftermath will be examined at greater length at the end of this chapter.

In *North Carolina v. Butler*,[63] the Court again faced the issue of an intelligent waiver. Butler was arrested by the FBI on a North Carolina fugitive warrant. After agents determined that Butler had an eleventh-grade education, he was handed an FBI "Advice of Rights" card, which he read. Butler refused to sign the waiver at the bottom of the form but agreed to talk with agents, whereupon he made some incriminating statements. Butler neither requested counsel nor asked to terminate the questioning. The North Carolina Supreme Court ruled that Butler's statement could not be used as evidence without an explicit statement of waiver, but the Supreme Court reversed. The Court ruled that in agreeing to answer questions, Butler had implicitly waived his right to counsel and his protection against self-incrimination.

Two other cases merit mention. In *Rhode Island v. Innis*,[64] the Court faced a situation similar to that in *Brewer v. Williams*. Innis was arrested for the murder of a cab driver, but the murder weapon, a shotgun, was not found. After being given the *Miranda* warnings, Innis was driven to the police station. Enroute, one officer remarked about how it would be unfortunate if some child in the neighborhood discovered the weapon. Innis asked the police to return to the place where he was arrested. After being warned a third time of his rights, Innis told the police where they could find the murder weapon. Unlike *Brewer,* however, the Court ruled that the casual conversation of the officers did not constitute "express questioning" or its "functional equivalent" and ruled that Innis had intelligently waived his rights.

Finally, in *New York v. Quarles,*[65] the Court created a "public safety" exception to the *Miranda* rule. Police followed Quarles, a rape suspect, into a supermarket and arrested him. The victim had told police that Quarles was armed, but a search produced no weapon. When asked about the gun, Quarles replied, "The gun is over there." No *Miranda* warnings had been given. The Supreme Court ruled that the gun posed enough danger to public safety to warrant an exception to the *Miranda* rule.

The cases examined here involving the right to counsel indicate an erosion of the *Miranda* decision and illustrate the game, or contest, approach to criminal justice. The police, for their part, try to devise clever ways to elicit incriminating evidence from defendants without violating the letter (but not the spirit) of *Miranda.* Criminal defendants try to devise clever ways to show how police tricked or otherwise deceived them into offering incriminating evidence. But criminal justice should not be a game of "Trickery and Deceit" or "Catch Us If You Can." Yet, as these cases illustrate, that is what the process often becomes.

Self-incrimination. The privilege against self-incrimination was already well established at common law when the Bill of Rights was added to the Constitution. Under English law, individuals charged with crimes could not be compelled to testify against themselves at trial. The privilege reflects, in part, a reluctance to force individuals to provide the means of their own destruction. That is, we are opposed to forcing people to condemn themselves to prison or death. It also reflects our accusatory approach to law: The accused does not have to prove his innocence; the State must prove his guilt. Surely the accused cannot be expected to assist the State in making a case against him. Finally, the privilege reflects concern over the reliability of confessions, especially if any evidence of coercion is involved. Recall that in *Mallory v. United States,* the Supreme Court was concerned not only with the failure of the police to arraign Mallory, but also with Mallory's inability to make an intelligent confession because of his limited mental capacity. Of course, the Constitution does permit the accused to confess, but there must be an intelligent waiver of the right to remain silent.

Despite some valid arguments for protection against self-incrimination, the privilege is not without its critics. The major criticism centers around this argument: If the accused is innocent, why should he be afraid to take the stand in his own defense? If, the argument runs, the accused has nothing to hide, why should he be afraid to take the stand to deny his guilt or to explain away the State's evidence against him? The problem, of course, is that this argument shifts the burden of proof to the defendant. The defendant is told, in effect, that he must prove his innocence and should therefore be willing to take the stand in his own defense. This argument is valid, and some criminal defendants do take the stand in their own defense, but only voluntarily and only with the advice of counsel.

Until fairly recently, some states allowed a prosecutor to comment on a defendant's failure to take the stand even when state law protected the defendant's right to refuse to testify. In two early cases, *Twining v. New Jersey*[66] and *Adamson v. California*,[67] the Supreme Court ruled that the Constitution did not prohibit a state jury from drawing negative inferences from a defendant's failure to take the stand in his own defense. Nor is due process violated if a state judge calls the defendant's failure to testify to the attention of the jury, even though federal judges are not allowed to do so. In *Malloy v. Hogan*,[68] however, the Court overturned *Twining* and ruled that the same protections against self-incrimination apply to both state and federal prosecutions.

The privilege against self-incrimination is closely related to both the right to counsel and protection against unreasonable searches and seizures. After being placed under arrest, the accused is usually told of his right to remain silent and then informed of his right to have an attorney present during questioning. This is done so that the accused will not inadvertently admit something that incriminates him since, as we have seen, the right to the advice of counsel is useless if the accused has already made incriminating statements. Likewise, the privilege against self-incrimination is related to search-and-seizure issues. In *Boyd v. United States*,[69] for example, the police seized invoices that showed that Boyd had imported cases of plate glass without paying the duties on them. The Supreme Court overturned Boyd's conviction on both Fourth and Fifth Amendment grounds, saying, ". . . we have been unable to perceive that the seizure of a man's private books and papers to be used in evidence against him is substantially different from compelling him to be a witness against himself."[70] Although *Boyd* has been modified considerably since 1886,[71] private papers, such as diaries, cannot be used to incriminate the accused.

As we have seen with other constitutional rights of the accused, time and technology have forced the courts to reconsider and reinterpret the privilege against self-incrimination. Although it is clear that the accused cannot be forced to admit his guilt, does the privilege extend to nonverbal forms of communication? For example, in *Rochin v. California*,[72] the police saw Rochin swallow some capsules they believed to be morphine. They took Rochin to a hospital and ordered physicians to pump his stomach against his will. The contents did contain morphine, and Rochin was convicted of its possession, but the Supreme Court reversed. In addition to condemning the act as an unreasonable search and seizure, the Court considered the act tantamount to a coerced confession. Calling the stomach pumping a method "too close to the rack and the screw," the Court ruled that the actions of the police "shock the conscience." However, in *Breithaupt v. Abram*[73] and *Schmerber v. California*,[74] the Court allowed a blood test to be admitted as evidence of drunk driving. In *Breithaupt*, the accused was unconscious and the test was done under medical supervision. The Court contrasted the relatively painless blood test to the stomach-pumping procedure used in *Rochin*. In *Schmerber*, the Court ruled that a blood test could be required even over the objections of the accused. The Court stated:

> We hold that the privilege protects an accused only from being compelled to testify against himself, or otherwise provide the State with evidence of a testimonial or communicative nature, and that the withdrawal of blood and use of analysis in question in this case did not involve compulsion to these ends.[75]

The "testimonial and communicative nature" requirement has led the Court to permit the admission of a number of types of nonverbal incriminating evidence. The Court has ruled that the accused may be forced to give handwriting samples, fingerprints, voice identifications, and dental records. Although the Court has ruled that the accused must submit to a lineup, it has also ruled that the accused has the right to have counsel present at postindictment lineups to ensure that no irregularities occur.[76]

TWO CASE STUDIES IN CRIMINAL LAW

In the introduction to this chapter, we noted the controversial nature of both substantive and procedural criminal law. In this section we will examine two Supreme Court cases that illustrate that controversy. The first case, *Rummel v. Estelle*,[77] deals with a question of substantive law—specifically, when does the punishment fit the crime? The second case, *Brewer v. Williams*,[78] raises the difficult question of protecting the constitutional rights of a factually guilty person.

Rummel v. Estelle.[79]   Texas, like many other states, had a habitual-offender statute which imposed a mandatory life sentence on anyone who was convicted of three felonies. In addition to having been convicted, the defendant must also have actually served time in prison for the first two convictions. In 1964, William Rummel was convicted of fraudulent use of a credit card in the amount of $80 and was sentenced to three years in the state prison. In 1969, he was convicted of passing a forged check for $28.36, for which he received four years in prison. In 1973, Rummel was convicted of receiving $120.75 by false pretenses. The total value of all three of Rummel's crimes was less than $230. At Rummel's 1973 trial, the prosecutor chose to proceed under the Texas habitual-offender statute, and Rummel received a life sentence. Rummel challenged the constitutionality of the life sentence on the grounds that it "was so disproportionate to the crimes he committed as to constitute cruel and unusual punishment."[80] The district court rejected Rummel's claim of cruel and unusual punishment, but a panel of the Fifth U.S. Court of Appeals reversed the district court judge. The case was reheard *en banc,* and the full Court of Appeals reversed the panel; that is, it upheld the original judgment of the district court against Rummel's claim. The U.S. Supreme Court, in a 5–4 decision, also ruled against Rummel.

Justice William Rehnquist authored the Court's majority opinion. Rehnquist began by noting that Rummel was not challenging the Texas recidivist statute per se. Rummel challenged the act only as it applied to him. Nor did Rummel challenge the fact that he could constitutionally have received sentences totalling 25 years for his three crimes. Rummel challenged only the State's ability to impose a life sentence in his particular case. Rummel based his challenge both on *Weems v. United States,*[81] in which the Supreme Court reversed the conviction of a Philippine official imprisoned at hard labor for 12 years for the crime of falsifying public records, and on some of the Court's previous decisions in death-penalty cases.[82] The Court rejected both in ruling against Rummel.

Justice Rehnquist noted the uniqueness of the *Weems* case. In addition to the lengthy sentence, Weems was chained at the ankle and wrist and forced to do hard labor for the 12 years. When viewed in its totality—the minor crime of falsifying public records and the harsh sentence—the Court in 1910 found no difficulty in ruling that the sentence was disproportionate to the crime. In Rummel's case, because of the State's liberal "good time" policy, he could be eligible for parole in 12 years. The Court also refused to apply its rationale in death-penalty cases to Rummel's situation. Justice Rehnquist noted that the irrevocability of the death sentence gave the death penalty a uniqueness that did not apply to Rummel.

Having stripped Rummel of his precedents, Justice Rehnquist proceeded to explain why the Eighth Amendment was not offended in this case. First, exercising judicial deferrence, he noted that the length of prison sentences is a legislative prerogative and that the determination of appropriate punishments for various crimes is too subjective for courts to decide. If Rummel's crimes had totalled $5,000 instead of a mere $230, would the life sentence be fairer? That, Justice Rehnquist said, is for a legislature, not the courts, to decide. Second, Rehnquist rejected Rummel's argument that the life sentence was excessive because his crimes were nonviolent. The presence or absence of violence has nothing to do with society's interest in deterring crime. Pollution, for example, is nonviolent, but society may impose harsh penalties to deter it. Third, Justice Rehnquist noted that Rummel was *not* being punished just for receiving $120.75 under false pretenses. As a habitual offender, Rummel had shown an inability to conform to the norms of society. Fourth, the penalty imposed by Texas, though severe, is not grossly out of line with recidivist statutes in other states. Finally, the fact that Rummel would be eligible for parole after serving 12 years indicated the unlikelihood of his remaining in prison for the rest of his life. These factors led the majority to conclude that the life sentence did not constitute cruel and unusual punishment.

Justice Lewis Powell, joined by three other justices, wrote a dissenting opinion in *Rummel.* Justice Powell disagreed with the majority's analysis on a number of points. First, in the death penalty cases, the Court ruled that the death sentence is an excessive punishment for certain crimes, such as rape.[83] Powell saw no reason that the disproportionality analysis of death-penalty cases should not apply to noncapital cases since there is no basis for such a distinction in Eighth Amendment jurisprudence. Powell also believed that the Court's restriction of *Weems* to its unique facts was not warranted. The *Weems* Court emphasized the number of years Weems received for a minor offense as much as the conditions of hard labor imposed. Nor did Powell accept the notion that society's interest in deterring repeat offenders justified a mandatory life sentence for Rummel's crimes. Powell observed, "A statute that levied a mandatory life sentence for overtime parking might well deter vehicular lawlessness, but it would offend our felt sense of justice."[84] In other words, the fact that Rummel's sentence might meet a societal goal does not make it less offensive to the Eighth Amendment.

Powell attacked the majority's reasoning on another point: the seriousness of Rummel's crimes. It is hard to imagine crimes that pose less danger to the safety of society than Rummel's, Powell argued. Forged checks, misuse of credit cards, and receiving money under false pretenses are hardly on a par with rape and murder. Yet under Texas law, the maximum sentence on a rape conviction is 20 years and the minimum is two years. At the time, the same sentence applied to a person convicted of involuntary manslaughter. The only first-time offense subject to a mandatory life sentence is capital murder. Powell noted that even Texas admits that Rummel's third offense was not a serious crime since in 1980 the state reduced it to a misdemeanor.

Finally, Powell argued that the fact that Rummel might become eligible for parole after 12 years should not be a consideration. Prison inmates have no legal right to a parole. Powell noted that in 1979, Governor William Clements of Texas denied parole to 79 percent of the inmates recommended by the state's pardon and parole board.[85] Therefore, Powell argued, the question of the disproportionality of Rummel's sentence should be judged independently of any hypothetical chance of parole.

The *Rummel* case did not end the debate over the practice of imposing life sentences on habitual offenders. Just three years later, in *Solem v. Helm,*[86] the Court reviewed the imposition of a mandatory life sentence on a person convicted of seven felonies. Helm's offenses, like Rummel's, were nonviolent property crimes, with the last one being the writing of a $100 "no account" check. However, this time the Court reversed its previous position somewhat. This time, with Justice Powell writing for the majority, the Court ruled that the imposition of a life sentence with no chance of parole did violate the Eighth Amendment's prohibition against cruel and unusual punishment. Making many of the same arguments he used in *Rummel,* Justice Powell asserted that the Eighth Amendment does forbid excessive punishment in noncapital cases. Powell also argued that objective criteria could be developed to guide courts in determining whether a given penalty was excessive. These criteria include the gravity of the offense versus the harshness of the penalty, whether sentences imposed on others for more serious crimes are less harsh, and whether sentences imposed for the commission of the same crime in other jurisdictions are less harsh.[87] Applying the criteria to Helm's case, the majority concluded that the life sentence he received was excessive for the crimes he had committed. In addition, Powell emphasized that in *Rummel* the prisoner had a possibility of parole after 12 years, whereas in *Helm* the sentence contained no chance of parole unless the governor commuted the sentence, a possibility the Court considered unlikely.

The *Rummel* and *Helm* cases raise some of the questions about the nature of substantive criminal law discussed earlier in the chapter. Individuals disagree over the appropriate punishment for habitual offenders. They also disagree, as did the justices of the Supreme Court, over what constitutes excessive or cruel and unusual punishment. It is because reasonable people disagree over the substance of criminal law that one must understand the political nature of the criminal justice system and, as discussed in Chapter 6, the lack of finality of constitutional questions. Suffice it to say that the debate over life sentences for habitual offenders is far from over.

Brewer v. Williams.   On Christmas Eve in 1968, a 10-year-old girl named Pamela Powers disappeared while attending a wrestling match at a Des Moines, Iowa, YMCA. A teenager opened the door of the YMCA for Williams, who was carrying a large bundle wrapped in a blanket. When the teenager opened Williams's car door, he noticed two "white and skinny legs" protruding from the bundle. Williams immediately became a suspect in the abduction of Pamela Powers. Later, Williams's car was discovered in Davenport, 160 miles east of Des Moines. A warrant was issued for Williams's arrest.

On December 26, a Des Moines lawyer named Henry McKnight informed police that he had been contacted by Williams from Davenport and that he had advised Williams to turn himself in to the Davenport police, which Williams did. Upon his arrest, Williams was given the *Miranda* warnings. In the presence of the Des Moines chief of police and a police detective named Leaming, McKnight informed Williams over the telephone that two Des Moines detectives were coming to Davenport to return him to Des Moines. McKnight also told Williams that he was not to discuss Pamela Powers with the detectives during the return trip. Williams was arraigned in Davenport and again given the *Miranda* warnings. Kelly, a Davenport attorney, also advised Williams not to say anything until he spoke with McKnight in Des Moines. When Detective Leaming arrived, he again gave Williams the *Miranda* warnings. At one point, Kelly asked Leaming for permission to accompany Williams back to Des Moines but was informed that the police department had a "no passengers" rule.

On the trip back to Des Moines, Detective Leaming made what was later termed "the Christian burial speech." Under the guise of giving Williams "something to think about," Detective Leaming pointed out that the weather was becoming worse and that snow was predicted before the day was over. Leaming pointed out that if it snowed, it might be impossible for anyone, even Williams, to find Pamela's body and that her parents were at least entitled to give their daughter a Christian burial. Williams asked if the police had found the girl's shoes, and when Leaming replied that he was unsure, Williams directed them to a service station where he claimed to have left them. However, a search failed to turn up the shoes. Later Williams inquired about the blanket and directed the detectives to a rest area, but the blanket was not found. Finally, Williams led the detectives to the body of Pamela Powers. Williams was later indicted for first-degree murder, and his motion to suppress all evidence resulting from his statements to Leaming was denied. The trial judge ruled that Williams had waived his right to counsel and his protection against self-incrimination.

The Supreme Court, in a bitterly divided vote, ruled that Williams had not waived his right to counsel and that Detective Leaming's "Christian burial speech" was a form of interrogation forbidden by the Sixth Amendment without the presence of counsel. Justice Potter Stewart, writing for the majority, found that Detective Leaming deliberately set out to elicit incriminatory information from Williams. Leaming, after reading Williams the *Miranda* warnings, said to Williams, "We'll be visiting between here and Des Moines."[88] Although Leaming had been warned not to interrogate Williams, the "Christian burial speech" was designed to appeal to Williams's deep religious beliefs. Moreover, at Williams's trial, Leaming admitted that that was his purpose. In response to a question, Leaming replied, "I was sure hoping to find out where that little girl was, yes, sir."[89] More important, the Court ruled, the State bears the burden of proving that a defendant has waived his right to counsel. Williams repeatedly told police that he would tell everything when they reached Des Moines. The Court interpreted that to mean that Williams did not intend to waive his right to counsel until he had a chance to speak with his lawyer, McKnight, in Des Moines. Finally, the fact that Williams had called McKnight in Des Moines and had secured Kelly's services in Davenport provided further proof of his reliance on the assistance of counsel. In light of these factors, Justice Stewart found that the State had failed to meet the burden of proving that Williams had intelligently waived his right to counsel.

In a concurring opinion, Justice Thurgood Marshall shed additional light on Leaming's actions. If, as indicated, Williams promised to tell the whole story back in Des Moines, why didn't the police just wait? If Williams were allowed to tell McKnight the location of the body, McKnight could then have told the police and Williams would not have been forced to incriminate himself directly—that is, by "directly demonstrating his knowledge of the body's location."[90] If finding Pamela Powers's body were truly the main objective, "this scenario would accomplish all that Leaming sought from his investigation except that it would not produce incriminating statements or actions from Williams."[91] In other words, eliciting incriminating statements from Williams, and not finding Pamela's body, was Leaming's real objective. Justice Marshall defended the majority's decision by noting, "The heinous nature of the crime is no excuse, as the dissenters would have it, for condoning knowing and intentional police transgression of the constitutional rights of a defendant."[92] Justice Marshall concluded his opinion by quoting Justice Louis Brandeis's dissent in *Olmstead v. United States:*

> In a government of laws, existence of the government will be imperilled if it fails to observe the law scrupulously. Our Government is the potent, the omnipresent teacher. For good or for ill, it teaches the whole people by example. Crime is contagious. If the Government becomes a lawbreaker, it breeds contempt for law; it invites every man to become a law unto himself; it invites anarchy. To declare that in the administration of the criminal law the end justifies the means—to declare that the Government may commit crimes in order to secure the conviction of a private criminal— would bring terrible retribution. Against that pernicious doctrine this Court should resolutely set its face.[93]

Lawyers like to say that "hard cases make bad law"; *Brewer v. Williams* is undoubtedly a hard case, but whether it made bad law depends on one's perspective. The dissenters in *Williams* saw Leaming's actions as "good police work," while the majority condemned them. There can be no doubt that Williams killed Pamela Powers, but it is important to remember that the Supreme Court does not deal with questions of guilt or innocence per se. The Court is interested in due process of law and in making sure that government obeys its own laws. Although that point may be difficult to understand and to accept, especially when an innocent little girl has been brutally murdered, it may be, to paraphrase Justice Oliver Wendell Holmes, Jr., that due process of law is the price we pay for civilization.

If the reader is still troubled by the decision in *Williams,* there is more to the story. The Supreme Court's decision did not mean that Williams was set free, but only that the State must retry him without using the incriminating evidence secured by Leaming's unlawful interrogation. In 1977, Williams was again tried for first-degree murder and was again found guilty. The prosecution introduced evidence concerning the condition of Pamela Powers's body when it was found, and the defense sought to suppress it as the "fruit" of Leaming's illegal interrogation. The trial court ruled that searchers would have come upon the body eventually even without Williams's help and that it would have been essentially in the same condition. Therefore, the trial judge allowed the evidence. Williams again appealed his case to the Supreme Court, but in *Nix v. Williams,*[94] the Court ruled against him and upheld his conviction and life sentence.

These two case studies, *Rummel v. Estelle* and *Brewer v. Williams,* were included in this chapter to illustrate aspects of substantive and procedural criminal law. In a real sense, justice prevailed in both cases. Rummel was paroled just eight months after his appeal was denied by the Supreme Court,[95] and Williams was sentenced to life in prison. However, the questions raised by the two cases are fundamental ones that may never be answered because they deal with our sense of justice and fairness. The debate over these issues will continue, for, as Yogi Berra aptly observed, "It ain't over till it's over."

CONCLUSION

As noted in this chapter's introduction, no topic in law is as controversial as criminal law. There is perhaps nothing that tells as much about a society as the way it treats those who are accused of crime. In a sense, then, crime is not only a social problem but a political one as well. In this chapter we have discussed both substantive and procedural criminal law. Substantive criminal law concerns what constitutes criminal behavior, what the elements of a crime are, and what punishment is appropriate for a given criminal act. Procedural criminal law concerns the "rules of the game" by which government must abide before it can deprive one of its citizens of life, liberty, or property. Both topics raise difficult questions that have elusive answers. Perhaps in the final analysis we must determine the answers individually. The one certainty is that the questions will not go away, and it is our hope that we have added to the reader's understanding of an enormously complex area of law.

NOTES

[1] Chapter 1.

[2] Thomas J. Gardner, *Criminal Law: Principles and Cases,* 3rd ed. (St. Paul, Minn.: West Publishing Company, 1985), p. 140.

[3] *Champion v. Ames,* 188 U.S. 321 (1903) quoted in Gerald Gunther, *Constitutional Law: Cases and Materials,* 10th ed. (Mineola, N.Y.: Foundation Press, 1980), p. 130.

[4] Henry C. Black, *Black's Law Dictionary,* 4th ed. (St. Paul, Minnesota: West Publishing Company, 1968), p. 55.

[5] Ibid., p. 1481.

[6] David W. Neubauer, *America's Courts and the Criminal Justice System,* 2nd ed. (Monterey, Calif.: Brooks/Cole, 1984), p. 64.

[7] Gerald Gunther, *Constitutional Law,* 11th ed. (Mineola, N.Y.: Foundation Press, 1985), p. 1157.

[8] Gardner, p. 9.

[9] Ibid.

[10] *Robinson v. California,* 370 U.S. 660 (1962).

[11] *Powell v. Texas,* 392 U.S. 514 (1968).

[12] Black, p. 1137.

[13] David Eliot Brody, *The American Legal System: Concepts and Principles* (Lexington, Mass.: Heath, 1978), p. 290.

[14] Gardner, p. 39.

[15] Justin Miller, *Handbook of Criminal Law* (St. Paul, Minn.: West Publishing Company, 1934), p. 228.

[16] Ibid.

[17] Ibid., p. 229.

[18] Ibid., pp. 229–230.

[19] Jesse R. Pistole, *Criminal Law for Peace Officers* (Reston, Va.: Reston, 1976), p. 148.

[20] Ibid., p. 145.

[21] Miller, p. 237.

[22] Pistole, pp. 144–145; Miller, pp. 226–227.

[23] Miller, p. 239.

[24] Pistole, p. 144.

[25] Miller, p. 242.

[26] U.S. Constitution, Amendment IV.

27 *Warden v. Hayden*, 387 U.S. 294 (1967).

28 *Warden v. Hayden* quoted in Lloyd L. Weinreb, *Leading Constitutional Cases on Criminal Law*, (Mineola, N.Y.: Foundation Press, 1981), p. 187.

29 *Weeks v. United States*, 232 U.S. 383 (1914).

30 Quoted in Robert F. Cushman, *Cases in Constitutional Law*, 6th ed., (Englewood Cliffs, N.J.: Prentice-Hall, 1984), p. 321.

31 *Mapp v. Ohio*, 367 U.S. 643 (1961).

32 *Olmstead v. United States*, 277 U.S. 438 (1928), at 485 (Brandeis, J., dissenting).

33 *Mapp v. Ohio* quoted in Cushman, 6th ed., p. 326.

34 *Rochin v. California*, 342 U.S. 165 (1952).

35 *Chimel v. California*, 395 U.S. 752 (1969).

36 John C. Klotter and Jacqueline R. Kanovitz, *Constitutional Law for Police*, 3rd ed. (Cincinnati: Anderson Publishing Company, 1977), p. 213.

37 Ibid.

38 *Terry v. Ohio*, 392 U.S. 1 (1968).

39 *Terry v. Ohio* quoted in Weinreb, p. 330.

40 *Carroll v. United States*, 267 U.S. 132 (1925).

41 *Chambers v. Maroney*, 399 U.S. 42 (1970).

42 *United States v. Robinson*, 414 U.S. 218 (1973).

43 *South Dakota v. Opperman*, 428 U.S. 364 (1976); *Cady v. Dombrowski*, 413 U.S. 433 (1973).

44 *Harris v. United States*, 331 U.S. 145 (1947).

45 Klotter and Kanovitz, p. 226.

46 Ibid., p. 227.

47 *Olmstead v. United States*, 277 U.S. 438 (1928).

48 *Goldman v. United States*, 316 U.S. 129 (1942).

49 *Katz v. United States*, 389 U.S. 347 (1967).

50 *Mallory v. United States*, 354 U.S. 449 (1957).

51 *Escobedo v. Illinois*, 378 U.S. 478 (1964).

52 *Escobedo v. Illinois* quoted in Harold W. Chase and Craig R. Ducat, *Constitutional Interpretation: Cases, Essays, Materials*, 2nd ed. (St. Paul, Minn.: West Publishing Company, 1979), p. 945.

53 Ibid.

54 Ibid., pp. 945–946.

55 *Miranda v. Arizona*, 384 U.S. 436 (1966).

56 See Richard H. Seeburger and R. Stanton Wettick, Jr., "*Miranda* in Pittsburgh: A Statistical Study," *University of Pittsburgh Law Review*, Vol. 29 (Oct. 1967), pp. 1–26.

57 *Mathis v. United States*, 391 U.S. 1 (1968).

58 *Orozco v. Texas*, 394 U.S. 324 (1969).

59 *Beckwith v. United States*, 425 U.S. 341 (1976).

60 *Oregon v. Mathiason*, 429 U.S. 492 (1977).

61 *Estelle v. Smith*, 451 U.S. 454 (1981).

62 *Brewer v. Williams*, 430 U.S. 387 (1977).

63 *North Carolina v. Butler*, 441 U.S. 369 (1979).

64 *Rhode Island v. Innis*, 446 U.S. 291 (1980).

65 *New York v. Quarles*, 467 U.S. 649 (1984).

66 *Twining v. New Jersey*, 211 U.S. 78 (1908).

67 *Adamson v. California*, 332 U.S. 46 (1947).

68 *Malloy v. Hogan*, 378 U.S. 1 (1964).

[69] *Boyd v. United States,* 116 U.S. 616 (1886).

[70] M. Glenn Abernathy, *Civil Liberties Under the Constitution,* 2nd ed. (New York: Dodd, Mead, 1972), p. 112.

[71] See *Matter of Grand Jury Empanelled,* 597 F. 2d 851 (3rd. Cir., 1979) and *United States v. Payner,* 447 U.S. 727 (1980).

[72] *Rochin v. California,* 342 U.S. 165 (1952).

[73] *Breithaupt v. Abram,* 352 U.S. 432 (1957).

[74] *Schmerber v. California,* 384 U.S. 757 (1966).

[75] *Klotter and Kanovitz,* p. 353.

[76] *United States v. Wade,* 388 U.S. 218 (1967).

[77] *Rummel v. Estelle,* 445 U.S. 263 (1980).

[78] *Brewer v. Williams,* 430 U.S. 387 (1977).

[79] Unless otherwise noted, all facts pertaining to the case are taken from the Supreme Court's written opinions.

[80] *Rummel,* at 267.

[81] *Weems v. United States,* 217 U.S. 349 (1910).

[82] See *Furman v. Georgia,* 408 U.S. 238 (1972); *Gregg v. Georgia,* 428 U.S. 153 (1976); and *Coker v. Georgia,* 433 U.S. 584 (1977).

[83] *Coker v. Georgia,* 433 U.S. 584 (1977).

[84] *Rummel,* at 288.

[85] Ibid., at 294.

[86] *Solem v. Helm,* 463 U.S. 277 (1983).

[87] Ibid., at 292.

[88] *Brewer,* at 391.

[89] Ibid., at 399.

[90] *Brewer v. Williams,* 430 U.S. 387 (1977), at 408 (Marshall, J., concurring).

[91] Ibid.

[92] Ibid.

[93] *Olmstead v. United States,* 277 U.S. 438 (1928), at 485.

[94] *Nix v. Williams,* 104 S.Ct. 2501 (1984).

[95] *Solem,* footnote 25 at 297.

8

Administrative Law

The twentieth century has seen a tremendous growth in the number and power of bureaucratic organizations in the United States. Despite the attempts of the Reagan Administration to deregulate the U.S. economy and to shift governmental power from the national government to the states, bureaucracies continue to flourish, seemingly immune from the forces that would weaken them. For better or worse, bureaucratic government is a political and legal fact of life. The growth of administrative government can be attributed primarily to two of its strongest features: expertise and efficiency.

As the U.S. economy became more complex, there developed a greater need for expertise in the management of our economic system. The victims of the abuse of unchecked economic power by the railroads and other monopolies turned to government for relief. The first federal regulatory agency, the Interstate Commerce Commission (ICC), was created by Congress in 1887 to regulate railroads and to protect farmers from unjust rates and other unfair practices. Similarly, when the labor movement became politically strong enough, workers demanded some form of government protection for the rights of workers. As a result, the National Labor Relations Board (NLRB) was created to regulate labor relations and to prevent such practices as blacklisting, yellow-dog contracts, lockouts, and union-busting. The Great Depression taught us how damaging the consequences of an unregulated economy can be.

The realization developed that government must guarantee the existence of the free-enterprise system by regulating banks and the stock market to prevent the recurrence of conditions that led to the Depression. In each of these areas of economic activity—monopolies, labor relations, banking, and stocks—the issues had become so complex that experts were needed to regulate them effectively. These activities, as well as many others, require public administrators with sufficient expertise to handle the myriad of problems associated with each. Thus, Congress responded to the demands for more government regulation by establishing agencies staffed by experts who were better qualified to deal with the problems of a modern industrial society. Administrative expertise soon became the justification for leaving major policy decisions to those most familiar with the problems—the administrators themselves.

The need for administrative expertise was paramount due to another aspect of our society. As Lief Carter has noted, "We live surrounded by very dangerous things—elevators, cars, airplanes, industrial wastes and chemical products, and recombinant DNA."[1] As technology provided us with new products and inventions, it also provided new ways to injure and kill people. People understandably wanted guarantees that airplanes and elevators were safe to use. The private sector, concerned more with profits than with safety, could not be trusted to take the necessary steps to ensure safety. Hence, people again turned to government to guarantee the safety of dangerous products through regulation. Similarly, people wanted guarantees that their food was pure, their prescription drugs safe, their workplaces safe, and their environment clean. Once again government responded to these demands by calling upon public administrators who possessed the expertise to handle the problems of our modern society. In short, then, abuses and changes in our economy and technology led to increased demands for government action, which in turn resulted in the growth of administrative government based upon expertise.

A second feature of administrative government that has contributed to its growth is its efficiency. In a sense, efficiency is related to expertise because expertise increases a government agency's efficiency. However, efficiency has another dimension. Because of the growth of the welfare system in the United States, the government receives hundreds of thousands of applications for Social Security benefits, veterans' benefits, food stamps, Aid to Families with Dependent Children (AFDC) benefits, and workers' compensation claims each day. In addition, the government issues licenses, ranging from liquor licenses at the state level to licenses for nuclear power reactors at the national level. Each year, thousands of students apply for student loans from state-supported colleges and universities. Without highly trained personnel to process these claims and applications, the system would quickly break down. Thus, a bureaucracy must be created to handle the large numbers of applications as expertly and efficiently as possible.

What do the need for expertise and efficiency have to do with administrative law? One often hears of Mussolini's Italy that "at least the trains ran on time." This comment is normally used to illustrate a political system that has sacrificed other values such as freedom, justice, and human dignity for efficiency. While administrative expertise and efficiency are important, we must be careful that they do not outweigh other cherished values such as justice and fundamental fairness. Anglo-American law tends to view justice and fairness in terms of what is called "due process of law." Our Constitution guarantees that "no person shall be denied life, liberty, or property without due process of law."[2] But problems arise, as they often do, with constitutional guarantees. What is a property right? Does a person have a "right" to public employment? Food stamps? Welfare? How much "process" is "due"? How many rights is a person entitled to? What kind of hearing is required before welfare benefits can be terminated? These and other issues are questions of administrative law. Administrative law concerns itself with the prevention of arbitrary and capricious action at the hands of public administrators. It is concerned with the abuse of official power and the overstepping of official authority. It is also concerned with the rights of citizens in a modern welfare state. In the constitutional language of checks and balances, administrative law deals with how the political system checks the exercise of discretion by public administrators and balances the rights of citizens with the rights of government. Without an understanding of this fundamental aspect of administrative law, we may find ourselves in a bureaucratic state in which the trains run on time, but in which there is little emphasis on human dignity or fundamental fairness.

In this chapter we will examine several facets of administrative law. Specifically, we will examine the legal source of administrative law, some procedural aspects of administrative law, and the role of judicial review. Finally, we will take a closer look at one substantive area of administrative law: public employment. We begin with the legal source of administrative authority.

DELEGATION THEORY

As previously noted, bureaucratic growth has occurred because of the need for expertise and efficiency in handling the problems posed by an increasingly complex economic system, new technology, and the advent of the modern welfare state. Throughout most of American history, the federal bureaucracy was small for a very simple reason: The federal government did not do very much. The New Deal period, as we have seen, sparked increased demands for positive government action in the management of the economy. This resulted in public pressure to create agencies for the regulation of everything from nuclear energy to the safety of the workplace. In so doing, Congress has created what is often termed the "fourth branch of government." The influence of bureaucratic government has become so pervasive that virtually no aspect of the average American's life is unaffected. In order to understand the role of the bureaucracy in our political system, we must first have an understanding of what is known as *delegation theory.*

Under the American Constitution, all sovereignty ultimately resides in the people. In drafting and ratifying the Constitution, the people of the United States have collectively vested their sovereignty in the hands of their government. In so doing, however, the American people created three distinct branches of the national government—legislative, executive, and judicial—allocating to each certain powers presumably to be exclusively exercised by each. This is known as the doctrine of separation of powers.

It was the decision of the people to vest the Congress with the lawmaking power. The people, through the Constitution, delegated to the Congress the power to make the laws of the nation on their behalf. Congress thus became the agent of the people, exercising only the powers that the people thought proper to give it. At common law there is a maxim, *Delegatus non protest delegare*—"a delegate cannot delegate." What this means in terms of constitutional law is that Congress may not redelegate the powers that have been delegated to it by the people. There are some very good reasons for adhering to this doctrine. Suppose Congress wished to relieve itself of the burden of deciding when a state of war exists between the United States and another nation. Could the Congress enact legislation authorizing the president to declare war? Certainly not, since such an act would be a clear violation of the Constitution. If the people had wanted the president to be the one to decide whether or not to go to war, they would have given the president that power in the Constitution. Instead, the people chose to let Congress make the decisions concerning war and peace. To allow such a law to stand would undermine the doctrine of separation of powers since, theoretically, Congress could transfer all of its power to the president, thus achieving a result that the people sought to avoid—the concentration of governmental power in the hands of a single individual.

Despite the theory that Congress may not redelegate powers delegated to it under the Constitution, the reality of the situation is that Congress is simply incapable of making the countless governmental decisions that must be made on a daily basis. Consequently, Congress has developed the practice of authorizing administrative agencies and executive officials to act on its behalf. Such authorization consists of allowing administrative agencies to "fill in the details" of a general law. Congress will enact legislation setting forth its policy goals in very broad language and allow an administrative agency to deal with specifics. For example, Congress has authorized the Federal Communications Commission (FCC) to regulate the broadcasting industry "in the public interest." The FCC, staffed by professionals familiar with the workings of the broadcasting industry, makes rules governing the licensing of stations as well as numerous other aspects of the industry. Acting as the agent of Congress, the FCC makes rules and regulations that are just as binding on broadcasters as if Congress itself had enacted them. Realistically, then, Congress must either delegate its lawmaking authority to administrative agencies or abandon altogether any attempt to regulate highly complex and technical industries.

If delegation is a political reality, how does our legal system get around the constitutional prohibition against delegation? It does so by simply maintaining the legal fiction that delegation does not occur. In modern constitutional law, the myth of nondelegation is circumvented by the assertion that the Constitution forbids only "excessive delegation." The Supreme Court has ruled that although some delegation is desirable and permissible under the Constitution, there is a line which may not be crossed in delegating power to administrative agencies. Once the line is crossed, delegation is termed "excessive," in violation of the constitutional doctrine of separation of powers. Unfortunately, the line to be crossed is not always a bright one, and Congress can never be sure when it has crossed it.

The Supreme Court, in determining issues of excessive delegation, decides when the line has been crossed on a case-by-case basis. In the 1930s, for example, the Supreme Court ruled in a series of cases[3] that Congress had crossed the line in delegating excessive legislative authority to either the president or his subordinates. In still other cases, the Court has upheld very broad delegations of legislative power to the very same individuals. In the final analysis, the Court's approach to excessive delegation is similar to that of Justice Potter Stewart's view of obscenity— that is, the Court "knows it [excessive delegation] when it sees it."

In the performance of its duties as an agent of Congress, an administrative agency is primarily bound by two legal authorities. First, administrative agencies are subject to the same constitutional restraints as the general government. That is, anything the Congress or the president are forbidden to do, an administrative agency is also forbidden to do. Just as the Congress may not force people to attend church, neither may a government welfare agency require church attendance as a condition for receiving welfare. Similarly, if the national government is forbidden to deny any person of "life, liberty, or property without due process of law," neither may a government agency deny due process. As we will learn later, much controversy in administrative law centers around how much process is due.

A second constraint on administrative agencies is their authorization statute, which is the law that creates and empowers an administrative agency. Although some state administrative agencies are provided for in their state's constitution, federal administrative agencies are the creations of Congress. It is Congress that determines the structure, personnel, and powers of all administrative agencies and executive departments of the federal government. Consequently, an administrative agency may exercise only those powers given to it by Congress. When an agency attempts to exercise powers beyond its statutory authorization, it is said to be acting **ultra vires.** If an agency is allegedly acting *ultra vires,* those wishing to challenge the agency's action may seek judicial review. The court will be asked to decide whether the agency is acting within the limits of its legislative authority. The legislative authority is often vague, resulting in a judicial interpretation which attempts to ascertain the "intent of Congress." Should a court wrongly interpret the intent of Congress, the lawmakers can simply amend the authorization statute in such a way as to clarify their intentions. Ultimately, then, Congress possesses the authority to curb *ultra vires* actions of administrative agencies and incorrect judicial interpretations of congressional intent.

Delegation of power to administrative agencies takes three forms. As we have already noted, Congress may authorize an agency to promulgate rules and regulations on behalf of Congress by filling in the details of legislation. This is called **rule-making.** Second, Congress may authorize the employees of the agency to enforce the rules made by the agency. For example, Federal Aviation Administration (FAA) inspectors may make periodic safety checks to ensure that FAA safety regulations are being obeyed by the airlines. This is referred to as **rule enforcement.** Finally, disputes over the promulgation or enforcement of the agency's rules may necessitate **adjudication.** Adjudication may occur, for example, if an airline believes that it has been wrongly fined for violating FAA regulations. Each of the three types of delegation bring into play questions of administrative law. Therefore, let us examine each type separately to see just how each shapes administrative law.

Rule-Making.   Modern administrative law accepts the practice of allowing Congress to delegate its rule-making authority in general and sweeping terms. The first regulatory agency, the Interstate Commerce Commission (ICC), was authorized to set "just and reasonable rates" for railroads, and the definition of "just and reasonable" was left to the ICC itself. Similarly, other agencies are allowed broad delegations of authority. The FCC may issue licenses to broadcasters if doing so is "in the public interest." The Occupational Safety and Health Administration (OSHA) may adopt rules that are "reasonably necessary to provide safe and healthful employment and places of employment." Finally, the Consumer Product Safety Commission (CPSC) may make rules "reasonably necessary to prevent or reduce risk of injury" to consumers. Literally thousands of rules are promulgated each year by the myriad of administrative agencies. In fact, the number of rules passed by administrative agencies each year far surpasses the number of laws enacted by Congress. As already noted, the rules thus promulgated are just as binding on citizens as if they had been passed by Congress itself.

Administrative law develops in the realm of rule-making in primarily two ways. First, reviewing courts must ascertain whether the agency has the authority to promulgate the rule in question. That is, was the agency acting *ultra vires* by promulgating a rule that it had no authority to issue? Recall our discussion of *Bob Jones University v. United States*[4] in Chapter 1. Bob Jones University argued that the IRS had no authority to promulgate Revenue Ruling 71–477 without specific authorization from Congress. Although the Supreme Court ruled that 71–477 was valid, *Bob Jones University* illustrates how the authority to issue a rule can be the basis for challenging that rule.

The second way in which administrative law develops in regard to rule-making centers around the procedures used to promulgate the rule. The question here is, Did the agency follow the statute's procedures for enacting administrative rules? The rules of administrative procedure require (1) that proposed rules be published in advance of their consideration, (2) that interested and affected parties be allowed to comment either orally or in writing on the proposed rule, and (3) that any decision on the rule be based on the findings of "the whole record." These procedural requirements seek to prevent agencies from arbitrarily passing rules without giving opponents of the rules a fair opportunity to be heard. There is a certain "process" which is "due," and it is for the courts to determine whether the procedural rules were followed. It is not only important that the rules themselves be fair, but also that the rules be enacted in a fair manner.

Rule Enforcement.   A second way in which administrative agencies exercise authority delegated by Congress is through rule enforcement. Once an administrative agency has promulgated rules that deal with the substantive area within the agency's jurisdiction (for example, aviation, food and drugs, broadcasting), the agency may promulgate rules for the enforcement of its substantive rules. For example, OSHA has established regulations designed to ensure the safety of the workplace. OSHA has also established rules of procedures governing the inspection of factories and other workplaces to ensure compliance with its regulations. Failure to comply with OSHA regulations can result in civil penalties for the company involved. Thus, the agency responsible for issuing the original regulations is also responsible for the enforcement of those regulations. The procedures used in the enforcement of agency regulations are concerns of administrative law. As we have noted in relation to rule-making, procedures employed in rule enforcement must be within the agency's power to enact; otherwise the agency is proceeding *ultra vires.* In addition, the agency's procedures may not violate the Constitution.

Administrative enforcement may take a variety of forms.[5] Some regulatory agencies require their regulatees to keep records for inspection. The FAA, for example, requires airlines to keep maintenance records of their airplanes. The Equal Employment Opportunity Commission (EEOC) requires certain industries to keep employment records for the enforcement of job discrimination laws. Finally, the IRS requires individuals to keep records of income. Physical inspections constitute another type of administrative enforcement. As previously noted, OSHA inspectors may conduct physical inspections for safety violations, and the Mine Safety and Health Administration (MSHA) inspects mines to ensure safety. At the local level, public health officials may inspect dwellings for potential health hazards, fire inspectors may inspect for fire hazards, and welfare workers may investigate the home environment of welfare recipients. Finally, even such individuals as airline passengers are required to submit to X-ray and metal detector searches.

Rule enforcement by administrative agencies tends to raise the same kinds of constitutional questions common to other fields of law enforcement. In terms of mandatory record keeping, the question of self-incrimination can be raised. That is, does a law that requires a person or company to keep certain records allow them to be used as evidence in an administrative procedure? Suppose, for example, that an airline's maintenance record revealed that the airline was in violation of FAA regulations. Can the maintenance records be used to assess a fine against the airline? Suppose the IRS required persons engaged in illegal gambling to report the earnings from their illegal occupation. Would such persons, by paying the tax, be incriminating themselves by admitting their participation in an illegal activity?

The Supreme Court has ruled that administrative agencies may require record keeping under certain conditions. First, the records must be "of a kind customarily kept." Second, the records must be reasonably related to a public concern. Third, the records must pertain to a noncriminal area of activity. Thus, in the case of the airlines, because maintenance records are routinely kept, air safety is a public concern, and the records pertain to a noncriminal activity, the airline's maintenance records may be used to uncover violations of FAA regulations.[6] In the case of the gambler, however, the Supreme Court ruled in

Marchetti v. United States[7] that the IRS requirement violates the Fifth Amendment's prohibition against mandatory self-incrimination. Marchetti was being forced to choose between reporting the gambling income, thereby subjecting himself to prosecution for state gambling violations, or not reporting the income, thereby subjecting himself to charges of federal income tax evasion. The Constitution, the Court ruled, forbids forcing a person to make such a Draconian choice.

The Fourth Amendment's prohibition against unreasonable searches and seizures is another area of special relevance to administrative enforcement. In regular law enforcement, searches require a search warrant issued by a magistrate upon probable cause. The search warrant must describe the places to be searched and the persons or things to be seized. Not all searches require search warrants, however. The Supreme Court has upheld numerous exceptions to the warrant requirement (warrantless searches) when it was shown that a particular search was not "unreasonable" within the meaning of the Fourth Amendment.

There are a number of problems associated with warrantless searches in administrative enforcement. First, it is almost impossible for an administrative agency to meet the probable-cause standard required for search warrants. When OSHA agents go out to check factories for safety violations, they almost never have probable cause to believe that a particular factory is in violation of OSHA rules. Similarly, when fire marshals inspect neighborhoods for fire hazards, they have no way of knowing which individual residences may constitute a fire hazard. Second, unlike other forms of law enforcement, administrative searches do not always have as their objective the detection of a "crime." OSHA agents and fire marshals are more concerned about correcting a dangerous situation than about punishing the offender. While it is true that civil and even criminal liabilities are possible, administrative enforcement of the type we are discussing is meant to be preventive and corrective rather than punitive. Finally, administrative enforcement often involves issues of public safety. Public health inspections and FAA inspections of airplanes are two notable examples. Because of the grave danger to the public posed by unsafe airplanes and unchecked health hazards, warrantless searches may be "reasonable" even if they do not meet the strict probable-cause standards necessary for the issuance of a search warrant.

The Supreme Court's solution to warrantless administrative searches has been to take a middle-ground approach. The Court recognizes that requiring administrative agencies to meet the probable-cause standard required in criminal cases would defeat the purposes of administrative enforcement. However, the Court has also been aware of the need to protect the privacy rights of businesspeople and individuals. Consequently, the Court's middle-ground approach is to uphold, at least initially, the individual's right to privacy. That is, when a person is first asked to submit her home or business to a warrantless search, permission may be denied. After a refusal, however, administrative officials may seek a search warrant from a court without meeting the probable-cause standard. If the agency can show that a particular dwelling or business is being searched as part of an overall administrative plan to enforce the agency's regulations, then a search warrant may be issued without probable cause.[8] The practical effect of this approach is that the individual might merely delay a search until a warrant has been secured. The Court has ruled that concern over public health and safety outweighs any absolute right of privacy of an individual.

A final area of Fourth Amendment rights that has been somewhat controversial involves mandatory home visits in welfare cases. *Wyman v. James*[9] illustrates the problem. New York state law requires welfare recipients to allow welfare workers to conduct home visits in order to determine the recipient's continuing eligibility. Barbara James, a welfare mother receiving AFDC, refused to allow such visits on Fourth Amendment grounds. Ms. James agreed to provide any information the welfare agency requested but refused to allow the home visit. The Supreme Court, in ruling against Ms. James, found that the home-visit requirement was not "unreasonable" within the meaning of the Fourth Amendment. According to the Court, the purpose of the AFDC program is to ensure that the children of welfare recipients are receiving adequate care, and assessment of the home environment is crucial to that end. The purpose of the visit was not to detect welfare fraud, since the welfare worker was not a law enforcement officer and the visits were announced in advance. Despite the finding of reasonableness, critics of the *Wyman* decision claim that it is just another example of discrimination against welfare recipients.

The problems with administrative enforcement point to a continuing concern of students of administrative government. As more agencies—state, local, and national—are created, there is an increasing number of "faceless bureaucrats" with authority over our lives and happiness. The delicate balance between the rights of individuals and the rights of society is a constant concern of courts responsible for curbing overzealous administrative enforcement.

Administrative Adjudication. The final type of delegation takes the form of what has been termed the "quasi-judicial" function of administrative agencies. In the normal course of an agency's duties, disputes will arise over the application of agency rules to a particular individual. For example, welfare laws and agency rules set forth the criteria for welfare eligibility. When an individual applies for welfare, agency personnel must make an initial determination of the person's eligibility based upon the agency's guidelines. Suppose that the person is denied benefits and wishes to appeal the denial. The agency usually has a procedure specifying the steps to be followed in appealing a denial of benefits, and the aggrieved person will be required to follow the procedure. This constitutes an adjudicatory procedure. Or, suppose a person who has already been receiving welfare benefits is informed that he is no longer eligible. If he appeals the loss of benefits, that too is an adjudicatory procedure. Similarly, a loss or denial of a license, loss of public employment, or even a denial of a passport can lead to an adjudicatory procedure.

As in other areas of administrative law, the main thrust of administrative adjudication is the prevention of arbitrary and capricious action at the hands of an administrative agency. Many people believe that they have been the victim of an unfair and arbitrary decision made by someone in authority over them. Administrative law seeks to reduce the risk of arbitrary decisions by requiring administrative agencies to observe fair rules of procedure in settling disputes that arise under their jurisdiction. In recent years, administrative law has seen what has been termed a "due process explosion." With increasing frequency, individuals who once meekly accepted the adverse actions of administrative agencies are demanding and receiving hearings on their complaints. Administrators who were once able to make decisions without fear of being questioned now find that their decisions are, in poker parlance, being "called" more frequently. While some observers applaud this more aggressive assertion of rights, others fear that too much emphasis on adjudication will bog down administrative agencies, leaving them unable to perform their functions adequately.

Administrative adjudications run the gamut from a simple disciplinary action in school to the dismissal of a public employee. The range of formality in adjudication also spans a wide range. At the informal end there is the unilateral decision of a person in authority; the more formal process involves adjudication by an administrative law judge. In this section, we will focus on the more formal aspects of adjudication in order to ascertain how administrative law is brought to bear on this "quasi-judicial" function.

One of the leading cases in administrative adjudication is *Goldberg v. Kelly*.[10] Kelly, a New York welfare recipient, was notified that her benefits were being terminated. Although several New York welfare administrators reviewed Kelly's eligibility before her benefits were actually terminated, Kelly was given no opportunity to present her side of the issue until *after* her benefits were terminated. At that point Kelly was entitled to a post-termination evidentiary hearing. If she prevailed at the post-termination hearing, her benefits would be restored and she would receive back payments. Pending the hearing, however, Kelly's benefits were cut off and she was practically destitute. Kelly argued that she should be granted a hearing before the termination of benefits, and the Supreme Court agreed. In the process of deciding the case, the Court outlined the "Goldberg ingredients" essential for due process of law.

Justice William Brennan, author of the *Goldberg* decision, outlined ten "ingredients" required to meet the minimum standard of due process of law in an administrative procedure.[11] The first *Goldberg* ingredient is (1) *adequate and timely notice.* A person subject to an agency action must be given notice of a change in status. For example, if an agency is preparing to terminate a benefit or suspend a license, the person affected (called the "person aggrieved") has a right to be informed in advance of the nature of the adverse action. Two related *Goldberg* ingredients are (2) the *right to confront adverse witnesses* and (3) the *right to cross-examine adverse witnesses.* Suppose a liquor retailer has been notified that her license is being suspended for selling liquor to a minor. The retailer has a right to confront the witnesses against her and to cross-examine them concerning their testimony.

The next two *Goldberg* ingredients are also related. The person aggrieved has (4) the *right to present arguments orally* and (5) the *right to present evidence orally.* Under the American system of law, persons aggrieved are not required to stand silently before their accusers. They have the right to present orally any relevant arguments or evidence in their favor. This ensures that those who are entitled to a "hearing" do indeed enjoy the right to be "heard."

(6) *Disclosure of opposing evidence* is the next *Goldberg* ingredient. In Chapter 4, a process called *discovery* was introduced. Discovery is the process whereby each party "discovers" the evidence upon which the other party plans to rely in presenting a case. In an administrative procedure, the person aggrieved has the right to know what evidence the agency is using to make its decision. For example, a person faced with the loss of welfare benefits has the right to see the evidence upon which the agency is basing its decision to terminate benefits. Disclosure of opposing evidence places the person aggrieved in a better position to present his or her case to the agency.

The next *Goldberg* ingredient is (7) the *right to retain an attorney.* Although administrative adjudications are not criminal in nature, the loss of a privilege or benefit can cause the person affected a great deal of emotional and financial hardship. Therefore, the person aggrieved has the right to have an attorney present to assist in the presentation of his or her case.

The last three *Goldberg* ingredients are (8) the *right to an impartial decision maker,* (9) a *determination on the record,* and (10) an *explanation of the decision.* The requirement of an impartial decision maker may seem self-evident. However, public administrators, like other humans, may prejudge a case or have a conflict of interest. An administrator is guilty of prejudgment if her mind appears to be made up even before the evidence is presented. Conflict of interest means that an administrator has a personal stake in the outcome of a case. Determination on the record is designed to ensure that no extraneous or impermissible evidence is used to make the decision. In criminal cases, for example, lawyers are often concerned that pretrial publicity in a sensational case will influence prospective jurors. That is, lawyers do not want prospective jurors to be influenced by newspaper or television reports containing evidence that is inadmissible in court. Newspapers may report hearsay evidence which is inadmissible at trial. Determination on the record seeks to ensure that only relevant, permissible evidence forms the basis for the decision.

Finally, the person aggrieved is entitled to a written explanation of the reasons for an adverse decision, the evidence upon which the decision was based, and the reason that other evidence was not relied upon by the decision maker. Basically, this ingredient serves to inform the person aggrieved why he or she lost. The written explanation can serve as the basis of further administrative appeal or even judicial review by an appellate court.

A cautionary note is in order here. The ten *Goldberg* ingredients represent an "ideal" model of administrative due process. A person aggrieved by an administrative agency may find all or none of the *Goldberg* ingredients in place. How is this possible? Lief Carter provides an answer, writing that "the bureaucratic world hardly marches in lockstep with the occasional prouncements of the Supreme Court."[12] In other words, an administrative agency may continue on its merry way, adjudicating disputes as it has always done, totally oblivious to Supreme Court rulings. Even though *Goldberg v. Kelly* serves as a precedent for future cases, if an agency's procedures go unchallenged, the agency may never have to adopt the *Goldberg* ingredients for its own procedures. This situation serves to remind us that the law is an evolutionary process that sometimes proceeds at an excruciatingly slow pace.

JUDICIAL REVIEW AND ADMINISTRATIVE LAW

In Chapter 6, judicial review was defined as the power of a court to review the actions of other governmental bodies in order to determine whether or not those actions are consistent with the Constitution. The actions of administrative agencies are, of course, included among those subject to judicial review. However, judicial review of administrative agencies poses problems for courts that may not be present in other areas of the law. First, administrative agencies are highly specialized bodies with highly specialized personnel. Members of the Nuclear Regulatory Commission (NRC), for example, are experts in a highly technical field. It would be presumptuous for a judge to try to second guess the NRC's decisions about nuclear power. Similarly, most judges are not in a position to question the expert judgment of the FAA or the FCC. Second, as noted in the introduction to this chapter, some government agencies process hundreds of thousands of applications for all kinds of government benefits and programs. Excessive judicial meddling into the operations of an agency may paralyze it and undermine its efficiency. In *Goldberg v. Kelly*, for example, the Supreme Court ruled that Kelly must receive an evidentiary hearing prior to the termination of her benefits instead of after termination, as had previously been the welfare agency's practice. Although at first glance it might not seem to make any difference whether the hearing preceded or followed the termination of benefits, consider the possible consequences. If someone is receiving benefits to which he is not entitled, the benefits must continue to be paid until after a hearing is held. If every ineligible recipient chooses to exercise the right to a hearing, it might tax the ability of the welfare agency to conduct timely hearings, resulting in long delays. Meanwhile, recipients who may eventually prove to be ineligible for benefits continue to receive, at the taxpayers' expense, benefits to which they are not entitled. Consequently, the number of termination hearings increases for agency employees, and the government continues to pay benefits to ineligible recipients.

Despite the problems associated with judicial review of administrative agencies, supporters of judicial review in administrative law argue in favor of it. First, supporters argue that public administrators are just as susceptible to abuse of discretion as any other public official. Indeed, because most administrators are not elected, the potential for abuse of discretion may be even greater. The courts should serve as checks on public administrators to guard against arbitrary and capricious actions. Second, supporters of judicial review argue that an administrative agency is frequently "captured" by the agency's clientele group. Capture occurs when an agency begins to place the interests of the regulated industry above the public interest. Critics of the now defunct Civil Aeronautics Board (CAB) complained that airfares were set more to guarantee the airlines a profit than to keep the consumer's traveling costs down. In light of such charges, supporters of judicial review argue that judicial intervention may be necessary to protect the public interest. Finally, supporters of judicial review argue that bureaucrats tend to see problems from a narrow perspective, while judges tend to see the "big picture." In *Goldberg*, for example, Justice Brennan's opinion tended to stress the bigger picture of the role of welfare in our society, whereas a welfare worker might see only that the decision will increase the number of termination hearings for the agency. In the rest of this section we will examine some of the limits of judicial review in administrative law.

Preclusion of Judicial Review.

There are some areas in which the courts are precluded from reviewing the decisions of administrative agencies. Congress, for whatever reasons, has chosen to take the review of some administrative decisions out of the jurisdiction of the courts. One such area is veterans' benefits. Consider the preclusion language of this statute concerning veterans' benefits:

> [t]he decisions of the Administrator [of Veterans' Affairs] on any question of law or fact concerning veterans' benefits or payments under any law administered by the Veterans' Administration shall be final and conclusive and no other official or any court of the United States shall have power or jurisdiction to review any such decision.[13]

This section of the statute clearly precludes judicial review of a *denial* of veterans' benefits. However, in *Wellman v. Whittier*[14] and several other cases, appellate courts held that although courts were precluded from reviewing denials of claims, the statute did not preclude judicial review of the *termination* of claims. In other words, a person denied veterans' benefits could not seek judicial review, whereas a person already receiving benefits could appeal a decision to terminate benefits.

As a general rule, a determined Supreme Court can find a way to get around most preclusion language. The Court is able to do this because, as we discussed in Chapter 6, it is the final arbiter of the meaning of the Constitution. For example, Congress amended the above statute on veterans' benefits:

> [t]o make it perfectly clear that the Congress intends to exclude from judicial review all determinations with respect to noncontractual benefits provided for veterans and their dependents and survivors.[15]

In *Johnson v. Robison*,[16] however, Johnson was a conscientious objector who performed alternate service in lieu of his military obligation. Johnson sought veterans' education benefits but was denied under a law passed by Congress. Johnson challenged the denial of benefits on First Amendment and equal protection grounds, and the Supreme Court agreed to hear the case. Since Johnson was challenging the *statute* which denied benefits to all conscientious objectors and not the *decision* of the VA administrator, the Court said that it was not precluded from exercising judicial review. The Court ultimately ruled against Johnson's claim for benefits, but at least it agreed to hear the case on the merits. *Johnson* makes clear that no statutory language can preclude judicial review of an administrative decision when a constitutional right or issue is at stake.

Judicial Restraint. Although courts can and do intervene in the administrative process, they are often reluctant to do so and tend to show great deference to administrative expertise when intervention is necessary. Courts have traditionally practiced judicial restraint when exercising the power of judicial review. Requirements of standing, ripeness, and mootness are just a few of the methods used by courts to avoid the use of their judicial power. In addition to these traditional methods, courts have adopted several other procedural devices to prevent premature judicial intervention into the administrative process. The first of these is the ***exhaustion of administrative remedies doctrine.*** Courts prefer that formal litigation be looked upon only as a last resort for settling disputes. Consequently, courts insist that a person avail himself of all administrative remedies before seeking judicial ones. For example, a person who has had a license revoked must follow the agency's procedure for appealing the revocation before initiating a lawsuit against agency officials. Similarly, a student who has received an unsatisfactory grade must exhaust all university appeals before turning to a court for relief. Courts feel that the individual agency is better equipped to handle these disputes and that judicial intervention should be limited to those few cases that cannot be resolved at the agency level.

A doctrine related to exhaustion of remedies is the ***primary jurisdiction doctrine.*** Primary jurisdiction holds that litigants should take their disputes to the agency that has primary responsibility for the dispute rather than to a court of law. In *Texas Pacific Railway Co. v. Abilene Cotton Oil Co.,*[17] for example, the cotton oil company sued the railroad to recover $1,951.83 in unreasonable overcharges. Even though the Interstate Commerce Act specifically permitted the company either to file a complaint with the ICC or to file a suit in a federal district court, the Supreme Court ruled that the ICC had primary jurisdiction and that the cotton oil company should have filed its complaint with the ICC first. The Court believed that uniformity and fairness could best be achieved by allowing the ICC to make the initial decisions about the reasonableness of rates.[18]

The difference between primary jurisdiction and exhaustion of administrative remedies is subtle but important. Primary jurisdiction requires a party with a dispute that falls within an agency's jurisdiction to go to the agency before taking the dispute to court. Exhaustion of administrative remedies states that a party already subject to the jurisdiction of a governmental agency must give the agency an opportunity to resolve the dispute before taking it to court.

One final way that courts practice judicial restraint is by observing the ***substantial evidence rule.*** This rule states that conclusions of fact, if supported by substantial evidence based on the whole record, are to be regarded as final. In other words, an agency's finding of fact is considered final if there is substantial evidence to support it. In *Consolidated Edison v. National Labor Relations Board*,[19] the Supreme Court stated that substantial evidence ". . . means such relevant evidence as a reasonable mind might accept as adequate to support a conclusion."[20] In other words, if there is any plausible evidence to support an agency's conclusion of fact, the court has a duty to defer to the judgment of the agency.

Judicial review of the actions of administrative agencies is still relatively new compared with other areas of the law. It should be recalled that the modern administrative state is a fairly recent development in the United States, so it is not surprising that many areas of administrative law are as yet undeveloped. In the next section we will focus on one particular area of administrative law—the law of public employment—to illustrate some of the features we have discussed thus far.

THE LAW OF PUBLIC EMPLOYMENT

Throughout most of the nineteenth century, public employment in the federal government was based upon the so-called *spoils system.* The spoils system was an outgrowth of democratic theory, which held that any reasonably intelligent person could perform satisfactorily in most government jobs. Therefore, after each election, the winning candidate would remove the former officeholder's appointees from their jobs and replace them with his own supporters. Since most government jobs were clerical to begin with, it was not necessary to have highly skilled people in most positions. The winning candidate used these jobs—called patronage jobs—to reward his supporters for their help in winning public office. Thus the saying "To the victor go the spoils" was applied to political campaigns as well as military ones.

American presidents, although the chief beneficiaries of the spoils system, found the task of filling patronage positions tedious. Supporters tended to exaggerate their importance in helping the president win office. President William Howard Taft once remarked that every patronage appointment created "nine enemies and one ingrate." When President James A. Garfield was assassinated in 1881 by a disgruntled office-seeker, public opinion turned against the spoils system. In 1883, Congress enacted the Pendleton Act, which created the first civil service positions in the United States. Since the passage of the Pendleton Act, more and more government jobs have been added to the list of civil service positions, until today all but a few thousand of the 2.8 million federal jobs are civil service. Civil service jobs are characterized by merit selection, tests for promotion, and job security. Under civil service, public employees are chosen on the basis of merit, not party affiliation, and do not have to worry about losing their jobs after each election.

The initial approach to the rights of public employees was basically that they had none. As Justice Oliver Wendell Holmes, Jr., remarked in *McAuliffe v. Mayor of New Bedford*, "The petitioner may have a constitutional right to talk politics, but he has no constitutional right to be a policeman."[21] Holmes went on to say that all employees agree to forfeit some of their rights as a condition of their employment, and public employees were no exception to that rule. However, public attitudes about the rights of public employees have changed since Holmes's day, and there is greater recognition of their rights. In the rest of this section we will examine several of the constitutional questions associated with the rights of public employees. The reader is cautioned to remember that we are discussing *public* employment and that many of the restrictions that apply to public employees do not apply to persons employed in the private sector.

The Right to Public Employment. One problem associated with public employment centers around the right/privilege distinction. That is, is public employment a right which cannot be denied without due process of law, or is it a privilege granted or withheld at the pleasure of the government? The answer, as is often the case in law, is somewhere in between. While it is still true that no one has an affirmative right to a government job, it is also true that certain rights can accrue *after* one has been hired by the government. It should not come as a surprise that many of the cases concerning public employment are ones surrounding the dismissal of public employees. In the language of due process, a public employee who is dismissed must assert and show either a property interest or a liberty interest. In other words, a public employee must show that her public job is her property which has been denied to her without due process or that her dismissal has infringed upon some liberty interest. To illustrate, let us examine some of the case law surrounding the rights of public employees, keeping in mind administrative law's special concern for questions of due process.

Board of Regents of State Colleges v. Roth[22] raised important questions of employees' rights. Roth was hired as an assistant professor of political science at Wisconsin State University–Oshkosh, under a one-year contract. Roth was on a "tenure track," which meant that after a probationary period—in this case, four years—he would receive tenure and be subject to dismissal only for cause. At the end of the academic year, however, he was informed that he would not be rehired. Roth filed suit against the University, alleging that his outspoken criticism of the University's administration was the real reason for his dismissal. Thus, Roth claimed that his right to freedom of speech had been abridged, constituting a denial of his "liberty" without due process of law. Second, Roth claimed that failure to afford him an opportunity for a hearing also violated due process.

The major issue before the Supreme Court was whether Roth was entitled to a hearing, and the Court ruled that he was not. In terms of his "liberty" claim, the Court noted that Roth had received no injury because he had no legal right to reemployment by the University. If Roth had been terminated during the term of the contract, he would have had a right to a hearing. But both Roth and the University upheld their ends of the contract for the specified one-year period. In addition, Roth was not precluded from seeking employment at another public university in Wisconsin. Finally, the Court ruled that Roth never proved that his dismissal was based on his free-speech activities. As for any "property" interest, the Court ruled that Roth had none. A property interest requires more than Roth's unilateral expectation of reemployment. Consequently, Roth was not entitled to a hearing when the University decided not to renew his contract.

On the same day that *Roth* came down, the Supreme Court decided *Perry v. Sindermann*.[23] Sindermann had taught at a community college in Odessa, Texas, for four years. Although the college had no formal tenure policy, the faculty handbook stated that an instructor should feel that he has "permanent tenure" as long as his work is satisfactory and "he is happy in his work."[24] Sindermann was terminated after he made a number of public statements that were highly critical of the college's Board of Regents. No official reasons for nonrenewal of his contract were given, and no hearing was held. Sindermann argued that the college's unofficial tenure policy vested him with a property right and entitled him to a hearing. The Supreme Court ruled that Sindermann must be given the opportunity to prove his claim to a property right. If Sindermann could prove that he had such a right, he was entitled to a hearing before being dismissed. The Court remanded the case to the lower court with orders that Sindermann be allowed to prove his claim to a property right. Sindermann ultimately prevailed, receiving a $48,000 judgment from the college in November 1972.[25]

A third case dealing with the right of public employment is *Bishop v. Wood*.[26] Bishop was a police officer on the Marion, North Carolina, police force. He began his employment in June 1969 and, after serving a six-month probation, became a permanent employee. He was dismissed by the city manager in March 1972 without a hearing. Bishop alleged that, as a permanent employee of the city, he was entitled to a hearing, that the grounds for his dismissal were false, and that his ability to seek future employment as a police officer was jeopardized by his illegal dismissal, thus abridging his liberty. The Supreme Court ruled against Bishop on all counts.

Bishop lost on the first issue, that of employment as a property right, on a technicality. Although the Supreme Court indicated that Bishop might have a legitimate claim, interpretations of North Carolina's public employment laws by state courts ran counter to Bishop's position, and the Supreme Court was obligated to abide by North Carolina's precedents. On the falsity of the grounds for his dismissal, the Court took the unsympathetic view that it was not their function to correct every personnel mistake made by public administrators. Finally, the Court ruled that he had no liberty claim. At most, Bishop could claim that his reputation had been damaged, reducing his chances of employment. But the Court noted that the charges against Bishop were not made public until he himself forced them to be made public during the pretrial discovery process. Consequently, any damage to his reputation as a result of the charges becoming publicly known was self-inflicted.

Roth, Sindermann, and *Bishop* illustrate that, depending on the circumstances, public employment may or may not be viewed as a "right." It is clear that public employees may not be dismissed for exercising constitutional rights such as freedom of speech. However, it is often difficult to prove violations of constitutional rights. The existence of a property right will depend on whether a court feels there is some entitlement. In *Roth* and *Bishop,* the Court ruled, for different reasons, that no entitlement existed, whereas in *Sindermann,* it did. As is so often true with case law, the unique circumstances of individual cases makes it difficult to generalize. These three cases merely scratch the surface of a very complicated area of administrative law.

Loyalty Oaths.   One of the most difficult areas of public employment law is the issue of loyalty oaths. Most states require its employees to sign a loyalty oath as a condition of their employment. The typical oath requires employees to swear that they have never been a member of a subversive organization. A major problem of such oaths is vagueness. As we saw in Chapter 6, the Supreme Court will invalidate legislation that is too vague. How is an employee to know which organizations are subversive? The government itself admits that some organizations are "fronts" for communist organizations. If someone innocently joins a communist-front organization, has he violated his loyalty oath?

The Supreme Court has struck down loyalty oaths that are overbroad. Some states required their employees to list every organization to which they had belonged. The Court found that such a requirement had a "chilling effect" on freedom of association. The Court did uphold prospective loyalty oaths in *Cole v. Richardson.*[27] A prospective loyalty oath obligates the employee to promise only future, not past, loyalty. Finally, in *Torcaso v. Watkins,*[28] the Court struck down a Maryland law that required all public officials to express a belief in God in order to hold public office.

Other Issues. A number of issues surrounding the rights of public employees involve the exercise of rights enjoyed by employees in the private sector. Public employees argue that what they do on their own time is not the business of their governmental employer. For example, most private employers do not care where their employees live, but cities and school districts often required their employees to live within the city limits. The Supreme Court upheld the right of cities to make residency a condition of city employment in *McCarthy v. Philadelphia Civil Service Commission,*[29] although many cities have done away with the requirement. The Supreme Court has also upheld regulations prohibiting the cohabitation of unmarried employees. In *Kelley v. Johnson,*[30] the Court ruled that a city could require its male police officers to keep their hair cut short. The Court said that the general public has an image of police officers as clean-cut and that it is reasonable for the city to maintain that image.

It is clear that the next major constitutional battle over the rights of public employees will involve undergoing mandatory drug testing as a condition of public employment. President Ronald Reagan was an outspoken supporter of drug testing, even submitting to the test himself. However, public employees argue that drug testing violates their constitutional right to privacy. As of this writing there has not been a definitive Supreme Court decision on the constitutionality of mandatory drug testing, but the likelihood that the Court will be called upon to resolve this question is almost certain.

CONCLUSION

Administrative law is one of the most fascinating and fastest growing areas of American law. As government gets bigger, the chances for government intrusion in our daily lives increases. If we are to remain "a nation of laws, not men," then we must keep vigilant watch over the rapidly growing government bureaucracy. Administrative law is the law that governs the people in government. We must not let those in government lose sight of the fact that they are the servants of the people, not their masters. Administrative law is one method we use to accomplish this goal.

NOTES

[1] Lief H. Carter, *Administrative Law and Politics: Cases and Comments* (Boston: Little, Brown, 1983), p. 11.

[2] U.S. Constitution, Amendments V and XIV.

[3] See *Schechter Poultry Co. v. United States,* 295 U.S. 495 (1935); *Carter v. Carter Coal Co.,* 298 U.S. 238 (1936); and *Panama Refining Co. v. Ryan,* 293 U.S. 388 (1935).

[4] *Bob Jones University v. United States,* 461 U.S. 574 (1983).

[5] See Florence Heffron and Neil McFeeley, *The Administrative Regulatory Process* (New York: Longman, 1983), pp. 173–197.

[6] In *Oklahoma Press Publishing Co. v. Walling,* 327 U.S. 186 (1946), the Supreme Court ruled that Fifth Amendment rights do not apply to corporations.

[7] *Marchetti v. United States,* 390 U.S. 39 (1968).

[8] See *Marshall v. Barlow's Inc.,* 436 U.S. 307 (1978).

[9] *Wyman v. James,* 400 U.S. 309 (1971).

[10] *Goldberg v. Kelly,* 397 U.S. 254 (1970).

[11] Carter, p. 125.

[12] Ibid., p. 124.

[13] Walter Gellhorn, Clark Byse, and Peter L. Strauss, *Administrative Law: Cases and Comments,* 7th ed. (Mineola, N.Y.: Foundation Press, 1979), p. 943.

[14] *Wellman v. Whittier,* 259 F. 2d 163 (D.C. Cir. 1958).

[15] Gellhorn, Byse, and Clark, p. 944.

[16] *Johnson v. Robison,* 415 U.S. 361 (1974).

[17] *Texas Pacific Railway Co. v. Abilene Cotton Oil Co.,* 204 U.S. 426 (1907).

[18] Heffron and McFeeley, pp. 308–309.

[19] *Consolidated Edison v. National Labor Relations Board,* 305 U.S. 197 (1938).

[20] Heffron and McFeeley, p. 277.

[21] Quoted in William W. Van Alstyne, "The Demise of the Right–Privilege Distinction in Constitutional Law," *Harvard Law Review,* Vol. 81, No. 7 (May 1968), p. 1439.

[22] *Board of Regents of State Colleges v. Roth,* 408 U.S. 564 (1972).

[23] *Perry v. Sindermann,* 408 U.S. 593 (1972).

[24] Ibid., p. 600.

[25] Gellhorn, Byse, and Clark, p. 464, footnote 3.

[26] *Bishop v. Wood,* 426 U.S. 341 (1976).

[27] *Cole v. Richardson,* 405 U.S. 676 (1972).

[28] *Torcaso v. Watkins,* 367 U.S. 488 (1961).

[29] *McCarthy v. Philadelphia Civil Service Commission,* 424 U.S. 645 (1976).

[30] *Kelley v. Johnson,* 425 U.S. 238 (1976).

Torts

A *tort* is a private, or civil, wrong in which the defendant's actions cause injury to a person or to property. Tort law provides redress for wrongs between individuals, while criminal law seeks to punish offenses against the public at large. A tort lawsuit involves only the persons involved in the tort; the state is neutral in regard to the outcome (unless, of course, the state is a party to the lawsuit). There are elementary dissimilarities between torts and crimes: (1) In the civil action of tort, the injured person himself initiates and maintains the lawsuit, whereas in criminal trials, the State prosecutes; and (2) the goal of each differs. Criminal law seeks to prevent wrongdoing and to punish the miscreant, while tort law aims to place the victim in the same position he would have been in if the tort had not occurred.

The same act often spawns both civil and criminal sanctions. Suppose that you are loitering in the hall before class when, without provocation, Joe suddenly comes up and hits you in the face. Joe is subject to criminal sanctions for this attack. However, you will also wish to file a tort action against Joe to recover money to pay for your new front teeth, your dentist's bill, your pain and suffering, and your mental anguish. The purposes of the two suits, which will be heard separately, are different. Society is punishing Joe for his antisocial behavior in the criminal trial, while you are seeking money from him. The usual remedy for tort liability is monetary reimbursement for the harm suffered.[1]

Tort law is fluid; it changes as society's values shift. New torts are today being recognized where no cause of action had previously existed, and the boundaries of tort liability are constantly in flux. One example is the expansion of liability in regard to drivers who injure someone while intoxicated. Traditionally, only the drivers themselves were responsible, but courts are now finding liable for damages employers who release their intoxicated employees to go home as well as drinking establishments whose customers leave and subsequently injure someone.[2] New causes of action may be created by the courts to provide remedies for perceived wrongs, or they may be established through statutory law by the various legislative bodies.

Tort law establishes certain legal standards of conduct by which all members of society must abide and then provides a remedy when such a standard is violated. It is primarily designed to protect three types of interests: (1) the person, (2) tangible property, and (3) intangible interests, including relational interests such as business, family, and social relations. The person who breachs the standard of conduct is known as the *tortfeasor.* Generally, the tortfeasor cannot be held liable for damages unless he has violated the prescribed standard of conduct.

The plaintiff in the suit decides on the theory of tort recovery and draws the complaint to reflect the theory. Each theory contains certain elements that the plaintiff must prove in order to collect damages from the defendant. It is not unusual for a plaintiff to plead alternative theories of recovery, which may contain contradictory elements, in the complaint. Then, through discovery, it can be determined which is the strongest, and the plaintiff then proceeds to trial on that theory. The only requirement is that defendants be given adequate notice in the complaint of the possible causes of action in order that they may properly prepare the defense. In our discussion of tort law, we will look at the theories of negligence, intentional torts, strict liability, and product liability.[3]

NEGLIGENCE

Negligence is the reckless or careless failure of the tortfeasor to exercise the degree of care that the law deems appropriate in a particular situation. A common example is that of an automobile accident in which a driver recklessly drives too fast on an icy road, loses control, and slams into another car, causing both personal injuries and property damage. The driver was imprudent and did not exercise the usual standard of care. However, she did not set out to inflict injury; this absence of malicious intent is one of the characteristics of negligence cases. Recovery in negligence cases is not predicated on proving the tortfeasor morally at fault. The elements that the plaintiff must prove in order to win at trial are the following: (1) that the defendant owed a duty of care to the plaintiff; (2) that the standard of care was breached; (3) that defendant's action was the proximate cause of the injury; and (4) that the plaintiff suffered some compensable damage as a result of defendant's actions. These four elements compose the *prima facie* case in a negligence cause of action; that is, the plaintiff is required to prove each of the elements in order to win the case. The issue of negligence is primarily a question of fact, and it is therefore a matter to be decided by the jury.[4]

Duty of Care. The plaintiff must initially show that the defendant owed a legally recognized duty of care. There are two subsidiary issues involved: what is the level of care the defendant must exercise, and to whom is the duty of care owed. In most cases, the test for the appropriate level of care is whether, under the circumstances of the case, the defendant acted as a "reasonably prudent person" would have acted to prevent the injury. The **reasonably prudent person** is a fictitious individual who has been created by the courts as an objective standard by which to measure a defendant's actions. This cautious and careful person is considered to be of ordinary intelligence and to have a normal memory and normal sensory perceptions. This ubiquitous paragon of virtue has been humorously described by one commentator, A.P. Herbert, in the following manner:

> He is an ideal, a standard, the embodiment of all those qualities which we demand of the good citizen . . . He is one who invariably looks where he is going, and is careful to examine the immediate foreground before he executes a leap or bound; who neither star-gazes nor is lost in meditation when approaching trapdoors or the margin of a dock . . . who never mounts a moving omnibus and does not alight from any car while the train is in motion . . . and will inform himself of the history and habits of a dog before administering a caress . . . who never from one year's end to another makes an excessive demand upon his wife, his neighbors, his servants, his ox, or his ass . . . who never swears, gambles or loses his temper; who uses nothing except in moderation . . . this excellent but odious character stands like a monument in our Courts of Justice vainly appealing to his fellow citizens to order their lives after his own example.[5]

The fact-finder considers the events of the case and decides whether the defendant exhibited the due care that a person of ordinary intelligence would have. A child is not held to as high a standard of care; each is judged against a child of like age, intelligence, and experience.[6] On the other hand, a person who has a special skill or knowledge is judged by a higher standard of care. For example, architects, engineers, and physicians must exhibit the same skills and care that others in the profession do.[7] Certainly one expects a higher degree of medical knowledge and skill from a physician than one does from a layperson. The physician is required by law to act as a reasonably prudent *physician* would in providing treatment. If the professional does not act in accordance with the standard, the usual result is a malpractice suit. Typically, the only way to prove negligence in this type of action is through the use of expert testimony, and professionals are often hesitant to testify against each other.

Another issue in regard to the standard of care is the relationship between the plaintiff and defendant. It is this relationship which determines just how careful one must be toward another person. Generally, the law does not impose a duty on a person to go to the aid of someone who is in danger, even though there may be a moral duty to do so. However, such a duty may be imposed when there is a special relationship. Although a stranger is probably not *legally* required to assist a drowning child, the parent might well be expected to do so in the eyes of the law.[8] Similarly, occupiers of land usually owe different levels of care to trespassers and to business visitors. The occupier must extend the greater level of care to business visitors or *invitees*—the duty of ordinary care. Social guests or *licensees* and trespassers, those on the land without the owner's consent, are owed a lesser degree of care— the duty to refrain from wilful or wanton misconduct. Suits involving homeowners and their guests are quite common, and most people buy insurance to protect themselves financially in case of such accidents.[9]

Breach of duty. The second element the plaintiff must establish is that the standard of care owed to her was violated by the defendant. There are two prongs to this element of a negligence action. The plaintiff must convince the fact-finder (1) that the act or omission actually occurred and (2) that such action was a breach of the standard of care owed to this particular plaintiff. Such a breach can be through commission or through omission—that is, through a positive act of the defendant or through a failure of the defendant to act. An example of a positive act is someone dropping a flowerpot from a third-story window without regard for the passerby below; an example of an omission is the failure of a store clerk to pick up a banana peel from the floor after seeing it.

Courts have provided shortcuts for plaintiffs in proving the lack of ordinary care in limited circumstances. The first of these is ***negligence per se.*** In a typical case, the legislature passes a statute regulating certain activities in the interest of safety—for example, traffic or working conditions in industries. The plaintiff alleges that the defendant violated such safety standard and that the plaintiff's injury is a result of such violation. If the judge agrees that the defendant violated the safety regulation, the decision is conclusive and the issue of negligence does not even go to the jury. The jury is then called upon only to decide the amount of damages.[10]

The second of these shortcuts is the doctrine of **res ipsa loquitur**— "the thing speaks for itself." Here, the plaintiff is required to prove that the accident is of a type that ordinarily would not occur without negligence (an airplane crash) *and* that all instrumentalities that would probably cause the accident were under the control of the defendant at the time (crew of airplane and aircraft maintenance were under the control of the airline). This doctrine resembles circumstantial evidence in that the trier of facts is asked to infer the result from separate pieces of evidence. Again, the jury's task is limited to determining the truth of these allegations rather than actual negligence. If the jury agrees with the plaintiff on these two points, they find for the plaintiff.[11]

Proximate Cause.   The plaintiff must also show that the defendant's action was the proximate cause of his injury. In other words, there must be some reasonable connection between the negligent act of the defendant and the plaintiff's injury. Suppose that Sue and her husband have an argument at breakfast; that Sue unjustifiably criticizes her secretary, George, during the day; and that George is upset and, as a result, is careless while driving home and has an accident. In one sense, it is possible to trace the cause of the accident back to the spat between Sue and her husband because "in a philosophical sense, the consequences of an act go forward to eternity, and the causes of an event go back to the discovery of America and beyond."[12] However, courts have declined to enter into this hornet's nest and have limited liability to "those causes which are so closely connected with the result and of such significance that the law is justified in imposing liability."[13]

This concept of legal responsibility based on a reasonable connection between the tortfeasor's action and the victim's injury is known as *proximate cause.* The plaintiff must establish not only that the defendant's conduct was *factually* one of the causes of the injury, but also that the defendant should be *legally* responsible for his actions. Additional limitations on liability have been developed. If the defendant could not reasonably have foreseen any injury to the plaintiff as a consequence of the act, there is no liability.[14] For instance, a tortfeasor involved in an automobile accident could not reasonably foresee that the sirens of the emergency vehicles would startle someone into dropping a pot of boiling water and scalding herself. Also, a defendant will be relieved of liability if there is an independent force intervening between the action and the injury.[15] To illustrate, assume that Sanders Gravel constructs a fence around its lake that is adequate to prevent the neighborhood children from straying in; however, a tornado strikes and blows down the fence, and a child drowns in the lake later that day. The tornado is considered to be an independent intervening cause in such a case.

There are often several contributing causes in a single accident, which will result in shared liability among the various tortfeasors. Consider a fairly typical automobile accident. Charles is driving east, is speeding, and is trying to get through the intersection before the light changes to red so that he does not slow down. Daniel, who is travelling west on the same street, is obeying all the traffic laws; however, his attention is diverted by his two children, who are squabbling in the back seat. Richard is going north on the intersecting street. The three cars collide at the intersection; personal injuries and property damage result. In addition to the foregoing facts, eyewitnesses will testify at the trial that the light was malfunctioning and was showing green on all sides. The trio will sue one another and the city for failing to properly maintain the traffic control device, the light. Each of them contributed to the accident, and it will be the jury's responsibility to apportion responsibility for the accident.

Damages.   The fourth element the plaintiff must prove is that of **damages,** a sum of money which the law imposes as pecuniary compensation. The plaintiff is required to establish both the nature of the injury and an amount that would fairly recompense him for the injury. The emphasis is on placing the plaintiff in the same position, insofar as is possible, as he was in before the accident. Of course, it is difficult to place a monetary value on pain and suffering or on the loss of an arm or leg or to predict a person's lifetime earnings; however, juries, utilizing the precedents of previous awards and the evidence adduced at trial, decide these formidable questions each day in rendering verdicts in tort cases.

Plaintiffs' attorneys have been successful in having courts recognize the various ramifications of an injury and in thereby expanding the recovery in tort actions. Assume that John is a football player who has signed a contract to play professional ball when he is paralyzed in an automobile accident. He would likely sue to recover for his pain and suffering, his medical expenses (which will be ongoing), his present loss of wages, his loss of future earnings, loss of value of his car, and mental anguish (if the state courts have recognized the latter).

Assume that Peter died in the same accident. His estate would have a common-law action for personal injury resulting in death and could recover for his consciousness of impending death, physical pain and suffering, and medical and funeral expenses. Peter's family—wife, children, and/or parents—could also file suit for damages for the loss of the monetary value that they could reasonably have expected to receive from Peter if he had not been killed.

The monetary value of these losses is quite troublesome for juries. The easier questions are those involving the loss of value to property such as automobiles, livestock, or buildings. Putting a price tag on someone's pain and suffering or anticipating the amount of future earnings of a child is subjective. Juries rely heavily on the testimony of experts, particularly economists, to assist them. Lawyers work throughout the trial to educate the jurors about the issue of damages; the plaintiff's counsel seeks to demonstrate how horrific the injury is and how only a large sum will adequately recompense the victim, while the defense seeks to minimize the possible award. The same kinds of damages are available for all torts including intentional torts and those involving product liability.[16]

Defenses. Once the plaintiff has established a *prima facie* case by presenting the four elements, the defendant has the opportunity to present his case and to rebut the plaintiff's arguments. Several methods of attack are available to the defendant, including challenging the plaintiff's proof on the four elements of negligence, claiming that the plaintiff was aware of the risk, or establishing that the plaintiff himself was negligent and thereby contributed to his own injury. For instance, a common defensive tactic is to dispute the seriousness of plaintiff's injury, thereby reducing damages; but the same approach, that of controverting fact questions, may be directed to each prong of the plaintiff's case. In addition, the defendant may also employ the affirmative defenses of contributory negligence and voluntary assumption of risk. In utilizing the defense of **voluntary assumption of risk,** the defendant attempts to prove that the plaintiff was cognizant of the danger and voluntarily chose to encounter it. A typical example is a person who, with knowledge that she may be hit by a flying puck, attends an ice hockey game. In other words, the plaintiff, either expressly or impliedly, consented to the risk of possible injury.

In contrast, the defense of contributory negligence alleges that the plaintiff's actions contributed to his own injury. Every person is charged with the legal duty to avoid exposing oneself to injury—that is, to exercise due care in regard to their safety as would the reasonable, prudent person in the community. The defendant bears the burden of proof to establish that the plaintiff acted in violation of this standard. The common-law rules of *contributory negligence* barred the plaintiff from *any* recovery if he was found to have contributed, even slightly, to his own injury. Modern courts and legislatures have tempered the harshness of this legal precept, however, through the adoption of *comparative negligence*. Under the doctrine of comparative negligence, the negligence is apportioned between the plaintiff and the defendant, with the result that the plaintiff may recover a certain portion of the damages even if he contributed to his own injury. Again, the burden rests on the defendant to prove that the plaintiff's own actions caused the injury.[17]

INTENTIONAL TORTS

Unlike torts based on negligence, which involve recklessness or a breach of the standard of care, intentional torts are based on wilful and knowing misconduct. The tortfeasor knows or is substantially certain that her actions will result in injury either to a person or to property. To hold the defendant liable for damages, tort law does not require the tortfeasor to harbor a malicious desire to harm someone; instead, courts will imply the requisite intent if the harm suffered was the predictable result of the defendant's actions.

Intentional torts, such as assault and battery and false imprisonment, are often repeated in criminal statutes, and the tortfeasor may also be subject to criminal penalties in a separate lawsuit. Because intentional torts are more culpable than negligence, the defendant faces the possibility of greater liability. Again, the key for distinguishing intentional torts from negligence is that the tortfeasor *intentionally* performed the acts *knowing* that injury would be likely to occur.

Assault and Battery. To paraphrase a popular song, assault and battery go together like love and marriage. However, the two are separate and distinct intentional torts. **Battery** is a harmful or offensive contact with another, whereas **assault** is the apprehension of an unwanted contact with another. The former is the actual physical touching; the latter is the mental awareness of the unwanted invasion. A battery may be committed without an assault and vice versa. A person struck in the back of the head may not be aware of the attacker's presence (battery without assault), and someone who throws a punch and misses has committed assault without battery. Technically, one cannot be assaulted by words alone; there must be an accompanying physical act that places one in apprehension of impending contact.

Consent is the primary defense for the torts of assault and battery. A boxer agrees or consents to have the opposing fighter touch him during the bout. Similarly, you might accept the contact as a caress from one person and yet be highly offended if a stranger touched you in the same manner. Certain persons are deemed to have a privilege to touch another; examples are a police officer making a valid arrest or a physician giving emergency treatment.[18]

False Imprisonment. The social policy underlying the tort of false imprisonment is concern about one of the most treasured of American rights—the freedom to move about freely, or, in constitutional terms, one's liberty interest. The plaintiff's *prima facie* case must include proof that the defendant intentionally restrained the plaintiff's freedom against the plaintiff's will and that the plaintiff was aware of such restraint. The victim need not necessarily be incarcerated or locked behind physical barriers; impediments of the freedom to proceed on one's way, including holding one's property, are included. Moral pressure or threats of future action alone are insufficient to create the required restraints. Store security personnel who prevent an alleged shoplifter from leaving the premises are treading a very fine line, although there is some statutory and case-law guidance available. Police personnel who exceed their authority in making arrests or who do so maliciously are also subject to suit for false imprisonment, but it is a defense that the defendant had legal authority to restrain the plaintiff.[19]

Infliction of Mental Distress. A person who wilfully and intentionally causes *serious* mental distress to another can be held liable for his actions. This tort is limited to cases involving extreme misconduct—for example, telling a mother that her child had been killed when, in fact, the tortfeasor knows the child is fine. It involves more than hurt feelings, disappointment, or worry; there must be actual and severe mental anguish. Courts have traditionally required that mental distress be linked with some other tort and actual physical harm; however, the trend is away from both these requirements. Many jurisdictions now recognize the infliction of mental distress as a separate tort.[20]

Invasion of Privacy. The concept of privacy is zealously guarded in the United States; it is protected by the courts against invasion from either the government or the private sector. In today's world, in which personal information about all persons is listed on computers that are subject to being tapped, the right to privacy is assuming even more importance. Two related torts deal with the right to be shielded from the public eye and the right to preserve one's reputation. The first, *invasion of privacy,* covers three broad areas: (1) the intentional invasion of privacy by wiretapping a phone or shadowing a person, (2) the appropriation of a person's name or likeness without permission for advertising purposes, and (3) the unwarranted publication of information about an individual's private matters.

The test that courts use to gauge the tortfeasor's actions is whether a reasonable person would find the act to be highly objectionable.[21] For example, Jones is having difficulty collecting a debt from Smith, so Jones creates a billboard sign that informs the world, "Smith owes me $1,000 and will not pay it." Most people (who are also debtors) find this obnoxious, and Smith would likely succeed in a tort action for invasion of privacy.

The second action, **defamation,** also concerns the issue of one's reputation in the community. Defamation is the injury of one's reputation in the community by derogatory or defamatory comments. There are two distinct branches of defamation: **slander,** in which the comment is usually spoken; and **libel,** in which it is written or is in some permanent form. The underlying public policy is the strong emphasis on protecting people from malicious or untrue attacks on their good name in the community.

In order for the plaintiff to recover in a slander suit, he must establish that the statement was made in the presence of a third party, that it subjected him to ridicule or contempt, and that he suffered pecuniary damages as a result of the tortfeasor's statements. Libel is easier to prove in that the defamation is in writing, pictures, videotape, or something of a permanent nature. Public figures, those in the public eye, must prove an additional element—that the defendant made the statement either with knowledge that it was false or with a careless disregard for its truth. The defendant may rely upon one of three primary defenses: (1) that the statement is true; (2) that the defendant was protected by a privilege to speak, such as that given legislators speaking on the floor of the legislature; or (3) that the plaintiff consented to the statement.[22]

Intentional Torts Against Property.   Although property damage can and does result from negligence, the law also recognizes intentional torts directed against property interests; among these are conversion, trespass, and nuisance. **Trespass to land** occurs when a person enters the land or building of another without consent. This intrusion must be physical; that is, the trespasser must actually walk on the ground or poke a stick through a fence. But even though the damage might be as minimal as a bent blade of grass, the owner can recover because of the interference with possession of the property.[23]

Nuisance is the use of the *defendant's* land in such a way that it interferes with the *plaintiff's* use of his land. Suppose, for example, that the defendant owns a quarry where blasting occurs and the shock waves shatter the windows in plaintiff's home; or, the defendant runs a chemical plant that produces a noxious odor. Courts must balance each party's right to use his own land as he chooses against the injury sustained by the other landowner. Factors to be considered in nuisance suits include the frequency of the intrusion, the value to society of the defendant's action, and the plaintiff's knowledge, if any, of the nuisance when he bought the property.[24] Even though nuisance is included here under intentional torts, the nuisance could be caused by the negligent or hazardous activities of the defendant, and therefore the plaintiff could proceed under the theories of negligence or strict liability. In addition to damages, the plaintiff in a nuisance suit may also be awarded the equitable remedy of injunction.

Personal property, as distinguished from real property or land, may also be damaged. A second type of trespass, *trespass to chattel,* occurs when the tortfeasor damages a *chattel,* which is an item of tangible, personal property such as jewels, money, or automobiles. For instance, Bill Bully intimidates his classmate, Stephen, into allowing Bill to ride Stephen's bicycle by breaking the headlight. Bill has damaged or impaired the bicycle, which is trespass to a chattel, and has also committed conversion by interfering with Stephen's possession of the bicycle. *Conversion,* then, is defined as depriving an owner of possession of tangible property. The person who borrows an item without permission or an employee who sells copies of the company's bid on a new construction project to a competitor has interfered with the owner's possession of the property and is subject to tort liability (that is, damages) as well as criminal penalties.[25]

Defenses. There are many other causes of action in tort law— including fraud, unfair competition, malicious prosecution, and alienation of affection—which permit the plaintiff to recover damages for the defendant's intentional infliction of injury. Each theory carries with it specific defenses that are applicable only to it. However, there are defensive tactics that are common to some, if not all, intentional torts. The defendant will initially attack and seek to rebut the plaintiff's *prima facie* case—those facts and elements that the plaintiff must prove in order to succeed at trial. The second front on which the defendant will do battle is the presentation of the general defenses; for example, the defendant would allege that the plaintiff consented to the action (that the football player agreed to be struck during the game) or that the defendant had a privilege to take the action (that the fireman trespassed on the land in order to put out a fire which was threatening other property). The third line of attack is the particular defense that is linked to a specific tort. For example, the defendant in an assault and battery case may counter with the argument that he struck the plaintiff only to protect and defend himself or another against the plaintiff's aggression.

STRICT LIABILITY

We have previously used the concept of fault as one of the distinguishing marks between intentional torts and negligence. In the former, the tortfeasor who knows and intends the consequences of the act is found liable for the injury it causes; and in the latter, the person who fails to exhibit ordinary care or who is reckless toward the welfare of others is required to make good on the damage that was inflicted. However, *fault*, in the eyes of the law, is not synonymous with moral blame. Instead, it implies that the actor has not lived up to the standard of conduct imposed by society.

Originally, the law would not impose liability on the tortfeasor unless it found "fault." However, courts, in the familar traditions of common law, have developed a new doctrine of "strict liability" whereby the tortfeasor may be responsible for the loss or injury of another even if there has been no violation of the reasonable standard of conduct. Legislatures ratified the theory through statutory enactment.

The concept of strict liability was initially applied against the owners of animals that escaped and damaged another's property, but it has been expanded to cover hazardous activities, such as blasting or moving explosive and inflammable liquids. Questions involved in such suits include the locale of the dangerous activity, the customs of the community, and the fitness of the premises or machinery for these purposes. In these situations in which neither party is at fault, society, through the courts, imposes the costs for the loss on the party who is most able to afford it.[26]

A relatively new area is that of *product liability,* wherein the manufacturer of a defective product or instrumentality is responsible for any injuries caused by the product. The plaintiff must prove that the product was defective as marketed in one of the following ways: (1) There was a defect in the construction of the product; (2) There was a defect in the design of the product; or (3) There were inherent dangers in the product about which the ultimate purchaser was not warned. A plaintiff who suffered serious injuries as a result of food poisoning because the food was improperly canned might allege the first, whereas those suing an automobile company because the gasoline tank of their cars exploded upon minimal impact would probably proceed on the second premise. An example of the third cause of action would be a patient who is suing a pharmaceutical company because the company did not warn that a certain medicine aggravated high blood pressure even though it was aware of the problem.

Other remedies are also available to a person who is injured because of a malfunction of a product. The first of these is negligence, but there is the practical problem of establishing the failure to exercise the standard of care. Another possibility is to proceed on a breach of warranty under contract law. The seller of a product is deemed by the law to have either expressly or impliedly warranted that the product is fit for its intended use. A plaintiff may wish to file suit against the seller for breach of the warranty and against the manufacturer for a defective product under tort law, thereby enhancing the possibility of establishing liability and obtaining damages. Jurors are consumers too, and they are awarding increasingly larger judgments against manufacturers and sellers of defective products.[27]

IMMUNITIES

A basic premise of American jurisprudence is that no one is above the law. Actually, that principle is not absolutely true in tort law. Tort liability may be moved from the actual tortfeasor to another (innocent) party under the theory of *vicarious liability;* thus, parents are responsible for some torts committed by their children, and employers are responsible for the torts of their employees committed during the course of employment. The legal theory for shifting the responsibility from the employee to the employer is known as *respondeat superior.* Vicarious liability is actually a "rule of policy, a deliberate allocation of a risk."[28] It places the monetary punishment on the person or organization with the "deep pockets," the one who is profiting from the enterprise or who is able to pay larger judgments. In police misconduct cases, the plaintiff typically sues the city as well as the individual officer because the city has the deeper pockets.

One of the largest employers in the country has limited liability for the torts of its employees, however. The U.S. government is subject to suit only for the negligent torts of its employees and not for intentional torts. This is an offshoot of the traditional sovereign immunity of governments, a concept which dates from the absolute monarchies in Europe. Congress and many state legislatures recognize the injustice of this immunity and have passed statutes designed to permit tort actions to be filed against the government. These same legislative bodies may also adopt special legislation allowing a particular plaintiff or class of plaintiffs to petition for redress from the courts even in the face of the immunity laws.[29] Other immunities exist as well. Public officials who are acting in the performance of their duties, such as judges, are also shielded from tort liability. Of course, these officials are not absolved from liability for personal torts or for torts outside the scope of job responsibility. In order to be protected from liability, the official must show that he is acting as a public official *and* that the activities fall within his job responsibilities.

CONCLUSION

Tort law is controversial today because of the number of suits and the large awards to victims. Some claim that the explosion of tort suits is unwarranted and that Americans are too inclined to sue on frivolous claims. They argue that proximate cause has been overexpanded, and as evidence, they point to the cases in which establishments serving liquor have been held responsible for damages caused by patrons who have injured others in traffic accidents. There has been a barrage of publicity about the high costs of insurance and the difficulty that those costs are causing for municipalities, physicians, and even bars and clubs.

There is a strong movement in state legislatures to fix a ceiling on tort recoveries. The opponents argue that the innocent parties, the victims, should not be required to go uncompensated for the wrongs done to them, and that the wrongdoers should be forced to assume responsibility for their actions. In addition, opponents point to enhanced safety in consumer products that are the result of tort litigation, such as the withdrawal from the market of Ford Pintos, the Dalkon shield, and flammable baby clothes. Others counter that the courts should not be making social policy and that consumer protection should be left to the other branches of government.

Tort law closely resembles criminal law in its effort to avenge the victim. In criminal law, the punishment as set by the state is incarceration or a fine, which is funneled into state coffers; in tort law, however, the money flows to the victim. Tort law involves intentional wrongdoing as well as negligence. It seeks to protect the consumer from wrongful acts by manufacturers. The social policy that is the foundation for tort law focuses on compensating the innocent victim, in a personal way, for injuries caused by third parties.

NOTES

[1] William P. Statsky, *Torts: Personal Injury Litigation*, (St. Paul, Minn.: West Publishing Company, 1982), pp. 1–8.

[2] *Otis Engineering Corp. v. Clark*, 668 S.W.2d 307 (Tex. 1984).

[3] Statsky, pp. 1–8.

[4] William L. Prosser, *Handbook of the Law of Torts*, 4th ed., (St. Paul, Minn.: West Publishing Company, 1971), pp. 141–142.

[5] Ibid., pp. 150–151.

[6] *Rudes v. Gottschalk*, 159 Tex. 552, 324 S.W.2d 201 (1959).

[7] *Cook Consultants Inc. v. Larson*, 700 S.W.2d 231 (Tex. App.—Dallas, 1985).

[8] Statsky, pp. 313–315.

[9] Prosser, pp. 351–415.

[10] *Richardson v. Gregory*, 281 F.2d 626 (D.C. Cir. 1960).

[11] *Sweeney v. Erving*, 228 U.S. 233 (1912).

[12] Prosser, p. 236.

[13] Ibid., p. 237.

[14] *Palsgraf v. Long Island R. Co.*, 248 N.Y. 339, 162 N.E. 99 (1928).

[15] *Garner v. Prescott*, 234 S.W.2d 704 (Tex. Civ. App.—Eastland, 1950).

[16] Statsky, pp. 380–394.

[17] Prosser, pp. 417–457.

[18] Ibid., 37–41.

[19] Statsky, pp. 521–527.

[20] Ibid., pp. 510–517.

[21] P. Allan Dionisopoulos and Craig R. Ducat, *The Right to Privacy* (St. Paul, Minn.: West Publishing Company, 1976), pp. 19–30.

[22] Raymond L. Yasser, *Torts and Sports* (Westport, Conn.: Quorum Books, 1985), pp. 86–116.

[23] Prosser, pp. 71–76.

[24] *Commerce Oil Refining Corp. v. Miner*, 281 F.2d 465 (1st Cir. 1960).

[25] Prosser, pp. 76–97.

[26] Ibid., pp. 492–497.

[27] Irwin Gray, Albert L. Bases, Charles H. Martin, and Alexander Sternberg, *Product Liability: A Management Response* (New York: Amacom, 1975), pp. 12–31.

[28] Prosser, p. 459.

[29] Peter H. Schuck, *Suing Government* (New Haven: Yale University Press, 1983), pp. 29–53.

10

Contracts

Contracts are binding agreements that have legal consequences and can be enforced in court. Noted contract scholar Samuel Williston defines a contract as "a promise, or set of promises, for breach of which the law gives a remedy, or the performance of which the law in some way recognizes as a duty."[1] Contracts provide stability and allow society to carry out its transactions in an orderly fashion; however, contracts are not limited to serious business ventures. For example, siblings who enter into bargains to divide the household chores between them are creating contracts. While some contracts are rather elaborate and formal, others are informal and even implied.

Ensuring stability and certainty is the quintessential goal of contracts. Those who enter into these agreements do so with the knowledge that failure to live up to one's part of the bargain may result in a court order for specific performance or for monetary damages as well as damage to one's reputation in the community. The importance of contract stability is emphasized by Article I, Section 10 of the U.S. Constitution, which provides that "No State shall . . . pass any . . . Law impairing the Obligation of Contracts." In earlier days, freedom of contract was virtually uncircumscribed by government restrictions; people contracted as they pleased, with the only real restraint being that contracts for illegal purposes were not enforceable by the courts. For example, an employee hired for the sole purpose of murdering his employer's wealthy spouse could not successfully petition the court to claim his unpaid fee. That rule is still valid; however, other restrictions have been added. Consider, for example, employment contracts, which are governed by regulations barring discrimination, requiring minimum wages, limiting hours, and providing workers' compensation, to name only a few. As society becomes more complex and more litigious, legislatures, administrative agencies, and courts at all levels of government are placing greater restrictions on the freedom to contract. Contract law permeates our daily lives in such diverse areas as sales, credit, employment, and commercial transactions.

FORMATION OF CONTRACTS

The requirements for formulating a contract appear relatively uncomplicated. First, there must be two or more parties, each of whom have the legal *capacity* to enter into an agreement. Second, there must be an *offer* and *acceptance,* or consent, which reflects a mutual understanding between the parties as to the essential elements of the contract. Third, the agreement must be supported by *consideration* or obligation.[2] Determining the existence of each of these elements is not as simple as it might appear at first glance.

Parties. Two or more parties must be involved in a contract.[3] One cannot enter into a legally enforceable contract with oneself. Parties to such agreements include both natural and *artificial persons* (corporations). The law creates a legal fiction that corporations are persons.[4] This allows corporations to sue and be sued and to conduct business transactions as entities without involving individual shareholders.

Each party involved in the contract must have the legal capacity to enter into the agreement.[5] Incapacity may result from the age of the individual or from a party's being mentally incapable of understanding the ramifications of the contract. At common law, a person under the age of 21 was considered an infant, or minor. Today, many states establish the *age of majority* at 18, the age at which citizens may vote. State laws often provide that minors may enter into contracts but that they retain the ability to withdraw from the agreement.[6] Assume that Patricia, age 17, buys a $750 stereo, but upon bringing it home and discussing the matter with her parents, she decides to return the stereo to the store. As a minor, she may disaffirm the contract, and the store must take the stereo back if there is a timely disclaimer on her part. Minors are under an obligation to return any consideration received under the contract. The fact that minors may avoid contracts causes many people to refuse to contract with them. Minors who contract for necessities such as food, shelter, and clothing are not usually permitted to avoid such agreements after the goods or services have been delivered; however, the minor is liable only for the reasonable value of the goods or services, which may not be the same as the contract price.[7] **Emancipation,** or the removal of one's disabilities as a minor, can occur by court order, by entry into the armed forces, or by marriage, according to state law provisions regarding emancipation.

Mental competency is another issue relating to capacity. The mental capacity to contract can be defined as the ability to understand the nature and effects of the business being transacted. Some people, such as the severely mentally retarded, are not capable of understanding the effects and obligations of contracts. These people are generally released from any contract they enter.[8] On the other hand, courts are hesitant to intervene in contractual relationships and are reluctant to release people from contracts merely because they were foolish for entering into them. For example, a person who abuses credit cards and charges large amounts that he will be unable to pay will not be protected simply because of bad judgment. Adults are presumed to have the legal capacity to contract, and those seeking to be excused from contractual obligations on this ground would be required to prove that they lacked legal capacity. It is incumbent on those contracting to determine the legal capacity of the other party.[9]

Mutual Assent.   Cases less frequently turn on the question of whether there are two parties to the contract or whether the parties had legal capacity than on the issue of mutual assent. The question is whether the two parties have a true "meeting of the minds"; that is, "the parties must reach an agreement on the same bargain on the same terms and at the same time."[10] The mutual agreement is generally measured on an objective standard, and the subjective intent of the parties is usually irrelevant. Courts examine the language of the contract and construe it by the usual meanings of the words. A great jurist, Learned Hand, clearly stated this principle of judicial construction when he wrote, "If, however, it were proved by twenty bishops that either party, when he used the words, intended something else than the usual meaning which the law imposes upon them, he would still be held, unless there was some mutual mistake, or something else of that sort."[11] For this reason, complex contracts often contain sections that clearly define certain terms. It is critical that both parties have the same understanding of the terms. To illustrate, merchants involved in international trading would specify the currency for payment as U.S. dollars rather than merely as dollars, which could drastically affect the amount paid if some other nation's dollars were involved. The test used by the courts to measure the party's intention is whether a reasonable person in the position of the other party would also interpret the words and actions in the same light.

The mutual understanding usually follows negotiations in which parties argue back and forth as to the terms of the contract. For example, assume that Joe Starr is a nationally known athlete and winner of his sport's highest honor, and that he wishes to parlay that recognition into a lucrative professional career. Starr and the team owners may enter into extended talks about the terms of his contract. The team owners may offer a $2,500,000 compensation package with a yearly salary of $100,000 and the remainder to be paid into a pension plan if Joe plays for the team for a period of five years. Joe may counter with an offer to play for $5,000,000 and a yearly salary of $150,000, with the other terms to remain the same. Such bargaining may continue until a compromise acceptable to both is reached. The final contract could have Joe playing for $3,000,000 with a yearly salary of $125,000, a no-cut provision, and a percentage of the team's profits. When one party (**the offeree**) accepts the terms offered by the other (the **offeror**), the negotiations are completed and the contract then be drafted in final form.

Surprisingly, most newspaper or catalog advertisements that state that goods will be sold for a certain price do not constitute offers in this sense. Instead, they are technically considered to be an invitation for the consumer to offer to pay this price for the goods. The merchant, although not required to have an unlimited supply of the items, is expected to have enough to meet the demand; if he intentionally lacks the needed number and tries to substitute another, he may run afoul of certain consumer protection laws. The language of some advertisements does constitute an offer. In these days of corporate raiders and takeovers, it is not uncommon for raiders to advertise to buy shares at a fixed rate, say $30 per share, which is interpreted as an offer. The issue of whether the specific advertisement or circular constitutes an offer depends on the intent of the parties, the specific language, and the circumstances.[12]

Offers are often accompanied by a restriction that the offer will remain open only for a given number of hours or days. When that time has lapsed, the offer is terminated. If no time limit is provided, a reasonable time, as determined by the judge or the jury, will be imposed. Offers may also be terminated by revocation or retraction of the offer, such as when a property owner removes her home from the market. An offer may be rejected by the offeror, and that rejection must be communicated to the offeree directly.[13]

Like rejection, acceptance of the offer must be manifested directly to the offeree by words—either oral or written—or by action, such as performance of one's part of the contract. If the offer is to paint a house and the painter does, in fact, paint the house, that performance is considered acceptance of the offer. The acceptance must be in the format demanded by the offeree, if any, to be valid.[14] The person accepting the offer must be the one to whom it was directed, but a ***third-party beneficiary*** may be entitled to enforce the contract even though a stranger to the offer and acceptance.[15] A typical third-party beneficiary contract is one in which parents agree to pay tuition for a student to a university. The student could sue the university for failing to place her name on the roll if the fees have been paid. The student did not participate in the bargaining process, but it was the clear intent of the parties that she was the intended beneficiary of the contract, and the law therefore provides an avenue of redress for her.

Valid contracts are accompanied by ***consideration.*** Consideration is not limited to money but instead is usually defined in terms of an exchange of benefits or detriments; that is, the parties agree to do something they are not legally obligated to do or refrain from carrying out some activity that they are bound by law to do.[16] This consideration may include the exchange of mutual promises, such as one party's agreeing to perform household tasks this week in exchange for a promise that the other party will do so next week, or the exchange of money or goods, such as trading one car for another. The consideration must be the result of the bargaining, and past consideration is not sufficient. The fact that one party did a favor for another last week is not valid consideration for this week's contract. Generally, even economically inadequate consideration will be sufficient to support the bargain, but the key is that both parties must suffer a detriment. Again, the courts are hesitant to correct the foolish errors or bad judgment of the parties if there has been no fraud or duress involved in the bargaining.

In determining the formation of a contract, courts look to three factors: the capacity of the parties, the offer and acceptance, and consideration. These factors are measured by an objective-person standard, which often requires the judge or the jury to reconstruct the negotiations. This is often difficult, particularly in the case of oral contracts. Oral contracts are as valid as written contracts, with a few exceptions, as we will discuss later; and simple contracts are as valid as the most laboriously drawn ones.

Parties often enter into contracts without realizing the full ramifications of their actions; therefore, it is imperative that both parties read the entire written contract and carefully consider all aspects of it. To illustrate, suppose that Samantha buys an automobile from a dealer with the understanding that she is to make monthly payments to him. However, a provision may allow ***assignment*** (a present transfer of a contractual interest to a third party) of the contract to a financial institution or to someone else without the permission of the obligor.

Samantha could owe the bank or some other unknown party; this frequently occurs with notes for consumer goods, which may be considered assets of the business and are often sold. Another example would be hiring a particular carpenter and then discovering that he had assigned the contract to someone else. In order to avoid the possibility of assignment, the contract should clearly state that it is not assignable.[17]

Rules of Construction. Despite the well-known need for clarity in contract language, the terms of contracts are frequently disputed. Courts and, to some degree, legislatures have devised tools to deal with these controversies. One of the foremost tools is the statute of frauds, which requires that certain contracts be in writing in order to be enforceable; this is contrary to the general rule that oral contracts are valid. Depending on state law, a writing is required when the contract involves any of the following: (1) contracts affecting interests in land, such as the sale of real property or the creation of a lien; (2) prenuptial agreements or agreements made in contemplation of marriage; (3) contracts that cannot be performed in one year, such as a construction project that will take three years to complete; (4) agreements involving a surety, such as when the executor of an estate repays the debts of the deceased from her own pocket; and (5) contracts involving the sale of goods valued over a set amount ($500 under the Uniform Commercial Code). If such agreements are not written and signed by the parties, the contract is generally unenforceable, although equity may step in to provide remedies.[18]

If the contract is written, the ***parol evidence rule*** is a critical rule of construction. It provides that only those terms stated in the contract will be considered, or that the court will look at only what is contained within the four corners of the document. Earlier negotiations or contemporaneous oral agreements are irrelevant. The purpose of the parol evidence rule and the statutes of frauds is to ensure certainty and stability in contractual relationships.[19]

Courts have developed other rules of construction to help them when the terms of contracts are not clear; an example of such a rule is the requirement that language will be interpreted in its usual meaning or in accordance with previous court decisions if the interpretation cannot be determined from the contract. Courts sometimes strain to interpret conflicting terms as consistent and to give validity to as much of a contract as possible. Courts may even provide missing terms of contracts if they can derive them from the facts of the cases. The policy position is to uphold contracts, and courts are sometimes quite creative in determining the intent of the parties or in dealing with ambiguities in contracts in order to reach that goal.[20]

BREACH OF CONTRACT

Defenses.   Failure to carry out the terms of one's obligations may result in a lawsuit for a **breach of contract,** defined as any failure to perform a contractual duty. Just as in other areas of law, certain recognized defenses are available that may protect one from liability for breach. Two of these excuses for nonperformance have been previously discussed: that the contract contravenes the statute of frauds and that the contract is for illegal purposes. In addition, a party may claim impossibility of performance and repudiation as protection from legal liability. **Repudiation** is when one party withdraws from performing the contract based either on his positive statement to the other party that he is unwilling or unable to perform, or on a voluntary affirmative act that makes his compliance impossible or seemingly impossible. If the act is involuntary and renders contract performance impossible, then the party may be relieved of the contractual obligations without liability. For example, an opera diva who permanently loses her voice due to an accident may repudiate future singing contracts with impunity because the loss of her voice was involuntary rather than voluntary. If the repudiation occurs before the other party has suffered any detriment, there is total protection; however, if the other party has complied or changed positions in reliance on the contract, the court may assess damages. Voluntarily failing to perform under the contract or claiming an impossibility that is the result of one's own acts may result in an award of damages.[21]

Other defenses involve the genuineness of the mutual assent. If there has been an inadvertent, material mistake of fact, the contract may be voided, depending on the stage in the transaction at which the mistake is discovered. Recession of the contract will be denied to one who is negligent if the other party is innocent and changed positions in reliance of the contract. The same policy is applied to those who fail to read contracts and are then bound by their terms.[22] If fraud or duress is involved, however, the courts will nullify the contract, and tort remedies may also be available. Allegations of this nature allow juries to examine the negotiation process despite the parol evidence rule.[23]

Remedies for Breach of Contract.   The most common remedy for breach of contract is for the court to assess monetary damages against the wrongdoer. Many contracts provide for liquidated damages—that is, a predetermined sum to be paid in the event of nonperformance. Compensatory damages, as discussed in Chapter 4, are designed to place the aggrieved party in the economic position in which he would have been had the contract been performed; they constitute the most frequent type of award. Punitive damages, which are designed to punish intentional or malicious wrongdoers by heaping additional costs upon them, are generally not awarded in traditional contract cases.[24] In contract law, the plaintiff may recover those damages which "may fairly and reasonably be considered . . . arising naturally, i.e., according to the usual course of things, from such breach of contract itself" as well as those damages "such as may reasonably be supposed to have been in the contemplation of both parties, at the time they made the contract, as the probable result of the breach of it."[25]

The result is that damages will be assessed only for the harm that was foreseeable when the contract was made. A corollary legal rule imposes an affirmative duty on the aggrieved party to mitigate damages stemming from the breach and not to sit idly by allowing the damages to mount. The courts do not look kindly upon such procrastination and may reduce the amount of damages awarded; on the other hand, the aggrieved party is required to take only reasonable steps that do not lead to undue expense or humiliation.[26]

Damages are the traditional remedy for contract breaches; however, because damages are not always adequate recompense, equity has stepped in to formulate two additional remedies. The first is **promissory estoppel,** which is applied in cases in which the promisee has substantially changed positions in reliance on a gratuitous promise from the promisor, and the promisor is now claiming inadequate consideration as an excuse for nonperformance. The court will step in to prevent injustice and to force the promisor to comply with the terms of the agreement.[27]

Another remedy for breach of contract is specific performance; that is, the court orders the party breaking the contract to comply with its terms. It is particularly appropriate when an item with unique attributes is involved. To illustrate, suppose that you contract to buy the Hope diamond. Another diamond with the same number of carats and the same cut is not an acceptable substitute. The remedy for breach is for the court to reject the offer of another diamond and to order the seller to deliver the Hope diamond or to void the contract if compliance is not possible. Specific performance is not the proper remedy for breach of employment contracts. A musical group that declines to honor its contract to perform on a certain date in a certain city because of a more lucrative order could not be placed under a court order to perform that evening. Such an order would resemble involuntary servitude or slavery, which is prohibited by the Constitution; the court could enter an injunction prohibiting the group from performing elsewhere, however, as well as awarding damages to the concert backers.[28]

Unfortunately, breach of contracts, with resulting litigation, is a frequent occurrence. Some of these cases are quite complex, requiring years to complete and involving the expenditure of many thousands, if not millions, of dollars on discovery and attorneys' fees. Other contract suits, such as a creditor's suing someone for failure to make a car payment, are relatively easy to resolve. Nevertheless, both types of lawsuits exact a toll on the judicial system in terms of the time both of court personnel and of other litigants, whose cases remain on the docket unheard.

UNIFORM COMMERCIAL CODE

Contracts are the core of most business transactions, and the law governing such agreements is primarily case law, which has developed over hundreds of years. However, various legislative bodies have entered the fray and codified many of these rules. The *Uniform Commercial Code* (UCC) is an example of a set of laws governing commercial transactions that has been enacted by state legislatures. The initial draft was proposed by the National Conference of Commissioners on Uniform State Laws, but each legislature may modify the provisions when adopting the Code. The goals of the Code are "(a) to simplify, clarify, and modernize the law relating to commercial transactions; (b) to permit the continued expansion of commercial practices through custom, usage, and agreement of the parties, and (c) to make uniform the laws among the various jurisdictions."[29] In order to facilitate the uniformity of statutes governing commercial transactions, relatively few changes have been enacted by state legislatures.

The UCC contains ten articles:

Article 1.	General Provisions
Article 2.	Sales
Article 3.	Commercial Paper
Article 4.	Bank Deposits and Collections
Article 5.	Letters of Credit
Article 6.	Bulk Transfers
Article 7.	Warehouse Receipts, Bills of Lading, and Other Documents of Title
Article 8.	Investment Securities
Article 9.	Secured Transactions; Sales of Accounts, Contract Rights, and Chattel Paper
Article 10.	Effective Date and Repealer

Most of the latter articles deal only with commercial transactions between merchants, but the first five articles are relevant in varying degrees, to the average consumer. However, a note of warning must be issued at this point. The UCC does not cover all commercial transactions, nor does it render contract law obsolete. The UCC is concerned primarily with the sale of goods and does not cover various service and real estate contracts. Previously developed common-law contract principles are codified and not abolished. In addition, there is ongoing interpretation by the courts of the various provisions. Different courts, in interpreting the provisions and applying them to specific situations, attribute different meanings and constructions to phrases. Thus, while uniformity is a desired goal, it is not automatic.

Many law students spend an entire semester studying the UCC, but our scope here is much more limited. We will briefly examine Article 2 because of its common applications. Article 2 deals with contracts for the sale of goods and applies to sales between consumers and merchants as well as between merchants. Goods are defined in Section 2-105 as all things that are "moveable at the time of identification to the contract for sale other than the money in which the price is to be paid, investment securities and things in action." Contracts for real property and services are not covered by this provision. Article 2 covers such topics as the formation of the contract and discusses the offer and acceptance. The major differences from the common law are the expansion of the form of acceptance to any "reasonable" manner and to allow the existence of new terms in the acceptance, rather than considering it a counteroffer if the sale is between merchants. Again, the policy is to uphold contracts whenever possible.

An important aspect of Article 2 is the warranty provisions it contains. A *warranty* is "an assurance by one party to a contract of the existence of a fact upon which the other party may rely . . . [and] is intended to relieve the other party of any duty to personally ascertain the fact."[30] Under the UCC, the seller automatically warrants the title as being good; that is, he warrants that he owns the property and has the legal right to transfer ownership. It also guarantees that the goods are being transferred free of a lien or other interest in the property by a third party unless the buyer is notified of the existence of such interest.

Warranties may be either express or implied. *Express warranties* are created by statements or promises made by the seller regarding the durability or other characteristics of the goods or by technical descriptions of goods. No specific language is required to create an express warranty, but the statement must have been a part of the bargaining process and must have become a basic assumption for entering the contract.

The UCC also contains two very important implied warranties. The first is the *Implied Warranty of Merchantibility*. This implied warranty applies only to sales in which the seller is a merchant and is a rich source for tort actions. In order to collect, the plaintiff must show the following: (1) that the seller is a merchant; (2) that this merchant sold these goods; (3) that the goods were not merchantable at the time of sale; (4) that the plaintiff or his property were injured; (5) that such injuries were proximately and actually caused by the defective goods; and (6) that notice of the injury was given to the merchant. Merchantable goods are defined as goods which minimally

(a)   pass without objection in the trade under the contract description; and

(b)   in the case of fungible goods, are of fair average quality within the description; and

(c)   are fit for the ordinary purposes for which such goods are used; and

(d)   run, within variations permitted by the agreement, of even kind, quality and quantity within each unit and among all units involved; and

(e)   are adequately contained, packaged, and labeled as the agreement may require; and

(f)   conform to the promises or affirmations of fact made on the container or label if any.[31]

The effect of the inclusion of this provision is to allow the consumer to sue not only the manufacturer but also the middleman or the merchant for injuries sustained because of defective goods. For example, plaintiffs injured because of defective automobiles may sue the car dealer as well as the manufacturer.

The second important implied warranty, the *Implied Warranty of Fitness,* applies to all sellers of goods, be they merchants or not. Here a seller is warranting that the goods are fit for a particular use, which is a narrower warranty than the previous one. In order to collect, the plaintiff here must prove many of the same elements, such as that this seller sold these goods and made certain representations about them, as well as that the injury was the result of the defective goods. In addition, however, the plaintiff must show that, as the buyer, he relied on the seller's skill or judgment in selecting these particular goods to perform these specific tasks. It is relatively easy for a plaintiff to show that he has less knowledge about the goods and their suitability than the seller and to show that he relied on the seller's expertise and superior knowledge; this, however, is an issue for the jury to decide.[32] These warranties may be specifically disclaimed—which is another reason to read all contracts carefully and completely. The UCC provisions regarding warranties and their possible waivers are bolstered by federal legislation.[33]

The UCC provides remedies for the breach of contracts. Generally, although the UCC Code distinguishes between solvent and insolvent buyers, the seller may withhold the goods, stop delivery, and sue for the price of the goods. The seller may sue for the price of the goods (Sec. 2-709) and for incidental damages (Sec. 2-710), for the difference between the contract price and resale price of the goods (Sec. 2-706), for damages (Sec. 2-708), and to cancel the contract. The usual formula for computing the seller's damages is the difference between the market price at the time of performance and the contract price, plus the costs incurred in mitigating the damage, minus any expenses saved as a result of the buyer's breach.[34] The buyer's remedies for breach are also provided. If the goods do not conform to the contract, the buyer may reject the goods and advise the seller in a timely fashion.[35] If the buyer keeps the goods, the usual formula is the difference between the value of the goods as they are and the value of the goods had they conformed to the contract. The buyer is also entitled to incidental and consequential costs (Sec. 2-715) and to the costs of obtaining substitute goods (Sec. 2-712), or to specific performance if the goods have unique qualities (Sec. 2-716). The buyer may also deduct damages from the unpaid portion of the price for the goods.[36]

The UCC is another attempt to add stability to commercial transactions. In our mobile society, uniformity of laws among the various jurisdictions greatly facilitates that goal. In addition, the codification of these provisions into one statute, rather than having the principles scattered throughout legislative enactments and court decisions, allows merchants, consumers, and lawyers to more easily identify the rules and obligations governing such transactions.

CONSUMER LAW

Since the 1960s, new laws and court decisions have expanded protections for consumers. Consumer law is not actually a separate field; rather, it comprises a conglomeration of elements from torts, contracts, the UCC, usury and bankruptcy, and other areas of law. Heightened awareness on the part of citizens, nurtured by consumer advocates like Ralph Nader, has resulted in major changes in the legal system's approach to the consumer. No longer is the purchaser of goods or services left to fend for himself; instead, because of the inherent imbalance between a single consumer and a large corporation, legislatures and courts have stepped in to enhance the fairness of the marketplace. That benefit is offset by the volume of government regulation to which businesses must adhere, and for many people, the benefits for individuals greatly outweigh the burden of regulation.

The Constitution gives Congress the power to "regulate Commerce" and to "provide for . . . general Welfare." The government has taken seriously that charge to regulate for the safety and well-being of the American people.[37] Scores of Supreme Court cases deal with monopolies, labor and employment laws, and other aspects of commerce.

Administrative agencies regulate the sale of securities under the SEC, the safety of the skies under the FAA, and new medications and food items under the Food and Drug Administration (FDA). Corporate America is accustomed to government regulation of entire industries, but the expectation that they will answer directly to individual consumers for problems with contracts and faulty goods really bloomed in the last two decades. The process was furthered by the willingness of the courts to entertain such large class-action suits as the asbestos and Dalkon Shield cases. New statutory remedies were fashioned to offer the consumer additional protection against the corporations and merchants of goods.

The area of deceptive-trade-practices statutes that have been enacted on both the state and national levels exemplifies legislative reform. Merchants are forbidden to include in advertisements misleading statements about, for example, geographic origin or condition of goods. A grocer cannot advertise Florida oranges when, in fact, they are California oranges. The "bait and switch" tactic, or advertising a particular piece of merchandise for a low price in order to draw customers in and then substituting another in its place, is barred.[38] In addition to the implied warranties in the UCC, many deceptive trade practices acts require truthfulness in statements about the condition of goods and allow the consumer to recover damages, attorney's fees, and court costs as damages. In order to allow recovery of additional damages, suits under the deceptive-trade-practice acts may be filed in conjunction with other types of suits, such as those for violations of tort law, breach of contract, or violations of the UCC.

A related issue is that of home solicitation sales. Assume, for example, that a salesperson comes to your home uninvited and persuades you to buy something. Once the person leaves, you reconsider and decide that you do not want or need the goods. You have the right to cancel that sale within a specified time period in some jurisdictions, and the salesperson must provide you with the forms and addresses necessary to revoke your acceptance and to notify the company. Many cities have ordinances prohibiting door-to-door solicitation, but these are aimed at controlling the traffic flow and not at guaranteeing the trustworthiness of the solicitors or the value of goods.

UCC Section 2-302 also provides that *unconscionable contracts* are unenforceable. The conscionability of the contract or a clause therein is a question for the courts; the UCC provides little direction because it does not define unconscionability, but it has generally been invoked in cases in which the buyer has been taken advantage of by the seller. Because courts are so reluctant to overturn contracts, they hesitate to state that a contract is unconscionable, and they infrequently do so when two merchants are involved in the transaction. This clause is used most often to benefit consumers, particularly those who are poor and uneducated. Courts have voided contracts that contained exorbitant prices for consumer goods or clauses waiving all warranties when the implied warranty of fitness existed. As discussed earlier, fraud and duress may cause a court to nullify a contract.

Lending laws have also been revised, and more information is now available to consumers who are borrowing money. The Federal Truth-in-Lending Act and similar pieces of state legislation require that the debtor be advised of all finance charges, figured annually and expressed at the annual percentage rate. The statute is not all-encompassing; it applies only to those transactions in which (1) the debtor is a natural person who is borrowing the money for personal, household, or agricultural expenses and (2) the creditor is in the business of extending credit in connection with sales, loans, or services. Individuals can now examine their own credit records for accuracy and may include letters explaining that a bill has not been paid because of some dispute with the merchant or provider of the service. In addition, lenders are not permitted to discriminate on the basis of age, sex, race, or ethnic origin.[39]

The pace of adoption of consumer-protection legislation has slowed, and many of the adopted statutes have been weakened, in part because of the efforts of business-oriented incumbent policymakers who favor few restrictions on the right to contract. The imbalance between large corporations and consumers is not as lopsided as it once was because many of the revisions and policies remain a vibrant part of consumer law.

CONCLUSION

In this chapter we have discussed the formation of contracts, outlining the required elements of multiple parties, mutual assent as evidenced by the offer and acceptance, and consideration. The courts have created certain tools, such as the parol evidence rule and the statute of frauds, to help them resolve disputes concerning the creation and interpretation of contracts. Breach, or failure to perform one's obligations under a contract, may result in the aggrieved party's collecting damages or in an order for specific performance issued against the nonperforming party. The UCC codifies many of the provisions of the common law in regard to contracts, but its coverage is limited. Elements of various branches of law, including contract law and tort law, have been combined with the UCC to create new areas of protection for consumers, exemplifying a shift from a policy of unswerving sanctity of contracts to a recognition of individual rights and concerns.

The overall purpose of contract law and its subsidiaries is to ensure stability in commercial and private transactions. As Justice Swayne wrote:

A compact lies at the foundation of all national life. Contracts mark the progress of communities in civilization and prosperity. They guard, as far as is possible, against the fluctuations of human affairs. They seek to give stability to the present and certainty to the future. They gauge the confidence of man in the truthfulness and integrity of his fellow man. They are the springs of business, trade and commerce. Without them society could not go on.[40]

NOTES

[1] Joseph D. Calamari and Joseph M. Perillo, *The Law of Contracts* (St. Paul, Minn.: West Publishing Company, 1970), p. 1.

[2] *Dartmouth College v. Woodward*, 4 Wheat. 518 (1819).

[3] *Fletcher v. Peck*, 6 Cranch 87 (1810).

[4] *Dartmouth College v. Woodward*, 4 Wheat. 518 (1819).

[5] *Davis v. Concordia*, 9 How. 280 (1850).

[6] *Tucker and Thompson v. Moreland*, 10 Pet. 58 (1836).

[7] Calamari and Perillo, pp. 212–215.

[8] *Board of Regents of Univ. of Tex. v. Yarbrough*, 470 S.W.2d 86 (Tex. App.—Waco, 1971).

[9] *Nguyn Ngoc Giao v. Smith & Lamm, P.C.*, 714 S.W.2d 144 (Tex. App.—Houston [1st Dist.], 1986).

[10] David Eliot Brody, *The American Legal System: Concepts and Principles* (Lexington, Mass.: Heath, 1978), p. 126.

[11] *Hotchkiss v. National City Bank of New York*, 200 F. 287 (S.D.N.Y. 1911) at 293.

[12] Calamari and Perillo, pp. 21–26.

[13] Arthur Linton Corbin, *Corbin on Contracts* (St. Paul, Minn.: West Publishing Company, 1952), pp. 141–142.

[14] Laurence P. Simpson, *Handbook on the Law of Contracts* (St. Paul, Minn.: West Publishing Company, 1965), pp. 41–45.

[15] *German Alliance Insurance Co. v. Home Water Supply Co.*, 226 U.S. 220 (1912).

[16] *Gary Safe Co. v. A.C. Andrews Co.*, 568 S.W.2d 166 (Tex. App.—Dallas, 1978).

[17] Calamari and Perillo, pp. 403–404.

[18] Simpson, pp. 131–161.

[19] Corbin, pp. 534–537.

[20] Simpson, p. 209.

[21] Calamari and Perillo, pp. 278–302.

[22] Corbin, p. 607.

[23] *Nguyn Ngoc Giao v. Smith & Lamm, P.C.*, 714 S.W.2d 144 (Tex. App.—Houston [1st Dist.], 1986).

[24] Simpson, pp. 392–399.

[25] *Hadley v. Baxendale*, 156 Eng. Rep. 145 (1854).

[26] Calamari and Perillo, pp. 345–346.

[27] Simpson, p. 112.

[28] Ibid., pp. 405–406.

[29] UCC Sec. 1-102.

[30] Brody, p. 188.

[31] UCC Sec. 2-314.

[32] UCC Sec. 2-315.

[33] 15 U.S.C Secs. 2301–2302.

[34] UCC Sec. 2-709.

[35] UCC Secs. 2-601–2-603.

[36] UCC Sec. 2-717.

[37] U.S. Constitution, Art. I, sec. 8.

[38] 16 CFR Sec. 228.114(a), 238.

[39] 15 U.S.C Secs. 1601–1691.

[40] *Farrington v. Tennessee*, 5 Otto 679 (1878).

11

Property

Of all legal subfields, property law is perhaps the area in which the principles and terminology of the past are most dominant. The concepts and language used today to create and describe property interests originated during the feudal era of England and have remained virtually unchanged.

> The imprint of the past is still discernible in the present. In this branch of the law more than any other we can time and time invoke the often quoted statement of Mr. Justice Holmes: "Upon this point a page of history is worth a volume of logic."[1]

One of the most basic principles of our system of government is private ownership of assets, and its preservation is secured by constitutional provisions: "No person shall . . . be deprived of life, liberty, or *property*, [emphasis added] without due proces of law."[2] We must not overlook the fact that there is public ownership of certain government assets, such as battleships and parks, which theoretically belong to all of us; however, most of the means of production and capital in the United States are held by private investors.

If you were asked whether you own property, what would be your response? Perhaps you would say no, based on the fact that you do not own land. That answer is likely to be incorrect. You own clothes or school supplies; you probably have money in your pocket or bank account. These items are your possessions, and title to them has legally vested in you. Technically, the word *property* means "an aggregate of rights" or "that dominion or indefinite right of use or disposition which one may lawfully exercise over particular things or subjects."[3] Thus, the legal definition of property is one of dominion and control over certain items, whether tangible or intangible. In common parlance, property usually means a thing that is owned or possessed, and judges and lawyers also use the word in that sense.

Two dominant methods are used to classify property. The first is to distinguish between real property and personal property. Real property, or *realty,* is legally interpreted as the land itself and the appurtenances thereto, such as structures constructed on the tract or timber growing on it. In addition, items of personal property that have been securely affixed to the structures or to the land are also considered real property. For example, huge pieces of machinery that are permanently installed in factories lose their character as personal property and assume that of realty. Personal property, or *personalty,* is everything other than realty and includes those items of real property that can be severed without injury to the realty, such as minerals. It includes such diverse items as cash, model airplanes, personal computers, and stocks and bonds.[4]

The second method of classification is to designate property as being tangible or intangible. *Tangible property* includes land and other material items that can be touched, such as paintings and automobiles. Items of *intangible property* are those things that cannot be perceived by touch. For example, debts are intangible even though the promissory note which is the legal acknowledgment of such debt is tangible. A patent or copyright is another illustration of intangible property, although, again, inventors may be given written documentation of their claims.

ESTATES

The Anglo-American notion of estates is based on the concept of ownership measured in terms of time. The duration of ownership determines both the legal rights of the owner and the manner in which he may dispose of the item. A *fee-simple estate* is the maximum estate; it potentially may last through infinity because one is permitted to pass it to one's heirs. The owner of a fee simple may divide it into smaller estates and into nonfreehold estates. The concepts and terms of property ownership are mired in the traditions of the past, particularly the feudal era.

Feudalism.   The word *feudalism* is used by historians to describe the social characteristics of Western Europe from the eighth to the fourteenth centuries. It describes a complicated social hierarchy of reciprocal obligations. For example, a tenant might have owed certain military services to his lord in exchange for the lord's protection against attack. Feudalism developed partly because of the dissolution of the Roman Empire caused by the Barbarian invaders. Chaos replaced the order and rule of law imposed by the Romans. It became necessary for private individuals to obtain higher levels of protection than they could provide by themselves. They were willing to give up some degree of personal independence and private ownership of land in order to secure the protection offered by the great lords. The effect was to convert Europe from a place where individuals owned land absolutely in prefeudal days to a place where individual and communal ownership of land was destroyed.

Feudalism existed in England before the Norman Conquest, but it was the doctrines and rules of William the Conqueror and his followers that came to dominate English land law. In 1066, William defeated the Saxon King Harold at the Battle of Hastings, and confirmed his somewhat shaky claim to succession from Edward the Confessor by his victory on the battlefield. William's attitude was that because the English landowners had disputed his claim to the throne and required him to assert it by force and because he was justly affirmed as monarch, the Saxon landowners who opposed him should forfeit their land. The King himself became the true owner of every acre of land by right of conquest. As a reward for loyalty and as a tool for maintaining order, William granted dominion over certain manors and castles to his followers with the reservation of ultimate ownership in himself. In exchange for being granted these properties and their revenues, the holders agreed to provide certain services or funds to the King.

A complex structure of reciprocal obligations eventually developed to deal with various social needs. A lord might hold several manors in widely separated areas of the country, and he would have tenants who owed him services for use and occupancy of an estate. This system of holding land in subordination to some superior was known as the *tenure* system; the king was considered to hold the dominion of the soil, while the tenant held the possessory title and the right to the use and profits of the soil, *seisin.* Thus, C might hold of B, who held of A, who held of the King. As more tenancies were created, it eventually became quite bewildering, and in 1290 the *Statute Quai Emptores* was passed. This statute recognized the right of freemen to dispose of their land, but the new holder was obligated to the same person for the same services as the prior holder. In other words, it substituted the new owner for the old in terms of services rather than creating a new level of services.

The services due from tenants varied considerably in nature, importance, and duration depending on one's social status.

The tenure system of holding land continued in England until this century, although it was substantially altered by the Statute of Tenures in 1660, which converted most obligations into a simple rent payment. Major land reform legislation was enacted by Parliament in the first quarter of this century, and while land is still theoretically held in tenure and not owned absolutely, it is essentially an empty concept.[5] In the American colonies, land was initially held in tenure. William Penn, for example, was obligated to render two beaver skins annually for his grant.[6] Although lands in the United States were originally held under the feudal concepts of tenure, it is, as a practical matter, not pertinent to land ownership today. Despite the fact that tenure itself is no longer important, the theories that it generated are the basis of modern property law.

Freehold Estates.   There are three types of freehold estates: estates in fee simple, estates in fee tail, and life estates. Each has its own unique characteristics. An estate in fee simple is the most durable of all estates and connotes the maximum of legal ownership. The holder has the right to possession of the property and the right to dispose of it at will. The title remains fixed in the owner until some affirmative divestment occurs, and title can be passed to heirs. This power of the holder to alienate or transfer the land evolved slowly from the feudal system, in which the lord controlled any changes. By the thirteenth century, however, it was established that the holder could transfer the interest, and that if the holder had conveyed the title with a warranty for both himself and his heirs, then the heirs could not overturn the transfer.[7] Today, land conveyances often include the same language, to the effect that the **grantor** and his or her heirs give up all claims of ownership and warrant good title to the purchaser; in addition, land transferred as a fee-simple estate is frequently given "to the purchaser and his or her heirs" although this does not give the heirs a present interest in the property.[8]

Another vestige of feudal law is the **estate in fee tail.** The purpose of the fee tail is to preserve large estates and to keep the property within the family. A fee tail conveys property to a person and the *heirs of his or her body*—that is, descendants of the **grantee.** The effect is to prevent transfer of the property by sale or inheritance outside the family. Like all property transfers, the fee tail may be created by a conveyance of property or by a will. The fee tail, coupled with the system of **primogeniture,** kept many of the major landholdings in England intact and safe from the ravages of dissolute heirs. The grantor could convey the property to a person and the heirs of the body by a particular spouse or limit the lineal descent either through the female line *(fee tail female)* or the male line *(fee tail male)*. Such an arrangement may pose difficulties for families if there are adopted children or if the family wishes to sell the property. Fee tails are disfavored by the law, and many courts will dissolve the fee tail so that land can be transferred and then create an equitable trust from the proceeds from the sale. In our egalitarian society, fee tails are relatively rare.[9]

The *life estate* is of limited duration, during the life of the holder or some other person. If the estate is for the duration of the life of a third party, it is known as an *estate pur autre vie*. A daughter's will might read "to Mother during her life and then to my children." The purpose here is to provide for the mother's welfare during her lifetime and to ensure that the property will ultimately pass to the grandchildren. Life tenants have the right to possession of the property and the right to receive any income and profits from it. They are under an affirmative duty to refrain from any act that would diminish the value of the property and are required to perform ordinary maintenance and repairs. Although a life interest may be transferred, there often is not a market for such limited estates.[10]

Modern conveyances of property employ the same terminology as ancient land deeds in identifying the type of estate created in the grantee. It is ultimately the grantee's responsibility to ensure that the grantor has good title to the property that he is conveying, although the grantor usually warrants that the title is clear. Most buyers delegate the duty of checking the title to trained professionals, such as title companies or attorneys, who examine the courthouse records to determine whether there is any cloud on the title. Many purchases of land involve real estate agents, and their responsibilities and charges should be clarified early in the relationship. The realtor should be looking after the seller's interest and not that of the other party to the transaction. Ethical realtors will be completely open and honest about all fees, closing costs, and real estate prospects in an area. Lending institutions are frequently involved in real estate transactions; in exchange for lending the money to purchase the property, the institution takes a mortgage or puts a lien on the property. If that loan is not repaid in a timely fashion, the institution may force the sale of the asset. The financial institution from which a loan is taken should be selected carefully. All documents involved in the transaction should be studied and questions should be asked without hesitation because these are important commitments.

Nonfreehold Estates.   Nonfreehold estates are leasehold estates that frequently involve periodic payments from a tenant to a landlord; that is, the owner of the fee-simple estate carves out a smaller and temporary estate and keeps the reversion interest in herself. There are three types of leasehold estates: an estate for years, a periodic estate, and an estate at will. The estate for years, which is expressed in terms of a multiple or fraction of a year, has a definite termination date and ends with the expiration of that time or by surrender. The periodic estate resembles the estate for years in that it endures for a year or a fraction thereof and for successive periods of that length until terminated by proper notice by either party. The estate at will has no specified period of termination. It continues at the will of the *lessor* and the *lessee.*

The basis of these arrangements is the *lease,* which is "neither fish nor fowl"; that is, it is neither wholly a contract nor is it wholly a property conveyance. It is based on a series of covenants or promises made by the parties to the lease and is tailored to suit the particular transaction. Typically, the lessor promises the tenant the right of "quiet enjoyment" of the premises; in addition, the landlord may agree to furnish certain services or to maintain the premises in reasonably good repair. In exchange, the lessee agrees to pay rent; to use the premises in the specified manner, such as for residential and not business purposes; to refrain from subleasing or assigning the lease without the landlord's permission; and to refrain from causing any damage beyond the normal wear and tear on the premises.[11]

Leases may be either oral or written. Leases for residential property are often standard forms and are frequently much less complicated than are commercial leases. The lessor, as the person with the largest estate, was favored by the common law if a dispute arose, but statutory enactments now offer the residential tenant much more protection than was previously available. State laws and municipal ordinances vary regarding the landlord's responsibilities, but typically the lessor must maintain the premises in a safe and habitable condition. Failure of either party to comply with the terms of the lease may result in litigation. If a tenant causes excessive deterioration to the property or fails to make timely rent payments, the landlord may evict the tenant under the state's statutory scheme, which may include court action. On the other hand, if lessors do not live up to their part of the bargain, tenants may also sue and punitive damages may be involved. Those who rent property should become familiar with their state and city laws regarding the landlord–tenant relationship. In addition, before a lease is signed, it should be *read.* For the tenant's protection, any preexisting damage, such as stains on the rug, should be listed on the lease itself, and the landlord or its agent should initial it. In addition, any and all provisions relating to the rental of the property should be included in the written lease, and there should be no oral modifications as to the tenant's obligations.

Concurrent Ownership. There are a number of schemes for owning property in common with other people. One of the most frequent is the marital estate. As discussed in Chapter 12, marital property comes in two varieties: the ***community-property*** system and the so-called common-law system. In community-property states, the husband and wife each own an undivided half of the marital estate. Property that was owned by either of them before marriage or that is received as a gift or by inheritance is considered to be separate property.[12] In the common-law states, each spouse has an individual estate; the wife's salary belongs to her and to her alone, although the couple may create cotenancies by mutually contributing money to buy an asset, such as a home. These tenancies are usually treated as tenancies in common.

Tenancies in common are interests in property that are concurrently held by two or more parties. Each has the right to use and enjoy the property; that is, each has a possessory interest. The separate and distinct ownership interests may be created at different times in different instruments, and the rights thereunder pass to the owner's heirs. In contrast, joint tenancies carry a right of survivorship, which means that the co-owner will inherit the interest. ***Joint tenancies*** are created by one instrument at the same time, and all the owners have the right to possess and enjoy the property.[13] Joint tenancies terminate with the death of one owner, with divorce if it is a marital estate, or by a ***suit to partition,*** which is a lawsuit requesting the court to divide the property into separate and distinct segments and to assign it to the owners individually.[14]

Limitations on Ownership Interests.   The traditional rule is that the holder of the fee-simple estate owns not only the surface of the land but also the area below it to the center of the earth and the area above it into the skies. Today, however, the perceptions of ownership are more limited.[15] One such restriction is an ***easement,*** which is a right to use some or all of the property of another and may be created by custom, agreement, statute, or court order. Typical easements include a right-of-way to reach one's land which is surrounded by another's property and easements to prevent the blocking of light, air, and the flow of water.[16] A second development is recognition of limit on the owner's authority over air space above the land; a landowner cannot, for instance, prevent a satellite from being stationed in outer space above his land.

A third limitation is the effect of formally separating the property into surface and subsurface estates. The usual reason for severing the two is to allow for the exploration and production of minerals, often oil and gas. Once severance has taken place, the mineral interest is the dominant one, and its owner has the right to develop that interest even if the surface is damaged. The surface owner may not collect for damage done to his or her interest which is "reasonable" in light of the current industry practices; in other words, the type of injury sustained would have to be unusual or malicious in order for the surface owner to receive compensation.[17]

A fourth limitation is the power of the government over private owners of land. Government has the power of *eminent domain*, or "the power to take private property for public use."[18] This allows government to seize land to construct new housing projects, sports arenas, highways, or other public facilities even over the owner's objections; however, the Fifth Amendment guarantees that "private property [shall not] be taken for public use, without just compensation." Those owners who are dissatisfied with the price offered by the government may file suit and ask for a jury determination as to the fair value of the property.

In addition, local governments frequently restrict the use and occupation of property through zoning ordinances. Zoning determines the type of activity that may be conducted on the property. Typical of such schemes would be delineated areas that are designated for single residences, multiparty residences, commercial purposes, or heavy industry, and landowners would be required to match the use of the land to the appropriate zone and would be barred, for example, from placing a large factory with the resulting traffic in the middle of a residential district and across the street from a school. The owner's freedom to use the land as he sees fit may also be hampered for environmental reasons, for historical preservation, or for aesthetic purposes, such as landscape ordinances. The justification for all of these land controls is in the government's power to protect the general welfare.[19]

SUCCESSION

The old adage "You can't take it with you" succinctly frames the legal problem of what happens to a person's property after death. The law, like nature, abhors a vacuum, and a vast and complicated system of laws has evolved to deal with the troublesome issue. Many of the terms and concepts regarding inheritances are borrowed from property law. For instance, statutes provide for different distributions of the decedent's property depending on whether it is realty or personalty. A person who is foresighted enough to prepare a *will* in accordance with the legal requisites is described as dying *testate*, whereas a person who dies without a will is considered to have died *intestate*. In the latter instance, the state will allocate the property in compliance with the intestacy statute. The *testator*, or person making the will, can control "from beyond the grave" who gets the property; otherwise, the state will make that decision.

Provisions relating to succession were a natural outgrowth of individual property ownership. Intestate succession, based on familial or clan relationships, probably preceded testamentary provisions, but the

Egyptians were designating their beneficiaries in writing as early as 2548 B.C. The Book of Genesis contains references to testamentary distributions, and the rules governing succession were included in the codes of both Jewish and Islamic religions. The Greeks, during the height of their civilization, had limited testamentary powers, but it was the Romans who fully developed the concept. The Roman traditions were incorporated into English law through the ecclesiastical courts, which retained dominion over matters of inheritance until the mid-nineteenth century. As discussed in the previous section, laws such as the estate-in-fee tail and primogeniture were designed to ensure succession within families and therefore to preserve the family's base of power. Although American laws regarding succession to property are founded in English principles, there are numerous differences. One of the most obvious is the failure to adopt the system of primogeniture and instead to adhere to the Roman principle that the children inherit equally from a parent.[20]

Intestate Succession. The laws of descent and distribution determine the manner in which a decedent's property will be distributed if he dies without making a will, if the will is invalid, or if it does not cover the entire estate. In effect, the law makes wills for those who do not make their own. The statutes disburse the property by fixed formulations based on consanguinity and affinity rather than dependency, age, household connections, need, or other factors. The two key elements in most of the intestacy statutes are the structure of the decedent's family and the categorization of property as realty or personalty. Such laws are blind to the individual needs or equities in a particular family because they are drafted to provide certainty and stability in a wide variety of situations. For instance, if you were deciding how your assets would be allocated after your death, you might want to provide for an aged parent or a handicapped sibling; however, the statute might assign all of your property to your minor children with a reservation of a life estate in your spouse.

The rules governing descent and distribution vary from state to state, but there are patterns in the various schemes. First, descendants receive favored treatment over all other blood relatives. The decedent's children, natural and adopted, inherit the property subject to the interest, if any, of the decedent's spouse. The children are given equal shares without regard to age or sex, and the children of any of the decedent's predeceased children receive the share that their parent would have received if still living. If the decedent leaves no surviving spouse or descendants, the property often goes to the parents, to the siblings, to the children of the siblings, and then to the descendants of the decedent's grandparents, in successive steps. The presence of *heirs* at any of those levels would stop the process. If there are no heirs, then the property will escheat to the state.[21]

Second, every state has some protection for surviving spouses. In community-property states, the spouse already owns half of the marital estate, and the succession laws may omit the spouse entirely in favor of those related by consanguinity.[22] A surviving husband may wind up owning his undivided half of the marital home, with the other half being owned by the children of his wife's first marriage (which can be a most uncomfortable situation). Another favorite statutory provision is to allow the surviving spouse to take one-half, one-third, or some other fractional share of the estate if the decedent left children; if there are no issue, then the spouse may inherit the entire estate.[23]

To iterate, each sovereign state has a different statutory scheme regarding intestacy and the guardianship of minor children. Disposition of the children can be predetermined by a testator, but without testamentary provisions, the state will decide the guardianship of the children. Many of the problems common to intestate succession rear their heads here. You might wish your best friends to have custody of your children instead of your aged parents or your disreputable sibling, but the law gives preference to relatives. The court will base its decision on the objective standard of the best interest of the children in a contested case, but blood relatives are often the preferred choices.

Testate Succession. A person who drafts a will determines the fate of his or her family and disposes of any assets rather than leaving such important issues to the sometimes cold and unfeeling state. No one has a better understanding of a person's wishes in this regard than the person herself, and despite what clairvoyants and mediums proclaim, the law is skeptical of communications "from beyond the grave" and will not give effect to any postdeath property dispositions. Drafting a will is really quite simple, but the process does demand that the testator carefully assess the situation and his own emotions and then make preparations based on that assessment.

Most of us think of a written instrument that has been executed with certain formalities when we hear the term *will.* However, there are other types of wills—holographic and nuncupative—which may be recognized by the law. A *holographic will* is one written entirely in the testator's handwriting and signed by him or her.[24] A *nuncupative will* is an oral will. These are not favored by the law because of the inherent difficulties in a will contest of determining the exact intent of the testator and the disposition of the property due to the fleeting nature of the will. Typically, statutes governing nuncupative wills set out stringent requirements for validity and may include such provisions as the following: (1) that the testator was aware of impending death; (2) that the witnesses cannot claim under the will; and (3) that only personalty, and not realty, may be affected.[25] Not all states accept holographic and nuncupative wills, and, as previously noted, the validity of the will is determined by the laws of the domicile of the testator. Louisiana, in particular, has unique provisions relating to succession, both testate and intestate, because of its civil-law heritage.

A testator executing a will—of whatever kind—must have **testamentary capacity,** which is defined as being of "sound mind" or understanding "the nature and extent of his property, the persons who are the natural objects of his bounty, and the disposition he is making of his property," and the nexus between all of these.[26] The moment at which the will is executed is the pivotal time, and the fact that one's mental capabilities fade in and out is not determinative of one's capacity. The testamentary capacity needed to make a will is not tantamount to the legal ability to contract. A somewhat related issue is the question of voluntariness. The will is void if the testator was acting involuntarily or under duress, or if there was fraud or undue influence involved. However, disinheriting one's family members, supposedly the natural objects of one's bounty, in favor of someone else does not automatically cast doubt on the validity of one's capacity.[27]

Other formalities must be observed in executing a written will. It is patent that the testator must sign the will for it to be effective. It must be signed in front of competent witnesses whose number and competency, usually age, are determined by state law, and it is axiomatic that someone taking under the will must not sign as a witness. The witnesses must be advised as to the nature of the ceremony they are observing, although they do not read the will and often do not know the testamentary provisions (unless the witness is the attorney who drafted the will or the secretary who typed it). The witnesses sign the will after the testator but in his presence. The will should be stored in a safe place until it is needed.[28]

Wills must be updated periodically as life circumstances alter. People marry, divorce, have children, and see those children become independent while once independent parents become dependent. One method of changing one's will is to add a **codicil,** which is a formal modification or addition to the existing instrument. A second method is to execute a new will, in which case the old one should be revoked through language in the new document or, even better, by destruction of the original, or both.[29]

It is relatively inexpensive to have a simple will prepared by an attorney, although it is not absolutely necessary to do so. We heartily recommend the avoidance of self-help methods or popular "how-to" books. It is true that one might follow these guides with no particular problems, but on the other hand, disaster can strike if one fails to understand all the ramifications. Remember, too, that each state has a different testamentary scheme and requirements for validity. A corollary issue is that of the "living will," which allows you and your family freedom of choice in regard to medical treatment for the terminally ill. Some states mandate a particular format and language in order for the will to be effective; therefore, if you are interested in executing such a document, be sure that you are aware of the law in your state, and do not assume that a standard form will suffice.

Probate. The purpose of probate proceedings is to ensure that the heirs and beneficiaries receive good title to the property they receive. Probate is conducted in accordance with the laws of the domicile of the decedent or with the laws of the state where realty is located.[30] Probate is generally much simpler (and often cheaper) if there is a will appointing an executor or administrator of the estate; otherwise, the court will appoint someone to carry out these responsibilities. It is this person's duty to gather the assets, prepare the inventory for the court's approval, pay the debts, prepare the estate tax return, if any, and disburse the assets to the beneficiaries or heirs.[31] Creditors of the decedent have priority over the heirs or beneficiaries, although state laws provide some protection for the surviving spouse and minor children. Again, this is not the ideal time to employ self-help methods or to ignore probate if one wishes to have legal title to any property one inherits.

Although dying testate is obviously meritorious, it is no guarantee that everything will be copacetic following a demise. Those who are omitted may be disgruntled, and the dispositions can generate enmity among relatives. Nevertheless, a prudent and considerate person protects those he cares for by preparing a will and engaging in estate planning. This includes maintaining an up-to-date list of all assets and debts, of the location of important documents, and of current advisors such as accountants, insurance agents, stockbrokers, and attorneys. The existence of this list and its whereabouts should be made known to family members. While many of us think of only the elderly as needing wills, it is perhaps more critical for younger people with dependent children to have a will in order to specify the guardianship of those children if something happened to the parent.

TRUSTS AND GIFTS

The laws relating to succession are designed to ensure the preservation of property. Another way to do so is through a *trust,* which is a transfer of property from the *trustor* or settlor to the *trustee* as trustee to manage the property for the benefit of the settlor or a third party, known as the beneficiary.[32] Trusts may either be created in a will—a testamentary trust—or during the lifetime of the settlor—an *inter vivos* trust.[33] Trusts are created for a variety of reasons. There may be certain tax advantages to this type of property transfer. The trustor may wish to transfer the problems of managing the trust assets to a financial institution while reserving the right to withdraw any or all of the money whenever it is needed. Perhaps the most common reason for creating a trust is to place the management of assets in the hands of an impartial party as a form of protection for children or grandchildren. Such appointment may be desirable because the person is a spendthrift and the assets can be protected from creditors, or because the trustor wishes to guarantee the beneficiary an income long after the trustor is gone.[34]

The provisions of the trust can be tailored to suit the trustor's wishes, and while it does allow for extended control "from beyond the grave," all trusts must eventually terminate, and none can last more than 21 years past the lives of the persons living and specified at the time of creating the trust. This is known as the **rule against perpetuities.**[35] A frequent testamentary arrangement is for the surviving spouse to receive the income from the trust, and after the spouse's death, the children or grandchildren would receive the **corpus,** or the principal. This provides the spouse with an income, and at the same time prevents him from wasting the children's inheritance or conveying it to a second spouse. Trustors have been quite creative in the restrictions and control they have exerted.

In contrast, gifts come with "no strings attached." **Gifts** are voluntary transfers of property to the recipient. The **donee** receives full legal title to the property and has full management of it. These are gratuitous transfers; that is, there is no exchange of consideration.[36] An estate planner may recommend a plan of annual gifts to reduce a person's estate below the state or federal inheritance tax levels. Gifts are tax-free to the donee. In other words, substantial gifts to individuals and to charities not only warm the **donors'** hearts but may also provide tax advantages to them, although the tax advantages of charitable contributions are now more limited under the 1986 tax-reform measures.

CONCLUSION

The maintenance of a system of private property has been of paramount importance in this country from its earliest days. It is entrenched social policy to preserve wealth in the hands of individuals, and the laws reflect that commitment. Americans look askance at those who attempt to limit the use of their property, especially land, and some only grudgingly comply with various zoning and building codes and with corporate regulation. They view these as interference with their God-given right to own and control their property as they see fit.

This chapter conforms to the traditional approach to property law. It discusses the creation of property rights, the traditional classifications, the means of preserving such interests, and the methods of transferring the property from one person through another. The nature of this work precludes an in-depth discussion of the complexity of landlord–tenant relations, financing land purchases, or tax issues related to property. The cursory treatment is not intended to minimize the importance of any of these issues, however.

Although we opted for the traditional approach, you should be aware of emerging trends in property law. Real property is no longer the dominant form of wealth in the United States; instead, billions of dollars are invested in pension and profit-sharing plans, mutual funds, stock markets, and government-backed securities. The result is that more attention by the government and courts is being directed toward these forms of wealth and toward civil and individual rights than was the case in the past. This focus is producing two shifts in American law. First, the courts are employing a balancing test of the owner's right to unfettered use of his land versus the interests of the other party.[37] In First Amendment and other cases, there is no longer an automatic reaction to rule in favor of the landowner, and the proprietor's use and enjoyment of the land are being circumscribed. Second, the concept of property is being expanded. Courts have held that one's means of livelihood, income, or career are defined as property for due-process purposes, which means that certain procedural requirements must be met before a person is deprived of his property interest.[38] Thus, as society evolves, the law of property is changing.

NOTES

[1] Cornelius J. Moynihan, *Introduction to the Law of Real Property* (St. Paul, Minn.: West Publishing Company, 1962), p. 1.

[2] U.S. Constitution, Amend. V; see also Amend. XIV.

[3] Henry C. Black, *Black's Law Dictionary*, 4th ed. (St. Paul, Minn.: West Publishing Company, 1968), p. 1382.

[4] Harold F. Lusk, *Law of Real Estate Business* (Homewood, Ill.: Richard D. Irwin, 1965), pp. 48–49.

[5] G. C. Cheshire, *The Modern Law of Real Property* as cited in John E. Cribbet, William F. Fritz, and Corwin W. Johnson, *Cases and Materials on Property*, 3rd ed. (Mineola, N.Y.: Foundation Press, 1972), pp. 1377–1385.

[6] Moynihan, p. 25.

[7] Ibid., pp. 28–35.

[8] John E. Cribbet, William F. Fritz, and Corwin W. Johnson, *Cases and Materials on Property*, 3rd ed. (Mineola, N.Y.: Foundation Press, 1973), p. 29.

[9] Ibid., pp. 52–53.

[10] Moynihan, pp. 48–62.

[11] John W. Wyatt and Madie B. Wyatt, *Business Law*, 3rd ed. (New York: McGraw-Hill, 1966), pp. 716–722.

[12] Robert Kratovil, *Real Estate Law* 6th ed. (Englewood Cliffs, N.J.: Prentice-Hall, 1974), pp. 212–213.

[13] Ibid., p. 190.

[14] Ibid.

[15] Kratovil, pp. 5–10.

[16] Ibid., pp. 18–42.

[17] David Eliot Brody, *The American Legal System: Concepts and Principles* (Lexington, Mass.: Heath, 1978), p. 202.

[18] Black, p. 616.

[19] *Village of Euclid v. Ambler Realty Co.*, 272 U.S. 365 (1926).

[20] Thomas E. Atkinson, *Handbook of the Law of Wills*, 2nd ed. (St. Paul, Minn.: West Publishing Company, 1953), pp. 7–30.

[21] Eugene M. Wypyski, *The Law of Inheritance in all Fifty States* (Dobbs Ferry, N.Y.: Oceana Publications Inc., 1976), pp. 5–7.

[22] Ibid., p. 17.

[23] Ibid., pp. 10–11.

[24] Gilbert Thomas Stephenson and Norman Adrian Wiggins, *Estates and Trusts* (Englewood Cliffs, N.J.: Prentice-Hall, 1973), p. 41.

[25] Albert M. Lehrman, *Complete Book of Wills and Trusts* (Englewood Cliffs, N.J.: Institute for Business Planning, Inc. 1978), pp. 35, 480–484.

[26] Atkinson, p. 232.

[27] Ibid., pp. 255–270.

[28] Ibid., pp. 291–354.

[29] Lehrman, pp. 48–55.

[30] *In re Barrie's Estate*, 240 Iowa 431, 35 N.W.2d 658 (1949).

[31] Stephenson, p. 219.

[32] George G. Bogert and George T. Bogert, *Handbook on the Law of Trusts*, 5th ed. (St. Paul, Minn.: West Publishing Company, 1973), p. 1.

[33] Stephenson, p. 95.

[34] Ibid., pp. 98–103.

[35] Bogert, p. 183.

[36] Black, p. 817.

[37] *Amalgamated Food Employees Union Local 530 v. Logan Valley Plaza Inc.*, 391 U.S. 308 (1968).

[38] *Goldberg v. Kelly*, 397 U.S. 254 (1970); *Board of Regents of State Colleges v. Roth*, 408 U.S. 564 (1972).

Family Law

Families in this country generate a great deal of litigation. Few lawsuits match the magnitude of the impact on the individuals involved, with the exception of more serious felony cases. These suits impinge upon the most sensitive and personal of relationships; these are the cases that dissolve marriages and determine the custody of children. Many are decided without blazing courtroom battles (the arguments have usually gone on earlier, behind closed doors). Many family-law cases are settled by agreement between the parties, and the courtroom proceedings may seem routine and bland to the detached observer, but the emotional impact on the parties is immeasurable.

Laws that affect familial relationships span many fields, including property law, wills and estates, contracts, torts, and criminal law. This chapter focuses on the creation of the family relationship by marriage, by paternity suits, and by adoption; on the legal principles governing such relations; and on the dissolution of the spousal and parent–child relationship through various types of court action. State legislatures and courts bear the primary onus of dealing with the sometimes complex, often time-consuming issues of family law. It is rare for the U.S. Supreme Court to consider a case involving these matters, although a few involving constitutional questions, such as equal protection, have reached the Court. It is state courts, often specially created domestic-relations courts, which try and then decide the overwhelming majority of such cases.

ROLE OF THE STATE IN FAMILY RELATIONSHIPS

The role of the state in regulating family relationships is so firmly entrenched in jurisprudence that it is virtually unchallenged by today's litigants. It began in Rome during the Republic where the law allowed two alternatives—a ceremony symbolizing the purchase of a bride or a religious ceremony—for the creation of the monogamous marital relationship. The wife and her property were fully under the husband's control, and only he could obtain a divorce. The formal requirements for the creation of a marriage were eventually relaxed, and marriage required only the reciprocal consent of the couple, a precursor of today's informal marriages. During this time, the parties were essentially equal; the husband controlled neither the wife nor her property, although he was obligated to maintain her financially, and either party could end the marriage.[1]

The first formal requirements for obtaining a divorce occurred during the reign of Augustus Caesar in A.D. 40. There were two grounds for divorce: mutual divorce or "no fault," in which the spouses agreed to everything and divorce "for cause," such as adultery. If fault was involved, then the innocent party was favored in the property settlement, and the case was heard by one of the praetors. In the mutual divorce, no judge was involved and the couple settled the matter between themselves.

Under Roman law, there was complete freedom in matters of marriage and divorce, and they were not justiciable matters unless there was controversy over the property settlement. The precepts of Christianity contravened such attitudes, particularly regarding divorce, because marriage was considered to be permanent and to remain indissoluable until death. The Emperor Justinian, a Christian who codified the Roman laws in the sixth century, confronted these countervailing views and chose the moderate path of compromise. The Codes contained limited grounds for divorce—mutual agreement, amicably without cause imputed to either party, and for cause—but the major change was that an agreement between the parties would no longer suffice for a divorce. That was revoked by Justinian's son who, like most of his subjects, shared neither his father's Christian beliefs nor his concern about divorce. However, Justinian's Code served as the basis for the legal systems of most European countries and for canon, or church, law, and his position that divorce by agreement should be barred has prevailed in the western world.[2]

Initially, Christianity had little effect on marriage under Roman law. The major change was in limiting freedom to marry by imposing additional barriers such as age requirements (14 for males and 12 for females) and by forbidding marriages within certain degrees of *consan-*

guinity (related by blood) or of *affinity* (by marriage). Eventually, however, the domination by the Catholic Church in the Middle Ages led to the replacement by canon law of many of the previous legal traditions, but it certainly did not obliterate them, and many remnants linger today. As early as the seventh century, marital laws in England included many of the Church's precepts. Among these was the principle that marriage was of divine origin and the attendant corollary that ecclesiastical courts should have exclusive jurisdiction over marriage, a situation that lasted until the mid-nineteenth century and the passage by Parliament of the Matrimonial Causes Act of 1857. The wife was essentially a chattel, and her property rights were not protected until the equity courts interceded beginning in the seventeenth century.

Divorce was also regulated by canon law, which offered few opportunities to escape from an unhappy marriage. One alternative was to have the marriage dissolved because the husband and wife were related within forbidden degrees of consanguinity. Henry VIII used this strategy to end his marriage to Catherine of Aragon in order to marry Anne Boleyn. The other alternative, available after 1660, was divorce by special Parliamentary act on the grounds of adultery. Both alternatives were possible only for the rich and the powerful.

The colonists transported English legal traditions along with their worldly goods to the New World. The rules governing the creation of marital relationships, such as the form of the ceremony and age requirements, remained virtually unchanged. However, the colonies, populated primarily by Protestants following the teachings of Martin Luther and John Calvin, regarded divorce as a legal rather than religious matter, and most adopted general divorce statutes. As new areas opened up and the population migrated westward, the domestic relations laws in the western states and territories became more liberal, to the point of allowing, for a short time, the practice of polygamy, or having a plurality of spouses at the same time.[3]

Some states deliberately enhanced their liberal divorce laws and became havens for those seeking simple and speedy divorces in states with stringent requirements. Those states, like New York, that retained arcane and harsh divorce laws often turned a blind eye to the perjury and exaggerated claims that were prevalent in divorce suits.[4] This atmosphere of chicanery and the recognition of class discrimination against the poor, who could afford neither a trip to Nevada nor the purchase of witnesses to perjure themselves, eventually led to the enactment of no-fault divorce statutes by 49 states.[5]

The role of the state in regulating family relationships has strong historical roots, and it is therefore virtually uncontroverted today. The rationale for such involvement is succinctly explained in the following excerpt:

Marriage is more than a personal relation between a man and a woman. It is a status founded on contract and established by law. It constitutes an institution involving the highest interests of society. It is regulated and controlled by law based on principles of public policy affecting the welfare of the people of the state.[6]

Families are perceived not only as social but also as legal entities, and government therefore issues rules governing the creation and dissolution of those relationships. Politicians, sociologists, and others frequently claim that today's American families are "under attack" and subject to destruction, and many conservatives argue that the government maintains too much involvement in family life. On the other hand, many of these same people would abhor the idea of complete freedom to marry because that might include homosexual marriage. However, the traditions and laws are so strong and society's interest so important that withdrawal of all government involvement is most unlikely.

MARRIAGE

Marriage is a legal status founded on contract law in American jurisprudence. As such, states have created certain rules and regulations to govern the creation of such status, just as the law establishes certain requirements for the existence of contracts. In both instances, for example, parties must have the legal capacity to enter into the bargain, and there must be a mutual assent in order to establish each. There are two methods for creating a valid marriage relationship: informal, or the so-called common-law marriage, and formal, whereby the couple is married by someone authorized to do so by law. In determining the validity of the marriage, it is critical to examine the local laws of the jurisdiction in which the marriage occurred. If the creation of the marital relationship satisfied the local requirements, then it is valid everywhere in the United States.[7]

Each state has control over those who marry within its boundaries; regulating marriage is essentially outside the sphere of Congress.[8]

Marriage, as creating the most important relation in life, as having more to do with the morals and civilization of a people than any other institution, has always been subject to the control of the legislature. That body prescribes the age at which parties may contract to marry, the procedure or form essential to constitute marriage, the duties and obligations it creates, its effects upon the property of both, present and prospective, and the acts which may constitute grounds for its dissolution.[9]

The minimum age requirement for marriage has several bases: biology, as the age is generally related to the time of puberty; tradition, such as the age requirements set by canon law; and contract law, which provides that those entering into a contract must be able to comprehend the event. The ages of 18 for men and 16 for women were common requirements, although many states have revised the law so that the same age requirement is applicable to men and women.[10] Beyond the age of majority (which often does not match the age requirements for marriage), couples may freely enter into the relationship; however, for those who are unemancipated minors, permission to marry is required from parents or the courts. In the same vein, those who are mentally incompetent lack the legal capacity to contract, and they are barred from marrying.

In addition to the age requirement, laws also prohibit marriage between those who are related within certain degrees of consanguinity and of affinity. That is, one is barred from marrying one's parents, brothers and sisters (both full- and half-blood), children and other descendants, and direct ancestors, such as grandparents or great-grand-parents. Individual jurisdictions may add to the list of those who cannot marry because they are related.[11] Marriage between persons of the same sex is legally not permitted.[12] This stems in part from society's traditional objections to homosexuality and in part from the premise that one of the reasons that people marry is procreation, which obviously will not occur in a homosexual or lesbian relationship. An additional restriction that states place on the freedom to marry is the requirement of monogamy, or having only one spouse at any given time; this requirement is a remnant of Roman and canon law.[13] In other cultures, such as in some African and Islamic countries, polygamy is legal. Obviously, each jurisdiction has wide authority in governing the marriages within its boundaries. The major exception is that states cannot prohibit interracial marriages. In 1967, the miscegenation statutes, which forbade marriage between blacks and whites in 16 states, were struck down by the landmark case of *Loving v. Virginia.*[14]

Assuming that the parties have the capacity to marry and are not barred from doing so by statutory provisions, there are two methods of creating a legally binding marriage in the United States. All states have standards for formal marriages, while only a few make provisions for informal marriages, but the validity of a marriage is determined by the local law. *Informal marriages* are sometimes called "common-law marriages," a term that may refer to their nonstatutory origin. The basis of an informal marriage is the *present* consent or agreement between the parties that they are married. An agreement to marry in the future is not sufficient. Most statutes additionally require cohabitation and a public declaration of marriage.[15] This declaration may consist of sharing a joint bank account, introducing the other party as the spouse, or some other indication that the couple considers themselves married. The fact that the woman keeps her own name is not a determining factor if the elements are otherwise met.

An informal marriage is a valid marriage, requiring divorce for dissolution. A spouse who enters into an informal marriage and later formally marries without first obtaining a divorce may be subject to bigamy charges. Proving the existence of an informal marriage is sometimes difficult, however; it is particularly difficult to prove the element of intent. Spouses may try to disclaim intent in a divorce suit in order to avoid a property settlement, but the requisite intent may be shown indirectly by other evidence. Informal marriages are disfavored in part because there is seldom a record of such relationships, which complicates such legal matters as receipt of insurance or social security benefits if one spouse dies; nevertheless, they are valid marital relationships if all other prerequisites are met.[16]

The vast majority of couples are joined through ceremonial marriages. Typically, they begin the process by paying a fee and obtaining a license from a public official, often the county clerk. Both parties generally must appear to apply for the license and are required to provide certain basic information, including full names, birthdates, and present marital status. Many states impose a short waiting period, and the licenses generally expire within a given time period. Physical examinations, particularly blood tests for venereal disease and rubella, may be required. In addition to requiring marriage licenses, statutes specify those with authority to perform marriage ceremonies, including ministers, rabbis, priests, or others authorized by religious organizations, as well as certain public officials such as justices of the peace and judges. Once the couple is married, the marriage license must be returned to the proper official, whereupon it becomes a matter of public record.[17]

DISSOLUTION OF MARRIAGE

States regulate not only the creation of the marital relationship, but also its dissolution. **Divorce** by consent alone is not allowed in the United States, and some type of judicial action is necessary to dissolve marriages. The adoption of **no-fault** grounds both facilitates obtaining a divorce and reduces the involvement of the judicial system to a minimum. For example, California statutes provide that couples who have been married less than five years, have no minor children, and have less than $10,000 worth of community property may avoid court entirely and may merely advise the proper authorities of their divorce.[18] In many other instances, judicial approval is purely *pro forma,* an acceptance of the parties' agreements in regard to custody of minor children, if any, and to the property division. Couples are often urged to enter into such agreements because, like a plea bargain in criminal law, it removes the issues from the vagaries of a judge or jury and provides for certainty. Courts favor these agreements for two reasons: (1) More cases can be processed through the system in a shorter period of time than would be the case if the judge had to consider the evidence and merits of each situation; and (2) courts avoid having to decide complex issues such as child custody, as well as the tiresome minutia of which spouse gets the towels and pots and pans.

Annulments. Marriages may be dissolved either by divorce or by **annulment.** Divorces are much more common than annulments because of the extremely limited grounds for annulments. An annulment differs from a divorce in that the legal basis of an annulment is that the marriage was invalid from its inception, whereas a divorce acknowledges the initial validity of the marital relationship. The goal in both cases is to dissolve the legal ties between the spouses.[19] Some statutes distinguish between **void** and **voidable** marriages. Voidable marriages are those which do not meet the requirements for a valid marriage and which can be dissolved on that basis. For example, Jane and Peter were both underage when they wed. If this is considered a voidable marriage, either could file for annulment based on that ground, or they could continue their marriage as if they had met the prerequisites. On the other hand, if Peter were married to Sally at the time that he married Jane, the second marriage would be void, or totally invalid.

The grounds for annulment are rather limited and vary from jurisdiction to jurisdiction. They are generally directed to the capacity or the intent to marry. Those who are underage or mentally incompetent may lack the necessary understanding to enter into a marriage relationship, much as they lack the capability to enter into a binding contract. Mental incompetency may be an issue for the trier of fact. Those who have been treated for mental illness and those who are slightly mentally retarded may have the requisite competency. Those who marry during an involuntary state of intoxication such as persons who have been drugged against their wills generally have grounds for annulment; the key here is that the intoxication is not voluntary. (Those who wish to disclaim their marriage vows because of a nip or two before their wedding are out of luck in qualifying for an annulment.)

Couples related to each other within prohibited degrees of consanguinity or affinity may file for annulments; some of these marriages are void while others are voidable according to state law. In addition, some of the relationships will also fall afoul of such criminal laws as incest statutes. Fraud and duress are other grounds for annulment. *Fraud* involves knowingly making false statements about a material and essential fact in order to induce someone into marriage, such as denying that one is currently married. *Duress* results from employing coercion or force in persuading someone to marry.[20] A facetious example is the reluctant groom who is marrying with the bride's father's loaded shotgun pointed squarely at his back.

Logically, declaring a marriage void from its inception leads to extremely harsh results. Any children born of the marriage are bastardized, and the economic results could be devastating. The effects have been mitigated by laws that legitimize the children and provide for equitable property division; these issues are decided in accordance with the rules that apply in divorce actions.[21] It is important to recognize that annulments are rather rare because most couples do not meet the statutory grounds for filing such a suit.

Divorce. The prevalent method for terminating a marital relationship is divorce. Three issues are generally involved in such suits: (1) the procedural aspects, such as residency and the technical grounds for divorce; (2) the property settlement; and (3) the custody of the children, if any. The result of a divorce suit is to dissolve the legal ties between the couple. As a practical matter, parties often remain connected to each other because of children or mutual property interests, including debts, which frequently cause them to reappear in court as litigants against each other. Some divorce-related issues may drag on for many years; the failure to pay alimony or child support in accordance with the court order is a common example. Divorce rarely resolves all the issues or complaints that couples have against each other, which is somewhat deceptive to many people who anticipate otherwise.

Procedural Aspects of Divorce. A court must have jurisdiction to grant a divorce, to enter a property settlement, and to decide custody of the couple's children. This jurisdiction stems from state constitutional and legislative provisions. A typical requirement is that one or both parties must meet residency requirements. Nevada is famed for its short residency period of 6 weeks, while Texas requires 6 months in the state and 90 days in the county preceding the filing of a divorce suit. Venue is generally in the county of residence of the parties.[22]

Divorce petitions must allege the grounds for the action. Most proceed on no-fault grounds, which merely allege incompatibility, marriage breakdown, or similar circumstances that indicate that the parties are no longer getting along and wish to end the marriage. This greatly simplifies the proof required to obtain a divorce; a simple statement to that effect by one of the parties while on the witness stand usually suffices to prove the grounds for divorce.[23]

The practice of claiming fault as a ground for divorce has fallen into disfavor because of the problems of proof. The party who alleges adultery must introduce evidence and persuade the trier of fact that such activity did occur. This is often an expensive (and somewhat embarrassing) procedure. Typical grounds of fault are adultery, desertion, and cruelty. One reason to allege fault in a divorce petition is to affect the property division against the wrongdoer. In contested cases, the allegations will generally be brought out in testimony and may be considered by the judge in allocating the marital resources. In uncontested cases, they may be used in negotiations as a bargaining chip. The fact that many couples do not wish their private lives to be revealed to public scrutiny, coupled with the difficulty of proof in fault cases, results in most divorces proceeding under the no-fault provisions of the statute.[24]

Property Division. During the existence of the marital relationship, the parties are required to financially support each other. When they decide to divorce, a grant of temporary alimony or maintenance for a spouse who needs it during the pendency of the divorce is usually authorized by state legislatures. Such maintenance orders are entered by the court after adequate notice and the opportunity for a hearing on the matter. Of course, that may be circumvented by agreement between the parties.[25]

At the time of the divorce hearing, the property and the debts are divided between the spouses. This aspect of divorce is often the one that causes the most bitterness and ill-will. Spouses may control the property division by entering into a prearranged property settlement which is generally ratified by the court, but few agreements satisfy both parties. Some couples anticipate the possibility of divorce and enter into a *prenuptial agreement* outlining the property division even before they marry. According to the Statute of Frauds, such contracts must be in writing.[26] Prenuptial agreements are frequently employed by wealthy individuals who are concerned about preserving their assets. The courts scrutinize such arrangements carefully to ensure that no overreaching or coercion was involved. Others who are likely to use prenuptial agreements are older couples who are marrying for the second time and who want their children from their first marriage, rather than their second spouse's children, to inherit their property. In either event, the goal of the prenuptial agreement is to predetermine the disposition of assets at the time of divorce or death.

Marital property is generally defined as all property acquired by either spouse during the marriage relationship, except for gifts or inheritances. In the eight community-property states (Arizona, California, Idaho, Louisiana, Nevada, New Mexico, Texas, and Washington), community property belongs equally to both spouses, regardless of whose efforts garnered the property. Each has an undivided interest in the property; the husband's or wife's salary belongs equally to both, and the issue of who holds the title to the property is irrelevant if it is community property. In contrast, property owned before marriage or property one inherited or was given during marriage belongs only to that spouse. In the so-called common-law states, the early rule was that the wife had no property rights and that her estate was under the control of her husband. The husband's control was abolished in many states by statutes usually known as the Married Women's Act, which often gave married women the right to own property and often to enter into contracts on their own behalf.[27] In these states, ownership of the property still vests in one of the parties unless specifically created in both; for instance, the wage earner has sole ownership of wages. In other words, "under the common-law system, a housewife who does not also work outside the home has no legal right to any marital asset, unless her husband puts it in her name or adds her to the title as a tenant in common or joint tenant."[28]

In both the community-property and common-law states, the same factors are typically considered in the property settlement. These factors include age, health, occupation, other assets, and the earning capacity of the respective parties. For example, Barbara completed one year of college before marrying James, after which she dropped out of school and worked as a bank teller to pay for his undergraduate and dental training. During the 25 years that their children attended public schools, Barbara did not work outside the home. Now Barbara and James, both age 50, are divorcing. He has an annual income of $60,000, while she has no income and no assets other than the marital property. Her age and lack of recent work experience will hinder her efforts to obtain employment, and any job she finds will probably not pay well. On the other hand, James enjoys a relatively secure income which is likely to continue for some time. The court may consider these factors in dividing the property and in setting *alimony* if permitted by state law (Texas, for example, does not allow the payment of alimony once the divorce is finalized).

Most statutes provide that the property be divided in a fair and equitable or reasonable manner. This is not tantamount to requiring that property be divided equally between the spouses. In addition to the aforementioned factors, courts may also consider other items, such as the allocation of debts and custody of minor children, in determining the final property division.[29]

Few topics stir up as much calumny as the subject of alimony. "No one likes alimony. Not the men who pay it, nor the women who receive it. But men are louder in their complaints . . . There are some women . . . who believe . . . it stifles women, both socially and professionally."[30] Charles V. Metz, in his polemic *Divorce and Custody for Men,* writes:

Of all the sadistic shackles that the modern, freed, equalized woman has placed upon men, alimony is the worst. Because alimony can never pay for services rendered, and because alimony inevitably results in mutual hatred, it should be abolished altogether . . . We can presently only hope that the courts which wantonly place men in bondage have their hell-fires stoked by the victims.[31]

Such rhetoric obscures the ultimate question about the justice and fairness of alimony.

Technically, there are differences between orders relating to the division of property and alimony. Property orders relate to marital property already in existence. Alimony, on the other hand, is a payment for support and maintenance usually payable from future income, although the court may approve a lump-sum payment; further, alimony may be founded on the couple's present standard of living as well as on the factors previously discussed in connection with the property settlement. In some instances, installment payments of the property settlement are permitted, but these must be distinguished from alimony. To illustrate, George and Lucy worked together to build a chain of stores now valued at $350,000. The court, having considered all of the factors and all of the couple's assets, orders Lucy to pay George $250,000 for his share of the business. Withdrawing that amount of money from the business at one time might well destroy it; therefore, Lucy may be permitted to pay George $25,000 plus interest for each of the next 10 years. This is not alimony, but instead represents a division of existing assets. In addition to saving her source of income, such installment payments offer certain tax benefits as well.

Differentiating alimony from property settlements is important for several reasons. Court decrees dividing the property generally cannot be modified at a later date, where as alimony orders can be changed upon proof of a change in the circumstances of the payor or recipient. Alimony payments automatically terminate upon remarriage in many states, but the obligation to make the installment payments for the property continues. The IRS treats the two differently for tax purposes. Property orders typically cannot be enforced by civil contempt, whereas alimony orders can be. Any court order involving both alimony and property division should clearly distinguish one from the other.[32]

Custody and Support of the Children. Deciding the custody of children is often a difficult decision for a judge or jury, who are well aware that however tormenting the decision is for them, it is much worse for the parties, especially the youngsters. Children, even those who have been mistreated, usually feel loyalty and affection toward their parents, and custody battles exact more from them than from anyone else. Custody arguments generally arise through two types of litigation: (1) cases in which the state is alleging that the children should be separated from their parents and (2) divorce actions. For a fact-finder, it is relatively easy to decide the issue if one spouse is a model parent and the other is not, but that is rarely true in contested cases.

The current standard used in awarding custody—that of the **best interest of the child,** rather than the old standard of proving the parent unfit for custody—shifts the emphasis from the parent to the child's overall well-being.[33] This intentionally vague standard of best interest allows a number of factors to be considered: (1) the parenting skills of the person seeking custody, (2) the physical safety of the child, (3) the stability of the home and parent, (4) the present and future emotional and physical needs of the child, (5) present and future plans for the child, (6) acts or omissions of the parent that would affect parenting performance, and (7) the child's preference, which is not binding on the court. The items on this list indicate that the parent with the highest earning potential or the most assets does not automatically receive custody, although the ability of each contestant to support the child is considered.

The last two decades have seen major revisions in custody laws, and a large number of them have come about through the feminist movement. One of these changes is the general abolishment of a sex preference in granting custody. The old common-law rule that the father's claim to custody should be paramount was supplanted by a preference for giving custody to the mother, particularly when the case involved girls or children under the age of 6, whereas fathers were generally awarded custody of older sons. Today, most statutes are neutral, and juries are instructed that the sex of the parent is not to be a determinative consideration. More fathers are seeking and obtaining custody today, either by agreement with their spouses or by court order in contested cases.[34] This is partly due to recognition of three factors: (1) that fathers often have parenting skills equal to or better than those of mothers; (2) that couples share household tasks, including the rearing of children, more equally than in the past; and (3) that both parents are employed in many American families, and no longer do mothers automatically stay at home with the children. Economic reality usually dictates that most single mothers must work outside the home, and there is essentially no difference in the amount of time that a working parent, male or female, could spend with the children. Thus, women's search for legal equality and fair treatment under the law has reaped an important benefit for men as well.

Custody orders are not immutable; they can be modified. The typical requirement is that there must have been a substantial and material change in the circumstances of either the parent or the child before the court will modify the original order.[35] The requirement is intended to discourage frequent relitigation of custody orders in order to promote stability in the children's lives. One unfortunate trend that has been somewhat checked is for noncustodial parents to snatch the children, move them to another state, and litigate in a more favorable forum, with the frequently fulfilled hope that the new court will change custody. It is axiomatic that in order to consider the matter, the court had to have jurisdiction; jurisdiction in child custody cases, as frequently defined by statute, vests not only in the court where the order was originally entered, but also in states where the child is presently located or where the most recent and best evidence of the child's care is located. Thus parents who snatch their children and remain undetected for a substantial period of time can invoke the new state's jurisdiction. The enactment by the states of uniform child custody laws that acknowledge the validity of sister states' original orders and promote compliance with those orders, along with the adoption of the Parental Kidnapping Prevention Act (28 U.S.C. Sec. 1738A), has strengthened the enforcement of original orders and curbed the tendency to modify orders or issue new ones.

When parents live apart and a court order is entered regarding custody, one parent is granted possession of the child and the right to determine the child's domicile, while the other is granted visitation rights. Typically, visitation is specified for certain weekends, for longer periods during summer school vacation, and for holidays. Visitation rights may be withheld or circumscribed at the court's discretion. An abusive parent or one who has previously snatched the child may be limited to visits with the child in a grandparent's home or in the offices of the state social service agency. There is a growing trend toward providing visitation rights for the grandparents as well. Custody and visitation rights may be tailored to fit the needs of the children and can be rather creative; an example is a decree that allows the children to remain in the family home while the parents move in and out rather than moving the children.

Parents are legally obligated to support their unemancipated children, and while courts generally do not intervene to enforce this provision if the parents and children are living together, they frequently do so in suits affecting the parent–child relationship, including paternity suits and divorces. The parties may set the amount of child support by agreement, subject to ratification by the court, or the court will assess the amount after considering the relevant evidence. The following factors are often considered in such decisions: actual and potential earnings and other assets of the parents, especially the obligor; division of property and debts; life-styles of the parties and the children; the children's age(s); health of both the parents and children; and the cost of living.[36]

Child-support orders, like custody orders, may be modified if there are substantial and material changes in the circumstances of the children or the parents. A well-paid executive who has lost her position because of economic depression in a particular industry may seek to decrease her child support; or, the custodial parent of a child who develops severe medical problems may seek to increase the support. These are extreme examples, but modification of child-support orders may be triggered by increases in the cost of living or by increased demands as children become older.

Determining the initial amount of support or modifying it are seldom as difficult a legal problem as enforcing the court order. Both visitation orders and child support are enforceable primarily through contempt proceedings and are a fertile source of litigation. Visitation and child support are parallel rights and are not tied to each other. Failure to pay child support on a timely basis does not authorize the custodial parent to withhold visitation as punishment; self-help methods are not favored by the courts in this regard. Both parties in such a situation could be held in contempt of court, which is punishable by fines or by jail sentences, or both, after a hearing that involves adequate notice and the opportunity to present any defense. True inability to pay child support is a valid defense, but courts carefully scrutinize such claims. A parent who claims that he is unable to pay because he lost his job, but who is not looking for work, is unlikely to find favor with the courts; nor is the parent who supports his new wife's children. However, parents who are unable to work because of injury or who are actively seeking work may win a reprieve and time to catch up on the payments at a later date.

Other remedies for nonpayment of support include reducing the amount to judgment and putting a lien on the obligor's property, garnishment of wages, and criminal nonsupport charges. To facilitate collection of child support when the obligor has moved outside the state, states have enacted the Uniform Reciprocal Enforcement of Support Act or its revised form; in addition, treaties provide for collection across international borders. The lawsuits are initiated in the children's home state in the required format and mailed to the site of the parent's new home. Authorities there file the papers, give legal notice and an opportunity to be heard to the parent, collect the support payments, and remit them to the children, all without forcing any of the parties to incur travel expenses.

Intense concern about the spiraling costs of welfare, along with increasing awareness that nonpayment of child support was reaching epidemic proportions, led Congress to enact P.L. 93-647, the Social Security Amendments of 1974 (42 U.S.C. Secs. 651–666). The statute encourages the states to create child-support programs by threatening to withhold federal AFDC funds if such a program is not created. The scheme is primarily directed toward the absent parents of children collecting AFDC; if the monthly amount of child support collected equals the amount of the monthly AFDC grant, AFDC is denied. These child-support programs also assist nonwelfare parents in establishing and enforcing child-support obligations. These state agencies also have access both to the parent-locator service, which uses Social Security numbers to locate absent parents, and to additional methods, such as intercepting tax returns and applying them to unpaid child support.[37]

The dissolution of a marriage is an emotion-laden, if not traumatic, event for most people. Many initiate the process hoping that it will be a cathartic experience, and are therefore disappointed in the detached and apparently insensitive attitudes of judges and attorneys. The parties often want the courts to allocate blame and to punish the other person for perceived injustices and grievances, but that rarely happens. The courts are there only to resolve the legal issues of dissolution, property, custody, and support in accordance with the statutes and legal precepts.

THE PARENT–CHILD RELATIONSHIP

The relationship between parents and children is both biological and legal. The two may not be identical, however. The potential difference arises because of legitimacy statutes, adoption, and, oddly enough, modern medical technology, which allows artificial insemination. Legally, the parent–child relationship may be created by operation of law; by contract, as in the case of surrogate parents; and by court order. As used here, the term *parent* refers to the legal, rather than biological, parent. Parents owe certain duties and responsibilities to their minor children, including the duty of care, support, and supervision. Whereas the biological relationship lasts as long as the parties live, legal parent–child relationships end. Children who reach the age of majority are no longer legally under the control of their parents. This is true of the mentally handicapped as well; most jurisdictions require the appointment of a guardian, who essentially carries out the parental responsibilities and, in fact, often *is* the parent. In addition, the relationship can be terminated by court order.

Establishment of the Parent–Child Relationship. Traditionally, illegitimacy, or birth out of wedlock, has been both a social and legal handicap. For many years, bastards (in the legal sense only) could not claim support or inherit from their natural fathers. Today, illegitimacy no longer makes one a social pariah, nor is it an absolute bar to enforcing legal rights. Children whose biological parents are married to each other at the time of conception or at the child's birth are legitimate. Over the years, laws have evolved that grant that status to children whose natural parents subsequently marry.[38] Children who are conceived by artificial insemination and born of married women are considered the legitimate children of her husband; in some states, the written prior consent of the husband is required before the procedure is performed. Legitimate children are allowed by the law to claim support from both parents as well as to inherit from them.

Relationship of Child to Mother.   In the past, the biological mother was considered the parent without further action and the child was considered as her legitimate offspring until the relationship was terminated by court order.[39] However, this situation has been altered by the use of artificial insemination to impregnate so-called surrogate mothers who contract with infertile couples on the basis that the child will be turned over to the couple to raise. In exchange, the couples generally agree to pay the woman a set fee, pay her medical bills, and perhaps pay her living expenses. There have been several instances in which the natural mother has refused to turn over the child after the birth. Although the famous "Baby M" was awarded to her father by a lower court, there has been no definitive court decision on the respective rights of the parties, but the emerging pattern is to uphold the contract. These arrangements apparently establish parenthood by contract.

Relationship of Child to Father.   Establishing the parent–child relationship between a child and the natural father may be more difficult. Many states provide a mechanism by which the father may voluntarily acknowledge the relationship. In addition, there are paternity statutes— the bases for judicial determination as to the existence of the relationship. Texas was the last jurisdiction in the United States to incorporate a paternity statute in its laws; wags in the state always claimed that it was to prevent the legislators from being sued, and, in fact, the legislature enacted the law only after the U.S. Supreme Court decided in *Gomez v. Perez*, 409 U.S. 535 (1973) that denial of paternal support to illegitimate children was a violation of the equal protection clause and therefore unconstitutional.[40]

Paternity suits, as do all other suits, require that the putative father be given adequate notice and an opportunity to present a defense. Typical defenses include denying sexual intercourse with the mother at the pertinent time or alleging that she was also having intercourse with other men during that time period. A crucial factor in many paternity suits is the results of tests run on blood drawn from the alleged father, the mother, and the child.[41] These sophisticated blood tests can exclude over 98 percent of the male population from being the natural parent—

a remarkable feat. They cannot prove that a particular individual *is* the father, however. Taken together, the facts that the man had access to the mother at the relevant times and that he falls within the 2 percent who could be the father is amazingly persuasive for most fact-finders. Many cases settle out of court once the blood tests are returned. Establishment of paternity invokes rights to visitation or custody and the obligations attached to such relationships, including financial support for the child.[42]

Adoption. Another method of establishing the parent–child relationship is by adoption. *Adoption* is defined in *Black's Law Dictionary* as "the act of one who takes another's child into his own family, treating him as his own, and giving him all the rights and duties of his own child" and as "a juridicial act creating between two persons certain relations, purely civil, of paternity and filiation."[43] As used here, the term refers to formal adoptions (which are court-approved, as opposed to merely taking a child into one's home for succor) and to adoptions of children rather than adults. The process legally substitutes one set of parents, the adoptive set, for another, the biological ones. The chief limitation on the right to adopt is the child's status in regard to his biological parents; that is, the child's relationship to his biological parents must have been terminated by court order before adoption may occur.

The criterion used by the court to judge whether to grant an adoption petition is whether the adoption will be in the child's best interest. As previously discussed, the best interest of the child is a nebulous standard which allows judges to exercise a great deal of discretion. The focus in applying the standard is the *fitness* of the proposed parent or parents, another rather vague term. Statutes and case law provide some guidelines, and judges frequently call upon neutral social service agencies to investigate the parents and the home environment and to file a report with the court or even to testify. It is firmly established that, if other prerequisites are met, an adoption cannot be denied solely on the basis of different religious backgrounds or even on the basis of the parents' lack of belief in a Supreme Being.[44] An absolute bar on interracial adoptions is also unconstitutional. In addition, many states now allow single persons to adopt, reflecting the legislatures' awareness that many families in the United States are headed by single parents. Another recent modification is the relaxation of the rule that the adoptive parents must meet certain physical specifications; those who have been deemed unfit by adoption agencies merely because of physical handicaps or obesity have successfully challenged those rejections in court.[45]

Thus, there are two traditional methods of legally establishing the parent–child relationship: by being the biological parent and having legitimate offspring or by obtaining a court order through paternity suits or adoption. We may be seeing the emergence of a third method: by contract, in situations of artificial insemination or with surrogate mothers. Accompanying the initiation of such relationships are certain duties and responsibilities.

Parental Rights and Obligations.   The obligations and responsibilities of parents, or of those having custody of children, are many and varied. The primary right is to have physical possession of the child and to establish its legal domicile without interference by third parties. The state may intercede to assume physical possession if child abuse is suspected or proven, or under other circumstances ordered by the court. Parents also have the power to make legal decisions for the child and to sue and be sued on the child's behalf. They have authority to consent to medical, surgical, and psychiatric treatment for a child and to approve of marriage or military enlistment for minor children.

The primary parental responsibilities toward children are twofold: (1) to provide the basic necessities of food, shelter, and clothing and (2) to provide care, control, supervision, education, and reasonable discipline. Violation of either of these obligations by the parents may result in the state's intervening in the situation. The parent–child relationship is a privileged one in the eyes of the law, and legislatures and courts hesitate to intervene, as indicated by the following quote from the U.S. Supreme Court.

> It is cardinal with us that the custody, care, and nurture of the child reside first in the parents . . . And it is in recognition of this that these decisions have respected the private realm of family life which the state cannot enter . . . But the family itself is not beyond regulation in the public interest.[46]

The law imposes a duty on parents to supervise children and allows a corollary right of discipline. Failure to adequately supervise children may lead to either civil or criminal liability on the parents' part as well as removal of the children from the home by the state. The duty to control one's offspring is offset by restrictions limiting the punishment a parent may dole out to children. Statutes generally employ such language as "reasonable" discipline. Locking children in closets for days, withholding food or water, and burning them with cigarettes do not fall within this category. Corporal punishment is permitted, but it must not be excessive, an issue which sometimes becomes a fact question at child-abuse trials.

Parents are also obligated to financially support their children and to provide the basics of life, including food, shelter, and clothing.[47] Generally, the standard of living within each home is outside the state's sphere, but if there is a complaint that children are being neglected, the family will be investigated by representatives of the state social service agency. A destitute family may be offered emergency or long-term assistance from private or public sources. If the neglect is intentional, however, a suit may be filed to remove the children from the home and to place them under the care of the state, either temporarily or permanently.

The societal goal is the protection and best interest of the children, but balancing that against the parents' interest is often difficult, even when there is common agreement on what constitutes the best interest of the children. Those instances in which a parent severely injures a child demand that the child be protected. Where is the line to be drawn, though, between spanking a child for disciplinary purposes and physically abusing the child? Parents are given the primary responsibility for the moral and religious instruction of children, but there is a public interest in seeing that children are educated.[48] A growing number of parents are deliberately flaunting compulsory school attendance laws and teaching their children at home because of dissatisfaction with public schools or for religious reasons. If the parents are prosecuted, then the court must attempt to balance the competing interests. Such complex and weighty matters are politically sensitive issues for legislators and judges.

Termination of Parental Rights.   The parent–child relationship may be ended by the child's being emancipated or by court order. Parents may accede to the termination of parental rights or it may be involuntary. As previously discussed, a child cannot be adopted until the rights of the biological parents have been terminated. Voluntary relinquishment is common among unwed and often young parents in order that the child may be placed for adoption. Generally, the written assent of both natural parents is required even if paternity has not been legally established, and a "cooling off" period is imposed, often 30 days, during which the parents may revoke their consent. That the parent who is relinquishing the child is a minor does not invalidate the consent.[49] Voluntary termination also frequently occurs is when the noncustodial parent agrees to adoption by the custodial parent's new spouse.

Suits to involuntarily terminate a parent's rights are usually generated by the state. These stem from abuse of the child—physically, mentally, or sexually—from neglect of the child, or from failure to properly supervise the child.[50] Permanently removing the child from the home by the state on these grounds requires a court order, but legislation provides for immediate removal without court approval if there is a serious or life-threatening emergency; in such a case, judicial review must take place as quickly as possible, often within 24 hours. Again, it is necessary to square the rights of the children with those of the parents and also to protect against hasty, ill-considered state action or excesses on the part of overzealous social service agency representatives, many of whom are under a statutory charge to assist in keeping families together. Involuntary termination may be, but much less frequently is, initiated by a custodial parent against a divorced spouse. The basis of the suit is often an alleged failure to financially support the child or an allegation that the parent ignored the child and has failed to visit or establish contact. The impetus behind such suits often is to facilitate adoption by the petitioner's new spouse.

The effect of terminating the parent–child relationship is to sever all connections between parent and child. It relieves parents of all duties and obligations toward their children, but it also means that the parents are to have no contact at all with their offspring. It voids the original legal relationship, and in adoption cases, the court records are sealed and new birth certificates may be issued.

CONCLUSION

Domestic-relations law touches every American because it deals with family issues. It is an area in which the state is reluctant to intrude, and for many people, the minimal intrusions are accepted and seldom controverted. Most citizens accept the necessity of meeting certain statutory requirements, such as those of obtaining a marriage license and attending school. They applaud the intervention of the state to protect abused children and battered spouses. They recognize the rationale for accurate government records regarding marriages, births, and dissolutions of marriage. The need for a neutral third party to referee domestic disputes and to render impartial decisions is apparent.

The topics discussed in this chapter, including marriage and the parent–child relationship, are only a sampling of the issues involved in family law. For example, juvenile laws are often contained in family codes or are routinely decided by family-law judges. Family litigation often seems interminable because of various modification and enforcement orders. It is the area of law in which many have their only contact as parties with the legal system. Decisions made in these lawsuits have immeasurable and permanent effects on the lives of the spouses and their children.

NOTES

[1] Homer H. Clark, Jr., *Cases and Problems on Domestic Relations,* 2nd ed. (St. Paul, Minn.: West Publishing Company, 1974), pp. 2–3.

[2] Peter J. Riga, "Are We Copying Ancient Rome on Divorce?" *The Texas Lawyer,* December 18, 1985, p. 13.

[3] *Reynolds v. United States*, 98 U.S. 145 (1878).

[4] Clark, pp. 3–11.

[5] Riga, p. 13.

[6] *Fearon v. Treanor*, 272 N.Y. 268 (1936), at 272; 5 N.E.2d 815 (1936), at 816.

[7] *Patterson v. Gaines*, 6 How. 550 (1848).

[8] *Simms v. Simms*, 175 U.S. 162 (1899).

[9] *Maynard v. Hill*, 125 U.S. 190 (1888), at 205.

[10] Clark, pp. 102–104.

[11] Ibid., pp. 121–122.

[12] *Baker v. Nelson*, 291 Minn. 310, 191 N.W.2d 185, appeal dismissed, 409 U.S. 810 (1972).

[13] *Reynolds v. United States*, 98 U.S. 145 (1878).

[14] *Loving v. Virginia*, 388 U.S. 1 (1967).

[15] *In re Estate of Fisher*, 176 N.W.2d 801 (Iowa, 1970).

[16] Clark, p. 82.

[17] Ibid., pp. 58–60.

[18] Riga, p. 13.

[19] *Perlstein v. Perlstein*, 152 Conn. 152, 204 A.2d 909 (1964).

[20] Clark, pp. 170–171.

[21] *Sefton v. Sefton*, 45 Cal.2d 272, 291 P.2d 439 (1955).

[22] Clark, pp. 577–578.

[23] Riane Tennenhaus Eisler, *Dissolution* (New York: McGraw-Hill, 1977), pp. 12–13.

[24] Michael Wheeler, *No-Fault Divorce* (Boston: Beacon Hill Press, 1974), pp. 1–18.

[25] Clark, pp. 730–732.

[26] John D. Calamari and Joseph M. Perillo, *The Law of Contracts* (St. Paul, Minn.: West Publishing Company, 1970), pp. 460–461.

[27] Eisler, pp. 32–34.

[28] Ibid., p. 33.

[29] Ibid., pp. 34–40.

[30] Wheeler, p. 50.

[31] Charles V. Metz, *Divorce and Custody for Men* (Garden City, N.Y.: Doubleday, 1968), p. 67.

[32] Clark, pp. 752–753.

[33] Eisler, p. 56.

[34] Ibid., pp. 55–56.

[35] Clark, pp. 900–902.

[36] Robin Green, *Divorce without Defeat*, (Amarillo, Tex.: Cimarron Press, 1982), p. 152.

[37] Susan Coleman and Franci Smith, *Child Support Enforcement in Texas* (Austin: League of Women Voters of Texas, 1982).

[38] Eisler, p. 122.

[39] *Barnardo v. McHugh*, as cited in Sophonisba P. Breckinridge, *The Family and The State* (Chicago: University of Chicago Press, 1934), pp. 444–446.

[40] John J. Sampson, "Texas Family Code Symposium, Chapter 13, Determination of Paternity," *Texas Tech Law Review*, vol. 13 (1982), p. 898.

[41] Eisler, pp. 122–123.

[42] *Stanley v. Illinois*, 405 U.S. 645 (1972).

[43] Henry C. Black, *Black's Law Dictionary*, 4th ed. (St. Paul, Minn.: West Publishing Company, 1968), p. 70.

[44] *In re Adoption of "E",* 59 N.J. 36, 279 A.2d 785 (1971).

[45] Clark, pp. 328, 339.

[46] *Prince v. Massachusetts,* 321 U.S. 158 (1944), at 171.

[47] *Hunt v. Thompson,* as cited in Sophonisba P. Breckinridge, *The Family and The State,* (Chicago: University of Chicago Press, 1934), p. 242.

[48] *Wisconsin v. Yoder,* 406 U.S. 205 (1972).

[49] *Johnson v. Cupp,* 274 N.E.2d 411 (Ind. App. 1971).

[50] Eisler, pp. 59–60; Clark, pp. 290–296.

13

Conclusion

We began this book by observing that one who wishes to understand the American legal system must first understand the meaning of law. We noted that law can be defined in terms of the functions that it performs in a society, the sources of law, and the different kinds of law. This book has attempted to acquaint the reader with the many facets of law in our society. Viewing law can be compared to the pleasant pastime of cloud gazing. Most of us at one time or another have looked up at the sky and described what we thought we saw in the various cloud formations above—a kind of heavenly Rorschach test. If accompanied by others, we soon discover that there are differences of opinion about the pictures formed by the various combinations of clouds. We also discover that, unless it is an unusually calm day, the cloud formations begin to change, drawing new pictures across the sky. An image we once thought to be clear and distinct is soon misshapen. What is formed by the clouds is a function of time, space, and the perceptions of the viewer.

In a sense, looking at the law is like looking at cloud formations. Law has the same elusive qualities as a cloud. Like a cloud, the law has a real presence, and yet our understanding of it may evaporate in an instant. Like a cloud, the law is constantly changing, but often at a rate so slow that it is almost imperceptible. Like a cloud, the law may appear to be different to different people at various points in time. In this chapter, we will try to bring together some of the facets of the law that have been described either explicitly or implicitly in previous chapters. We will try to pull together the loose ends we have left untied. In so doing, however, we will remind the reader that others have spent a lifetime trying to define and explain the concept of law. The reader may conclude, as we have after years of studying it, that law, like beauty, is in the eye of the beholder.

LAW AS PROTECTOR AND OPPRESSOR

Abraham Lincoln once used the example of the shepherd, the wolf, and the sheep to illustrate the potential variety of perceptions of government. The sheep looks to the shepherd for protection from those who would prey upon him and even kill him. The wolf, on the other hand, sees the shepherd as an oppressor. After all, a wolf, like all living things, needs food to survive, and it is hardly his fault that nature made him carnivorous. To the wolf, the shepherd is an enemy who keeps him from the food he so desperately needs for survival. Lincoln's point was that government, like the shepherd, represents different things to different people. To some, government is the guardian of liberty and the protector of the weak from the strong. To others, government is a source of oppression that interferes with their "pursuit of happiness." To some extent, neither view is entirely incorrect. Government is indeed capable of being both protector and oppressor, as history certainly confirms.

Like the shepherd and government, the law can be viewed as a source of both protection and oppression. For example, consider how the divorced parents of a minor child might view child-support laws. To the custodial mother, the state's child-support laws may seem like the protector of the child's rights. Most children need the financial support of both parents. The law provides the custodial mother with the means (albeit often inadequate) to force her recalcitrant husband to pay his fair share of the financial burden of child rearing. On the other hand, the noncustodial father may see the state's child-support laws as a burden, particularly if there is a controversy about how the funds are spent. Forced to maintain a separate household, the father has living expenses that may make child-support payments an onerous burden. If he remarries, the father often finds himself drained by the job of trying to support two families emotionally and financially. Although he clearly has a legal and moral obligation to provide financial support for his child, he cannot help but feel that the law has placed an intolerable burden on his shoulders.

One more example should help clarify the view of law as protector and oppressor. In Chapter 10 we discussed contract law. A common form of contract is a rental agreement or lease. To the landlord, such agreements are designed to protect the rights of the property owner against abuses by renters. That is, the law serves as the protector of property rights. To the renter, the typical lease gives the landlord unfair advantages, especially if the renter is desperate to find a place to live. Although the law assumes that the two parties entered into the rental contract as equals, the renter often feels that he has no choice but to accept the terms set out in the lease. That the lease permits the landlord to profit from his advantage seems to the renter patently unfair. In the eyes of the law, however, the renter was not forced to sign the lease and consents to the terms of his free will.

More examples could be cited, and the reader can doubtless think of others. It is not our place to say who is right or wrong on these issues. Like most questions of law, there are two sides to every story. We will allow readers to decide for themselves which party is the wolf and which is the sheep in the examples we have cited. Suffice it to say that there will always be those who will use the law to their advantage or to exploit others. As we noted in Chapter 1, law is a function of the society that creates it. Consequently, law is only as good or as bad as the people who make it.

LAW AND POLITICS

It is almost impossible to escape the conclusion that law and politics are inseparable. The legal profession has a vastly disproportionate amount of influence on both our legal and our political institutions. A few examples will illustrate this point. Under normal circumstances, about half the members of Congress are lawyers. Compared to their percentage of the American population as a whole, lawyers are vastly overrepresented. Although there may be good reasons for this overrepresentation, the fact remains that lawyers have disproportionate influence over the making of national laws. The same is true, but to a lesser extent, at the state level. One authority on state government has noted that "Lawyers, farmers, and business owners are heavily represented in state legislatures."[1] Similarly, lawyers almost completely dominate the judicial branch of government. Although there is no constitutional requirement that a president's choice for the Supreme Court be a lawyer, the likelihood of a nonlawyer being approved by the lawyer-dominated Senate Judiciary Committee is remote. At the state level, the possession of a law license is a requirement for appointment or election to most judicial offices. Also, as noted in Chapter 3, the selection of judges at the state and federal levels is a highly politicized process. It makes little difference whether judges are elected, appointed, or chosen by merit; politics will always play a role. Different selection methods do nothing more than change the level of politics involved. As long as judges make political decisions, politics will enter into the selection process. It appears that the close relationship between law and politics will continue. Political science majors still constitute the largest single group of students taking the Law School Admissions Test (LSAT).

The dominance of the legal profession in our political institutions is not the only way that law and politics interact. Courtrooms are increasingly becoming the battlegrounds for causes won or lost in the political arena. Americans have a tendency to turn to courts to resolve the most controversial issues of our society. As noted in Chapter 8, the issues of abortion, discrimination, school prayer, and capital punishment are perennial issues before the courts of the nation. We can anticipate that controversies surrounding issues such as acquired immune deficiency syndrome (AIDS) and surrogate motherhood will require additional judicial resolution in the future. Civil rights, environmental, women's, and other special-interest groups often turn to courts to win the results they have failed to achieve in other political arenas. A loss today is a mere temporary setback for most groups because they know that in time the makeup of the courts could change in their favor. Today's loss is tomorrow's victory. They know that, with perseverance, they can eventually achieve the desired results. Law, then, becomes a never-ending battle between the status quo and the forces of change.

LAW AND SOCIETY

We noted in Chapter 1 that law is a function of the society that creates it, and we have already observed in this chapter that law is only as good or bad as those who make it. Law reflects the values of the lawmaker and the dominant political and economic forces in a society. In Chapter 7 we discussed this relationship in the area of criminal law. Just what kind of behavior society deems unacceptable is manifested by the acts it prohibits by its criminal law. Just how serious society deems that behavior to be is reflected in the vigor with which the law is enforced and the severity with which it is punished. Let's take littering as an example. While it is true that most American cities have ordinances prohibiting littering, it is equally true that these ordinances are infrequently enforced and that the punishment is a relatively small fine. What this seems to indicate is that while littering may be universally condemned and prohibited, it is generally not viewed as a serious offense in our society.

Other, more serious, examples could be cited to reflect upon the relationship of law to society. Only fairly recently have states begun to get really tough with drunk drivers. Although few, if any, rational persons would seriously defend drunk driving, it is not uncommon for drunk drivers to have been arrested several times for the offense before they are severely punished. Often this is because those in our judicial system have empathy for the drunk driver, especially the first offender. Few, if any, persons who drink have not at one time or another driven while legally under the influence of alcohol. Jurors are inclined to think, "There but for the grace of God go I." That is, any one of us could easily picture ourselves in a predicament similar to that of the defendant. Prosecutors and judges, knowing how difficult it is to convict first offenders, will allow the drunk driver to plead guilty to some other offense. When the repeat offender finally kills or injures someone, citizens ask in disbelief how a repeat offender could be allowed to drive at all. Fortunately, through the efforts of groups like Mothers Against Drunk Driving (MADD), states have begun to crack down on driving under the influence. But as long as alcohol use and abuse remain a part of our culture, drunk driving will remain a legal and social problem. Similarly, until such time as problems like abuse of children, spouses, and the elderly are viewed as serious by our society, the law will continue to treat them as relatively minor offenses.

We also noted in Chapter 7 that law reflects a society's attitude toward the lawbreaker. Critics of American criminal justice argue that our legal system is overly concerned with the rights of those accused of crime and almost totally unconcerned about the rights of the victims of crime. Our purpose here is not to reopen that debate. Suffice it to say that our Founding Fathers, themselves branded as "outlaws" by the British government, were sensitive to the ability of government to use its coercive power against the individual. Whether they "overreacted" by placing so many safeguards into the Constitution is also open to debate. The point is that we, as a society, are divided over the proper balance between the rights of the accused and the rights of society. Consequently, there is a constant struggle among law enforcers, civil libertarians, and the public at large over what is the proper balance. The likelihood of reaching a consensus on this issue seems remote.

Finally, we would like to reiterate the evolutionary nature of the law. Law, like the clouds we discussed earlier, changes over time as our society changes. Our ideas and ideals about decency, justice, and due process evolve over time. As noted in Chapter 7, we have narrowed the range of offenses for which a person can be put to death. Crimes that once resulted in hanging, such as horse stealing and bank robbery, are today treated like any other theft of property. It is true that there are still those in our society who would like to see harsher penalties imposed. Generally, however, we have reached a consensus on those offenses that merit the ultimate punishment. Perhaps someday we will reach a similar consensus on the decriminalization of a range of other activities, including gambling and marijuana use.

LAW AND ECONOMICS

One frequently overlooked facet of law is the relationship between law and economics. As previously noted, landlords have historically used the law of contracts to their economic advantage. In addition, landlords have used local city ordinances or state laws to evict tenants who failed to pay their rent on time. Disputes typically arose over the failure of the landlord to effect some needed repairs, and the tenant withheld the rent only to discover that the law favored the landlord. Fortunately, that situation is a thing of the past in most jurisdictions. Laws have been changed to guarantee the tenant the right to live in a habitable dwelling, and methods have been devised to mediate landlord–tenant disputes.

The use of eviction laws was just one way in which an economic group used the law to gain an advantage over another. During the early struggle between labor unions and management, the latter would use court injunctions as a weapon against striking workers. If an owner were able to convince a judge that a labor strike caused him "irreparable damage," the judge would issue an injunction ordering an end to the strike. Stripped of their principal weapon, the workers were fired and replaced by other workers desperately in need of employment. In this manner, employers were permitted to keep wages low, hours long, working conditions unsafe, and workers insecure. The use of the injunction as a strike breaker also illustrates the importance placed upon property rights in our legal system. Judges, often sympathetic to the views of the owners, placed property rights above the workers' rights to decent wages and working conditions. It is fascinating to read accounts of state and national efforts to enact laws to protect the rights of workers only to have those laws ruled unconstitutional by the courts.[2] In a sense, the law was a battleground in an economic class war.

The modern era can provide similar examples of the influence of economics on the law. Tax law is frequently cited as an example of how laws are written to benefit a particular economic class. Laws that provide tax breaks and tax incentives for wealthy investors in municipal bonds and other tax shelters are widely known. A common complaint of the average American is that the tax code gives unfair advantages to those in our society who are already wealthy. Whether this accusation is actually true or not is seldom questioned. The fact is that most

Americans believe it to be true. Another example of the relationship of economics and law is in the area of criminal law. Until the 1963 *Gideon v. Wainwright*[3] decision, indigent persons accused of noncapital offenses were forced in most states either to defend themselves at trial or to plead guilty. Until the *Gideon* decision ruled that states must provide counsel for indigent defendants, those who were economically disadvantaged were also legally disadvantaged.

One final example of the relationship of law and economics is in order. In recent years the medical profession has been plagued by an increase in both the number of malpractice suits and the amount of damages awarded to successful plaintiffs. The response to the crisis has been twofold. First, the cost of medical malpractice insurance premiums has skyrocketed to the point that the costs are nearly prohibitive for many physicians. Second, pressure has increased from both the medical profession and the insurance industry to put a ceiling on the amount of damages that can be awarded in a malpractice suit. These two groups have sought legislation in various states under the general label of "tort reform." Physicians and insurance companies have been opposed in their efforts to win tort reform by segments of the legal profession. Lawyers, especially those who represent plaintiffs, argue that the problem has been grossly exaggerated. Physicians argue that lawyers may not be totally neutral parties since they are often working on a contingency-fee basis. Consequently, physicians argue that lawyers have a financial interest in maintaining a system that encourages large awards. Lawyers counter that large awards are given only in cases of extreme or gross negligence, that they are usually justified, and that the jury system serves as a check on any abuses. Although strong arguments can be made on both sides, our point is that physicians, lawyers, plaintiffs, and insurance companies all seek to use the law to promote some economic self-interest. Despite disclaimers to the contrary, economics is central to this controversy.

We are not prepared to say, as perhaps an economic determinist would, that economics is the only or even the major force behind the enactment of every law. We are, however, prepared to say that the economic impact of the law is a powerful influence on the way that law in our society is shaped.

FINAL REFLECTIONS

We will conclude with a few final reflections on law in American society. As we noted at the beginning of this chapter, law is perceived differently by different people. In a sense, then, our perceptions about the nature and meaning of law have colored the contents of this book.

What we have chosen to emphasize or to ignore is a function of our own individual biases. The fact that hundreds of books have been written on law is a testimony both to its complexity and to the fascination with which law is viewed.

What is this fascination with the law? Part of it is due to the need for humans to have an ultimate answer. There is a finality in law that is comforting to most people. Even those who have lost a lawsuit are sometimes comforted by the fact that they did everything possible to prevail. Even in defeat, they know that they will never have to wonder what would have happened if they had not pursued their case to the fullest extent of the law. A losing litigant may analyze what went wrong and what might have been done differently, but in the final analysis there is the realization that the issue has at least been resolved.

Another reason for our fascination with the law is the feeling of righteousness that often accompanies our involvement with it. One usually hears the relative of a murder victim express satisfaction that "justice was finally done" upon learning of the killer's conviction. Despite the efforts of religion and philosophy to persuade us to rise above our human failings, the fact remains that the need for retribution is powerful in most humans. The old saying "Don't get mad—get even" appeals to many. Law provides us with a civilized way to exact revenge, because even if the individual victim is forgiving, society, in its role as avenger, is not. The same is true for litigants in civil cases. Although we would not entirely rule out avarice as a motivator, litigants in civil suits frequently disavow the desire for money as their reason for suing. Instead, they cite "the principle involved." Given the expense in time and money and the uncertainty of success, principle probably does play a major role in most lawsuits. Law, then, helps fulfill the basic human need for justice.

Finally, law is a source of comfort to most of us. In a world described by Thomas Hobbes as "solitary, poor, nasty, brutish, and short,"[4] it is comforting to realize that we have risen above the law of the jungle, where the strong prey upon the weak. As previously noted, the law really does serve as the sheep's protector. The popularity of the television series "The Equalizer" illustrates this point. People want a hero who will protect them from the injustices of life and the wrath of their enemies. To many, the law is such a hero—a great equalizer ready to come to our assistance if needed.

We hope this book has made its readers think about the law. Regardless of whether the reader accepts or rejects the ideas presented herein, we will have succeeded if each reader has reflected upon the nature and purpose of the law and perhaps has even grown to understand the law a little better.

NOTES

[1] Murray S. Stedman, Jr., *State and Local Governments* (Boston: Little, Brown, 1982), p. 118.

[2] See, for example, *Lochner v. New York,* 198 U.S. 45 (1905); *Hammer v. Dagenhart,* 247 U.S. 251 (1918); *Bailey v. Drexel Furniture Co.,* 259 U.S. 20 (1922); and *Adkins v. Children's Hospital,* 261 U.S. 525 (1923).

[3] *Gideon v. Wainwright,* 372 U.S. 335 (1963).

[4] Quoted in Kenneth Janda, Jeffrey M. Berry, and Jerry Goldman, *The Challenge of Democracy: Government in America* (Boston: Houghton Mifflin Company, 1987), pp. 8–9.

The Constitution
of the United States

WE THE PEOPLE of the United States, in order to form a more perfect union, establish justice, insure domestic tranquillity, provide for the common defense, promote the general welfare, and secure the blessings of liberty to ourselves and our posterity, do ordain and establish this Constitution for the United States of America.

ARTICLE I

SECTION 1. All legislative powers herein granted shall be vested in a Congress of the United States, which shall consist of a Senate and House of Representatives.

SECTION 2. (1) The House of Representatives shall be composed of members chosen every second year by the people of the several States, and the electors in each State shall have the qualifications requisite for electors of the most numerous branch of the State legislature.

(2) No person shall be a Representative who shall not have attained to the age of twenty-five years, and been seven years a citizen of the United States, and who shall not, when elected, be an inhabitant of that State in which he shall be chosen.

(3) Representatives and direct taxes[1] shall be apportioned among the several States which may be included within this Union, according to their respective numbers, which shall be determined by adding to the whole number of free persons, including those bound to service for a term of years, and excluding Indians not taxed, three fifths of all other persons.[2] The actual enumeration shall be made within three years after the first meeting of the Congress of the United States, and within every subsequent term of ten years, in such manner as they shall by law direct. The number of Representatives shall not exceed one for every thirty thousand, but each State shall have at least one Representative; and until such enumeration shall be made, the State of New Hampshire

---

[1]Modified as to income taxes by the 16th Amendment.
[2]Replaced by the 14th Amendment.

shall be entitled to choose three, Massachusetts eight, Rhode Island and Providence Plantations one, Connecticut five, New York six, New Jersey four, Pennsylvania eight, Delaware one, Maryland six, Virginia ten, North Carolina five, South Carolina five, and Georgia three.

(4) When vacancies happen in the representation from any State, the executive authority thereof shall issue writs of election to fill such vacancies.

(5) The House of Representatives shall choose their Speaker and other officers; and shall have the sole power of impeachment.

SECTION 3. (1) The Senate of the United States shall be composed of two Senators from each State, chosen by the Legislature thereof,[3] for six years; and each Senator shall have one vote.

(2) Immediately after they shall be assembled in consequence of the first election, they shall be divided as equally as may be into three classes. The seats of the Senators of the first class shall be vacated at the expiration of the second year, of the second class at the expiration of the fourth year, and of the third class at the expiration of the sixth year, so that one third may be chosen every second year; and if vacancies happen by resignation, or otherwise, during the recess of the legislature of any State, the executive thereof may make temporary appointments until the next meeting of the legislature,which[3] shall then fill such vacancies.

(3) No person shall be a Senator who shall not have attained to the age of thirty years, and been nine years a citizen of the United States, and who shall not, when elected, be an inhabitant of that State for which he shall be chosen.

(4) The Vice President of the United States shall be president of the Senate, but shall have no vote, unless they be equally divided.

(5) The Senate shall choose their other officers, and also a president pro tempore, in the absence of the Vice President, or when he shall exercise the office of President of the United States.

(6) The Senate shall have the sole power to try all impeachments. When sitting for that purpose, they shall be on oath or affirmation. When the President of the United States is tried, the Chief Justice shall preside: and no person shall be convicted without the concurrence of two thirds of the members present.

(7) Judgment in cases of impeachment shall not extend further than to removal from office, and disqualification to hold and enjoy any office of honor, trust or profit under the United States: but the party convicted shall nevertheless be liable and subject to indictment, trial, judgment and punishment, according to law.

SECTION 4. (1) The times, places and manner of holding elections for Senators and Representatives, shall be prescribed in each State by the legislature thereof; but the Congress may at any time by law make or alter such regulations, except as to the places of choosing Senators.

(2) The Congress shall assemble at least once in every year, and such meeting shall be on the first Monday in December, unless they shall by law appoint a different day.

[3]Modified by the 17th Amendment.

SECTION 5. (1) Each House shall be the judge of the elections, returns and qualifications of its own members, and a majority of each shall constitute a quorum to do business; but a smaller number may adjourn from day to day, and may be authorized to compel the attendance of absent members, in such manner, and under such penalties as each House may provide.

(2) Each House may determine the rules of its proceedings, punish its members for disorderly behavior, and, with the concurrence of two thirds, expel a member.

(3) Each House shall keep a journal of its proceedings, and from time to time publish the same, excepting such parts as may in their judgement require secrecy; and the yeas and nays of the members of either House on any question shall, at the desire of one fifth of those present, be entered on the journal.

(4) Neither House, during the session of Congress, shall, without the consent of the other, adjourn for more than three days, nor to any other place than that in which the two Houses shall be sitting.

SECTION 6. (1) The Senators and Representatives shall receive a compensation for their services, to be ascertained by law, and paid out of the Treasury of the United States. They shall in all cases, except treason, felony and breach of the peace, be privileged from arrest during their attendance at the session of their respective Houses, and in going to and returning from the same; and for any speech or debate in either House, they shall not be questioned in any other place.

(2) No Senator or Representative shall, during the time for which he was elected, be appointed to any civil office under the authority of the United States, which shall have been created, or the emoluments whereof shall have been increased during such time; and no person holding any office under the United States, shall be a member of either House during his continuance in office.

SECTION 7. (1) All bills for raising revenue shall originate in the House of Representatives; but the Senate may propose or concur with amendments as on other bills.

(2) Every bill which shall have passed the House of Representatives and the Senate, shall, before it become a law, be presented to the President of the United States; if he approve he shall sign it, but if not he shall return it, with his objections to that House in which it shall have originated, who shall enter the objections at large on their journal, and proceed to reconsider it. If after such reconsideration two thirds of that House shall agree to pass the bill, it shall be sent, together with the objections, to the other House, by which it shall likewise be reconsidered, and if approved by two thirds of that House, it shall become a law. But in all such cases the votes of both Houses shall be determined by yeas and nays, and the names of the persons voting for and against the bill shall be entered on the journal of each House respectively. If any bill shall not be returned by the President within ten days (Sundays excepted) after it shall have been presented to him, the same shall be a law, in like manner as if he had signed it, unless the Congress by their adjournment prevent its return, in which case it shall not be a law.

(3) Every order, resolution, or vote to which the concurrence of the Senate and House of Representatives may be necessary (except on a question of adjournment) shall be presented to the President of the United States; and before the same shall take effect, shall be approved by him, or being disapproved by him, shall be repassed by

two thirds of the Senate and House of Representatives, according to the rules and limitations prescribed in the case of a bill.

SECTION 8. (1) The Congress shall have power to lay and collect taxes, duties, imposts and excises, to pay the debts and provide for the common defense and general welfare of the United States; but all duties, imposts and excises shall be uniform throughout the United States;

(2) To borrow money on the credit of the United States.

(3) To regulate commerce with foreign nations, and among the several States, and with the Indian tribes;

(4) To establish an uniform rule of naturalization, and uniform laws on the subject of bankruptcies throughout the United States;

(5) To coin money, regulate the value thereof, and of foreign coin, and fix the standard of weights and measures;

(6) To provide for the punishment of counterfeiting the securities and current coin of the United States;

(7) To establish post offices and post roads;

(8) To promote the progress of science and useful arts, by securing for limited times to authors and inventors the exclusive right to their respective writings and discoveries;

(9) To constitute tribunals inferior to the Supreme Court;

(10) To define and punish piracies and felonies committed on the high seas, and offenses against the law of nations;

(11) To declare war, grant letters of marque and reprisal, and make rules concerning captures on land and water;

(12) To raise and support armies, but no appropriation of money to that use shall be for a longer term than two years;

(13) To provide and maintain a navy;

(14) To make rules for the government and regulation of the land and naval forces;

(15) To provide for calling forth the militia to execute the laws of the Union, suppress insurrections and repel invasions;

(16) To provide for organizing, arming, and disciplining the militia, and for governing such part of them as may be employed in the service of the United States, reserving to the States respectively, the appointment of the officers, and the authority of training the militia according to the discipline prescribed by Congress;

(17) To exercise exclusive legislation in all cases whatsoever, over such district (not exceeding ten miles square) as may, by cession of particular States, and the acceptance of Congress, become the seat of the government of the United States,[4] and to exercise like authority over all places purchased by the consent of the legislature of the State in which the same shall be, for the erection of forts, magazines, arsenals, dockyards, and other needful buildings; and

(18) To make all laws which shall be necessary and proper for carrying into execution the foregoing powers, and all other powers vested by this Constitution in the government of the United States, or in any department or officer thereof.

[4]Modified by the 23rd Amendment.

SECTION 9. (1) The migration or importation of such persons as any of the States now existing shall think proper to admit, shall not be prohibited by the Congress prior to the year one thousand eight hundred and eight, but a tax or duty may be imposed on such importation, not exceeding ten dollars for each person.

(2) The privilege of the writ of habeas corpus shall not be suspended, unless when in cases of rebellion or invasion the public safety may require it.

(3) No bill of attainder or ex post facto law shall be passed.

(4) No capitation, or other direct, tax shall be laid, unless in proportion to the census or enumeration herein before directed to be taken.[5]

(5) No tax or duty shall be laid on articles exported from any State.

(6) No preference shall be given by any regulation of commerce or revenue to the ports of one State over those of another: nor shall vessels bound to, or from, one State, be obliged to enter, clear, or pay duties in another.

(7) No money shall be drawn from the Treasury, but in consequence of appropriations made by law; and a regular statement and account of the receipts and expenditures of all public money shall be published from time to time.

(8) No title of nobility shall be granted by the United States: and no person holding any office of profit or trust under them, shall, without the consent of the Congress, accept of any present, emolument, office, or title, of any kind whatever, from any king, prince, or foreign State.

SECTION 10. (1) No State shall enter into any treaty, alliance, or confederation; grant letters of marque and reprisal; coin money; emit bills of credit; make anything but gold and silver coin a tender in payment of debts; pass any bill of attainder, ex post facto law, or law impairing the obligation of contracts, or grant any title of nobility.

(2) No State shall, without the consent of the Congress, lay any imposts or duties on imports or exports, except what may be absolutely necessary for executing its inspection laws; and the net produce of all duties and imposts, laid by any State on imports or exports, shall be for the use of the Treasury of the United States; and all such laws shall be subject to the revision and control of the Congress.

(3) No State shall, without the consent of Congress, lay any duty of tonnage, keep troops, or ships of war in time of peace, enter into any agreement or compact with another State, or with a foreign power, or engage in war, unless actually invaded, or in such imminent danger as will not admit of delay.

ARTICLE II

SECTION 1. (1) The executive power shall be vested in a President of the United States of America. He shall hold his office during the term of four years,[6] and, together with the Vice President, chosen for the same term, be elected, as follows:

(2) Each State shall appoint, in such manner as the legislature thereof may direct, a number of electors, equal to the whole number of Senators and Representatives to

[5]Modified by the 16th Amendment.
[6]Modified by the 22nd Amendment.

which the State may be entitled in the Congress: but no Senator or Representative, or person holding an office of trust or profit under the United States, shall be appointed an elector.

The electors[7] shall meet in their respective States, and vote by ballot for two persons, of whom one at least shall not be an inhabitant of the same State with themselves. And they shall make a list of all the persons voted for, and of the number of votes for each; which list they shall sign and certify, and transmit sealed to the seat of the government of the United States, directed to the president of the Senate. The president of the Senate shall, in the presence of the Senate and House of Representatives, open all the certificates, and the votes shall then be counted. The person having the greatest number of votes shall be the President, if such number be a majority of the whole number of electors appointed; and if there be more than one who have such majority, and have an equal number of votes, then the House of Representatives shall immediately choose by ballot one of them for President; and if no person have a majority, then from the five highest on the list the said House shall in like manner choose the President. But in choosing the President, the votes shall be taken by States, the representation from each State having one vote; a quorum for this purpose shall consist of a member or members from two thirds of the States, and a majority of all the States shall be necessary to a choice. In every case, after the choice of the President, the person having the greatest number of votes of the electors shall be the Vice President. But if there should remain two or more who have equal votes, the Senate shall choose from them by ballot the Vice President.

(3) The Congress may determine the time of choosing the electors, and the day on which they shall give their votes; which day shall be the same throughout the United States.

(4) No person except a natural born citizen, or a citizen of the United States, at the time of the adoption of this Constitution, shall be eligible to the office of President; neither shall any person be eligible to that office who shall not have attained to the age of thirty five years, and been fourteen years a resident within the United States.

(5) In the case of the removal of the President from office, or of his death, resignation, or inability to discharge the powers and duties of the said office, the same shall devolve on the Vice President, and the Congress may by law provide for the case of removal, death, resignation, or inability, both of the President and Vice President, declaring what officer shall then act as President, and such officer shall act accordingly, until the disability be removed, or a President shall be elected.[8]

(6) The President shall, at stated times, receive for his services, a compensation, which shall neither be increased nor diminished during the period for which he shall have been elected, and he shall not receive within that period any other emolument from the United States, or any of them.

(7) Before he enter on the execution of his office, he shall take the following oath or affirmation:—''I do solemnly swear (or affirm) that I will faithfully execute the office of President of the United States, and will to the best of my ability, preserve, protect and defend the Constitution of the United States.''

[7]This paragraph was replaced by the 12th Amendment.
[8]Replaced by the 25th Amendment.

SECTION 2. (1) The President shall be commander in chief of the army and navy of the United States, and of the militia of the several States, when called into the actual service of the United States; he may require the opinion, in writing, of the principal officer in each of the executive departments, upon any subject relating to the duties of their respective offices, and he shall have power to grant reprieves and pardons for offenses against the United States, except in cases of impeachment.

(2) He shall have power, by and with the advice and consent of the Senate, to make treaties, provided two thirds of the Senators present concur; and he shall nominate, and by and with the advice and consent of the Senate, shall appoint ambassadors, other public ministers and consuls, judges of the Supreme Court, and all other officers of the United States, whose appointments are not herein otherwise provided for, and which shall be established by law: but the Congress may by law vest the appointment of such inferior officers, as they think proper, in the President alone, in the courts of law, or in the heads of departments.

(3) The President shall have power to fill up all vacancies that may happen during the recess of the Senate, by granting commissions which shall expire at the end of their next session.

SECTION 3. He shall from time to time give to the Congress information of the state of the Union, and recommend to their consideration such measures as he shall judge necessary and expedient; he may, on extraordinary occasions, convene both Houses, or either of them, and in case of disagreement between them, with respect to the time of adjournment, he may adjourn them to such time as he shall think proper; he shall receive ambassadors and other public ministers; he shall take care that the laws be faithfully executed, and shall commission all the officers of the United States.

SECTION 4. The President, Vice President and all civil officers of the United States, shall be removed from office on impeachment for, and conviction of, treason, bribery, or other high crimes and misdemeanors.

ARTICLE III

SECTION 1. The judicial power of the United States, shall be vested in one Supreme Court, and in such inferior courts as the Congress may from time to time ordain and establish. The judges, both of the Supreme and inferior courts, shall hold their offices during good behavior, and shall, at stated times, receive for their services, a compensation, which shall not be diminished during their continuance in office.

SECTION 2. (1) The judicial power shall extend to all cases, in law and equity, arising under this Constitution, the laws of the United States, and treaties made, or which shall be made, under their authority;—to all cases affecting ambassadors, other public ministers and consuls;—to all cases of admiralty and maritime jurisdiction;—to controversies to which the United States shall be a party;—to controversies between two or more States;—between a State and citizens of another State;⁹—between citizens

⁹Restricted by the 11th Amendment.

of different States;—between citizens of the same State claiming lands under grants of different States, and between a State, or the citizens thereof, and foreign States, citizens or subjects.

(2) In all cases affecting ambassadors, other public ministers and consuls, and those in which a State shall be party, the Supreme Court shall have original jurisdiction. In all the other cases before mentioned, the Supreme Court shall have appellate jurisdiction, both as to law and fact, with such exceptions, and under such regulations as the Congress shall make.

(3) The trial of all crimes, except in cases of impeachment, shall be by jury; and such trial shall be held in the State where the said crimes shall have been committed; but when not committed within any State, the trial shall be at such place or places as the Congress may by law have directed.

SECTION 3. (1) Treason against the United States, shall consist only in levying war against them, or in adhering to their enemies, giving them aid and comfort. No person shall be convicted of treason unless on the testimony of two witnesses to the same overt act, or on confession in open court.

(2) The Congress shall have power to declare the punishment of treason, but no attainder of treason shall work corruption of blood, or forfeiture except during the life of the person attainted.

ARTICLE IV

SECTION 1. Full faith and credit shall be given in each State to the public acts, records, and judicial proceedings of every other State. And the Congress may by general laws prescribe the manner in which such acts, records and proceedings shall be proved, and the effect thereof.

SECTION 2. (1) The citizens of each State shall be entitled to all privileges and immunities of citizens in the several States.

(2) A person charged in any State with treason, felony, or other crime, who shall flee from justice, and be found in another State, shall on demand of the executive authority of the State from which he fled, be delivered up, to be removed to the State having jurisdiction of the crime.

(3) No person held to service or labor in one State, under the laws thereof, escaping into another, shall, in consequence of any law or regulation therein, be discharged from such service or labor, but shall be delivered up on claim of the party to whom such service or labor may be due.

SECTION 3. (1) New States may be admitted by the Congress into this Union; but no new State shall be formed or erected within the jurisdiction of any other State; nor any State be formed by the junction of two or more States, or parts of States, without the consent of the legislatures of the States concerned as well as of the Congress.

(2) The Congress shall have power to dispose of and make all needful rules and regulations respecting the territory or other property belonging to the United States; and nothing in this Constitution shall be so construed as to prejudice any claims of the United States, or of any particular State.

SECTION 4. The United States shall guarantee to every State in this Union a republican form of government, and shall protect each of them against invasion; and on application of the legislature, or of the executive (when the legislature cannot be convened) against domestic violence.

ARTICLE V

The Congress, whenever two thirds of both Houses shall deem it necessary, shall propose amendments to this Constitution, or, on the application of the legislatures of two thirds of the several States, shall call a convention for proposing amendments, which, in either case, shall be valid to all intents and purposes, as part of this Constitution, when ratified by the legislatures of three fourths of the several States, or by conventions in three fourths thereof, as the one or the other mode of ratification may be proposed by the Congress; Provided that no amendment which may be made prior to the year one thousand eight hundred and eight shall in any manner affect the first and fourth clauses in the ninth Section of the first article; and that no State, without its consent, shall be deprived of its equal suffrage in the Senate.

ARTICLE VI

SECTION 1. All debts contracted and engagements entered into, before the adoption of this Constitution, shall be as valid against the United States under this Constitution, as under the Confederation.

SECTION 2. This Constitution, and the laws of the United States which shall be made in pursuance thereof; and all treaties made, or which shall be made, under the authority of the United States, shall be the supreme law of the land; and the judges in every State shall be bound thereby, anything in the constitution or laws of any State to the contrary notwithstanding.

SECTION 3. The Senators and Representatives before mentioned, and the members of the several State legislatures, and all executive and judicial officers, both of the United States and of the several States, shall be bound by oath or affirmation to support this Constitution; but no religious test shall ever be required as a qualification to any office or public trust under the United States.

ARTICLE VII

The ratification of the conventions of nine States, shall be sufficient for the establishment of this Constitution between the States so ratifying the same.

Done in Convention by the unanimous consent of the States present the seventeenth day of September in the year of our Lord one thousand seven hundred and eighty-seven, and of the independence of the United States of America the twelfth. In witness whereof we have hereunto subscribed our names.

Go. Washington—

Presidt. and Deputy from Virginia

Articles in addition to and amendment of the Constitution of the United States of America, proposed by Congress, and ratified by the legislatures of the several States, pursuant to the fifth article of the original Constitution.

ARTICLE I[10]

Congress shall make no law respecting an establishment of religion, or prohibiting the free exercise thereof; or abridging the freedom of speech, or of the press; or the right of the people peaceably to assemble, and to petition the government for a redress of grievances.

ARTICLE II

A well regulated militia, being necessary to the security of a free State, the right of the people to keep and bear arms, shall not be infringed.

ARTICLE III

No soldier shall, in time of peace be quartered in any house, without the consent of the owner, nor in time of war, but in a manner to be prescribed by law.

ARTICLE IV

The right of the people to be secure in their persons, houses, papers, and effects, against unreasonable searches and seizures, shall not be violated, and no warrants shall issue, but upon probable cause, supported by oath or affirmation, and particularly describing the place to be searched, and the persons or things to be seized.

[10]The first ten Amendments were adopted in 1791.

ARTICLE V

No person shall be held to answer for a capital, or otherwise infamous crime, unless on a presentment or indictment of a grand jury, except in cases arising in the land or naval forces, or in the militia, when in actual service in time of war or public danger; nor shall any person be subject for the same offense to be twice put in jeopardy of life or limb; nor shall be compelled in any criminal case to be a witness against himself, nor be deprived of life, liberty, or property, without due process of law; nor shall private property be taken for public use, without just compensation.

ARTICLE VI

In all criminal prosecutions the accused shall enjoy the right to a speedy and public trial, by an impartial jury of the State and district wherein the crime shall have been committed, which district shall have been previously ascertained by law, and to be informed of the nature and cause of the accusation; to be confronted with the witnesses against him; to have compulsory process for obtaining witnesses in his favor, and to have the assistance of counsel for his defense.

ARTICLE VII

In suits at common law, where the value in controversy shall exceed twenty dollars, the right of trial by jury shall be preserved, and no fact tried by a jury shall be otherwise reexamined in any court of the United States, than according to the rules of the common law.

ARTICLE VIII

Excessive bail shall not be required, nor excessive fines imposed, nor cruel and unusual punishments inflicted.

ARTICLE IX

The enumeration in the Constitution, of certain rights, shall not be construed to deny or disparage others retained by the people.

ARTICLE X

The powers not delegated to the United States by the Constitution, nor prohibited by it to the States, are reserved to the States respectively, or to the people.

ARTICLE XI[11]

The judicial power of the United States shall not be construed to extend to any suit in law or equity, commenced or prosecuted against one of the United States by citizens of another State, or by citizens or subjects of any foreign State.

ARTICLE XII[12]

The electors shall meet in their respective States and vote by ballot for President and Vice-President, one of whom, at least, shall not be an inhabitant of the same State with themselves; they shall name in their ballots the person voted for as President, and in distinct ballots the person voted for as Vice-President, and they shall make distinct lists of all persons voted for as President, and of all persons voted for as Vice-President, and of the number of votes for each, which lists they shall sign and certify, and transmit sealed to the seat of the government of the United States, directed to the president of the Senate;—The president of the Senate shall, in the presence of the Senate and House of Representatives, open all the certificates and the votes shall then be counted;—The person having the greatest number of votes for President, shall be the President, if such number be a majority of the whole number of electors appointed; and if no person have such majority, then from the persons having the highest numbers not exceeding three on the list of those voted for as President, the House of Representatives shall choose immediately, by ballot, the President. But in choosing the President, the votes shall be taken by States, the representation from each State having one vote; a quorum for this purpose shall consist of a member or members from two thirds of the States, and a majority of all the States shall be necessary to a choice. And if the House of Representatives shall not choose a President whenever the right of choice shall devolve upon them, before the fourth day of March next following, then the Vice-President shall act as President, as in the case of the death or other constitutional disability of the President.—The person having the greatest number of votes as Vice-President, shall be the Vice-President, if such number be a majority of the whole number of electors appointed, and if no person have a majority, then from the two highest numbers on the list, the Senate shall choose the Vice-President; a quorum for the purpose shall consist of two thirds of the whole number of Senators, and a majority of the whole number shall be necessary to a choice. But no person constitutionally ineligible to the office of President shall be eligible to that of Vice-President of the United States.

[11]Ratified in 1795; proclaimed in 1798.
[12]Adopted in 1804.

ARTICLE XIII[13]

SECTION 1. Neither slavery nor involuntary servitude, except as a punishment for crime whereof the party shall have been duly convicted, shall exist within the United States, or any place subject to their jurisdiction.

SECTION 2. Congress shall have power to enforce this article by appropriate legislation.

ARTICLE XIV[14]

SECTION 1. All persons born or naturalized in the United States, and subject to the jurisdiction thereof, are citizens of the United States and of the State wherein they reside. No State shall make or enforce any law which shall abridge the privileges or immunities of citizens of the United States; nor shall any State deprive any person of life, liberty, or property, without due process of law; nor deny to any person within its jurisdiction the equal protection of the laws.

SECTION 2. Representatives shall be apportioned among the several States according to their respective numbers, counting the whole number of persons in each State, excluding Indians not taxed. But when the right to vote at any election for the choice of electors for President and Vice President of the United States, Representatives in Congress, the executive and judicial offices of a State, or the members of the legislature thereof, is denied to any of the male inhabitants of such State, being twenty-one years of age, and citizens of the United States, or in any way abridged, except for participation in rebellion, or other crime, the basis of representation therein shall be reduced in the proportion which the number of such male citizens shall bear to the whole number of male citizens twenty-one years of age in such State.

SECTION 3. No person shall be a Senator or Representative in Congress, or elector of President and Vice President, or hold any office, civil or military, under the United States, or under any State, who, having previously taken an oath, as a member of Congress, or as an officer of the United States, or as a member of any State legislature, or as an executive or judicial officer of any State, to support the Constitution of the United States, shall have engaged in insurrection or rebellion against the same, or given aid or comfort to the enemies thereof. But Congress may by a vote of two thirds of each House, remove such disability.

[13]Adopted in 1865.
[14]Adopted in 1869.

SECTION 4. The validity of the public debt of the United States, authorized by law, including debts incurred for payment of pensions and bounties for services in suppressing insurrection or rebellion, shall not be questioned. But neither the United States nor any State shall assume or pay any debt or obligation incurred in aid of insurrection or rebellion against the United States, or any claim for the loss or emancipation of any slave; but all such debts, obligations and claims shall be held illegal and void.

SECTION 5. The Congress shall have power to enforce, by appropriate legislation, the provisions of this article.

ARTICLE XV[15]

SECTION 1. The right of citizens of the United States to vote shall not be denied or abridged by the United States or by any State on account of race, color, or previous condition of servitude.

SECTION 2. The Congress shall have power to enforce this article by appropriate legislation.

ARTICLE XVI[16]

The Congress shall have power to lay and collect taxes on incomes, from whatever source derived, without apportionment among the several States, and without regard to census or enumeration.

ARTICLE XVII

The Senate of the United States shall be composed of two Senators from each State, elected by the people thereof, for six years; and each Senator shall have one vote. The electors in each State shall have the qualifications requisite for electors of the most numerous branch of the State legislatures.

When vacancies happen in the representation of any State in the Senate, the executive authority of such State shall issue writs of election to fill such vacancies: *Provided,* That the legislature of any State may empower the executive thereof to make temporary appointments until the people fill the vacancies by election as the legislature may direct.

This amendment shall not be so construed as to affect the election or term of any Senator chosen before it becomes valid as part of the Constitution.

[15]Adopted in 1870.
[16]Adopted in 1913.

ARTICLE XVIII[17]

SECTION 1. After one year from the ratification of this article the manufacture, sale, or transportation of intoxicating liquors within, the importation thereof into, or the exportation thereof from the United States and all territory subject to the jurisdiction thereof for beverage purposes is hereby prohibited.

SECTION 2. The Congress and the several States shall have concurrent power to enforce this article by appropriate legislation.

SECTION 3. This article shall be inoperative unless it shall have been ratified as an amendment to the Constitution by the legislatures of the several States, as provided in the Constitution, within seven years from the date of the submission hereof to the States by the Congress.

ARTICLE XIX[18]

The right of citizens of the United States to vote shall not be denied or abridged by the United States or by any State on account of sex.

The Congress shall have power to enforce this article by appropriate legislation.

ARTICLE XX[19]

SECTION 1. The terms of the President and Vice President shall end at noon on the 20th day of January, and the terms of Senators and Representatives at noon on the 3rd day of January, of the years in which such terms would have ended if this article had not been ratified; and the terms of their successors shall then begin.

SECTION 2. The Congress shall assemble at least once in every year, and such meeting shall begin at noon on the 3rd day of January, unless they shall by law appoint a different day.

SECTION 3. If, at the time fixed for the beginning of the term of the President, the President elect shall have died, the Vice President elect shall become President. If a President shall not have been chosen before the time fixed for the beginning of his term, or if the President elect shall have failed to qualify, then the Vice President elect shall act as President until a President shall have qualified; and the Congress may by law provide for the case wherein neither a President elect nor a Vice President elect shall have qualified, declaring who shall then act as President, or the manner in which

[17]Adopted in 1919. Repealed by Article XXI.
[18]Adopted in 1920.
[19]Adopted in 1933.

one who is to act shall be selected, and such person shall act accordingly until a President or Vice President shall. have qualified.

SECTION 4. The Congress may by law provide for the case of the death of any of the persons from whom the House of Representatives may choose a President whenever the right of choice shall have devolved upon them, and for the case of the death of any of the persons from whom the Senate may choose a Vice President whenever the right of choice shall have devolved upon them.

SECTION 5. Sections 1 and 2 shall take effect on the 15th day of October following the ratification of this article.

SECTION 6. This article shall be inoperative unless it shall have been ratified as an amendment to the Constitution by the legislatures of three-fourths of the several States within seven years from the date of its submission.

ARTICLE XXI[20]

SECTION 1. The eighteenth article of amendment to the Constitution of the United States is hereby repealed.

SECTION 2. The transportation or importation into any State, Territory or Possession of the United States for delivery or use therein of intoxicating liquors in violation of the laws thereof is hereby prohibited.

SECTION 3. This article shall be inoperative unless it shall have been ratified as an amendment to the Constitution by conventions in the several States, as provided in the Constitution, within seven years from the date of submission hereof to the States by the Congress.

ARTICLE XXII[21]

SECTION 1. No person shall be elected to the office of the President more than twice, and no person who has held the office of President, or acted as President for more than two years of a term to which some other person was elected President shall be elected to the office of the President more than once. But this Article shall not apply to any person holding the office of President when this Article was proposed by the Congress, and shall not prevent any person who may be holding the office of President, or acting as President, during the term within which this Article becomes operative from holding the office of President or acting as President during the remainder of such term.

[20]Adopted in 1933.
[21]Adopted in 1951.

SECTION 2. This Article shall be inoperative unless it shall have been ratified as an amendment to the Constitution by the legislatures of three-fourths of the several States within seven years from the date of its submission to the States by the Congress.

ARTICLE XXIII[22]

SECTION 1. The District constituting the seat of Government of the United States shall appoint in such manner as the Congress may direct:

A number of electors of President and Vice-President equal to the whole number of Senators and Representatives in Congress to which the District would be entitled if it were a State, but in no event more than the least populous state; they shall be in addition to those appointed by the states, but they shall be considered, for the purposes of the election of President and Vice-President, to be electors appointed by a state; and they shall meet in the District and perform such duties as provided by the twelfth article of amendment.

SECTION 2. The Congress shall have power to enforce this article by appropriate legislation.

ARTICLE XXIV[23]

SECTION 1. The right of citizens of the United States to vote in any primary or other election for President or Vice-President, for electors for President or Vice-President, or for Senator or Representative in Congress, shall not be denied or abridged by the United States or any state by reason of failure to pay any poll tax or other tax.

SECTION 2. The Congress shall have power to enforce this article by appropriate legislation.

ARTICLE XXV[24]

SECTION 1. In case of the removal of the President from office or his death or resignation, the Vice President shall become President.

SECTION 2. Whenever there is a vacancy in the office of the Vice President, the President shall nominate a Vice President who shall take the office upon confirmation by a majority vote of both houses of Congress.

[22]Adopted in 1961.
[23]Adopted in 1964.
[24]Adopted in 1967.

SECTION 3. Whenever the President transmits to the President pro tempore of the Senate and the Speaker of the House of Representatives his written declaration that he is unable to discharge the powers and duties of his office, and until he transmits to them a written declaration to the contrary, such powers and duties shall be discharged by the Vice President as Acting President.

SECTION 4. Whenever the Vice President and a majority of either the principal officers of the executive departments, or of such other body as Congress may by law provide, transmit to the President pro tempore of the Senate and the Speaker of the House of Representatives their written declaration that the President is unable to discharge the powers and duties of his office, the Vice President shall immediately assume the powers and duties of the office as Acting President.

Thereafter, when the President transmits to the President pro tempore of the Senate and the Speaker of the House of Representatives his written declaration that no inability exists, he shall resume the powers and duties of his office unless the Vice President and a majority of either the principal officers of the executive department, or of such other body as Congress may by law provide, transmit within four days to the President pro tempore of the Senate and the Speaker of the House of Representatives their written declaration that the President is unable to discharge the powers and duties of his office. Thereupon Congress shall decide the issue, assembling within 48 hours for that purpose if not in session. If the Congress, within 21 days after receipt of the latter written declaration, or, if Congress is not in session, within 21 days after Congress is required to assemble, determines by two-thirds vote of both houses that the President is unable to discharge the powers and duties of his office, the Vice President shall continue to discharge the same as Acting President; otherwise, the President shall resume the powers and duties of his office.

ARTICLE XXVI[25]

SECTION 1. The right of citizens of the United States, who are eighteen years of age, or older, to vote shall not be denied or abridged by the United States or by any state on account of age.

SECTION 2. The Congress shall have the power to enforce this article by appropriate legislation.

---

[25]Adopted in 1971.

Glossary

Acceptance. In contract law, compliance by the offeree with the terms of an offer and the manifestation of such compliance.

Accessory after the fact. A person who "receives, relieves, comforts, or assists another knowing that he has committed a felony."

Accessory before the fact. A person who, "although absent from the time and place of the crime, procured, counseled, commanded, or encouraged its commission."

Actus reus. The "guilty act"; the forbidden act or omission which is an element of a crime.

Adjudication. The resolution or settlement of a dispute between two parties by a third party.

Administrative law. Law which governs the actions of administrative agencies.

Adoption. The act of voluntarily assuming the rights and obligations of a parent over a child.

Adverse witness. Also called a hostile witness, an adverse witness is one who is providing prejudicial information against the party conducting the examination.

Affinity. Related by marriage, such as a mother-in-law and son-in-law or stepchildren or stepbrothers.

Age of majority. The age set by statute at which one loses the disabilities of minority and becomes able to enter legally binding contracts.

Alimony. Court-ordered support payments from one spouse to the other following the dissolution of a marriage.

Annulment.   Dissolution through judicial action of a marriage that was invalid from its inception.

Answer.   The defendant's response to allegations made by the plaintiff in the latter's complaint.

Appellant.   The party, usually the losing one, who seeks to overturn the decision of a trial court by appealing to a higher court.

Appellate court.   A court which hears appeals on points of law from trial courts.

Appellee.   The party, usually the winning one, against whom a case is appealed.

Arraignment.   The stage of the criminal justice process at which the defendant is formally informed of the charges and allowed to enter a plea.

Arrest warrant.   A court order which allows the police to take a person accused of a crime into custody.

Artificial persons.   Corporations that are given certain human attributes by legal fiction in order that they may sue and be sued.

Assault.   The apprehension of an offensive or unwanted contact from another person.

Assignment.   Transfer of a present contractual interest to a third party.

Battery.   Harmful or offensive contact with another person.

Bench trial.   A trial conducted without a jury in which the judge serves as the trier of fact.

Best interest of the child.   An objective standard used by the courts in determining custody of the child in contested cases.

Bond.   Something of value, either money or property, posted by a criminal defendant to ensure the defendant's appearance in court.

Bound over.   If, at the preliminary hearing, the judge believes that sufficient probable cause exists to hold a criminal defendant, the accused is said to be bound over for trial.

Breach of contract.   Failure to perform any aspect of a contract.

Brief.   A legal document in which an attorney outlines the facts, alleged errors, and precedents in a case appealed to a higher court.

Canon law.   A system of church law.

Capacity.   The ability of an individual who is not under some legal disqualification such as infancy or insanity to enter into legally binding agreements.

Case law.   Law that develops through the interpretation of statutes, constitutions, treaties, and other forms of written law.

Caveat emptor.   Literally, "let the buyer beware." At common law, the doctrine that purchasers of goods must inspect them to avoid being cheated by merchants.

Certification.   One method of appealing to the U.S. Supreme Court by which the lower court formally identifies questions of law for decision.

Challenge for cause.   Method for striking a potential juror because of specified reasons, such as bias or prejudgment.

Charge to the jury.   The instructions given to the jury by the judge whereby the judge outlines what the jury must find in order to rule for the plaintiff and then what they must find in order to rule for the defendant.

Chattel.   An item of tangible property other than realty.

Choice-of-law questions.   In conflict of laws, determining which state law will be applied when some or all of the operative elements occurred in a jurisdiction other than the forum state.

Circumstantial evidence.   An indirect method of proving the material facts of the case. Testimony that is not based on the witness's personal observation of the material events.

Civil action.   A civil lawsuit brought by one person or corporation against another.

Civil disobedience.   The theory that a person may disobey human laws that conflict with natural law or God's law.

Civil law.   There are two meanings of civil law. One is a system of laws in which the legislature is the ultimate lawmaker and which relies on codes rather than court precedent as the basis of decisions. The second defines civil law as regulating relations between private individuals and includes areas of law such as torts and contracts.

Closing statement.   Address in which the attorney summarizes the case for the jury at the end of the presentation of evidence.

Codicil.   A formal modification of the terms of a will.

Comity.   In conflict of laws, a willingness to accept judgments of foreign courts as a matter of courtesy or respect.

Common law.   Law developed, mainly in England, by judges who made legal decisions in the absence of written law. Such decisions served as precedents and became "common" to all of England.

Community property.   Property gained during marriage which belongs to each spouse equally unless it is a gift or inheritance as defined by the marital property laws in community-property states.

Comparative negligence.   A theory which allocates negligence between the plaintiff and the defendant and which allows plaintiffs to recover even if they contributed to their own injuries.

Complaining witness.   In criminal law, the person, often the victim, who swears out a complaint against another, leading to the issue of an arrest warrant against the latter.

Complaint.   In civil law, a legal document in which the plaintiff makes certain allegations of injury and liability against the defendant. In criminal law, it is the formal accusation of a criminal act against a criminal defendant.

Concurring opinion.   An opinion by an appellate court judge in which the judge agrees with the decision of the majority but not for the reasons given in the majority opinion.

Consanguinity.   Related by blood, such as parents and children, siblings, or cousins.

Consideration.   The inducement to contract, which may include money, mutual exchange of promises, or the agreement of parties to do or refrain from doing some act which they are not obligated to do.

Constitutional courts.   Federal courts created by Congress under its power under Article III of the Constitution to create courts inferior to the Supreme Court.

Constitutional law.   Law that consists of court decisions which interpret and expand the meaning of a written constitution.

Contingency fee. The normal fee arrangement in a civil suit in which the attorney receives a percentage of any award won by the plaintiff.

Contributory negligence. A legal theory which totally bars the plaintiff who contributed, even slightly, to his own injury from recovering damages.

Conversion. The deprivation of an owner of possession of tangible property.

Corpus. The principal of a trust, as opposed to the interest or income.

Court of last resort. At the state level, the highest court with jurisdiction over a particular case. At the national level, the U.S. Supreme Court.

Court of record. A court in which a record of the proceedings are kept, usually in the form of a transcript made by a court reporter.

Courts of general jurisdiction. The trial courts responsible for major criminal and civil cases.

Courts of limited jurisdiction. Lower-level state courts, such as a justice-of-the-peace court, whose jurisdiction is limited to minor civil disputes or misdemeanors.

Criminal law. Laws passed by government that define and prohibit antisocial behavior.

Cross-examination. At trial, the questions of one attorney put to a witness called by the opposing attorney.

Culpability. In law, the state or condition of being blameworthy or responsible in whole or in part for the commission of a crime.

Damages. Pecuniary, or monetary, compensation paid by the wrongdoer in a civil case.

Defamation. Injury to one's reputation in the community by defamatory comments.

Default judgment. A judgment awarded to the plaintiff because the defendant has failed to answer the complaint.

Defendant. The person against whom a lawsuit is brought.

Delegation theory. In administrative law, the theory which allows a legislative body to delegate its lawmaking power to administrative agencies.

Delegatus non protest delegare. Literally, "a delegate cannot delegate." A person who has been empowered by another to do something may not redelegate that power to another.

Demurrer. A motion by the defendant asking for dismissal of a case on the grounds that the plaintiff has insufficient grounds to proceed.

Deposition. A form of discovery which involves taking the sworn testimony of a witness outside of open court.

Direct causation. The causing or bringing about of an effect without the interference of an intervening variable or factor.

Direct evidence. Evidence derived from one or more of the five senses.

Direct examination. At trial, the questions asked of a witness by the attorney who called the witness to the stand.

Directed verdict. An order from a judge to the jury ordering the latter to decide the case in favor of one of the parties for failure of the other party to prove its case.

Discovery. A pretrial procedure in which parties to a lawsuit ask for and receive information such as testimony, records, or other evidence from each other.

Dissenting opinion. A written opinion of an appellate court judge in which the judge states the reasons for disagreement with the decision of the majority.

Diversity of citizenship suit. A specific type of federal lawsuit between citizens of two different states in which the amount in controversy exceeds $10,000.

Divine right of kings. The medieval theory that kings were chosen by God to rule, thereby establishing the king's legitimacy.

Divorce. Dissolution of the marital relationship through judicial action.

Domicile. A person's legal home.

Donee. One who receives a gift.

Donor. One who gives a gift.

Due process of law. Term appearing in the Fifth and Fourteenth Amendments which refers to the process that is due before government may deprive a person of life, liberty, or property.

Easement. The right to use someone else's property.

Emancipation. The removal of one's legal disability of being a minor, either by having reached the age of majority or by other statutory reasons, such as marriage or court order.

Eminent domain. The power of the government to take private property for public use.

En banc. A situation in which all of the members of an appellate court participate in the disposition of a case.

Equity. A branch of law which provides for remedies other than damages and is therefore more flexible than common law.

Estate in fee tail. A freehold estate which limits the succession to the "heirs of the body," or descendants of the donee or devisee.

Estate pur autre vie. An estate which is held during the lifetime of another.

Exclusionary rule. A judicially created rule which holds that evidence obtained through violations of the constitutional rights of the criminal defendant must be excluded from the trial.

Exhaustion of administrative remedies doctrine. In administrative law, the doctrine which requires persons aggrieved to avail themselves of all administrative remedies before seeking judicial relief.

Ex parte injunction. An injunction granted to one party in a suit in equity without the participation of the other party.

Ex post facto law. A law which makes a criminal act retroactive; that is, a law which allows punishment for an act performed before the act was illegal.

Express warranty. An explicit statement or promise that a certain fact in relation to the subject of the contract is true or accurate.

Fee-simple estate. An absolute interest in property; the fullest possible amount of control over property.

Fee tail female. An estate in fee tail which may only pass through the female line.

Fee tail male. An estate in fee tail which may only pass through the male line.

Feudalism. The social system of the Middle Ages, involving a series of reciprocal responsibilities from the king through the lords to the serfs.

Forum non conveniens.   A legal doctrine which allows a court to refuse to accept jurisdiction over a case.

Foundation.   Also known as "laying a predicate." Preliminary questions which establish the relevancy and admissibility of evidence.

Garnishment.   Process whereby money owed to one person as a result of a court judgment may be withheld from the wages of another person known as the garnishee.

General damages.   Damages, such as payment of medical bills, awarded to the plaintiff to restore him to his original condition before he was injured by the defendant.

General intent.   In criminal law, a general showing that the prohibited act was performed voluntarily, regardless of whether the person meant to do it.

General verdict.   A verdict in which the jury finds the defendant liable and awards the plaintiff the monetary damages he sought, less than what he sought, or more than what he sought.

Gift.   A voluntary transfer of property without consideration.

Grand jury.   A group of citizens who decide if persons accused of crimes should be indicted (true billed) or not (no billed).

Grantee.   The person to whom property is being conveyed.

Grantor.   The person who is conveying property.

Habeas corpus.   Literally, "you have the body." In criminal law, a judicial writ ordering a law enforcement official to bring a person before the court and show cause as to why the person is being detained.

Harmless error.   An error made during a trial which an appellate court feels is insufficient grounds for reversing a judgment.

Hearsay.   An out-of-court assertion or statement made by someone other than the testifying witness which is being offered to prove the truth of the matter stated. Hearsay evidence is excluded from trials unless it falls within one of the recognized exceptions.

Heir.   Generally, one who inherits property under a will or by intestate succession; technically, a person who receives a property interest through intestate succession.

Holographic will.   A will that is written entirely in the handwriting of the testator.

Hung jury.   Description given to a jury when the jurors are unable to reach a verdict. Especially significant in criminal trials in which an unanimous verdict is required.

Impanelled.   After jurors are sworn in, the jury is said to be impanelled and the defendant is placed in "jeopardy."

Implied warranty of merchantibility.   The warranty which is imposed on merchants that the goods are merchantible as defined in the UCC; the warranty is imposed even though the merchants do not actually make such claims.

Indictment.   A formal accusation of a criminal offense handed down by a grand jury.

In forma pauperis.   Literally, "in the manner of a pauper." Permission of the court for a poor person to seek judicial relief without having to pay the usual court fees.

Informal marriage. A type of legally recognized marriage that is created by informal means; also known as a common-law marriage.

Information. A formal accusation charging someone with the commission of a crime, signed by a prosecuting attorney, which has the effect of bringing the person to trial.

Initial appearance. During the initial appearance, the accused is informed of the charges against him, given his constitutional rights, informed of the amount of his bail, and given a date for a preliminary hearing.

Injunction. A court order directing a person to refrain from performing certain acts or carrying out certain activities.

In personum jurisdiction. Judicial jurisdiction of a court to enter a personal judgment or decree against a person.

In rem jurisdiction. Judicial jurisdiction of a court to enter a decree affecting property interests.

Intangible property. Those items of property which are not capable of being touched, such as debts owed.

Interrogatory. A form of discovery in which written questions about a lawsuit are submitted to one party by the other party.

Inter vivos. During life.

Intestate. Dying without a will.

Invitee. In tort law, a business visitor on one's premises.

Jeopardy. The point in the criminal justice process at which the accused is in danger of criminal liability. Once in jeopardy, the accused must be either aquitted or convicted and may not be placed again in jeopardy.

Joint tenancies. Concurrent ownership of property whereby the survivor inherits the entire property.

Judicial conduct board. An official body whose function is to investigate allegations of misconduct made against judges.

Judicial gatekeeping. Term used to describe how judges control access to the judicial system by either opening or closing the judicial "gates" to certain kinds of controversies.

Judicial notice. A method of providing trial evidence which allows the court to accept facts that are commonly known or verifiable without formal proof.

Judicial review. The power of a court to declare null and void acts of governmental bodies contrary to the Constitution.

Jurisdiction. The power and authority of courts to render a binding decision in a case.

Laying a predicate. Also known as laying a foundation. Preliminary questions which establish the relevancy and admissibility of evidence.

Leading question. A question whereby an attorney attempts to put words into the mouth of a witness; that is, a question which elicits the information to which the attorney wishes the witness to testify.

Lease. An agreement, oral or written, which governs the rental of property.

Legislative address. A method of judicial removal used in some states which allows the state legislature to remove a state judge, usually by a two-thirds vote.

Legislative courts. Federal courts created by Congress under one of its legislative powers; for example, military and territorial courts.

Lessee. Also known as the tenant; the person who is in possession of the property under a lease.

Lessor. Also known as the landlord; the person who owns the fee-simple estate and carves out a small estate for a tenant.

Libel. Defamation which is preserved in some permanent form.

Licensee. In tort law, a social quest on one's property.

Life estate. An estate in land which is held only during one's lifetime or during the life of another.

Long-arm statute. A legislative enactment which extends a court's jurisdiction to nonresident parties as long as there are "minimum contacts" between the litigant and the state, which is a requirement of due process.

Majority opinion. The opinion of a majority of appellate court judges in which the decision of the court and its reasons for that decision are given.

Malum in se. Literally, "wrong in itself." In criminal law, something which is made illegal because it is inherently or morally wrong.

Malum prohibitum. In criminal law, something made illegal because government has deemed it undesirable, thereby prohibiting it; for example, gambling.

Marriage. A legally recognized special relationship between a man and a woman which is founded in contract.

Mens rea. Literally, "the guilty mind." The wrongful purpose which is an element of a crime.

Missouri Plan. The name given to a method of judicial selection which combines merit selection and popular control in retention elections.

Mootness. Term used to describe a case that has become a dead issue because the controversy that gave rise to the case was resolved before a final judicial decision could be made.

Motion in limine. A written motion, usually filed before the trial, which bars prejudicial questions and statements on specified topics.

Natural law. The theory that human law must conform to the laws of God and nature, just as the physical world must conform to the laws of physics.

Negligence. A theory of tort recovery involving a legal duty, a breach of duty, proximate cause, and injury.

Negligence per se. A method of establishing the defendant's negligence by proving a violation of a safety statute or regulation.

No bill. Term used to describe the decision of a grand jury not to indict a person for a crime.

No-fault divorce. A divorce in which neither party must allege or prove fault (adultery, cruelty, and so on) in order to dissolve the marriage; the grounds are generally incompatibility or failure of the marriage.

Nolo contendere. Literally, "I will not contest it." A plea, tantamount to a guilty plea, in which the accused refuses to admit culpability but accepts the punishment of the court.

Nuisance. The use of the defendant's land in such a way that it interferes with the plaintiff's use or enjoyment of the plaintiff's land.

Nuncupative will. An oral will.

Obiter dictum. Also known as dicta; statements in a judicial opinion which were not essential to the resolution of the case and are not binding precedent.

Offer. A proposal to enter into a contract.

Offeree. The person to whom an offer is made.

Offeror. The person making an offer.

Opening statement. Address made by attorneys for both parties at the beginning of a trial in which they outline for the jury what they intend to prove.

Oral argument. The part of the appellate court decision-making process in which lawyers for both parties plead their cases in person before the Court.

Oral testimony. A form of evidence that is given by the witness on the stand in open court or in a deposition under oath.

Ordinance power. The power of cities and other local government units to enact regulations binding on citizens within their jurisdiction.

Panel. A group of appellate judges, less than the full membership of the court, assigned to review a case on appeal.

Parol Evidence Rule. A rule of contract construction which prevents modification of written contracts by any oral statements.

Party. One of the principals, either the plaintiff or the defendant, in a lawsuit.

Per curiam decision. Literally, "for the court." An unsigned Supreme Court decision, usually very short, in which the Court's judgment is announced.

Peremptory challenge. A method used to strike a potential juror from the jury without specifying the reason for doing so.

Personal service. A personally delivered notice to a party of pending litigation, or the personal delivery of a copy of a subpoena to a witness.

Personalty. All property except realty or those items which cannot be severed from the realty without damage to it.

Plaintiff. The party who initiates a lawsuit.

Plea bargain. An arrangement whereby the accused agrees to exchange a plea of guilty for a lesser sentence, a reduction of charges, or some other consideration by the court.

Plurality opinion. On the Supreme Court, any written opinion which reflects the views of less than a majority of the justices who heard the case.

Political question. The doctrine that courts will not decide cases that involve issues for which a final decision is clearly left to one of the political branches of government by the Constitution.

Positive law. The theory that law is merely a reflection of the will of the strongest in a society.

Precedent. A case previously decided which serves as a legal guide for the resolution of subsequent cases.

Preliminary hearing. Either a pretrial hearing at which motions are considered or, in criminal law, a pretrial hearing to determine whether there is probable cause to hold the accused for an indictment.

Prenuptial agreements. Also known as antenuptial agreements; these are contracts entered into by the spouses before marriage which outline certain conditions such as the division of the property in case of divorce.

Preponderance of the evidence. In civil law, the standard of proof required to prevail at trial. For a plaintiff to win, he must show that the greater weight, or preponderance, of the evidence supports his version of the facts.

Prima facie case. The plaintiff's version of the facts which, if taken at first glance, or "first face," seem to substantiate the plaintiff's allegations against the defendant.

Primary jurisdiction doctrine. In administrative law, the doctrine that requires litigants to take a dispute to the administrative agency with primary responsibility for handling the dispute before seeking judicial relief.

Primogeniture. A legal doctrine whereby the oldest son alone inherits the property of his ancestors.

Principal in the first degree. The person who actually commits, or perpetrates, a crime.

Principal in the second degree. A person who aids and abets another in the commission of a crime.

Prior restraint. A form of censorship which attempts to prevent the publication of a story or document.

Privilege. In evidence, a recognized right to keep certain communications confidential or private.

Probable cause. Standard used to determine whether a crime has been committed and whether there is sufficient evidence to believe that a specific individual committed it.

Procedural law. Law which outlines the legal procedures or process that government is obliged to follow.

Product liability. A subfield of tort law which imposes liability on the manufacturers of defective or unsafe products.

Promissory estoppel. A contract remedy whereby one party has changed positions in reliance of the other party's gratuitous promise.

Property. The legal right to use or dispose of particular items or subjects.

Proximate cause. The theory that the injury sustained by the plaintiff and the defendant's action were so closely connected that the defendant's act caused the injury and there were no intervening causes.

Punitive damages. Money beyond actual damages awarded against a defendant whose conduct was so wanton, reckless, or reprehensible as to justify additional punishment.

Quasi-in-rem jurisdiction. The power and authority of courts to enter a judgment affecting property interests to satisfy the owner's personal obligations, even though the owner is not otherwise subject to the court's jurisdiction.

Ratio decidendi. Those statements in a judicial opinion which are essential to the resolution of the case and are binding precedent.

Realty. Also known as real property; land and the appurtenances thereto.

Reasonably prudent person. A mythical person created by the courts to be used as the objective standard by which the party's conduct is measured.

Recall. A method used in some states to remove judges from office. Recall elections allow the voters to directly remove judges from the bench.

Recognizance. Term used to describe the release of an accused person from custody without requiring a property or money bond.

Recross-examination. Questions asked of a witness after direct examination, cross-examination, and redirect examination. Essentially a second series of questions asked of a witness called by the opposing attorney.

Redirect examination. Follow-up questions asked of his own witness by the attorney who originally called the witness to the stand.

Regulatory Law. Rules and regulations promulgated by administrative agencies which are just as binding as statutes passed by legislatures.

Remittitur. The process by which a jury verdict of money damages is reduced because the amount is excessive.

Renvoi. A legal theory applicable when there is a choice-of-law question and the forum state adopts the entire law of the sister state.

Repudiation. The contract remedy excusing one party from performance of the contract terms based on the other party's statements of prospective nonperformance.

Res ipsa loquitur. A method of showing the defendant's tort liability by proving that all the instrumentalities were under its control and that the accident is of a kind that would not have occurred without negligence.

Respondeat superior. A theory of vicarious liability in which the employer or master is financially responsible for the torts of employees or servants.

Reversible error. An error made at trial serious enough to warrant a new trial.

Ripeness. The doctrine that an appellate court will not review the decision of a lower court until all remedies have been exhausted. Courts will not decide an issue before the need to do so.

Roman Law. A system of laws created by the Romans and codified in the Code of Justinian.

Rule Against Perpetuities. The rule that interests in property must vest not later than 21 years after the lives of the persons specified at the time that the interests were created.

Rule enforcement. The power of an administrative agency to enforce rules promulgated by the agency under its rule-making power.

Rule-making. The power of an administrative agency to promulgate rules and regulations concerning matters that fall within its jurisdiction. Rules promulgated by administrative agencies have the force of law.

Rule of Four. The requirement that four Supreme Court justices must agree to hear a case before the Court will grant a writ of certiorari.

Scienter. An element of a crime which requires knowledge or awareness that a particular act is illegal.

Seisin. Possession of land under a claim of a freehold estate; akin to absolute ownership of land.

Senatorial courtesy. The custom in the U.S. Senate that requires the president to clear judicial appointments with the senators of the state wherein the appointment occurs when the senators are of the president's party.

Sequestered. A jury is sequestered when its members are isolated from the community until it has reached a final verdict.

Service. The process of formally delivering the complaint or a subpoena to the defendant or to a witness in a civil suit.

Shield law. A law which allows a newspaper or other reporter to refuse to disclose the source of information in a criminal case. Shield laws are a type of privilege.

Slander. Defamation which is spoken or not preserved in permanent form.

Small-claims court. A lower-level state court whose jurisdiction is limited to a specified dollar amount; for example, damages may not exceed $1,500.

Sociological theory of law. The theory that law is a function of the society that makes it and that law changes as society changes.

Special-issues verdict. A verdict in which the jury answers a series of questions rather than merely entering a general finding.

Specific intent. The requisite intent that must be proved as an element of some crimes, such as killing another "with malice aforethought."

Specific relief. Equitable remedies which are personally directed to the defendant and obligate him to do or refrain from doing some activity.

Spoils system. Term used to describe the awarding of public jobs to political supporters by victorious politicians because "to the victor go the spoils."

Standing. The doctrine requiring that a party bringing suit before a court must have a legal right to do so.

Stare decisis. The policy of courts to follow the rules laid down in previous cases and not to disturb settled points of law.

Statutes of limitations. Statutes which prescribe the time periods in which lawsuits must be filed.

Statutory law. Laws, called statutes, passed by legislative bodies that bestow benefits, impose obligations, or prohibit antisocial behavior.

Subpoena. An order from a court directing a person to appear before the court and to give testimony about a cause of action pending before it.

Subpoena duces tecum. An order from a court directing a person to appear before the court with specified documents which the court deems relevant in a matter pending before it.

Substantial Evidence Rule. Rule that says a finding of fact by an administrative agency is to be final if there is substantial evidence to support the agency's conclusion.

Substantive law. Law that deals with the content or substance of the law; for example, the legal grounds for divorce.

Substituted service. A notice of pending litigation or other legal matters which is not personally delivered to the person; an example would be publication of such notice in the newspaper.

Substitutionary relief. The award of money damages as compensation for legally recognized losses.

Suit to partition land. A lawsuit dividing land held by co-owners or joint tenants into separate and distinct parts.

Summary judgment. Decision by a judge to rule in favor of one party because the opposing party failed to meet a standard of proof. For example, if a plaintiff fails to present a prima facie case, the judge may enter a summary judgment in favor of the defendant.

Summons. A court order directing the defendant to appear in court at a specified time and place, either in person or by filing a written answer to the plaintiff's complaint.

Tangible evidence.   Any evidence that the trier of fact may touch or observe in the courtroom.

Tangible property.   Land and other material items that can be touched.

Taxpayer's suit.   A suit brought by a person who claims standing on the basis of status as a taxpayer.

Tenancies in common.   Current ownership of property which does carry a right of survivorship.

Tenure.   The system of landholding in the feudal era wherein land was held in subordination to a superior.

Testamentary capacity.   The mental ability of an individual to understand the legal consequences of the act of making a will.

Testate.   Dying with a will.

Testator.   The person making a will.

Third-party beneficiary contracts.   Contracts intended to benefit a third party—that is, one who is not a party to the contract.

Tort.   A private or civil wrong in which the defendant's actions cause injury to the plaintiff or to property; the usual remedy is money damages.

Tortfeasor.   The wrongful actor in a tort suit.

Trespass to chattel.   The damage to another's item of tangible,

Trespass to land.   The injury to another's real property by an unlawful entry.

Trial de novo.   Literally, a "trial from the beginning." Cases appealed from courts that have no transcript are reheard in their entirety "from the beginning."

Trier of fact.   The trier of fact is responsible for hearing and viewing the evidence at trial and evaluating the veracity of it. The trier of fact can either be the judge or a jury.

True bill.   A bill of indictment by a grand jury.

Trust.   A right or property held by one person for the benefit of another.

Trustee.   The person or institution which is vested, under an express or implied agreement, with property to be used for the benefit of another; also known as a fiduciary.

Trustor.   The person creating a trust.

Ultra vires.   Literally, "beyond the powers of." In administrative law, the doctrine that an administrative agency has exercised powers beyond those delegated to it by a legislative body.

Uniform Commercial Code (UCC).   A set of uniform statutes governing commercial transactions which have been enacted by state legislatures with some modifications.

Venire.   A group of citizens from which members of the jury are chosen.

Venireman.   A person called for jury duty.

Venue.   The geographic location of a trial, determined by constitutional or statutory provisions.

Vicarious liability.   The shifting of liability from the tortfeasor to another party, usually an employer.

Void.   Null, ineffective, not able to support the purpose for which it was intended.

Voidable.　Something, such as a contract or marriage, which is not void in and of itself but which can be voided at the option of the parties.

Voir dire.　Literally, "to speak truth." The process by which prospective jurors are questioned by attorneys to ascertain whether there is cause to strike them from jury.

Voluntary assumption of risk.　A defense used in tort law that the plaintiff was cognizant of the danger and voluntarily chose to encounter it.

Warranty.　A covenant or promise that a statement or fact is true.

Will.　The legal expression of one's wishes regarding the disposition of one's property which is to be effective after death.

Witness.　A person called to the stand to give testimony in a trial.

Writ of certiorari.　An order from a higher court to a lower court in which the former orders the latter to send up the record of case for review by the higher court.

Writ of execution.　A court order allowing a law enforcement official to seize the property or assets of a defendant against whom a civil judgment has been rendered.

Table of Cases

Index

Fortas, Abe 58–59, 132–33
Frankfurter, Felix, 58–59
Frauds, Statute of, 227
Free Exercise Clause, 16, 22, 123, 126–29
Full Faith and Credit Clause, 111

Gandhi, Mahatma, 5
Gardner, Thomas, 155, 156
Garfield, James A., 201
George III, 5, 163
Gifts, 250
Goldberg, Arthur J., 58
Goldberg ingredients, 196–97
Goldberg v. Kelly, 195–97, 198, 206n, 252n
Grand jury, 82
  indictment, 82
  no bill, 82
  true bill, 82
Greek law, 20, 246

Hamilton, Alexander, 116
Hammurabi, 19
Hand, Learned, 224
Harlan I, John M., 155
Harlan II, John M., 132
Harold (of England), 240
Haynesworth, Clement, 52, 54, 58–59
Hearsay, Rule against, 76, 90–91
Hearst, Patty, 157
Hebrew law, 20, 246
Henry of Bracton, 25
Henry I, 24
Henry II, 13, 24, 30
Henry VIII, 255
Herbert, A.P., 209
Hinckley, John W., 158
Hobbes, Thomas, 282
Holmes, Oliver Wendell, Jr., 13, 19, 57, 129,
  131, 148n, 181, 202
Home solicitation sales, 234
Hughes, Charles Evans, 114, 139
Hughes, Howard, 87
Humphreys, West H., 65

Immunities, 219
Implied Warranty of Fitness, 218, 232
Implied Warranty of Merchantibility, 218,
  231–32
Infliction of mental distress, 215
Informal marriages, 257–58
Inns of Court, 33
Intent, 157–58, 214
  general, 157
  scienter, 157
  specific, 157
Intentional Torts, 214–17
  assault, 214
  battery, 214
  conversion, 217
  defamation, 139, 144–46, 215–16
  definition, 214
  false imprisonment, 214–15
  infliction of mental distress, 215
  invasion of privacy, 215
  libel, 139, 144–46, 215–16
  nuisance, 216–17
  slander, 139, 144–46, 215–16
  trespass to chattel, 217
  trespass to land, 216
Internal Revenue Service, 14–16, 171, 172,
  192, 193, 263
Interstate Commerce Commission, 185, 190,
  200
Intestate succession, 246–47
Islamic law, 21–22, 246, 257

Jackson, Robert, 128, 129
Jefferson, Thomas, 4, 116–18

John (of England), 29
Johnson, Lyndon B., 53, 58
Joint tenancies, 244
Judges, removal of, 65–67
  federal judges, 65–66
  state judges, 66–67
Judicial conduct boards, 67
Judicial gatekeeping, 98–104
Judicial notice, 87
Judicial restraints:
  conflict of laws, 108–11
  exhaustion of administrative remedies, 200
  gatekeeping, 98–104
  jurisdiction, 105–7
  mootness, 100–102
  political questions, 102–4
  primary jurisdiction doctrine, 200
  ripeness, 100–102
  standing, 99–100
  stare decisis, 111–12
  statutes of limitations, 108
  substantial evidence rule, 200
  venue, 107–8
Judicial review, 11, 115–22, 197–201
Judicial selection, 51–64, 277–78
  appointment, 33, 51–60, 62
  election, 60–62
  federal, 52–60
  European, 21, 33
  Missouri Plan, 62–64, 66
  state, 60–64
Jurisdiction, 105–7
  appellate, 40–42, 50–51, 105, 197–201
  difference in venue and, 107
  elements, 105–7
  federal courts, 32–42, 44–46
  in personam, 106
  in rem, 105
  long-arm statutes, 106
  quasi-in-rem, 106
  state courts, 46–51
Jury:
  grand jury, 82
  history, 23, 74–75
  hung jury, 84
  role as fact-finders, 75, 86
  sequestered jury, 85
Jury selection, 74–76
  venire, 75
  voir dire, 75
Justice of the peace court, 47–48
Justinian, 21, 22, 254

Kennedy, John F., 53, 58
King, Martin Luther, Jr., 5

Law, compliance with, 4–5
Law, economics and, 280–81
Law, functions of, 2–3, 19
Law, kinds of, 7–14
  administrative law, 11–12, 16, 20, 185–206
  case law, 12–13, 30–31, 111–12
  civil law, 8–10, 36
  common law, 13–14, 16, 22–25
  constitutional law, 10–11, 16
  criminal law, 3, 6, 8–10, 151–52
  European civil law, 21–22
  natural law, 5–6, 11
  positive law, 6, 11
  procedural law, 7–8
  regulatory law, 12, 16, 191
  statutory law, 11, 16
  substantive law, 7–8, 37, 70, 151–52
  See also individual entries
Law, politics and, 277–78
Law, sources of, 4–7
Law School Admissions Test (LSAT), 101, 278
Lease, 242–43, 277

Legal profession, 31–34
American, 31–34
domination in political system, 277
European, 21, 31, 33
Legislative courts, 37, 44–46
Legitimacy:
of children, 267–69
of law, 4–5, 9
Libel, 139, 144–46, 215–16
Life estates, 242
Limitations, statutes of, 108
Lincoln, Abraham, 276
Living will, 249
Locke, John, 9
Long-arm statutes, 106
Loyalty oath, 204
Luther, Martin, 255

Madison, James, 116, 117
Magna Carta, 29
Maitland, Fredrick, 28
Majority, age of:
contracts, 223
emancipation, 223
marriage, 256–57
Mallory v. United States, 81–82, 95n, 170–73,
183n
Malum in se, 3, 8, 153, 155
Malum prohibitum, 3, 8, 153–55
Mantle, Mickey, 51
Marbury v. Madison, 114, 116–20, 146n
Marbury, William, 117–18
Marital property, 243–44, 261–63
Marriage, 256–58
ceremonial, 258
informal, 257
restraints, 257
Married Women's Act, 262
Marshall, James, 117
Marshall, John, 59, 114, 116–19
Marshall, Thurgood, 58, 180, 184n
Matrimonial Causes Act of 1859, 255
Mens rea, 156–58
Merit System Protection Board, 44
Mertz, Charles, V., 262–63
Mine Health and Safety Administration, 192
Miranda warnings, 13, 171, 173, 179–80
Missouri Plan, 62–64, 66
Mootness, 100–102
Mormon Polygamy Case *(Reynolds v. United
States)*, 127, 147n, 273n
Mothers Against Drunk Drivers, 279
Municipal courts, 47
Mutual assent, 224

Nader, Ralph, 233
Napoleonic Code, 21
National Labor Relations Board, 185
Natural law, 5, 6, 11
Negligence, 77, 209–14
breach of duty, 210–11
comparative, 77, 213
contributory, 77, 213
damages, 27, 72, 212–13
defenses, 213–14, 217
duty of care, 209–10
elements, 209
negligence per se, 210
proximate cause, 211–12
res ipsa loquitur, 211
standard of care, 209–10
Neubauer, David W., 155
Nixon, Richard, 52–53, 54, 58–59, 60, 104,
144
Noonan, John T., 32–33
Nonfreehold estates, 242–43
Nuclear Regulatory Commission, 198
Nuisance, 216–17

Obscenity, 142–44

Occupation, Health and Safety Administration,
191, 192, 193
O'Connor, Sandra Day, 53, 58–59
Offer, 223–26
acceptance, 223
invitation to, 225–26
rejection, 225

Palsgraf v. Long Island Railroad Co., 32
Parental Kidnapping Prevention Act, 265
Parent-child relationship, 263–72
Parol evidence rule, 227
Patent and Trademark Office, 44
Pendleton Act, 201
Penn, William, 241
Pentagon Papers Case *(New York Times Co. v.
United States)*, 139–40, 149n
People's Court, The, 48
Perpetuities, rule against, 250
Perry v. Sindermann, 203–4, 206n
Perry, William, 85
Personalty, 239
Persons and Masks of the Law, 32
Pickering, John, 65
Plato, 20, 31
Political question doctrine, 102–4
Positive law, 6, 11
Powell, Louis, 60, 177, 178
Precedent, 3, 13, 97, 111–12
Press, freedom of, 138–46
censorship, 138–39
libel, 139, 144–46
obscenity, 142–44
pre-trial publicity, 85, 107, 140–42
rights of reporters, 93, 142
Pritchett, C. Herman, 11, 130
Privacy, invasion of, 215–16
Privileges, 93–94
Probate, 249
Procedural law, 7–8, 40, 70, 71–80, 80–85,
151–53, 162–81, 187, 191, 195, 196, 202
Product liability, 218–19
Proof, standard of, 76, 81, 84, 158–60, 196–97
beyond a reasonable doubt, 81, 84, 152,
158–60
preponderance of the evidence, 76, 159
Property:
concurrent ownership, 243–44, 261–63
definition, 239
easement, 244
estates, 239–45
gifts, 250
intangible, 239
lease, 242–43, 277
limitations on interests, 244–45
marital, 243–44, 261, 263
mineral interests, 244
Statute of Tenures, 241
Statute Quai Emptores, 240
succession, 245–49
tangible, 239
tenure system, 240
trusts, 249–50
Proximate cause, 158, 211–12
Proxmire, William, 146
Public employment, 201–5

Rail Reorganization Court, 44
Raleigh, Sir Walter, 90, 96n
Reagan, Ronald, 46, 52, 54, 58–59, 158, 185,
205
Realty, 239
Rehnquist, William, 176–77
Religion, freedom of, 123–29
establishment, 11, 123–26
free exercise, 126–29
Remedies:
breach of contract, 27, 228–30, 232–33
damages, 26–27, 72–73, 212–13
specific relief, 27, 229